COTTAGE HOLIDAYING IN BRITAIN

COTTAGE HOLIDAYING
IN
BRITAIN

Compiled & Illustrated

by

GALE ARMSTRONG

Classic Media Publications
Searsport, Maine

Front cover pictures: PEEL TOWER (Durham), LITTLE MANOR (Gloucestershire), NYMET (Devon), THE TEMPLE (Yorkshire), GINGER-BREAD HOUSE (Somerset), LUNDY LIGHTHOUSE (Devon), LAMBARDS OAST (Kent).

Back cover pictures: THE LOFT (Cornwall) and APPLETON WATER TOWER (Norfolk)

Title page picture:: CLEMY COTTAGE (Scilly Isles)

Manufactured in the United States of America
First Edition/Second Printing

Library of Congress Catalogue Card Number 94-70762
ISBN 0-9644325-5-2

CONTENTS

Acknowledgments

The author would like to express appreciation for the boundless hospitality shown by cottage owners from the four corners of Britain over the many years and many sojourns that constituted the background for this book. Of more immediate importance is the cooperation from the the numerous property owners and rental agents whose assistance has made this book possible.

The author's thanks also go out to Eileen Marchini for her vigilant and tireless editorial eyes; to Greg Closter for his keen eye into the mysteries of computer digitization, and to Timothy Pearkes, *Our Man in Britain,* eyes and all!

PREFACE

It is probably a good idea to begin this book with a forthright confession; or perhaps this is more of a bold assertion. This pen-person, this paint brush-person, is a *dyed-in-the-wool* Anglophile....actually, I should say *Britophile,* because my everlasting affections (not to mention ancestral roots) extend to all the mystical Celtic corners of this endearing archipelago.

My love affair with the British Isles began as a teenager, when I first toured there as part of the Commonwealth Youth Movement. Our mission was a pretty solemn one; to honor the dead of the so-called *Great* wars. We toured for many weeks all over Britain and Continental Europe; placing wreaths on graves; standing all night, candlelit vigils in mournful places; and, of course, drinking gallons of tea with veterans' widows. Occasionally we were even invited to sip a bit of sherry with the old war heroes or bubbly wine in a continuous reception line that began with proudly bemedaled village burgermeisters and ended back in England with a handshake from the slightly bemused Prince Philip. Candlelight...sherry...handsome princes; all pretty heady stuff for a wide-eyed kilted lass from down-home Nova Scotia.

In the nearly thirty years since that youthful initiation, my infatuation with Britain has matured, but just a little bit. Adolescent thrill has toned down now to worldly exhilaration each time I step off the plane at Heathrow or Prestwick. Over the years, more sporadic trips were followed by longer working stays and eventually leisurely annual sojourns of a month (or two...or three). It helps having a spouse who is also a *Britophile,* though I never let him forget that he is a Johnny-come-lately, having only discovered Britain in 1972 when he went to work at the British Museum.

It isn't just me that has matured; Britain has, as well. Matured as a tourist destination. In retrospect, I guess Britain wasn't a very accommodating place back in the 60s. Oh, the hospitality was surely there, as were the historic and natural attractions, which, after all, had been around for eons. But the War (the latter of the aforementioned *Great* ones) wasn't so easily swept aside in Britain as it was back in North America. Travellers of the 50s & 60s brought back the obligatory pictures of the Tower of London, the White Cliffs of Dover, and Stonehenge, but what they remembered most was primitive plumbing ("no showers"), cold lodgings, warm beer, and expensive petrol. The good part was that the Brits spoke English, albeit with some rather curious accents; and, even though handling the money was a bit of a challenge for us then, one knew that all tradesmen and taxi drivers were completely honest and on our side.

Well, some things never really change. The British still speak a version of English (several absolutely delightful versions, in fact) and from the Isle of Wight to the Isle of Mull, West Country to East Anglia, the traveller is still in culturally safe territory, even when the coin of the realm is in the picture. The historic and natural attractions are still in place, which is very much a part of the appeal of Britain to North Americans, who sense that at home both historic and natural treasures go unprotected from mindless change. What *has* changed is the *quality of life* for the traveller; to wit, accommodation, food, and transport. Altogether it's a matter of *accessibility,* which is the key to a good holiday experience.

Without question, Britain is the most accessible *foreign* experience for the North American traveller. It's Europe, Western Civilization, and, in many cases, our ancestral roots in a venue which is friendly, relatively secure, open, affordable, and culturally enriching for visitors of all ages....in short, Britain is a *must-do* experience, and is eminently *do-able!*

The question then is how to *do* it. How to access the best of it, and, if economy is a concern, how to access the most for the least. Not surprisingly, our North American instinct is to rent a car and go...go...go. See it all! Alas, this is really a strategy to miss it all; to drive past England, Wales and Scotland. Of course, if driving is one's passion, then I suppose the open-ended touring approach may suit one best. No doubt, left-side driving and narrow lane roads will add an extra challenge to a frenetic holiday. Better get started. If you don't reach Penzance by Tuesday, you'll be late getting to Edinburgh on Saturday. There's lots to see; don't blink!

Of course, one never can *see it all* in Britain, though I am bound to say that it is our family's lifelong goal, however unattainable. But then, I've already confessed to a certain obsession as regards the British Isles, and we must assume that the *normal* readers of this guide have more sense than to share this bizarre quest. Therefore, let us start with a pretty simple proposition: One holiday taken into your heart and soul is preferable to ten holidays taken on Kodak, or a hundred holidays made memorable by a maze of yellow highlighter scrawl on your AAA Road Atlas and red ink punctuating your post-trip bank statement.

It takes a measure of stationary-ness to let the cultural rhythms sink in. It doesn't matter whether you plan a stay in busy London or choose to nestle into one of the thousands of bucolic villages of England, Wales and Scotland. The *feel* of the place comes from the little daily things and casual encounters; like buying your morning *pinta* (that's milk) from the old dear at the village shop, or hoisting an evening pint (that's what you think it is) amongst a friendly crowd of characters in a picture book pub. There's the fishmonger to chat with on his Tuesday morning rounds; and the newsagent, who has a nephew living in Iowa; and the greengrocer, who has saved you the best produce because you're the nice folks from America staying at Rose Cottage; and the vicar, whose other passion is trout, and who has a saintly disposition to share information about where best to wet one's line; and the retired colonel doing volunteer duty in the village library, who doubles as the local historian and is ever ready to answer queries about Roundheads, Celtic mounds, and Pilgrim origins. All in all, the real Britain is a mosaic of memorable humanity cast against a story-book landscape.

Oddly enough, the British think of themselves as a pretty reserved lot, which may just be a subtle way of distinguishing themselves from the Irish, who are, admittedly, God's most loquacious, open and friendly species. But the fact is, you can not stay for long anywhere in Britain without the *locals* taking some kind of amiable and genuine interest in you...and that is precisely the access point for you to get a real feel for the endearing and enduring quality of their land and culture. Ever lasting Kodacolor printed directly on the heart!

But what about the castles, museums, and photo opportunities, you say? Well, to be sure, one doesn't want to come back to North America with a bag full of unexposed film! Not to worry. No matter where you decide to rent in Britain you will have more marvelous historic sites, natural wonders, and tourist activity/attractions within a one hour driving radius than you will possibly be able to cover in a week, or even a month. The geographic concentration of points of interest in Britain is really beyond our North American experience or expectation. Really, it's just a matter of history (of making it, and keeping it!), and the forward thinking Britons have been busy for the past three or four thousand years creating those points of interest for today's visitors. Probably we should give God a little credit, as well, for giving those eons of Britons such a varied and beautiful landscape on which to build their culture. Incidentally, you will find *God Thanking Stations* in every village throughout the Land, and foreign visitors are always warmly welcomed.

Welcoming is really pretty close to the heart of cottage holidaying in Britain. You will find that this welcome feeling begins with the people offering you their accommodations. We have made a special point of selecting many properties for presentation in this book which are available for rent directly from the owners, who, after all, know their cottage and area best. Who better to call for answers to all your particular questions?

Somewhat less knowledgeable, but no less *welcoming,* are the cottage rental agencies operating, for the most part, at the regional level throughout Britain. Over the years we have personally used the agencies many times to book properties and have never been disappointed by the level of professionalism exhibited in all aspects of the relationships. There are, in fact, over two hundred such agencies operating in the UK, and we have selected properties from only a few of the best. Some of the agencies have more recently opened North American offices or offered their cottages through North American brokers specializing in self-catering properties in Europe. Likewise, we have screened these brokers for their professionalism, as well as the quality and good value of their offerings.

What about cost, you ask? Obviously, one of the great advantages of a self-catered holiday is the savings in food and accommodation, relative to hotels or even B&Bs. To be sure, there are up-market and down-market hotels, just as there are cottages across the full spectrum of "economy". *Best value* is the point, whether one is renting a luxury apartment in London, an historic castle in Scotland, or a modest thatch cottage in the West Country. Suffice it to say that, at what ever level, self catering will save hundreds of dollars relative to comparable hotel, resort, or B&B accommodations. Perhaps almost as important is the fact that renting a cottage base for your explorations will save hours and hours of searching and moving.

Time and Money Ahead...what a great way to begin a memorable holiday abroad!

4

THE PARTICULARS CODE

BEDROOM BATHROOM ARRANGEMENT

I. (ground floor); II. (2nd floor); III. (3rd floor); etc.

B (bedroom); -s (single); -b (bunks); -t (twin); -d (double);
-q (queen, approx. 60"); -k (king, approx. 74");
-t/q (joinable twins to form queen or king); -CS (convertible sofa)

F (bathroom facilities)
-1 (WC or WC with basin)
-2 (WC, basin, tub, possibly with hand-held shower)
-3 (WC, basin, shower (over tub or separate)
-4 (WC, basin, tub and/or shower + bidet)

[2] (two bedrooms or bathrooms of the same type)

SERVICES

*$ [added charge] -BA [by arrangement]   * [in some units] s [shared]*

E	(electric included); E-$ (flat charge); E-$m (metered); E-$c (coin)
H	(heat included); H-$ (flat charge); H-$c (coin); H-$m (metered)
FP	(fireplace, wood or coal supplied)
FPS	(with stove or wood stove); FPG (gas insert); FPE (electric insert);
LT	(bed linen and towels included); L (linen only); L-BA (by arrangement); T$ (extra charge for towels)
TELc	(telephone, coin); TELm (metered); TELin (incoming calls only)
TV	(color television[s]); TVV (with video)
W/D	(washer/dryer); W (washer only); D (dryer only); W/Ds (shared)
DW	(dishwasher)
MW	(microwave)

CONDITIONS, STAYS, AND RATES

NS	(non smokers please)
C-	(sorry, no children); C-BA (some conditions, usually age ranges)
P-	(sorry, no pets); P-BA (specific consent required).
E/HC	(suitably fitted for the elderly and/or physically impaired)
S-S	(Saturday to Saturday); F-F (Friday to Friday); Open (usually means open booking in the off season only)
MS	("mini-stays", generally 3 days, but varies)
INS	(cancellation insurance available from the owners or agents; almost always the premium is already included in the listed rental rate)
VAT$	(additional 17.5% tax will be charged)
BK$	(modest booking or overseas service fee will be charged by the agency)
TA	(will accept bookings through North American travel agents)
£	(low and high weekly rates in UK pounds sterling); OR
$	(low and high weekly rates quoted in US dollars)
S 5	(sleeping accommodation for five persons; range or maximum, etc.)

HOW TO USE THIS GUIDE

COTTAGE HOLIDAYING IN BRITAIN is essentially a **telephone book** and an **introductory handshake**. Our object is to get the reader as close as possible to making a personal, direct, and easy choice of a cottage base for a memorable holiday in Britain.

It's as simple as 1-2-3!

1. **Pick** the area(s) of Britain you want to explore.

2. **Pick** some prospective cottages from the selections offered for that area in the Map Indexes. Turn to the appropriate cottage entry, consider my more or less subjective comments and the more or less objective description coded into the Particulars Box. Couples and small families should not rule out larger properties (even castles!); often there are price breaks for more limited occupancy. Mini-stays under one week are available for the majority of properties during the off-season, and always worth inquiring about when booking at the last minute.

3. **Pick** up the phone and call the owners or agents directly for more detailed particulars and a personal feel for whether their cottage and location suits you. A few minutes of exploratory calling directly to the sources will cost only a few dollars. Take advantage of the 4-8 hour time difference with early morning and weekend rates. It's a small price to pay for the personal assurance that you are headed for a real holiday *home of your own!*

Key to Particulars Boxes

I. CS	First floor has a convertible sofa; also half/bath (toilet & basin).
F-1	Second floor has a bedroom with double bed and a bathroom with
II. B-d	shower over tub or shower room, in addition to toilet facilities.
F-3	Third floor has two twin-bedded rooms; no bathroom facilities.
III.B-t [2]	Electricity is metered and will be charged extra at end of stay. Heat
E$m H	is included in the weekly rate, as is the gas fireplace.
FPG	Bed linen is included, but towels will be charged extra if required.
L T$	Cottage has a coin operated telephone and at least one television.
TELc TV	Washer/dryer is included in rate, but is shared with owners or other
W/Ds	guests. There is a dishwasher and microwave.
DW MW	Non-smokers preferred; pets not allowed; age conditions apply for
NS P- C-BA	children. Some cottages are suitable for elderly or handicapped.
E/HC*	Normal start days are Saturdays; in off season stay may begin any
S-S OPEN	day. Stays for less than a week can be arranged, generally off-
MS INS	season, and cancellation insurance is provided. The weekly rate
£250-400	ranges from a low of 250 to 400 pounds sterling in high season,
S 6-8	and the cottage accommodates a maximum of eight persons.

OFFICIAL RATING SYSTEMS

England, Scotland and Wales each have official tourist boards which play a much more interventionist role in regulating and promoting holiday accommodations than is common in North America. In addition, there are very active regional tourist authorities, including one in London. Official ratings from these bodies mean something in Britain; inspections are annual and rigorous, albeit participation is voluntary and relatively expensive for the property owner.

The Official Ratings, designated as *Keys* (England), *Crowns* (Scotland), and *Dragons* (Wales) insure an ascending level of facilities and services in the self-catered unit. Somewhat facetiously, *One Key* guarantees you heat; *Two Keys* assures you won't miss your favorite BBC offerings in color; *Three Keys* gets you a heated towel rail; *Four Keys* puts you by way of a washer/dryer; and *Five Keys* secures you a telephone on which you can call the English Tourist Board if any of the other thousand items are missing on the check-off sheet. Perusing the property inventory may not be your idea of holiday time well spent, but presumably it is reassuring to know that someone does count.

Less precise, but perhaps more impressive are the Qualitative Grades which are added on top of the Ratings in England and Scotland. The designations *Approved, Commended, Highly Commended,* and *Deluxe* encompass a range of criteria including "quality" of furnishings and outdoor amenities; even the charm of the management may be assessed. It is tempting to suppose that the *Ratings* are objective and *Grades* are subjective, but in practice each tends to be a bit of both...the Welsh, in fact, explicitly meld the two, which no doubt makes the Welsh inspecting officer a force to respect! Bureaucratic though such schemes may be, there is no doubt that the upper ranges of the ETB, WTB, and STB ratings are unsullied by shoddy self-catering properties. *Deluxe* cottages are invariably just that; and one will have difficulty finding deficiencies in anything bearing the accolade *Highly Commended,* or even *Commended.*

Not all holiday property owners participate in the inspection system. In fact less than a quarter of the nearly 80,000 cottages available in Britain are officially rated. Many of these are, however, under the *discipline* of rental agencies who have jealously guarded quality standards of their own. And, most important is the self discipline and high standard of many of the property owners, themselves. You will meet many of these proud people in the pages of this book, as I have in my travels throughout Britain over the years. As with so much in the British culture, their virtue is a wonderful meld of professionalism and the amateur ideal. More than *hands-on,* these are *hearts-on* enterprises. Their house pride is your best guarantee of a comfortable and memorable stay.

Quite explicitly, none of the official schemes offer counsel on the matter of *good value,* nor, thank goodness, has the matter of *character* been reduced to an objective code. Character is, of course, in the eye of the beholder; and good value depends partly on whose pocketbook is being gored. Suffice it to say that in making my selection of properties I have sought to present a range of offerings from the distinctly economical to some quite luxurious and ostentatiously priced accommodations...but always there should be character, be it historic, contemporary, or uniquely regional. After all, it is for this that we go to Britain...again and again!

THE REGIONS OF BRITAIN

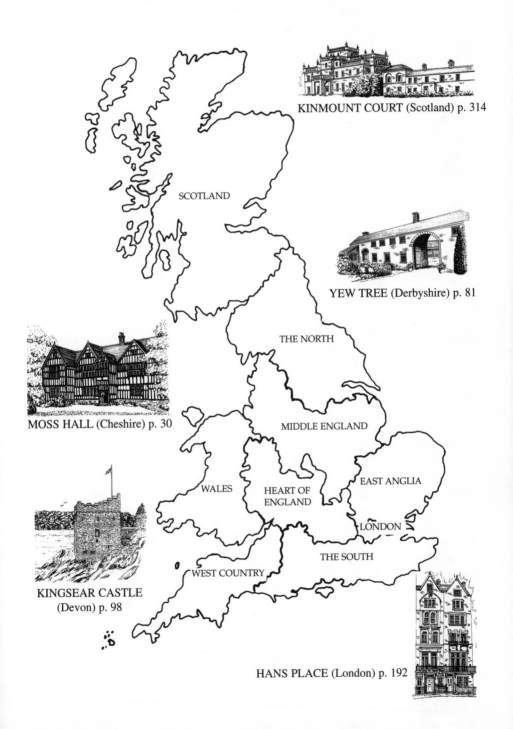

KINMOUNT COURT (Scotland) p. 314

YEW TREE (Derbyshire) p. 81

MOSS HALL (Cheshire) p. 30

KINGSEAR CASTLE
(Devon) p. 98

HANS PLACE (London) p. 192

SCOTLAND

THE NORTH

MIDDLE ENGLAND

WALES

HEART OF
ENGLAND

EAST ANGLIA

LONDON

THE SOUTH

WEST COUNTRY

THE WEST COUNTRY
Cornwall•Devon

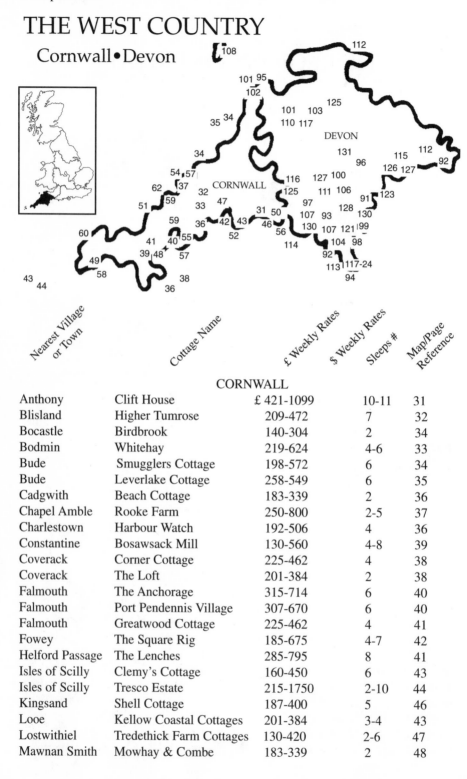

Nearest Village or Town	Cottage Name	£ Weekly Rates	$ Weekly Rates	Sleeps #	Map/Page Reference
		CORNWALL			
Anthony	Clift House	£ 421-1099		10-11	31
Blisland	Higher Tumrose	209-472		7	32
Bocastle	Birdbrook	140-304		2	34
Bodmin	Whitehay	219-624		4-6	33
Bude	Smugglers Cottage	198-572		6	34
Bude	Leverlake Cottage	258-549		6	35
Cadgwith	Beach Cottage	183-339		2	36
Chapel Amble	Rooke Farm	250-800		2-5	37
Charlestown	Harbour Watch	192-506		4	36
Constantine	Bosawsack Mill	130-560		4-8	39
Coverack	Corner Cottage	225-462		4	38
Coverack	The Loft	201-384		2	38
Falmouth	The Anchorage	315-714		6	40
Falmouth	Port Pendennis Village	307-670		6	40
Falmouth	Greatwood Cottage	225-462		4	41
Fowey	The Square Rig	185-675		4-7	42
Helford Passage	The Lenches	285-795		8	41
Isles of Scilly	Clemy's Cottage	160-450		6	43
Isles of Scilly	Tresco Estate	215-1750		2-10	44
Kingsand	Shell Cottage	187-400		5	46
Looe	Kellow Coastal Cottages	201-384		3-4	43
Lostwithiel	Tredethick Farm Cottages	130-420		2-6	47
Mawnan Smith	Mowhay & Combe	183-339		2	48

Mawnan Smith	Bosulla	250-655	7	48
Mawnan Smith	Little Bareppa	210-470	4-5	49
Millbrook	Venton House	818-1472	17	50
Penzance	Egyptian House	216-387	3-4	49
Perranporth	Reen Manor Farm	344-746	9	51
Polperro	Harbour View Cottage	200-480	2-6	52
Polperro	Bridge End House	200-450	8	53
Polperro	Osprey House	150-350	5	53
Port Issac	Homelands	154-406	5	54
Port Quin	The Fishcellars	170-300	6	54
Portscatho	Anchorage & Chapel	200-390	4	55
Rame Head	Fort Polhawn	895-2934	18-20	56
St. Endellion	Trevathan Farm	120-500	1-12	57
St. Mawes	Parc Vean	192-506	5	57
St. Mawgan	Tillers Meadow	198-512	6	59
St. Michaels Mt.	Acton Castle	187-819	4-8	58
Trevose Head	Redlands	351-943	8	62
Truro	Bosanneth	288-642	6	59
Zennor	Mermaid Cottage	250-420	5	60
Zennor	Treveglos Farmhouse	250-480	7	61

DEVON

Abbotskerswell	Willow Cottage	207-495	6	91
Axminster	Shute Gatehouse	288-613	5	92
Bigbury	Court Cottage	164-400	6	92
Blackawton	Sheplegh Court	135-378	2	93
Bolt Head	The Anchorage	840-1610	6	94
Bolt Head	Ringrone	575-1080	4-6	94
Cadbury	Fursdon	130-245	4	96
Clovelly	Leworthy Mill	182-395	5	95
Cornwood	Pigwigs Place	209-472	6	97
Dartmouth	Kingswear Castle	623-1175	6	98
Dittisham	Passage House	256-397	9	98
Dittisham	Smugglers Cottage	256-697	8	99
Drewsteignton	Gibhouse	233-612	4	100
Great Torrington	The Library	302-655	2-4	101
Hartland	Town's End Cottage	152-426	6-10	101
Hartland	Exmansworthy Farmhouse	400-970	10-12	102
Hartland	Southole	201-384	4	102
Ivybridge	The Garden Apartment	135-324	4	107
King's Nympton	Nymet	200-360	6	103
King's Nympton	Collacott Farm	135-775	2-12	103
Kingsbridge	Malston Mill Farm	156-636	2-6	104
Kingsbridge	Bolt House	276-609	6	105
Little Torrington	Church Ford House	107-271	5	110
Loddiswell	Stockadon Farm	156-495	4-6	107
Lundy Island	Lighthouse	205-624	4-5	108

THE WEST COUNTRY AVON•SOMERSET

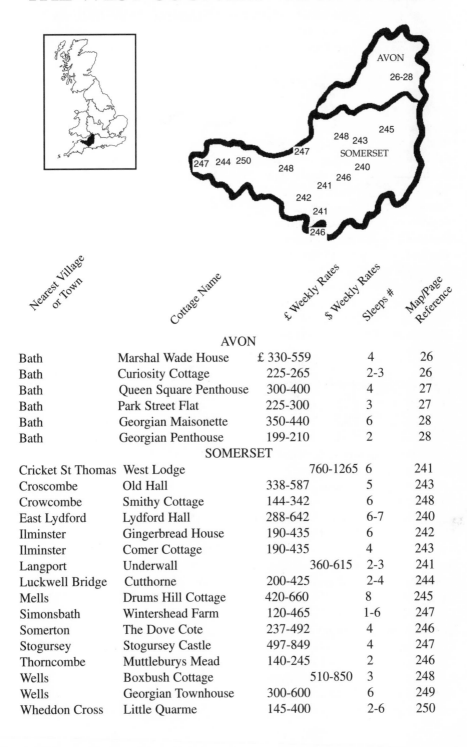

Nearest Village or Town	Cottage Name	£ Weekly Rates	$ Weekly Rates	Sleeps #	Map/Page Reference
AVON					
Bath	Marshal Wade House	£ 330-559		4	26
Bath	Curiosity Cottage	225-265		2-3	26
Bath	Queen Square Penthouse	300-400		4	27
Bath	Park Street Flat	225-300		3	27
Bath	Georgian Maisonette	350-440		6	28
Bath	Georgian Penthouse	199-210		2	28
SOMERSET					
Cricket St Thomas	West Lodge		760-1265	6	241
Croscombe	Old Hall	338-587		5	243
Crowcombe	Smithy Cottage	144-342		6	248
East Lydford	Lydford Hall	288-642		6-7	240
Ilminster	Gingerbread House	190-435		6	242
Ilminster	Comer Cottage	190-435		4	243
Langport	Underwall		360-615	2-3	241
Luckwell Bridge	Cutthorne	200-425		2-4	244
Mells	Drums Hill Cottage	420-660		8	245
Simonsbath	Wintershead Farm	120-465		1-6	247
Somerton	The Dove Cote	237-492		4	246
Stogursey	Stogursey Castle	497-849		4	247
Thorncombe	Muttleburys Mead	140-245		2	246
Wells	Boxbush Cottage		510-850	3	248
Wells	Georgian Townhouse	300-600		6	249
Wheddon Cross	Little Quarme	145-400		2-6	250

THE SOUTH Dorset•Hampshire•Kent
Surrey•Sussex(s)•Wiltshire

Nearest Village or Town	Cottage Name	£ Weekly Rates	$ Weekly Rates	Sleeps #	Map/Page Reference
		DORSET			
Bedchester	Well Cottage	£ 144-342		5	132
Bridport	The Chantry		515-735	2-4	132
Burton Bradstock	Rose Cottage	290-530		5	133
Chideock	Dawn Cottage	360-615		6	133
Corfe Castle	Knowle Barn	220-550		8	134
Corfe Castle	Scoles Manor Barn	175-775		4-8	135
Higher Bockhampton	Greenwood Grange	208-715		2-6	136
Longburton	Gate Lodge		620-1290	6	137
Lyme Regis	Armada House	168-636		6-10	137
Milton Abbas	Old Chapel Cottage		395-875	6	138
Puddletown	Higher Waterston Farm	215-410		2-6	138
Sherborne	Marsh Court	100-240		4-5	139
		HAMPSHIRE			
Bartley	Forest Glade Cottage	250-370		4	154
Beaulieu	Ladycross Estate	199-630		2-6	155
Droxford	Pond Cottage		305-525	2-3	154
Eaglehurst	Luttrell's Tower	578-954		4	156
Emery Down	Hawthorn Cottage	270-410		5	156
Lymington	Rose Cottage		490-855	3-5	157
Lymington	Kings Huts		305-525	4	159
Lyndhurst	Forest Bank Cottage	220-410		6	158
Rockbourne	Wisteria Cottage	144-342		5	159
Rockbourne	Old Stable Cottage		490-855	4	160

Stockbridge	Horsebridge Station	475-855	2-4	161

KENT

Bethersden	Brissenden Court	175-950	2-10	171
Boughton Monchelsea	Dove Cote	175-250	4	171
Canterbury	Knowlton Court	95-325	6	172
Canterbury	Dower House	575-1100	19	173
Canterbury	Prospect Tower	289-340	2	174
Cowden	Hole Cottage	408-600	4	174
Fawkham	Three Gates Stable Cottages	180-300	2-5	177
Goldhill Mill	Ciderpress & Walnut Tree	275-625	4-6	175
Goudhurst	Three Chimneys Farm	171-501	2-6	176
Sandwich	St. John's Cottages	155-195	2-4	178
Sevenoaks	Lambards Oast	555-605	2	177

SURREY

East Molesey	Hampton Court Palace	549-995	6-8	254

SUSSEX(s)

Brighton	Seapoint	255-485	4	255
Brighton	Hanover Crescent	225-995	2-8	256
Brighton	Eyebright Cottage	225-395	5	258
Brighton	Marine House	255-425	4	258
Charlton	Fox Hall	377-610	4	261
Chiddingly	Pekes Manor	290-1065	4-8	259
Chiddingly	Bull River Cottage	200-360	2	260
Crawley	Above Par	120-200	5	260
Hove	Brunswick Square	295-575	6	262
Lewes	Laughton Place	391-614	4	261
Lewes	Southerham Old Barns	365-1535	2-10	264
Litlington	Stable Cottage	370-790	5	265
Patcham Old Village	Glebe Cottage	160-300	6	263
Rottingdean	Blacksmiths Cottage	195-355	2-4	257
Rye	Cobble Cottage	395-720	6	267
Telscombe Village	Duck Barn	120-575	2-10	266
Wepham	Wepham Farm Stables	213-425	4-6	265

WILTSHIRE

Bradford-on-Avon	The Dower House	350-550	6	271
Manningford Bohune Common	The Old Church	450	6	270
Marlborough	Jasmine Cottage	490-855	4	272
Melksham	Coach House	320-615	2-5	272
Netheravon	The Stables	220-350	5	273
Salisbury	The Wardrobe	345-548	4	273
Tisbury	Academy Cottage	620-1090	6-8	274
Wootten Rivers	Mortimer Cottage	450-785	4-5	274

LONDON

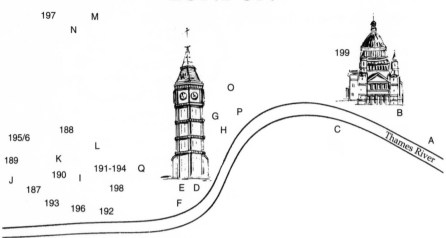

A. Tower of London	G. Picadilly Square	M. Regents Park
B. St. Pauls Cathedral	H. Trafalgar Square	& London Zoo
C. National Theatre	I. Natural History Museum	N. Lords Cricket
D. Parliament	J. Holland Park	O. British Museum
E. Westminster Abbey	K. Kensington Park	P. Theatre District
F. Tate Gallery	L. Hyde Park	Q. Buckingham Palace

LONDON

District	Street or Bldg. Name	£ Weekly Rates	Sleeps #	Map/Page Reference
Bayswater	Inverness Terrace	£ 650-950	3-6	188
Chelsea	Mallord Street	525	2	192
Earl's Court	Richmond Mansions	925	5	193
Earl's Court	Penywern Road	500	4	187
Holland Park	Ladbroke Square House	400-500	4	189
Kensington	Stratford Road	1075	4-6	190
Kensington	De Vere Mews	595	2-4	190
Knightsbridge	Cheval Place	400-500	3-4	191
Knightsbridge	Hans Place	975	4	192
Knightsbridge	Beaufort Gardens	1425	5	193
Knightsbridge	Beaufort House	785-2205	2-7	194
Notting Hill	Artesian Road	500	6	195
Notting Hill	Hereford Mansions	595	2-3	196
Park Walk	Stanley Mansions	795	4	196
St. John's Wood	Abbey House	250	4	197
Sloane Square	Service Suites	366-959	1-6	198
Smithfield	Cloth Fair	369-up	2-4	199
South Kensington	Brechin Place	500-600	4	189

EAST ANGLIA
Norfolk•Suffolk

Nearest Village or Town	Cottage Name	£ Weekly Rates	$ Weekly Rates	Sleeps #	Map/Page Reference
		NORFOLK			
Claxton	Lambs Court	£ 295-676		8-10	201
Cranworth	Old Gamebird Cottages	130-360		2-6	202
Burnham Market	Foundry Barn	250-468		6	200
Burnham Market	Foundry Cottage	250-468		6	200
Erpingham	Lees Farm	196-442		6	203
Fakenham	Hindringham Hall Cottages		480-865	4	202
Hickling	Old Chapel Cottage	170-210		4	204
Holt	The White House	272-510		6-8	204
Houghton St Giles	Giles Cottage		460-660	2-3	205
Merton	Rose Cottage	132-276		3	206
Mulbarton	The Long Barn	104-346		2-6	207
Norwich	Worsted Cottage	220-280		3	208
Norwich	Strangers Court	250-320		4	208
Plumstead	The Farmhouse	227-425		8-10	205
Sandringham	Appleton Water Tower	352-613		4	209
South Raynham	Vere Lodge	213-924		2-7	210
Sustead	Beck Farm	170-318		5	209
Syderstone	Harpers Cottage	124-248		4	211
Wiveton	Golden Goose Cottage	170-318		4	212
Wymondham	Stable Cottage	132-276		4	212
Wymondham	The Directors Saloon	132-276		4	213
		SUFFOLK			
Aldeburgh	Martello Tower	431-683		5	251
Badwell Ash	Lodge Cottage	250-420		8	252
Market Weston	Green Cottage	145-312		5	253
Otley Bottom	Primrose Cottage	450-640		4-7	253
Stowlangtoft	Old Rectory Flat	110-200		2	254

HEART OF ENGLAND
Berkshire•Gloucestershire•Hereford &
Worcestershire•Oxfordshire•Shropshire•Warwickshire

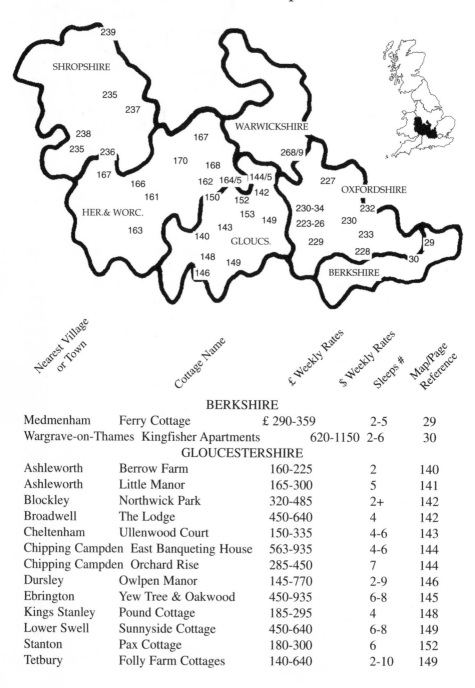

BERKSHIRE

Nearest Village or Town	Cottage Name	£ Weekly Rates	$ Weekly Rates	Sleeps #	Map/Page Reference
Medmenham	Ferry Cottage	£ 290-359		2-5	29
Wargrave-on-Thames	Kingfisher Apartments		620-1150	2-6	30

GLOUCESTERSHIRE

Nearest Village or Town	Cottage Name	£ Weekly Rates	$ Weekly Rates	Sleeps #	Map/Page Reference
Ashleworth	Berrow Farm	160-225		2	140
Ashleworth	Little Manor	165-300		5	141
Blockley	Northwick Park	320-485		2+	142
Broadwell	The Lodge	450-640		4	142
Cheltenham	Ullenwood Court	150-335		4-6	143
Chipping Campden	East Banqueting House	563-935		4-6	144
Chipping Campden	Orchard Rise	285-450		7	144
Dursley	Owlpen Manor	145-770		2-9	146
Ebrington	Yew Tree & Oakwood	450-935		6-8	145
Kings Stanley	Pound Cottage	185-295		4	148
Lower Swell	Sunnyside Cottage	450-640		6-8	149
Stanton	Pax Cottage	180-300		6	152
Tetbury	Folly Farm Cottages	140-640		2-10	149

Tewkesbury	Apple Tree Cottage	200-600	12	150
Tewkesbury	Stonemasons House	150-325	5	151
Winchcombe	Tythe Barn Cottages	160-500	2-6	151
Winchcombe	Sudeley Castle Cottages	153-495	2-7	153

HEREFORDSHIRE & WORCESTERSHIRE

Bredon	Bredon Hill	530-1485	5-6	162
Bridstow	Wye Lea Country Manor	234-865	2-8	163
Broadway	Broadway Court Cottages	260-385	2-4	164
Broadway	Stanton Court Cottages	485-1320	2-6	165
Canon Frome	Swiss Cottage	275-575	2	161
Crowle	The Cottages	132-240	3-4	167
Much Cowarne	Cowarne Hall	180-575	2-8	166
Pudleston	Ghorst Farm Cottage	306-326	4	167
Sedgeberrow	Hall Farm Cottages	115-430	2-6	169
Vale of Evesham	Abbots Court Cottages	155-1395	2-6	168
West Malvern	Cottages at Westwood	210-520	4-6	170

OXFORDSHIRE

Bruern	Aintree Cottage	328-530	6	223
Burford	The Mill at Burford	140-440	2-5	224
Chipping Norton	Badger Cottage	177-354	4	225
Churchill	The Little Cottage	160-255	2-4	226
Culworth	Cavaliers Cottage	215-363	4	227
East Hagbourne	The Oast House	360-700	8	228
Faringdon	Coxwell House	350-650	6	229
Great Tew	Bluebell Cottage	360-615	5	230
Islip	The Cottage	180-250	3	230
Kingham	Keen's Cottage	170-340	4	231
Minster Lovell	White Hall	150-340	4-6	232
Oxford	The Old Parsonage	546-852	6	233
Oxford	#7 St. Michaels Street	280-430	2	233
Swerford	Heath Farm	180-350	2-4	234
Tusmore	Pimlico Farm Cottages	140-395	2-6	232

SHROPSHIRE

Clun	The Bothy	290-425	2	235
Eyton-on-Severn	The Summer House	640-735	2	235
Ironbridge	Music Master's House	95-315	2-6	237
Lydbury North	Walcot Hall	168-250	2-8	238
Ludlow	Bromfield Priory Gatehouse	371-602	6	236
Whitchurch	Ashwood	185-369	6	239

WARWICKSHIRE

Stratford-upon-Avon	Hathaway Hamlets	475-695	2-3	268
Stratford-upon-Avon	Priest's House	570-855	4	268
Stratford-upon-Avon	The Bath House	313-481	2	269

MIDDLE ENGLAND

Cheshire•Derbyshire•Lancashire• Leicestershire•Lincolnshire & Nottinghamshire•Northamptonshire• Staffordshire•West Midlands

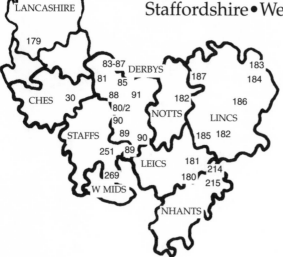

Nearest Village or Town	Cottage Name	£ Weekly Rates	$ Weekly Rates	Sleeps #	Map/Page Reference
		CHESHIRE			
Audlem	Moss Hall		$420-850	2-4	30
		DERBYSHIRE			
Ashbourne	Yeldersley Hall	£ 140-395		2-4	80
Ashbourne	Dairy House Farm	145-300		2-4	82
Ashford-in-the-Water	Kitty's Cottage	187-332		4	81
Barlow	Oxton Rakes Hall Farm	210-275		2-4	83
Blore	Blore Hall Cottages	216-866		2-8	84
Buxton	Cressbrook Hall Cottages		240-1070	2-6	84
Cromford	Wharf Cottage		570-1035	4	85
Edale	Sycamore Cottage		475-695	2	86
Hathersage	North Lees Hall		515-900	2-5	87
Ilam	Cottage by the Pond	110-385		2-6	88
Lullington	Rose Cottage	95-130		2-3	89
Mickleover	Bank Cottage	170		4	89
Ticknall	Swarkestone Pavilion	221-304		2	90
Snelston	Oldfield House Stable Wing	163-269		4	90
Wirksworth	Wisteria Cottage	118-197		2	91

THE NORTH
Cumbria•Durham•
Northumberland•
Yorkshire(s)

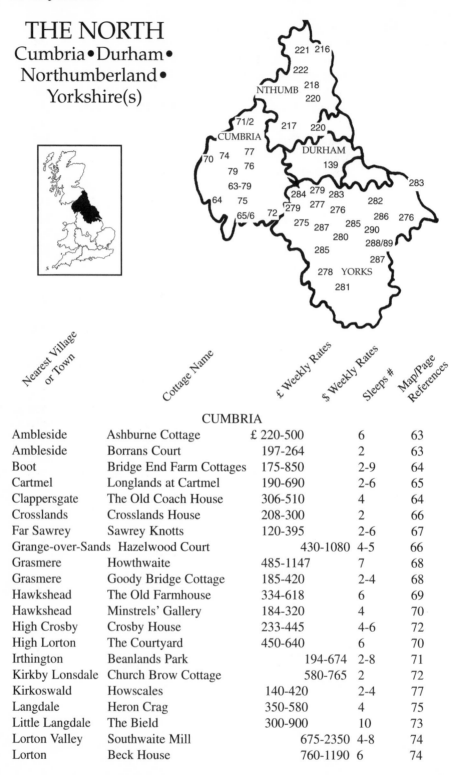

Nearest Village or Town	Cottage Name	£ Weekly Rates	$ Weekly Rates	Sleeps #	Map/Page References
CUMBRIA					
Ambleside	Ashburne Cottage	£ 220-500		6	63
Ambleside	Borrans Court	197-264		2	63
Boot	Bridge End Farm Cottages	175-850		2-9	64
Cartmel	Longlands at Cartmel	190-690		2-6	65
Clappersgate	The Old Coach House	306-510		4	64
Crosslands	Crosslands House	208-300		2	66
Far Sawrey	Sawrey Knotts	120-395		2-6	67
Grange-over-Sands	Hazelwood Court		430-1080	4-5	66
Grasmere	Howthwaite	485-1147		7	68
Grasmere	Goody Bridge Cottage	185-420		2-4	68
Hawkshead	The Old Farmhouse	334-618		6	69
Hawkshead	Minstrels' Gallery	184-320		4	70
High Crosby	Crosby House	233-445		4-6	72
High Lorton	The Courtyard	450-640		6	70
Irthington	Beanlands Park		194-674	2-8	71
Kirkby Lonsdale	Church Brow Cottage		580-765	2	72
Kirkoswald	Howscales	140-420		2-4	77
Langdale	Heron Crag	350-580		4	75
Little Langdale	The Bield	300-900		10	73
Lorton Valley	Southwaite Mill		675-2350	4-8	74
Lorton	Beck House		760-1190	6	74

Newby Bridge	Conegliano	275-490	4	75
Penrith	Kirkland Hall Cottages	210-415	6	76
Rydal	Rydal Mount Cottage	201-495	5	77
Skelwith Bridge	Riverside Cottages	295-786	2-6	78
Troutbeck	Betty's Cottages	250-550	6	79
Ullswater	Lakefield	255-685	8	79

DURHAM

Staindrop	Peel Tower	530-1225	5	139

NORTHUMBERLAND

Bamburgh	# 8 Front Street	150-450	6	216
Hexham	Gibbs Hill Farm Cottages	150-379	2-4	217
Longhorsley	Beacon Hill Farm	160-850	2-6	218
Newcastle-upon-Tyne	The Banqueting House	337-671	4	220
Whalton	Gallowhill Farm	190-385	4-6	220
Whitton	The Pele Tower	248-467	4	222
Wooler	Coupland Castle Tower	1280-1745	7-8	221

YORKSHIRE(s)

Bellerby	Vine Cottage	180-295	4-6	276
Buckden	Dalegarth Cottages	274-426	4-6	275
Buckden	The Ghyll	286-409	2-6	275
Countersett	Bee-Bole Cottage	175-265	3	277
Ebberston	Cliff House Cottages	160-630	2-6	276
Grinton	Virginia Cottage	690-1140	8	277
Haworth	Westfield Farm	130-300	2-6	278
Hebden Bridge	Great Burlees	250-665	2-6	278
Langstrothdale Chase	Low Greenfield Farm	244-349	2-6	279
Langthwaite	Hilltop Cottage	215-280	4	279
Luddenden Dean	Upper Mytholm Barn	260-450	6	281
Pateley Bridge	Rivulet Court	180-400	6-8	280
Richmond	Culloden Tower	403-741	4	283
Robin Hood's Bay	The Pigsty	289-512	2	283
Rosedale Abbey	Bell End Farm	208-813	2-6	282
Sedbusk	Jasmine Cottage	150-345	7	284
Selby	Cawood Castle	252-417	2	287
Skipton	Beamsley Hospital	470-784	5	285
Sowerby	Lime Tree Cottage	190-260	2	285
Swinnithwaite	The Temple	220-315	2	287
Wrelton	Beech Farm Cottages	225-1250	2-10	286
Yearsley	Baytree Cottage	215-280	4	290
York	Turks Head Court	400-900	4-6	288
York	# 45 Monkgate	400-875	4-6	288
York	Baile Gate House	180-620	6-8	289

WALES

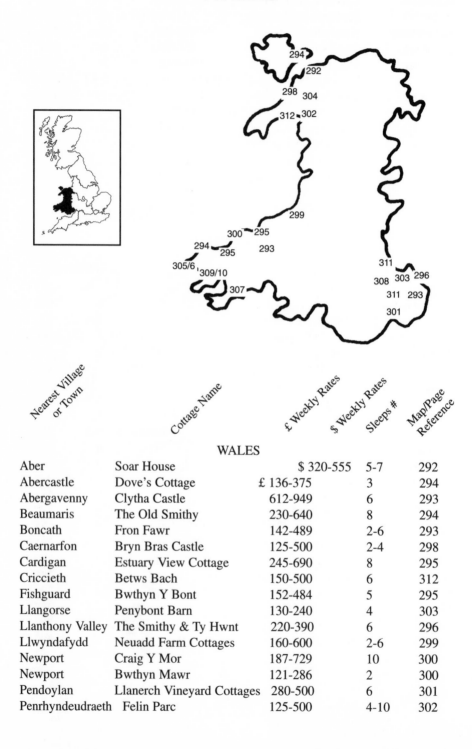

Nearest Village or Town	Cottage Name	£ Weekly Rates	$ Weekly Rates	Sleeps #	Map/Page Reference
		WALES			
Aber	Soar House		$ 320-555	5-7	292
Abercastle	Dove's Cottage	£ 136-375		3	294
Abergavenny	Clytha Castle	612-949		6	293
Beaumaris	The Old Smithy	230-640		8	294
Boncath	Fron Fawr	142-489		2-6	293
Caernarfon	Bryn Bras Castle	125-500		2-4	298
Cardigan	Estuary View Cottage	245-690		8	295
Criccieth	Betws Bach	150-500		6	312
Fishguard	Bwthyn Y Bont	152-484		5	295
Llangorse	Penybont Barn	130-240		4	303
Llanthony Valley	The Smithy & Ty Hwnt	220-390		6	296
Llwyndafydd	Neuadd Farm Cottages	160-600		2-6	299
Newport	Craig Y Mor	187-729		10	300
Newport	Bwthyn Mawr	121-286		2	300
Pendoylan	Llanerch Vineyard Cottages	280-500		6	301
Penrhyndeudraeth	Felin Parc	125-500		4-10	302

Rhostryfan	The Old Bakery	200-390		6	304
St. Davids	Calves Cot Cottage	245-750		9-10	305
St. Davids	Pebbles Cottage		600	4	306
St. Florence	Kingfisher Cottage	190-480		4	307
Scethrog	The Tower	350-600		4-6	308
Solva	Bridge View Cottage	190-499		5	309
Solva	Cerbid Farmhouses	215-799		8-10	310
Talgarth	Bronllys Castle House	180-325		4-6	311
Upper Llangynidr	Hope Cottage	180-295		4	311

THE CHANNEL ISLANDS

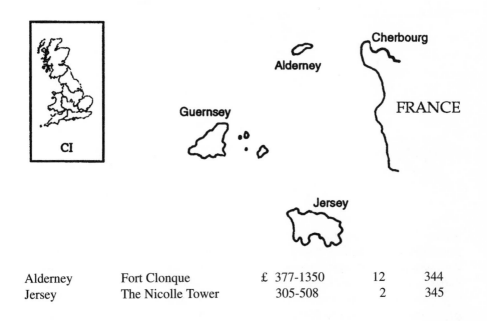

| Alderney | Fort Clonque | £ 377-1350 | 12 | 344 |
| Jersey | The Nicolle Tower | 305-508 | 2 | 345 |

SCOTLAND

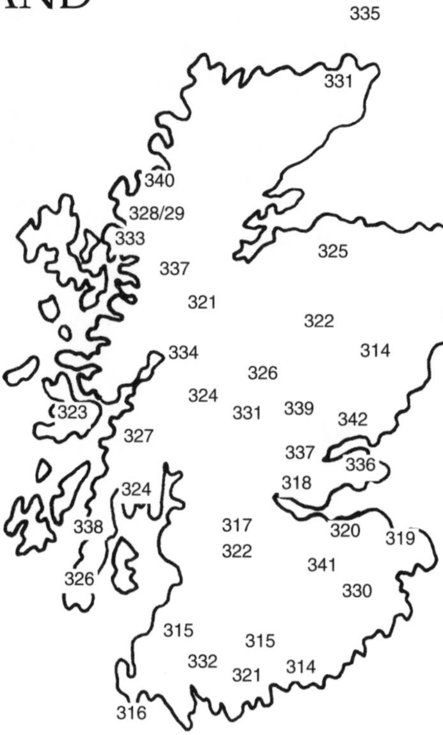

335

331

340
328/29
333
337
325
321
322
334
326
314
324
331 339 342
327
337 336
324
318
338
317 320 319
322
326
341
330

315
315
332 314
321
316

Nearest Village or Town	Cottage Name	£ Weekly Rates	$ Weekly Rates	Sleeps #	Map/Page Reference
		SCOTLAND			
Annan	Kinmount Court		$ 425-1870	2-6	314
Auldgirth	Barjarg Back Lodge	£ 135-205		4	315
Banchory	Village Cottage	275-375		4	314
Barrhill	Black Clauchrie House	710-1100		16	315
Castle Douglas	Barncrosh Farm	85-350		2-8	317
Drummore	Harbour Row	160-395		4-6	316
Drummore	Kirkmaiden House	850		10	316
Dunmore	The Pineapple	271-641		4	318
Dundee	Westbeach	280-420		6	342
East Linton	Traprain Cottage	199-415		4-5	319
Edinburgh	Rosslyn Castle	526-985		7	317
Edinburgh	Royal Mile Mansions	225-450		4-6	320
Fort William	Druimarbin Farmhouse	500		7	321
Girthon	The Millhouse	200-380		7	321
Glasgow	52 Charlotte Street	325-390		2-3	322
Glenbuchat	Coldstriffen Cottage		575-950	6	322

Isle of Bute	Arran View	575-1200	4	324
Isle of Mull	Tiroran House	150-364	2-7	323
Keith	Drummuir Castle Estate	172-314	2+	325
Kilchrenan	Larach Bhan	1180-2620	7-9	324
Kilmelford	Melfort Pier Harbour Lodge	395-895	2-6	327
Kintyre	Saddell Castle	718-1452	8	326
Lochearnhead	Earnknowe Cottages	100-335	2-6	331
Loch Shieldaig	Arrowdale	240-500	9	328
Loch Shieldaig	Innis Bheatha	240-500	7	329
Loch Tummel	Donlellan	300-700	7	326
Lyth	Barrock House	845-1870	10	331
Melrose	Eildon Holiday Cottages	180-380	2-5	330
Newton Stewart	Shennanton House	690-950	8-11	332
North Connel	Ardshellach	150-370	7	334
Orkney Isles	Skaill House Flats	230-430	5-7	335
Plockton	Achnandarach Lodge	850-1200	9	333
Rumbling Bridge	Pavilion Cottage	575-1200	4	337
Ratagan	Kintail	316-373	4-6	337
St. Andrews	Dron Court	140-495	2-9	336
Tarbert	Dunmore Villa	340-695	10	338
Tarbert	Dunmore Court	150-395	5-7	338
Trochry	Wester Ballachraggan	300-500	6	339
Ullapool	Rhidorroch Estate Cottages	360-480	2-10	340
West Calder	Crosswoodhill Farm	140-300	5	341

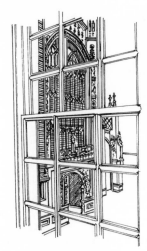

MARSHAL WADE HOUSE
Bath

If I were to say that Bath is the prettiest city in Britain I am quite sure someone would protest. Alright, I concede, maybe Bath is not really a *city*. Scale can be deceiving, and whether Bath is a large town or a small city, the fact is that Bath has more to see and do than any city I know twenty times its size, and this survey need not confine itself to Britain.

Certainly one of Bath's principal sights is the Abbey, dating from the late 15th century. There are many perspectives on this sacred building, but mid-elevation out your front window is not a viewplane enjoyed by most tourists. Call it your *private audience*.

Field Marshal George Wade built this splendid townhouse adjacent to the Abbey in about 1720, and the Landmark Trust now offers the beautifully restored third and fourth floors as a holiday flat. The rooms are nicely paneled, including the kitchen, which features a unique octagonal utilities island, thereby leaving the historic paneling unabutted. The rooms are not over furnished, but every piece contributes to the special historic atmosphere. There are interesting pictures on the walls and out the window.

III.F-1
IV.B-d
B-t
F-2
E&H
LT
P-
S-S   MS
INS
£330-559
S 4

Contact The Landmark Trust, Shottesbrook, Maidenhead, Berkshire SL6 3SW
TEL 01144-1628-825925 or FAX 01144-1628-825-417

CURIOSITY COTTAGE
Bath

If you can't see a mob of the finest BBC character actors milling about under the broad keyed arch of this *close* leading to the Old Curiosity Shoppe, then you just don't have a proper Dickensian imagination! This little Georgian shop, with its expansive small pane window, was said to have inspired Dickens to write *The Curiosity Shop*. I have no doubt that in its contemporary life as a holiday cottage it will inspire many a fond memory of a lovely visit to Bath. This is a residential area now, off a tree-filled square near the Royal Crescent. Curiosity Cottage has a private interior garden patio which contributes to the bright & airy atmosphere in the downstairs living room, just as the character window in front brilliantly lights the dining area. The upstairs bedroom shares in the perspective over the patio. Throughout, the furnishings are tasteful and comfy in floral motifs with several quite interesting antique pieces. If we can ever use the term *quaint* to describe a town property, this is it!

ETB 3 Keys; Commended

I. CS
F-2
II.B-d
E&H
LT
TELm TV
MW
C-BA P-
F-F
BK$
£225-265
S 2-3

Contact Celia Hutton, Bath Holiday Homes, 3 Frankley Buildings, Bath BA1 6EG, TEL 01144-1225-332-221

QUEEN SQUARE PENTHOUSE

Bath

Here we have a luxury penthouse at bargain basement rates. The dignified vine covered Georgian facade of the building promises something special. The elegant stairwell, with low risers, curved mezzanine landings and exquisite plaster work, all lit by Palladian windows, enhances the promise. Three flights up and you are in the private hall of the penthouse, though the sky-lighting lends a roof garden atmosphere.

III.B-q
F-3
B-t
F-4
E&H
LT
TELm
TVV
W/D
DW MW
C-BA P-
F-F
BK$
£300-400
S 4

The living room and kitchen are at opposite ends of a spacious open plan, with dining in the middle. Furnishings are eclectic, but all very tasteful and well suited to the handsome architectural detail. The view from the front is over the wooded square with the slopes of Beechen Cliff beyond. The kitchen and dining facilities are ultra modern, as are the bathrooms. The bedrooms are pleasingly furnished; understated really.
ETB 5 Keys; Highly Commended

PARK STREET FLAT Bath

High marks for the design choices in the conversion of the ground floor of this fine Georgian town house into a separate flat. Too often the statuesque old double parlors are rudely carved up to accommodate the spatial divisions needed for all the modern conveniences. In this case the designer's priority was to preserve and restore the back parlor as if it were still the principal room of a grand house. The result may be a bit skimpy in the bedrooms and compact in the kitchen and bathroom, but the living room is magnificently spacious, with all the Georgian proportions to revel in. The dining table is in the lovely bow end with massive 6/6 pane windows looking down into a garden. There are lovely dentil mouldings, lighted alcoves, a marble fireplace with a coal/gas fire, and a beautiful gilt mirror over the mantle. The soft furnishings are modern and cream, and the room is accented with nice plants and richly grained antiques. It is only a ten minute walk to the city center. ETB 3 Keys; Highly Commended

I.B-d
B-s
F-3
E&H
FPG
LT
TELm
TV
MW
P-
Sun-Sun
BK$
£225-300
S 3

Contact Celia Hutton, Bath Holiday Homes, 3 Frankley Buildings, Bath BA1 6EG
TEL 01144-1225-332-221

GEORGIAN MAISONETTE
Bath

This is not one of Bath's most perfect Georgian structures...lacking ornamentation it is, in fact, quite plain. Imagine your surprise were you to peek into the two street level windows to the right in the drawing! What royal personage lives here, you might ask? It is, indeed, a very courtly scene: creamy silk drapes beautifully swagged and tied back, finely paneled walls, ornately corniced ceiling, elegantly arched alcoves, and a statuesque marble fireplace. Suffice it to say that the furnishings are of the same standard, and plenty of attention has been paid to the details of decor, lighting, plants and the little pretty particulars. The street elevation also contains the kitchen with a dining area in the bay overlooking a secluded two tier patio garden in the rear. The garden, which may be accessed from the lower floor where the bedrooms are located, is for the exclusive use of this apartment and is equipped with a table and chairs. The bedrooms are prettily decorated, though not proportioned quite so regally as the upper rooms. The master bedroom is en-suite with shower and occupies the bay window perspective on the garden.
ETB 3 Keys; Commended

| I. B-d |
| F-3 [2] |
| B-t [2] |
| E&H |
| LT |
| TELm |
| TVV |
| W |
| DW MW |
| C-BA P- |
| S-S |
| BK$ |
| £350-440 |
| S 6 |

GEORGIAN PENTHOUSE Bath

As with the property above, this apartment is conveniently located in the very heart of Bath on a residential street quite near the Assembly Rooms. The apartment, which is on the third floor, is compact but exceptionally well lit, having window perspectives over the roof tops to both the east and west, as well as sky-lighting. Recent renovations have rendered a very cheery environ, with plenty of garden greenery in place around the pristine white rooms. Furnishings are modern and tasteful and there are colorful decoratives to give the apartment a very homey feel. The kitchen is galley style, joined by an open archway to the living room. There is a small counter and stools by the kitchen window.

This apartment is approached by a communal hallway and stairwell. All the flats in the house have video entry phone systems to screen visitors.
ETB 3 Keys; Commended

| III.B-t |
| F-3 |
| E&H |
| LT |
| TELc TV |
| W/D |
| MW |
| P- |
| S-S |
| BK$ |
| £199-210 |
| S 2 |

Contact Celia Hutton, Bath Holiday Homes, 3 Frankley Buildings, Bath BA1 6EG
TEL 01144-1225-332-221

FERRY COTTAGE

Medmenham

Medmenham is on the *Royal River*, six miles downstream from the famous regatta town of Henley-on-Thames. The parish church here dates from 650 AD and was rebuilt around 1150, just in time to have its church bell thrown into the ransom paid for King Richard I. The delightful village pub, The Dog & Badger, was built about the same time as the famous Medmenham Abbey (13th century), which was restored by the Hellfire Club in the middle of the last century (the Abbey, that is, not the pub, which has maintained its own restorative powers).

Entrance to Ferry Cottage is through electronically operated gates and up a large drive. This is a garden cottage, converted to a high standard, overlooking the owners' colorful garden surrounded by mature shrubs, apple trees and woods. To the rear of the cottage is a large patio with all the necessary furnishings for quiet alfresco dining. The brick built barbecue is also available for use by the guests.

The cottage is nicely laid out with the living area upstairs. At ground level one enters to a hall and thence a country style kitchen, fitted in pine cabinetry, tiled counters, and all the most up-to-date equipment. There is a dining area here; bench seating with comfortable cushions covered in Country Diary fabrics. Large prints and dried flower arrangements fill out the cozy atmosphere. A "stable" door leads out to the patio. Upstairs, the living room is spacious and bright under open (sloping) rafters, with deep pile wall to wall carpeting in cornflower blue to match the curtains. There is a sofa, as well as a three seater bed settee, plus assorted armchairs and wicker furnishings. The bedroom is also quite bright, with a large picture window overlooking the lawn.

The Thames from Oxford to Windsor, girdled by its many locks, is the most gentle byway in the land. Boats with paddles or power are for hire in Henley and Hurley and one need not be a veteran of the regatta to safely navigate these waters. I know of no better way of seeing this part of England than from the *Royal Canal*. Every bend in the river (and there are lots of them!) presents a brilliant picture worthy of hanging in the National Gallery...sometimes it's a Turneresque quick glimpse of nature being natural; other times the scene is Impressionist, a voyeur's misty perspective on humanity being natural.

ETB 4 Keys; Highly Commended

I. F-1
II.CS
B-d+s
E&H
LT
TVV
W/D-BA
DW   MW
S-S
TA
£290-359
S 2-5

Contact Cottage in the Country, Forest Gate, Frog Lane, Milton-U-Wychwood, Oxford OX7 6JZ
TEL 01144-1993-831-495 or FAX 01144-1993-831-095

KINGFISHER APARTMENTS
Wargrave on Thames

Britain offers great variety in holiday experiences. Certainly among the most memorable for us have been the times spent potting about on the Thames, culminating in *oarside* seats for the famous Henley Regatta. Seeing the English countryside from the water is a unique treat, very often like drifting quietly through a Turner painting. In our first go at a Thames holiday twenty plus years ago we rented a house boat to call home, which carried with it some nautical responsibilities that became increasingly burdensome. Today, I recommend waterside accommodations with a smaller power launch for day excursions and explorations. The *Royal Canal* is really just a lazy swan-filled stream up here; lined with historic sites from Windsor to Oxford (all accessible from the water); dotted by charming locks and pretty villages with friendly pubs, as well as grassy banks to pull over for a picnic. If you're curious about *how the other half lives*, there are plenty of waterside mansions exclusively screened from the land, but exposed to vicarious viewing from the water.

The over & under pair of Kingfisher flats are right on the water, with boats available for hire from the owner. The ground floor unit offers two bedrooms, the flat above has one bedroom with an additional sofa bed, sleeping two. The apartments are prettily furnished and decorated, with inviting outdoor amenities on the riverside terrace or garden.

E&H	
LT	
TV	
DW	MW
P-	
F-F	MS
INS	
BK$	
$620-1150	
S 2-6	

MOSS HALL Audlem

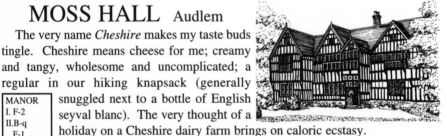

The very name *Cheshire* makes my taste buds tingle. Cheshire means cheese for me; creamy and tangy, wholesome and uncomplicated; a regular in our hiking knapsack (generally snuggled next to a bottle of English seyval blanc). The very thought of a holiday on a Cheshire dairy farm brings on caloric ecstasy.

Moss Hall is the manor house on a 140-acre dairy operation. This classic *magpie* structure dates from the early 1600s, and you will find the two guest wing apartments, named Tudor Rose & Manor Oak, rich in Tudor interiors: exposed timbers, oak paneling, and latticed window views. Furnishings are in a traditional idiom, reserved and tasteful, with a touch of *brass* in the queen size beds.

There are a number of touring opportunities from a base at Moss Hall. The Welsh Border attractions are a short drive, and the City of Chester, with its near perfect Roman Wall and splendid black & white architecture, is a must see. Or simply pack a wedge of Cheshire and a bottle of wine in your knapsack and stroll along the old Shropshire Union Canal towpath which passes the property.   3 Keys; Highly Commended

MANOR
I. F-2
II.B-q
F-1
B-t
FPE
$510-850
S 4
TUDOR R.
II.B-q
F-2
CS
MW
$420-750
S 2-3
BOTH
E&H
LT
TV
W
NS
S-S   MS
INS

Contact Meta Voyage, 1945 Pauline Plaza, Suite 14, Ann Arbor, MI 48103-5047
TEL 800-771-4771 (East) 800-538-6881 (West) or FAX 313-995-3464

CLIFT FARM
Antony

We are just across the River Tamar from Plymouth near the great Queen Anne masterpiece of architecture, Antony House...quite near, in fact just a short walk up the road. Indeed, the Carews of Antony House still own the land around Clift Farm. Clift Farmhouse is a rambling Grade II Listed property dating from the 13th century with its "modern" wing added about the time of the Civil War (that's Oliver Cromwell, not Robert E. Lee!). Actually, this house has grown with time rather than by design, beginning as a one-roomer, expanding into a longhouse inhabited by man and beast, and thence enjoying a monastic period of development.

The property is nicely situated on its own tidal creek flowing into the Lynher River estuary, a paradise for bird watchers and naturalists, generally. A dinghy is available for potting about the creeks and mud flats, and larger boats can be rented in the area for more ambitious explorations of St. John's Lake and the lower Tamar. There is good fishing for bass, mackerel and flounder.

Clift House is spacious, to say the least. The living room-cum-library is entered through a studded oak door...this is an impressive room for its architectural features (high beamed ceiling, massive stone fireplace, flagstone floor) and exceptional furnishings (grand piano, fine rugs, shelves of literature and walls covered with worthy paintings). All the furnishings are comfortable and some are quite extraordinary antiques, which tells one right away that this is a family home, not just a holiday let. The dining room has a wonderful window seat under Gothic windows and a log burning stove. There are two stairwells up to five bedrooms; one with king size bed and lovely views over the estuary, sharing a large bathroom with the twin next door. Another twin has an ancient carved door and a plasterwork frieze; another with fireplace; and a fifth bedroom may be had up the steep stairs to the third floor. Of the kitchen we need only say that it has Poggenpohl fixtures and an Aga...a four-oven Aga!

I. F-1
II. B-k
B-t [2]
B-d+s
F-4
F-2 [2]
III.B-d
E-$m
H-$
FPS-$
LT
TELc
TV
W/D
DW MW
P-BA
S-S MS
INS
BK$
£421-1099
S 10-11

Contact Helpful Holidays, Coombe, Chagford, Devon TQ13 8DF
TEL 01144-1647-433-593 or FAX 01144-1647-433-694

HIGHER TUMROSE   Blisland

It may be said that there are two kinds of Anglophiles: moor lovers and those who can't quite square the rugged grandeur of the moors with their highly *civilized* image of England. For the latter, the moors belong in Scotland. Among the former, that is the passionate aficionados of moor walking, moor history...and, most importantly, moor aura...it may be said that there is a hierarchy, or at least strongly defended loyalties. Partisans of Dartmoor and Exmoor will contest to the last pint of real ale the respective virtues of their moors, but would agree that Bodmin Moor isn't even in the running. *Wroooong!* In the moor-aura department Bodmin is definitely a heavyweight; perhaps this is because Cornwall is itself so full of primordial mystery and outlaw ghosts with long shadows. This is *Poldark* country! And don't forget all the evil doin's up at the *Jamaica Inn* on Bodmin Moor...begin to feel the moor aura? Exmoor's *Lorna Doone* sounds a sissy tale by comparison!...and Dartmoor's *Hound of the Baskervilles* might as well be a Disney pooch script!

If all this sounds a bit Stephen King*ish*, let me assure you that the village of Blisland is most appropriately named. With its long tree-shaded green, medieval church, and pretty cottages it is a truly enchanting place. The residents are no less inviting...indeed, I recollect my spouse nearly buying a house here after a casual gab with Postperson Patricia and the publican. Higher Tumrose, which is in the gentle woodlands at the edge of the moor, is a delightfully bright and spacious single story house. It began as a barn conversion and sort of kept growing, inside and out...and in-between, with terrace, patio, sunken garden, and a manicured lawn going to a cleverly built *ha-ha* which disguises the fact that the owners' considerable pastoral menagerie is not, in fact, grazing on the lawn. Inside, the house is nicely furnished with a mix of contemporary and antique pieces (note the grandfather clock), and a particularly good library. There are four large bedrooms with dreamy from-the-bed vistas.

Fifty yards away sits the stone built Tumrose Cottage, which sleeps four in comparable comfort and is suitable for the partially handicapped. And, a few yards further through the gate is...you guessed it...the moor, beckoning every romantic bone in your body, as well as some under-exercised muscles.

I. B-q
B-t
B-t/q
B-s
F-3 [2]
E$m
H
FP$
LT
TV
W/D
DW MW
S-S   MS
INS
BK$
£209-472
S 7

Contact Helpful Holidays, Coombe, Chagford, Devon TQ13 8DF
TEL 01144-1647-433-593 or FAX 01144-1647-433-694

WHITEHAY   Nr Bodmin

We are back in the area of Bodmin Moor, which we enjoy so much. Whitehay is not actually on the moor, but rather sits amidst lush pastures and woodlands, with the lovely little River Ruthern cutting through the property. By any standard, Whitehay is an impressive "farmhouse", being a very dignified Georgian home with lovely quoin-work and fenestration to set off the fieldstone walls. One of the two "cottages" offered is located in the wing of the big house; the other is the restored Mill House across the yard.

Owners Ian and Felicity Lock have gone about the development of these accommodations with an eye to perfection. I dare say that the elegance of The Wing could be no less than that of their own home. Beginning with the bright airy feel of the Georgian period style, the Locks have decorated and furnished The Wing in a luxurious fashion. The drawing room contains beautiful soft furnishings, accented by fine antique pieces, and features a baby grand piano at one end and a huge stone fireplace at the other. Beautiful wood grains seem to be everywhere, in the furnishings, in the gorgeously polished parquet floors, and above in one of the most impressive beam ceilings one will ever see in a domestic setting. Carefully chosen lighting, fine decoratives, quality rugs; The Wing is very refined, indeed. French doors lead to a private terrace which steps up into a raised garden.

The Mill House is particularly unique in that it still retains the working water wheel. Double doors lead out to a private garden alongside the mill pond and leat. There is also a small rowboat to pot about in the river. As one would expect, the interior of the Mill House is very handsomely fitted out. The placement of the living room up on the second floor under the high vaulted ceiling provides marvelous views over the valley. The ground floor kitchen, from the characterful flagstone floor up, is designed to please the most ardent *foodie*.

Walkers will want to have a go at the nearby Camel Trail (Bodmin to Padstow). Also very special is the National Trust's Lanhydrock Estate, which is open for special events even late in the season. We have most pleasant memories of caroling there one Christmas in the darkness of a power outage.

WING
II.B-q
B-d
B-t
F-2
F-F
£282-624
S 6
MILL
I. F-2
B-d
II.B-t
S-S
£219-447
S 4
BOTH
E
H$
FPS
LT
TV
W/D
DW MW
P-
INS

Contact Ian and Felicity Lock, Whitehay, Withiel, Bodmin, Cornwall PL30 5NQ
TEL 01144-1208-831-237

BIRDBROOK

Boscastle is one of those little Cornish villages that slipped off an impressionist painter's easel and fell into reality. On a foggy day, or even on a bright one with perhaps just a puff of clouds, strolling down to the tiny harbor can be so ethereal as to put you back in the painting. The village is a spread out series of levels and drops, of high ground always conceding to gravity and the rushing tide as it swirls laterally around the blackened old breakwater, threatening to carry the challenge right up the gorge.

Birdbrook is snuggled up behind the gate to its little walled garden. The cottage is a wing of a larger cottage, but is self-contained, with its terrace bounded by the mound of Bottreaux Castle and by a little stream making its way to the harbor, as eventually does every moving thing in Boscastle. Inside, the cottage is as inviting as that impressionist painting. Slate floors in the downstairs sitting/dining room; bare wood floors in the gallery above, with a double bed and en-suite facilities.

II.B-d
F-3
E&H
LT$
TV
F-F
INS
£140-304
S 2

Contact Cornish Traditional Cottages, Lostwithiel, Cornwall PL22 0HT TEL 01144-1208-872-559

SMUGGLERS

It isn't hard to conjure up images of smugglers, working here under cloud blackened night skies, furtively beaching their little boats laden with kegs of contraband brandy. On the bluffs above, red coated soldiers hunker over a struggling fire, more interested in warming their bone-cold fingers that giving chase to the Cornish rascals who would deny the King his due.

This is a dreamy place for holiday time-traveling, with endless surf-pounded beaches to pad along. The cottage, with its low beamed ceilings and ancient stone walls, is cozy and protected, just what a vicarious smuggler wants. A private electric generator supplies the light and conveniences unknown to occupants of that other era. Your time warped musings can continue in front of the big inglenook fireplace with its original bread oven and brass laden lintel. When day dreams want to become night adventures, one can retire to bedrooms where the sound of the surf never leaves the ear and where first light will burn in through the small pane windows as gold as a soldier's braid. No time to lose; it's grab a mug of coffee and head up the beach searching for fresh prints in the sand before tide and time erases the mystery. Later you may want to walk along the coastal footpath a mile or so to Bude, for a taste of last night's delivery in one of the pubs and for provisions to continue your vigil up the beach.

I. B-d
II.B-d
B-t
F-3
E
H$
FP
L
TELc
TV
W
NS
S-S MS
INS
BK$
£198-572
S 6

Contact North Devon Holiday Homes, 19 Cross St., Barnstaple, Devon EX31 1BD TEL 01144-1271-76322

LEVERLAKE COTTAGE   Nr Bude

Here is a cottage that a calendar artist would kill for! Leverlake Cottage oozes merry olde England character at the same time that it promises modern comforts approaching luxury.

Like virtually all the yeomen's cottages of the West Country, this one has grown by increments over the last four centuries. However, unlike many of its contemporaries, this cottage apparently enjoyed periods of real prosperity; witness the beautiful beamed ceiling crafted from ships timbers. It is worth noting that this coastline saw many shipwrecks, and, indeed, the nearby town of Bude made something of an industry out of the often suspicious business of *wrecking.* This is also a coast rich in adventure and romance. What story might the Armada vintage Spanish dagger, which was found in the inglenook during restoration, tell?   Indeed, if ever there was a storyteller's *court,* it is the sitting room of this cottage. Stoke up a blazing fire in the huge inglenook fireplace some evening as the moonlight shimmers in through the lattice paned windows...fix your eyes on the acrobatic shadows dancing across the undulating surface of the thick stone walls...in no time you'll begin to feel like a time-traveller in antiquity...Tintagel is just down the road, with its ghosts of Arthur, Merlin and the Knights of the Round Table. Cornwall is a magical place and this cottage is a waiting invitation to feel, as well as see, it.

Now, on to the more down-to-earth particulars. There are two cozily decorated bedrooms in the cottage proper, and an additional double en-suite bedroom in the annex, which is attached by an arched gateway. The cottage has lovely soft furnishings in floral patterns, wall sconce lighting, pretty pictures and plates, and fresh flowers in season. There is a small stream right out the front door and an ancient thatched covered well...care to make a wish?

I. B-t
F-3
II.B-d
F-2
B-d
F-3
E&H
FP$
LT
TELc
TVV
W
MW
S-S
£258-549
S 6

Contact Classic Cottages, Leslie House, Lady Street, Helston, Cornwall TR13 8NA
TEL 01144-1326-565-656 or FAX 01144-1326-565-554

BEACH COTTAGE
Cadgwith

Beach Cottage is a private window on another world; the world of weathered fisherfolk quietly going about their toil with a resolve that is generations deep. Life here follows the tide, and it is a soothing rhythm which can take you over very quickly...if you're smart! The cottage, which earlier saw service as a net loft, is perched right at the edge of Cadgwith's stoney beach. Your front *garden* is a display of gayly painted working boats, patiently waiting on the tide or some bit of refitting, first one, then the other, on and on...you'll get to know them like old friends; they'll be there when you return next year. The cottage is modestly, but comfortably, furnished and decorated with handsome prints done by the owner, a noted artist. There is plenty to see down here on the Lizard, Britain's most southerly point...but don't let your agenda get ahead of the tide...ever the rhythm!

Contact Classic Cottages, Leslie House, Lady Street, Helston, Cornwall TR13 8NA
TEL 01144-1326-565-656 or FAX 01144-1326-565-554

I.B-q
F-3
E&H
L
TV
P-
Sun-Sun
MS
INS
£183-339
S 2

HARBOUR WATCH Charlestown

This is a modest little cottage overlooking St. Austell Bay and strategically located for leisurely poking along the fascinating south coast from Plymouth to Falmouth, or up into Bodmin Moor, just a few minutes drive north. Charlestown, as a port town, was built in Georgian times, but never had the naturally endowed expansive harbors of Fowey and Falmouth which are just on its flanks.

Harbour Watch sits in a row of Victorian cottages looking down on the picturesque harbor. The property is approached by a road up from the harbor to a communal parking area, and thence through a gated path to the garden overlooking the fields behind the house. We enter via a small kitchen and pass through a pine fitted dining room with a coal effect gas fire. Beyond this, there is a modest sitting room, giving way to probably the most important, if tiniest, room in the cottage--the glass porch overlooking the sea. To soak up more of the view, there are chairs and a table set up on the front patio with the lawn sloping down toward the harbor. For a beach day, both Carlyon Bay and Porthpean are within five minutes' drive.

II.B-d
F-1
B-t
F-3
E
H$
FPG
TV
D
MW
NS P-
S-S
INS
£192-506
S 4

Contact Cornish Traditional Cottages, Lostwithiel, Cornwall PL22 0HT
TEL 01144-1208-872-559 or FAX 01144-1208-873-548

ROOKE FARM   Chapel Amble

Rooke Farm is part of the Prince's of Wales' Duchy of Cornwall Estate. No, Charles won't be here to check you in, but you'll receive no less a royal welcome from Gill Reskelly and her husband Rob, who operate the farm and the cottages as royal tenants.

Formerly part of an eighteenth century stable block, the two cottages have been thoughtfully converted by the Reskellys to combine traditional style with all the modern comforts. There is a tasteful blend of natural stone walls, flagstone floors, open beams and brilliant white plasterwork throughout. The cottages are impeccably furnished with handsome living room suites and coordinated floral patterned drapery. The rooms are uncluttered, bright, and airy, with the scent of fresh flowers to bring a bit of the country inside.

Honeysuckle Cottage is at the front end of the old stable block and accommodates two. There is a sitting/dining room with a stone fireplace and log burner. An archway leads to the kitchen with its characterful black slate floors. In the upstairs en-suite bedroom you will find a four-poster bed and French doors leading out to an iron-railed balcony.

Meadow Cottage is the larger, sleeping up to five. The floral and white motif of the bedrooms is particularly cheerful. The master bedroom, which is en-suite, has a wonderful canopy draped bed. There is a twin bedroom and another single with shared bathroom-shower and a separate WC. Downstairs, it is the Saunderson country colors again, and a cozy log fire.

The little village of Chapel Amble is only half a mile away and has a traditional pub, The Maltsters Arms, where I had my first and only oyster pie (loved it). The village also has an interesting pottery. The nearby market town of Wadebridge is noted for its seventeen arch medieval bridge, said to have been built on a foundation of compacted wool. At Rooke Farm you are strategically located to explore the incomparable beauty of the north Cornish coast. Golf, fishing, boating and biking facilities are all nearby.

ETB 5 Keys; Highly Commended

Contact Gill and Rob Reskelly at Rooke Farm, Chapel Amble, Wadesbridge, Cornwall PL27 6ES
TEL 01144-1208-880-368 or FAX 01144-1208-880-600

HONEY-SUCKLE
I. CS
II.B-d
F-3
MEADOW
II.B-d
B-t
B-s
F-3
F-2
F-1
BOTH
E&H
FPS
LT
TELc
TVV
W/D
DW MW
INS
TA
£250-800
S 2-5

CORNER COTTAGE Coverack

Saying you "holidayed on the Lizard" may take a bit of explaining back home, though don't count on being understood. Our first trip to this southernmost peninsula of England was with our (then) five year old son at the tail end of winter. *Lizard* is alternately taken to be Celtic for *high palace* or *outcast,* but our Robbie was having none of it. He clearly anticipated a kind of Galapagos Island. Nor was he actually disappointed, because on that occasion the Peninsula was fogged in all the way down to Lizard Point. You won't be disappointed either. With or without giant lizards or atmospheric fog, The Lizard is a wonderful place to holiday. Corner Cottage in Coverack could not be a more charming place to base your explorations. Brightly furnished in oak and pine, fine sea views over the harbor, secluded garden with barbeque...it's all here.

II.B-q
B-t
F-3
E&H
LT
TELc
TV
W/D
P-
S-S
INS
£225-462
S 4

THE LOFT

Coverack

Pristine white walls meet a crystal blue sky and emerald green sea. This is one of the most romantic cottages I have ever reviewed. Coverack is a picturesque fishing village, particularly as regards its traditional stone and thatch cottages, and none of these is more *calendar perfect* than The Loft. As the name suggests, this two hundred year old cottage was formerly a net loft. The conversion has been very tastefully done, without forgetting where the cottage is located. You are at the water's edge here and the view demands your attention at all times. If the owner hadn't put the dining table in front of the seaside window, the guests undoubtedly would. *On a clear day...you can see forever...!* Well, even without Robert Goulet, you get the idea. The cottage is entered via a stable door to the living room at road level and below this there is an attractively decorated bedroom...with more spectacular views of Coverack Bay. Nice galley kitchen, nice walks...nice stay!

I. B-d
F-3
II.F-1
E&H
LT
TV
MW
P-
S-S
INS
£201-384
S 2

Contact Classic Cottages, Leslie House, Lady Street, Helston, Cornwall TR13 8NA
TEL 01144-1326-565-656 or FAX 01144-1326-565-554

BOSAWSACK FARMHOUSE & MILL

Constantine

Constantine is situated above the headwaters of the Helford River, providing easy access to the many sophisticated amenities of Falmouth, as well as the marine pleasures of Helford and the old Cornish character villages of the Lizard Peninsula. Constantine, itself, is an up-market little village, with a commitment to the good life, as evidenced in its excellent bakery and wine shop.

Bosawsack Farmhouse is a Grade II Listed building in the vernacular style with thick granite walls, heavy stone lintels and broad small pane windows. Both the Farmhouse and the old flour Mill building have profited from very careful remodeling, and though they have shared entries off the farm courtyard, they enjoy separate and private perspectives on the surrounding countryside. While the Farmhouse has a handsome stone porch in front, the traditional entry is through the stable door off the courtyard which leads to the large cozy farm kitchen via a back hall. There is a breakfasting area here, but the main dining room, which accommodates eight, is further along the hall and offers very pleasant views over the orchard. The living room features a slate fireplace and is bright and airy, with comfortable furnishings and yet more fine views.

Upstairs we find four bedrooms, doubles and twins in equal measure, all with wall to wall carpeting (as with the downstairs reception rooms), and still more of those soothing country views. The upstairs bathroom has a bidet; shower facilities are downstairs.

The Mill, with sleeping accommodations on the ground floor, is actually entered via the balustraded stone steps to the upper level. Here we find an open plan living/dining room with fitted carpeting, pleasant furnishings and views into the garden. Interior stairs lead down to the bedrooms, one with a double bed and the other with full size bunks. As with the Farmhouse, there is a patio area for outdoor relaxation or dining, and pleasant walks into the orchard.

FARM-HOUSE
I. F-3
II.B-d [2]
B-t [2]
F-4
FP
TELc
DW
£180-560
S 8
MILL
I.B-d
B-b
F-3
MW
£130-360
S 4
BOTH
E
H$
L
TV
W
S-S

Contact Mrs. Ruth Austen, Cornish Holiday Cottages, Killibrae, West Bay, Maenporth Falmouth Cornwall TR11 5HP   TEL 01144-1326-250-339

THE ANCHORAGE Falmouth

Admiral's Quay is an impressive contemporary waterfront project, a *character* property of the future. The Anchorage is located right at the end, with a three-sided maritime panorama; a *peninsular apartment*, as it were. You can't get any closer to the water without being in it...or on it. Floor-to-ceiling windows bring everything from Penryn to the Carrick Roads right into your living room, day and night. Multiple sliding doors and a wraparound second floor veran- dah allow you to step out into the busy vista of harbor activity and sparkling lights. For those nights with a chilly breeze off the water, strike up the cozy gas-log fire. There are three lovely bedrooms and bathrooms in equal measure, one with jacuzzi, another with bidet. Sailing, fishing, golf, and a host of town cultural entertainments are easily accessible from this unique holiday base. Parking is in the basement of The Anchorage.

I.B-q
F-4 [2]
B-d [2]
F-3
E&H
FPG
L
TV
W/D
DW MW
NS C- P-
S-S
INS
£315-714
S 6

Contact Classic Cottages, Leslie House, Lady Street, Helston, Cornwall TR13 8NA
TEL 01144-1326-565-656 or FAX 01144-1326-565-554

PORT PENDENNIS HARBOUR VILLAGE

I don't think when Sir Walter Raleigh chose the site of Falmouth for his Queen's naval enterprise he quite foresaw it becoming the first class holiday and retirement center it has. Port Pendennis Harbour Village is a case in point. This is a large new development built around a lovely marina behind a tidal gate and offering slip space for seventy boats up to 38 feet. The Port Pendennis Village has a comfortable *Florida* feel about it, in the best sense. The whole Village is nicely laid out with limited car access and pretty walkways, not least being the wonderful boardwalk encompassing the marina. One may want to walk this by day and evening, like a commodore making his quiet rounds of inspection. Poor old Walt, would that he could have retired here, rather than to his Queen's Tower!

II.B-d
F-3
B-t
CS
F-3
E&H
FPG
LT
TEL
TV
W/D
DW MW
F-F
£307-670
S 6

This condominium is well positioned, with front views out into the openness of Falmouth Harbour and back views over the Marina. There is no direction you can turn on either floor without being rewarded with a handsome scene. The living room is prettily furnished with a teal green soft suite and matching wall to wall carpeting overlaid with colorful oriental rugs. The pristine white walls are hung with some tasteful prints and there is a handsome traditionally framed fireplace with gas log heating to complement the central heating system. An archway separates the living room from the dining area, where you will find French door access to a balcony (with seating and barbeque) overlooking the marina. Above, off the master bedroom, is another balcony where one can have a cup of tea and watch the early morning boat show.

Contact Mrs. Ruth Austen, Cornish Holiday Cottages, Killibrae, West Bay, Maenporth Falmouth
Cornwall TR11 5HP   TEL 01144-1326-250-339

THE LENCHES

Helford Passage

A modern bungalow with a touch of magic! Sound improbable? Well, it's true. The secret is in the plate glass (walls of it!) exploiting the most professional landscaping (featuring an ornamental fish pond) and an unsurpassable panorama over the Helford River countryside. The effect is extraordinary...inescapable, really, wherever you are in The Lenches: living/dining room, bedroom, even the kitchen. A view that *floods!* The other virtue of this "cottage" is its spaciousness. Start with a living/dining room that is over forty feet across...well the room had to be big to accommodate the window, after all (there is no doubt which went on the drawing board first). Furnishings are in a contemporary style; comfortable, if perhaps not quite living up to the promise of these rooms. There is an *all-in* luxury kitchen and an open fireplace to put a glow on central heating. Exterior amenities include a lovely south-facing terrace with plenty of seating, and a heated outdoor pool, automatically illuminated at night. If that sounds like a romantic invitation, you will find a couple bottles of complimentary bubbly in the refrigerator to get in the mood.

I.B-d [2]
B-t [2]
F-1
F-3 [2]
E
H$
FP
L
TELc
TVV
W/D
DW   MW
NS   P-
Th-Th
£285-795
S 8

Contact Mrs. Ruth Austen, Cornish Holiday Cottages, Killibrae, West Bay, Maenporth , Falmouth
Cornwall TR11 5HP   TEL 01144-1326-250-339

GREATWOOD COTTAGE   Nr Falmouth

This is an exceptional cottage, convenient to Falmouth and its surrounds, as well as for boating explorations up the famous Carrick Roads all the way to Truro. Greatwood is the end one of three cottages in this 18th century Grade II Listed terrace. The cottage sits prettily behind the hedge, a vision of tranquil dignity. Keen walkers will be delighted that the cottage is on the footpath between Mylor Bridge and Restronguet. More sedentary types will be content to pull up a chaise and watch the sailing races from the sunny back terrace. The cottage is handsomely furnished in beige & white fabrics and carpeting, and there is an open stone fireplace.

I. F-3
II.B-d
B-t
E
H$
FP$
L
TELc
TV
W/D
DW   MW
NS   P-
S-S
INS
£225-462
S 4

Contact Classic Cottages, Leslie House, Lady Street, Helston, Cornwall TR13 8NA
TEL 01144-1326-565-656 or FAX 01144-1326-565-554

THE SQUARE RIG
Fowey

I'll never forget my first sight of Fowey. Viewing the historic town from the ferry landing at Bodinnick across the river, I felt a Gothic mystical spell come upon me. I did not know it at the time, but I was standing not fifty yards from the young Daphne duMaurier's own house, seeing the medieval port town from the very same perspective that never ceased to move her imagination across eons of time into the soulful mysteries of the Cornish coast.

The ferry will land you at the town carpark. Except for deliveries, car traffic is restricted in the town. By the time you've walked the narrow cobbled streets to your destination at The Square Rig you too will surely get that special feel of this picturesque medieval town. Modern by Fowey standards, The Square Rig was built only 200 years ago in the Cornish tradition with massively thick walls. Though an unimposing little two-story house on the street, with quaint red shutters and gay flower boxes, The Square Rig becomes four modernesque levels on the harborside, with access to the water by steps and a slipway. It has been sympathetically converted into four self-contained flats, each with a captain's view of the harbor from their own balconies. There is free use of the boat house and a row boat for explorations of the historic River Fowey.

The apartment interiors are starkly modern; pristine white plaster meeting bulwarks of grey stone with up-to-date furnishings to match. The Tarquins Flat at river level sleeps five; the Lower Deck four; the Middle Deck six, including bunks for children. The Upper Deck is on two levels with a third en-suite bedroom in the rafters with panoramic views. Each flat has a fully fitted kitchen, and there is a communal laundry facility as well as a games room. Double beds are all queen-size.

Neither a village nor a city, Fowey is a true town, medieval in aspect, with staunchly independent traditions, not unlike a tiny Mediterranean city-state. The town has many historically interesting sites: Castle Dore, occupied over 2000 years ago; *The Haven*, home of novelist Sir Arthur Quiller-Couch, better known as "Q"; St. Fimbarrus Church; the Almshouse; and on it goes! Fowey is a town to walk in, day and night. It is also an ideal base for water enthusiasts, sailors and fishermen, with benefits of both the river and the sea. Hikers have a wide choice of charming and spectacular walks, and a day trip across on the Polruan ferry is a must.

ETB 4 Keys; Highly Commended

| E&H |
| FPG |
| LT |
| TELc |
| TVV |
| W/Ds |
| MW |
| F-F S-S |
| MS |
| £185-675 |
| S 4-7 |

Contact: Square Rig Holidays, Manor Works, 168 Worcester Road, Bromsgrove, Worcestershire B61 7AX   TEL 01144-1527-575-929 or FAX 01144-1527-833-466

KELLOW COASTAL COTTAGES Looe

Kellow Coastal Cottages take me back to Bermuda, where small family colonies-cum-resorts, such as this, offer an easy way to relax and turn the children loose to search the tide pools and build up a batch of new pen pals for the coming years. Perhaps the resemblance is in the little tile roofed white stucco buildings peeking out from behind tall hedges and flowering shrubbery....all that semi-tropical flora and fauna. Certainly it is in the amiable climate; coastal Cornwall and Bermuda are similarly blessed. There are eight cottages here, tucked away in two acres of grounds above Millendreath Beach. A private path takes one down to the beach and a popular leisure center where a temporary membership entitles one to enjoy a host of water activities, from paddle boating to parascending. Other routes will take one to more private beaches or around the headlands to the characterful town of Looe, with its narrow streets facing each other across the river, good shops, and quay-side fish market.

E$	
H$	
TV	V*
W*	D
MW	
P-	
F-F	S-S
INS	
£201-384	
S 3-4	

Contact Classic Cottages, Leslie House, Lady Street, Helston, Cornwall TR13 8NA
TEL 01144-1326-565-656 or FAX 01144-1326-565-554

CLEMY'S COTTAGE Isle of Scilly

Hugh Town on St. Mary's Island is the *metropolis* of the Scillies. The *axis* of the Scillies is perhaps more fitting, as Hugh Town is a good base for exploring the other islands via the continuous shuttle of launches coming and going from the Boatman's Association Quay. St. Mary's, itself, is a delight to explore; a tropical paradise only three miles across. In fact, you can take a leisurely walk around the perimeter of the island in a single day, dallying for a swim or picnic or to pick the wild flowers. Flowers, after all, are the stock and trade of the Scillies, as well as the perfect metaphor for these idyllic isles.

Clemy's Cottage is a modest granite building dating from the middle of the last century, when the islands were better known for smuggling than posy growing. The cottage is situated about fifty yards from Porthcressa Beach and five minutes from town. It has been modernized to a comfortable standard, and has electric fires upstairs and a Rayburn stove down for the off season visitors. Mind you, these Isles really only have two seasons, spring and summer. The "spring" flower harvest can begin in November! ETB 2 Keys; Commended

I. F-3	
II.B-d	
	B-b [2]
E$c	
H	
FPS	
LT	
TV	
P-	
S-S	MS
TA	
£160-450	
S 6	

Contact Mr & Mrs Peter Cattran, Tregarthen Farmhouse, Zennor, St. Ives, Cornwall, TR26 3BP
TEL 01144-1736-796-977

TRESCO ESTATE   Isles of Scilly

Ever spend a holiday on a small island? Ever listen to people who have spent their holiday on a small island? Notice the repeated use of the first person possessive pronoun? *My island...My beach...My quay!* For couples it comes in the plural possessive...*Our island...Our beach...Our quay!* Why is this? After a week in Paris, one doesn't go around saying *My Paris, Our Seine!* Hike to the bottom of the Grand Canyon or the top of Mount Washington...that doesn't make it *yours!* Nope, there is something wholly unique about an island experience...it's a *possessing* experience. I should hasten to add that size is a factor. Japan, Ireland and Hawaii are all islands; and, though I've enjoyed my stays, I have never, subliminally or other-wise, laid claim to them. No; a real *possessing island* is one you can walk the perimeter of in a day or so. That leaves out Bermuda, lovely as it is. Going back to Bermuda, which is always a pleasure for me, does not, however, engender those goose bumps associated with going *home.* This may sound a shade egocentric, but I really don't have the feeling that Bermuda has missed *me,* in my absence. If you can't relate to that, then it is definitely high time you spent a holiday on a *possessing* island. Personally, *I have* several such islands in my private collection, and I am prepared to share one of the most possessing with you...Tresco in the Isles of Scilly.

Tresco lies 28 miles off the Cornish coast in the balmy breezes of the Gulf Stream. You can't drive to it (via ferry) or on it, and that is very much part of its *possessing* charm. Tresco can be reached by commercial helicopter or by the open launch from St Mary's, the "big" island of the Scillies. *Our island* (remember, I'm sharing it with you) is only two miles long and a mile across; so get on your walking shoes, every inch of Tresco wants to meet you. If you are in a real big hurry to take possession of *your island* you may want to rent a bike from the Tresco Estate Office, but really there is no need to rush. Rushing is very un-Tresco! *Our island* is chocka-block with spectacular natural sights, from its many sandy beaches and crystal clear water to its caverns and romantic little paths; but they're not going away. *Our island* is also rich in historic sights, from the Bronze Age tomb to the medieval monastic and Civil War castle ruins; but these too are here to stay. So, take your time and assess *your* assets at a leisurely pace, and also get to know the islanders who take care of *your island* in your absence, harvesting the cut flowers for the London market, fishing and lobstering, and, of course, outfitting the accommodation awaiting your arrival...return.

Tresco is an island of immense variety, as dramatized in the Tresco Abbey Garden with its world-famous collection of exotic flora from every corner of the globe. Horticulturally inclined visitors will do well to tear themselves away from the acres of gardens, which have been developed over the past century and a half with both scientific enthusiasm and aesthetic sensitivity. In fact, there are special Spring and Autumn Gardener Holiday weeks, with organized lectures and demonstrations on various horticultural subjects (liberally interspersed, of course, with good eating, good wine, and the other island pleasures.)

Smugglers Cottage

```
E$m*
H
FP*
FPS*
LT
TV  V*
DW*
MW*
P-
OPEN MS
INS
£215-1750
S 2-10
```

There is, as well, great variety in holiday accommodation on the island. In addition to the new Island Hotel, there are a number of traditional granite built cottages scattered around the island for self catered holidays. These historic little buildings, such as Smugglers Cottage, are all neatly furnished with pretty Laura Ashley fabrics and polished pine, and have all the necessary modern conveniences. There are also ten cottage-cum-flats developed out of the old barn complex of the estate. And, if the *my island* feeling really gets hold of you, you may want to take up residence in the Tresco Abbey Tower, itself. The Tower of the huge mansion offers accommodation for eight in four double bedrooms, with imperial views across the bay to St. Martin's Island (*their* island). All of which raises a rather delicate question. Who lives in the rest of the Tresco Abbey mansion?

Well, the truth must come out. The fact is that *our island* has a prior claimant, a *pretender*, as it were. We must admit that Mr. Robert Dorrien-Smith's possessive affection for the island is no less than our own, and there may be some historical basis for his claim. His ancestor, Augustus Smith, leased the island from the Duchy of Cornwall way back in 1834, and over the next forty years transformed it from a lawless smuggler's lair into an enlightened and productive estate. Successive generations of the family, right down to Robert, have devoted themselves to the welfare of the island and its historic garden project. I suppose they really couldn't have done otherwise...after all, they were *possessed*...by the Island, that is. So, maybe it is *their* island, not *ours*. But there is a consolation prize for us; the Dorrien-Smiths are very good at sharing!

Contact Tresco Estate Holiday Cottages, Tresco, Isles of Scilly, Cornwall TR24 0QQ TEL 01144-1720-422-566

SHELL COTTAGE
Kingsand

A glowing sunrise over an endless sea of sunflowers on the hot plains of Provence. A burning red hot Navajo sunset on the high mesa of Northern Arizona. Yellow so golden it sizzles; red so burnt it steams. Colors so rich they can paradoxically stir the passions or slow the metabolism; not primary colors, these are primordial colors! Now what in the devil does all this have to do with a cottage in a little fishing village down in Cornwall, you ask? Plenty!

To be sure, Shell Cottage is designer decorated in bold strokes. Actually, sunburst yellow living rooms and ember red bedrooms are not entirely out of character for this particular little fishing village down in Cornwall. Our old friends, the Bowaters at Helpful Holidays, describe Kingsand as "something positively Italian". A compact village of sun bleached houses cascading down narrow old streets from a wooded hill to gang up at the edge of the broad tidal beach. Boats carelessly pulled up on the pebble beach as if their owners were in a hurry to find shade and refreshment in quay-side pubs, apparently unconcerned about the prospects of a returning tide. No Cinzano umbrellas, but plenty of fuschia and geraniums.

Shell Cottage is a few steps up from the waterfront, tucked in a narrow little street of row houses with a basket of trailing geraniums hanging by the big oak door. There are two floors, with the living room and kitchen/dining area on the ground floor and a small cobbled courtyard beside...a wonderful sun trap to snooze in, surrounded by a profuse jungle of floral color. Back to the living room...always with great anticipation! From all angles the pretty mirror over the coarse stone fireplace (a real deep blazer!) catches glimpses of the most eclectic assemblage of pretty particulars you will see this side of Britain's *Ideal Home Magazine* (which, not surprisingly, recently featured Shell Cottage). Nice bits of pottery and porcelain, bowls of dried flowers and violets, interesting pictures and off beat frameables; bright straw hats and family photographs...clutter that works! Multi-cultural and

II. B-d [2]
B-s
F-2
E$
H$
FP$
LT
TELin
TVV
W/D
DW MW
S-S MS
INS
BK$
£187-400
S 5

multi-multi-multi-color! Walls ragged and sponged into delicious textures. Rather steep stairs lead you to three bedrooms; a double with direct access to a bathroom with a boldly painted Victorian tub, and another quite small double with a starry ceiling. You will find a children's room, as well; and sea views from both the living room and one bedroom.

Kingsand is tucked into the side of the Rame Head Peninsula across the Sound from Plymouth, which can be reached by nearby passenger ferry. This has long been a personal favorite area for us. Nearby Antony House is one of the finest Queen Anne mansions in Britain; a *must see* if you fancy heritage architecture.

Contact Helpful Holidays, Coombe, Chagford, Devon TQ13 8DF
TEL 01144-1647-433-593 or FAX 01144-1647-433-694

TREDETHICK FARM COTTAGES

Nr Lostwithiel

Tim and Nicky Reed's 200-acre sheep farm is situated in the bucolic countryside that inspired Kenneth Graham's *Wind in the Willows*. The farm lies about half way between the idyllic creekside village of Lerryn with its old Inn, and historic Lostwithiel on the River Fowey. The sheer natural beauty of this countryside with its tidal creeks and woodlands has motivated the conservation minded Reeds to create a footpath from the cottages, wending a course along ancient hedgerows, past ponds and through the woods to the tiny hamlet of St. Winnow (very Kenneth Graham*ish!*), where there is a lovely church once featured in the *Poldark* series.

The cottages have been sympathetically converted from traditional Cornish stone barns around an open landscaped courtyard with a central fountain. Original openings and character features have been retained, such as dovecotes, granite pillars oak lintels, and the interior beams. There are six cottages sleeping two to six persons; all with ground floor bedrooms and showers, and most with queen-size beds. The cottages are designed with open plan living areas, taking every advantage of exposed beams and stonework. The Dairy, Hayloft, and The Granary Cottages each have large stone fireplaces with log burning wood stoves. All have central heating. The Granary and Hayloft are laid out on two floors, with the living/dining rooms and kitchens above, offering enhanced views. Liddicoat and Scantlebury Cottages have galleried lofts, good fun for children. Two of the cottages are designed for wheelchair access. All of the kitchens are nicely fitted in light oak, with waxed pine farmhouse tables and chairs. The same country styles are carried through in the rest of the furnishings featuring William Morris fabrics in warm terracotta, greens and yellows.

ETB 4 Keys; Highly Commended

E$c
H
FPS*
LT
TELc
TV V*
W/D
DW MW
E/HC*
F-F S-S
MS
TA
£130-420
S 2-6

Contact Nicky & Tim Reed, The Guild House, Tredethick, Lostwithiel, Cornwall PL22 0LA
TEL 01144-1208-873-618

MOWHAY & COMBE COTTAGES

Mawnan Smith

The Helford River cuts deeply across this southern promontory of Cornwall, rising and falling daily with the tide, shaping the landscape into a maze of little arterial creeks and secluded ravines lost under an umbrella of hardwood foliage. Helford, itself, is a lovely car-less village, much favored by yachtsmen for its cozy anchorage and equally cozy watering hole. Mawnan Smith is an attractive village north of the River, and I recommend taking the foot ferry from Passage Cove to Helford, rather than driving around.

Mowhay and Combe Cottages are situated down a country lane about a mile from the village. Mowhay sets in a secluded garden surrounded by azaleas and red and yellow flowering broom. The ground floor has a kitchen and separate dining room, as well as the double bedroom. Upstairs there is a spacious living room, with brightly white-washed walls under open rafters. Combe Cottage has an open plan kitchen/diner separate from the sitting/bedroom, and is comfortably furnished in soft florals and pretty pine. Heating in Combe is by way of the Aga...the coziest *warm* ever invented!

Contact Classic Cottages, Leslie House, Lady Street, Helston, Cornwall TR13 8NA
TEL 01144-1326-565-656 or FAX 01144-1326-565-554

MOWHAY
I.B-d
F-2
COMBE
I. B-d
F-2
BOTH
E&H
FPS$
L
TV
W   Ds
MW
C- P-
Sun-Sun
Sat-Sat
INS
£183-339
S 2

BOSULLA

Mawnan Smith

Bosulla sits in a commanding position a hundred feet above Navas Creek, which takes its tidal rhythm from the Helford River. The superlative view across is to Port Navas, which can be reached with the small boat tied up to Bosulla's dock. There is, as well, a mooring if one wants to rent a larger craft for exploring these wonderful estuaries. Bosulla, itself, is a picture of tidy convenience; a newer home, with character beams, fireplace and lattice pane windows which are filled with a truly glorious panorama. It is prettily furnished with comfort, not ostentation, in mind, and complete with all the modern amenities, telling us that Bosulla is more an owners' retreat than rental cottage. (Telephone with *honesty box!*) The house is single story and has a level entry, but there is some up and down walking in the acre of lovely garden and lawns (with summer house and barbecue) and quite a climb for those taking advantage of the water frontage.

I.B-d [2]
B-t
B-s
F-4
F-3
E   H$
FP
L
TEL TV
W
DW MW
NS
W-W
£250-655
S 7

Contact Mrs. Ruth Austen, Cornish Holiday Cottages, Killibrae, West Bay, Maenporth Falmouth
Cornwall TR11 5HP   TEL 01144-1326-250-339

EGYPTIAN HOUSE   Penzance

Penzance has the fascination of geography and geology, as well as the hearts of Gilbert & Sullivan enthusiasts around the world. The tourist tradition of this most westerly town of England is not quite as old as its pirate tradition, but there is a kind of 19th century Ripley's *Believe It Or Not* atmosphere here that is easy to get into. In fact, the Egyptian House was an early tourist trap, where, from about the time of Queen Victoria's coronation, one Mr. John Lavin did a swift trade in selling the holidaymakers a piece of the rock (Cornwall, that is) from his Geological Museum. Mr. Lavin certainly knew how to draw them in!

Since its thorough restoration by the Landmark Trust in 1968, Egyptian House has been drawing them in again. Three almost identical flats are offered on the second, third and fourth floors, with two bed-

F-2	
E&H	
FPE	
LT	
P-	
S-S	MS
INS	
£216-387	
S 3-4	

rooms each. Charmingly Victorian, with the usual Landmark Trust flair for decorative, as well as architectural, statements. The second floor apartment has two living room windows (center-left in drawing) overlooking the street; the fourth floor apartment gives one a crow's nest perspective on St. Michael's Mount! You will find compact kitchens to the rear and dining tables in the sitting areas. National Trust offices now occupy Mssr Lavin's ground floor.

Contact The Landmark Trust, Shottesbrook, Maidenhead, Berkshire SL6 3SW   TEL 01144-1628-825-925

LITTLE BAREPPA
Mawnan Smith

Little Bareppa is an attractive self-contained wing of a Grade II Listed Georgian country house. Its setting, in its own private gardens with a dear little stream running through, could hardly be more peaceful; indeed, this area around the hamlet of Bareppa near the picturesque village of Mawnan Smith is in every way an idyllic retreat. There is much to do, particularly in the marine line, at Helford Passage (just two miles away) or on the beach at Maenporth (just a half mile's walk from the cottage), but if you choose the delights of seclusion, Little Bareppa will be very accommodating.

I. F-2	
II.B-d+s	
B-t	
F-1	
E$c	
H	
FP	
LT	
TVV	
W/D	
MW	
F-F	MS
£210-470	
S 4-5	

The cottage is bright and airy and prettily furnished in a contemporary *country house* fashion, including the inviting soft chairs covered in spring floral fabrics. There is a separate dining room and a very workable kitchen. The cottage is centrally heated and has a fireplace, as well.

ETB 4 Keys; Commended

Contact Mr. & Mrs. Gaunt, Bareppa House, Bareppa nr Falmouth, Cornwall TR11 5EG
TEL 01144-1326-250-210 or FAX 01144-1326-250-278

·VENTON HOUSE   Millbrook

There are cottages that are *holiday lets,* and then there are those cottages that are *real homes,* which one enters and exclaims, "Boy! if this were mine, I'd never..." Venton House is such a home, and, lucky for us, it's owners are of a more sharing spirit.

This property has a long litany of virtues, but, at the risk of repeating myself, I must begin with lavish praise of the area itself. We never tire of this Rame Head Peninsula, with the St. John Lake entrance to the mighty Tamar on one side and gorgeous Whitsand Bay on the other. It is no coincidence that for centuries the well-to-do have built here...Antony House and Mount Edgcumbe being prime examples. And, just a short (walk-on) ferry ride across the Tamar is Plymouth, which is the cultural center of the West Country (sorry Exeter), with theater, symphony, galleries...even shopping if you must. Millbrook, itself, is a typical little Cornish village with a pleasant pub, and sits by a waterfowl conservation area with many options for peaceful walks.

I. F-1
II. B-q
B-d [3]
B-t
F-2
III.B-q
B-t
B-d+s
F-3
E&H
FP
LT
TELin
TVV
W/D
DW MW
S-S MS
INS
BK$
£818-1452
S 17

Venton House is a Grade II Listed Georgian building. It sits proudly amid its own gardens and sweeping lawn with an interesting variety of trees which will probably be new to North Americans (perfumed balsam poplar, and Turkey oak) as well as some which will simply surprise you to find in Cornwall (eucalyptus, magnolia and, yes, palms!). Inside, Venton House is full of pleasant surprises, as well...large well-proportioned rooms made all the more spacious by the floods of natural light coming through wide 8-over-8 Georgian windows. These rooms are complete melds of pretty particulars (lamps, flower-filled vases, brass candlesticks, grandfather clock, exceptional pictures and homey soft furnishings) and beautiful architecturals (a pair of marble fireplaces with large gilt mirrors, period chandeliers, deep casement windows, high moulded ceilings). The second and third floors give way to equally impressive bedrooms; eight in all, two with private showers. The excellent kitchen was made for large parties, and there is a games room in the cellar.

Contact Helpful Holidays, Coombe, Chagford, Devon TQ13 8DF
TEL 01144-1647-433593 or FAX 01144-1647-433694

REEN MANOR FARM   Perranporth

It was from the grassy dunes overlooking Perran Bay that Winston Graham wrote his famous *Poldark* novels...those deliciously comlex Gothic tales of Captain Ross and sweet Demelza's endless struggles against the evil and unscrupulous Warleggan clan, ever complicated by the dark shadowy fates that inhabit every stone crevice of the Cornwall landscape. There is something of a paradox in this for me. Quite frankly, looking up the miles of almost tropical sandy beach here on a bright and breezy day, I would have expected a literary output more in the order of Michener's *Tales of the South Pacific*. But then Cornwall is full of visual tricks. Less than a mile away, perched on a hill overlooking this very beach, is Reen Manor Farm. Poldark would be most at home here in these impressive granite buildings dating from the late 1500's; plenty of crevices for the ghosts of Cornwall to inhabit, and more honest to god Jacobean character than any novelist or film maker could ever conjure up. Everything at Reen Manor is special; very special!

Reen Manor's owner, Roger John Opie, offers four "cottages", all in the Listed historic buildings of the one-time farm; all furnished with impeccable taste that is anything but rustic. The smallest, Reen Court, sleeps two in a handsome four-poster-bedded room, plus a couple of children in a bunk-bedded room. One enters through a secluded courtyard and up the stairs to the sitting room with unobstructed views of the coastline.

Then there is Reen Cottage (left in drawing above) which sleeps four in bedrooms off an upper gallery. The downstairs living room is expansive, with stone walls and exposed beams. Leaded pane windows highlight the character of this 1656 building. Attached is Manor Barn (right in drawing), which really started out as a pre-Reformation church, went through its "barn period", and is now one of the most sublime holiday accommodations one will find anywhere. The ground floor features Norman arches and slate floors leading to four bedrooms. Note the arrow slits in the bathroom! Upstairs is an open beamed living/dining room, with polished wood floors and oriental carpets, a grand piano and a handsome Jacobean dining suite, complemented by a fine old dark oak welsh dresser and a period settle.

To round out a picture of perfection, Opie invites us to stay in the 1590 Manor House, sleeping nine. The combination of sea air, encroaching tropical flora and bare stonework of the Manor recalls fond memories of Bermuda. The sweet texture of those recollections are further enhanced by the antique furnishings and decor that lay within.

```
MANOR
HOUSE
I. B-t
   F-3
II.B-d [2]
   B-t
   B-s
   F-2
E    H$
FPS$
L
TV
W
DW  MW
P-
S-S  MS
£344-746
S 9
```

Contact Roger John Opie, Reen Manor Farm, Perranporth , Cornwall TEL 01144-1872-573-064

HARBOUR VIEW COTTAGE   Polperro

A travel writer friend once wrote that if Polperro didn't exist, Hollywood would have had to build it. It wasn't an entirely kind remark and reflects a certain brand of snobbism. Picturesque and undiscovered, becomes picture perfect for the cognoscenti, becomes a living picture postcard for the multitude. For better or for worse, Polperro may be too popular to be fashionable now, but my friend is quite wrong about one thing. Hollywood couldn't create a Polperro. Geography, history, the elements and, yes, even the multitude who have flocked here since the railroads breached Cornish seclusion, are all responsible for Polperro as we know it...and, in my case, love it. Movie magic may give us images, but Polperro is for real. It hasn't been ruined by a century and a half of gawkers and I doubt that it ever will. After all, it's a rock! A Cornish rock!

If you've ever thought you'd like to take up residence in a post-card...that is, actually put yourself inside one of those quintessential scenes which come to you bearing the inevitable inscription, *wish you were here*...then Harbour View is your chance. Post cards, calendars, even the cover of the *AAA Illustrated Guide to Britain*; Harbour View is an "image" you've seen many times. And, not to belabor the point, the image isn't a scratch on reality. Harbour View Cottage puts you in the view and gives you a unique perspective on the harbor, *across the bow* views of the fishing boats and all the associated activity. The cottage is one of the most ancient in Polperro, and is actually built on the harbor wall. It is the non-whitewashed building in the drawing above.

There are three bedrooms in Harbour View, comfortable steads for a party of six; and two full bathrooms, so that the six need not share all the

II. B-t
F-2
III.B-t
B-d
F-3
E$c
H
FP
LT$
TV
W/D
MW
S-S   MS
TA
£200-480
S 2-6

intimacies of being immediate family. The sitting/dining room has an open fireplace in addition to an electric fire and night storage heaters. Furnishings are modest, but comfortable, with much bright pine in evidence in wainscotting and window seats, as well as tables and chairs. It is important to remember that Polperro has restricted vehicular access, though provisions are made for loading and unloading. In the case of Harbour Cottage, it is possible to get within a short (level!) walk from the cottage, and a luggage trolley is provided.   ETB 4 Keys; Commended

Also on the harbor is **BRIDGE END HOUSE**, which was formerly the Harbor Master's quarters. This old stone building stands tall, like a sentinel, over the little Roman Bridge which crosses the tiny River Pol right at the edge of the tide. The Pol feeds into the upper harbor at this point, and is responsible for the deep geological crevice in which the village of Polperro is built. Over the years we have frequented the little galleon-affect restaurant across the cobbled street from Bridge End House and noted its twin high pitched dormers peering over roofs onto the inner harbor, with raised eyebrows like a suspicious eagle. More views! Really more than a view, this is a people watching motion picture of boatmen busy at work, of the comings and goings of trade in the little shops along the harbor front, and of the wash of tourists who flow down Polperro's narrow streets, inevitably arriving at the Roman Bridge overlooking the snug upper harbor, rising and falling like a municipal pond. Bridge End House is three stories high, with bedrooms in the peak, a double en-suite on the middle floor adjacent to the living room, and kitchen/dining on the ground floor, with access to a small and sunny private garden. For purposes of unloading one may get their car as far as the Roman Bridge, but then must park in the municipal lot at the upper end of the valley.   ETB 4 Keys; Commended

II. B-t
F-2
III.B-d
B-t
B-b
F-3
E$c
H
LT$
TV
W/D
MW
S-S   MS
TA
£200-450
S 8

MIRADOR
I.B-t [2]
B-s
F-1
F-2
E$c
H
FPE
LT$
TV
W/D
MW
S-S
TA
£150-350
S 5

High above the harbor are the pair of flats in **OSPREY HOUSE**. This is Talland Hill, on the south facing side of Polperro, and Osprey is set in its own half acre of gardens terraced into the steep hill, with access to the harbor area below. Osprey was built in 1825, no doubt with the same intent of capturing the view that it still delivers, right out to Eddystone Light. Mirador Flat sleeps up to five, while The Peak sleeps up to three. Both are self contained and have access to the garden, and both have immediate parking.   ETB 4 Keys; Approved

Contact Mr. & Mrs. Ian Ferguson, Luckmauree, Osprey, Talland Hill, Polperro, Cornwall PL13 2RX
TEL 01144-1503-72819 or FAX 01144-1503-72670

HOMELANDS Port Isaac

In sketching the West Country coastal villages I have often reflected that there were really two types: the ones that seem to creep down to the sea, like a timid bather approaching the icy water of May; and those that seem to have been cast up from the sea, like wind sprayed debris driven into the crevices of looming cliffs. Port Isaac is definitely one of the latter, and, though civilization isn't exactly hanging by its fingernails from a cliff here, the outstanding spatial quality of the village is definitely *vertical*. With horizontal space at a premium, lanes rather than roads snake their way up the hillside. The narrowest of these (according to Guinness, the narrowest in all England) is *Squeezebelly Alley*, and near the top of this character track is the character cottage called *Homelands*. The brightly whitewashed cottage, with its view-full porch, hangs on the hillside about 75 yards above the harbor. The old fisherman's cottage is entered through a stable door to a sitting room with a large stone fireplace and cloam oven. Old ships-timber beams overhead, wall sconce lighting, and bright Georgian windows sustain the character ambience and promise a memorable holiday.

I. B-s
II.B-d
B-t
F-3
E$
H
FP
TELc
TV
MW
S-S
INS
£154-406
S 5

Contact Cornish Traditional Cottages, Lostwithiel, Cornwall PL22 0HT
TEL 01144-1208-872-559 or FAX 01144-1208-873-548

THE FISHCELLARS
Port Quin

The Fishcellars, as the name suggests, saw service over the centuries as a pilchard processing building, and has more recently been converted into three character cot-

II.B-d+d
B-t
F-3
E$c
H
FP
L$
TV
W
MW
S-S
TA
£170-300
S 6

tages. This is Port Quin, a quiet and unspoiled hamlet on the rugged North Cornish coast. Much of the surrounding area is managed by the National Trust, and Fishcellars Cottage is an ideal base for doing the spectacular Coastal Footpath walks.

The cottage is entered at grade level from the back, but is on the second floor with perspectives over the slipway and harbor. It is furnished in a mix of older style sofa and chairs, with some antique pieces, including a dining table built by the owner's father from local elm. The living room has very handsome deep casement windows and an open fire. There is an up-to-date oak fitted kitchen and an attractive bathroom.

Contact Mrs P.E. Yelland, Dunveth Cottage, St. Breock, Wadebridge, Cornwall PL27 7JR TEL 01144-1208-814-550

ANCHORAGE & CHAPEL COTTAGES
Portscatho

Porthscatho is central to the so-called Cornish Riviera in more ways than one. This is a quintessential Cornish fishing village, down a steep road, perched on a ledge over a craggy indentation in the rocks that passes for a harbor, though generally only with the aid of a breakwater of sorts. There is always an interesting *mood* to these little hard won settlements, whether they are becalmed by sunny seas of tranquility or undergoing a furious battering. The mood is, of course, deeply ingrained in the character of the residents, but even the visitor may share in it and take some of it home as the kind of memory that is not so much an image as a *feeling*.

Anchorage Cottage is, itself, perched on the ledge, with its little walled garden going right to the high tide; indeed the garden wall is a seawall on those furious days. There is a wonderful privateness here, with your back to civilization you can almost step into the spectacular view out over Gerrans Bay. The late 18th century cottage is attached to the owner's home, but is completely self-contained. The sitting room has a beamed ceiling and a large inglenook under a formidable timber lintel, as well as an open stove that burns wood or coal (there is also central heating...for those who prefer to skip *mood* and go straight for heat). A good selection of books is provided, and there are days down here when nothing beats just sitting out on the rocks in the sun and sea breeze and reading something entirely frivolous. Anchorage has twin bedrooms, furnished in Liberty and Sanderson fabrics.

Across the lane is the Victorian vintage Chapel Cottage. It has two bedrooms, double and twin, with an open fire in the living room, a separate dining room and two full baths. There is a nice patio in front, with bay views, and a private sun-trap garden to the rear. You will find wonderful coastal walks in the immediate neighborhood, and for a bit more of that Cornwall *feeling* be sure to visit nearby Veryan, famous for its round houses (built so as to deny the Devil a corner to hide behind).
ETB 4 Keys; Highly Commended

ANCHOR
B-t [2]
F-3
FPS
C- P-
£200-360
CHAPEL
B-d
B-t
F-3 [2]
FP
£220-390
BOTH
TELc
TV
MW
INS
BK$
OPEN
S 4

Contact Mary Spivey, The Independent Traveller, Thorverton, Exeter EX5 5NT
TEL 01144-1392-860-807 or FAX 01144-1392-860-552

FORT POLHAWN

Rame Head

Lord Palmerston was not a complete fool. True, he went a bit nuts when the French came up with the first real iron-clad warship. Sure, in a panic he did commission the construction of Fort Polhawn to protect vital Plymouth without measuring the depth of Whitsand Bay, resulting in the guns of the fort being aimed the wrong way. Oh, and yes, there was all that confusion about building the spiral stairwells backwards, so that only left handed swordsmen could make a fight of it. But, as it turned out, not a gun was ever fired (in anger) nor a buckle ever swashed (left-handed or otherwise), and *Palmerston's Folly,* as it was called, has turned out to be one of the most extraordinary holiday properties anywhere. What is more, for a group of 15-20 it is an incredible bargain.

Enter from the roof (after you're across the drawbridge), down one of the aforementioned granite spiral stairs. Welcome to the 80 ft. long living/dining room, with the granite pillars, the wonderfully vaulted brick ceiling, and the flagstone floor "spotted" with gorgeous oriental style carpets replying to the brick red of the ceiling. The masonry in here is so impressive you just want to run your hand over it! Builder/romantic owners, John and Teresa Wicksteed, have furnished this *roooooom*

I. B-q
B-d [3]
B-d+s [2]
B-s [2]
F-4 [5]
F-2
E$m
H$m
FP$
LT
TEL   TV
W/D
DW MW
P-BA
F-F   MS
INS
BK$
£895-2934
S 18-20

handsomely; an open fire at one end, piano at the other, with cozy zones of sofas and chairs in between. The dining facilities can expand (or contract) to virtually any requirement, and the Fort has a commercial kitchen, with catering options for an occasion or an entire stay. Maid service is, likewise, an option. Two more granite spiral staircases to eight fabulous bedrooms; all en-suite (showers & bidets), and all with commanding views over Whitsand Bay through large granite framed gunports.

Exterior amenities include a private beach (down steep path), tennis, clay pigeon shooting, mountain biking, croquet, and the enclosed lawn to the cliff. Fort Polhawn only sleeps 20, but, by arrangement with the Wicksteeds, you can invite an additional eighty or so for dinner...or perhaps a wedding reception or corporate function.

Contact Helpful Holidays, Coombe, Chagford, Devon TQ13 8DF
TEL 01144-1647-433-593 or FAX 01144-1647-433-694

TREVATHAN FARM

St. Endellion

Trevathan Farm is still very much a working farm, though the outdated barns have found new life in the conversion to holiday accommodations; ten in all, and very spacious. These are exceptionally pretty stone buildings, with contemporary design interiors, comfortably furnished in the same homey idiom. There are one, two and three bedroom cottages; all are carpeted, central heated, and have bath/showers. Myrtle Grove Cottage (drawing above) is a Listed building and stands alone a short walk from the farm. It has open fires in both the living room and kitchen/dining area, and handsome French doors leading out onto a slate patio. Recreational amenities include a hard tennis court, a games hall, and a fitness room. The other thing that the Symons offer is critters of all sorts and sizes (lambs and calves, rabbits and peacocks, dogs, goat, hens, etc.), and, unlike some of the other farm holidays in our book, Henry & Shirley Symons are not adverse to the guests mixing a bit with the four-legged residents.

E$c H$c
FP*
LT$
TVV
W/D
DW*
MW
S-S   MS
£120-500
S 2-12

ETB 5 Keys; Highly Commended

Contact Shirley Symons, Trevathan Farm, St. Endellion, Port Isaac, Cornwall PL29 3TT TEL 01144-1208-880-248

PARC VEAN   St. Mawes

The ever popular St. Mawes has a very distinct Mediterranean ambience, reinforced by its mild climate and by water on three sides, which always seems to be busy with a colorful fleet of pleasure craft in all sizes and descriptions. Just across the Carrick Roads is Falmouth, rich in historic interest, as well as and contemporary cultural pursuits. This is a very nice place to be, holidaying or otherwise!

I. B-t [2]
F-4
F-2
II.B-s
F-1
E$
H$
TV
W/D
DW MW
NS
C-BA P-
S-S
INS
£ 192-506
S 5

Parc Vean is also a very nice place to be. The pristine little white house sits with three others through an archway around a cobbled courtyard, with long views over Falmouth Bay. It is never hard to find the sun in St. Mawes, and at Parc Vean there are little terraces fore and aft; the latter is accessed through French windows in the master bedroom, which is en-suite with shower and bidet. The living room is upstairs, with plenty of light and view pouring in through the front bay windows. Parc Vean also offers excellent kitchen facilities for guests who are want to cook, and St. Mawes offers plenty of good eateries for those who want nothing to do with pots and pans on their holiday.

Contact Cornish Traditional Cottages, Lostwithiel, Cornwall PL22 0HT
TEL 01144-1208-872-559 or FAX 01144-1208-873-548

ACTON CASTLE

Nr St. Michael's Mount

It is surprising how little we know about the origins of many of the great mansions; monuments which have outlasted the record of their beginnings, or, no doubt in many cases, records purposefully lost in the ennobling process. Greed and pride have doubtlessly given us most of our grander architectural heritage, but occasionally, as in the case of Acton Castle, love has motivated the builder.

John Stackhouse, the builder in question, was a rather sickly gentleman and a scientist by avocation, with a keen interest in the scintillating subject of seaweed. One might not think these attributes the makings of a great romantic, but Stackhouse proved otherwise in 1772 when he selected the high promontory east of Penzance with a fairyland view of St. Michael's Mount to build this wedding present for his betrothed, Miss Susanna Acton. This is, of course, a *domestic* castle...a wedding cake castle...in many ways a precursor of the great flights of amorous & Gothic imagination that characterized the romantic age of the succeeding century, but (gratefully) with a dignified modicum of Georgian restraint. Acton Castle is no less romantic today, with its formally laid out terraces, sunken garden, and the mirror pond with the requisite lily pads to accommodate frog princes.

The Grade II Listed building has been divided carefully into luxury flats, of which two in the central tower are offered as holiday lets. The larger, sleeping up to eight, occupies the top two floors with exclusive use of the castellated roof terrace (with appropriate outdoor furnishings). Unsurpassed views of the sea and St. Michael's Mount by day, and by night...*star light, star bright...wish I may...wish I might!* The penthouse floor below is a 40 ft. long open plan living/dining/kitchen with rich maple wood floors, recessed lighting and an all white decor. More romance! Three broad stone mullioned window bays bring in a wash of light and sea atmosphere (as if the apartment needed more atmosphere!). Downstairs (that is, three up from the garden terrace) there are three large en-suite bedrooms, two of which are queens with "sea-from-bed-views". And, here is the best part, if you are an aging romantic and the prospect of climbing up four floors is a bit daunting, there is a convenient rear entrance from the sloping ground at the level of this apartment.

The second apartment enters from the garden terrace (left of steps in drawing) into a small hall with a slate floor kitchen/dining area off to the side. Upstairs is a large living room with stone mullioned windows offering wonderful garden and sea views, and two bedrooms, one with bunks (perhaps not so romantic).　　ETB 4 Keys; Highly Commended

II. B-d
B-b
CS
F-3
F-1
£187-474
S 4
III.B-q [2]
B-t + b
CS
F-3 [2]
F-2
£310-819
S 8
BOTH
E$　H$
LT
TELc　TV
W/D
DW　MW
P-
S-S　MS
INS　BK$

Contact Helpful Holidays, Coombe, Chagford, Devon TQ13 8DF
TEL 01144-1647-433-593　or　FAX 01144-1647-433-694

TILLERS MEADOW   St. Mawgan

Up the Vale of Mawgan, about three miles from the beaches, is the exceptionally pretty village of St. Mawgan. Even by Cornwall standards this is an ancient village, as is evidenced by its old stone manor house, which was occupied by Richard of Arundel, Marshal of England, in the 13th century.

Tillers Meadow is a cozy detached cottage, albeit more spacious than most. The cottage has a comfortably furnished living room with parquet floors, an open fireplace, and sliding doors exiting onto a patio with picnic table and barbeque. There is a separate dining room, adjacent to the fitted kitchen, as well as a breakfast room. Upstairs is a large bathroom, with bidet, as well as three bedrooms, the master double being en-suite.

I. F-1
II.B-d [2]
F-1
B-t
F-4
E   H$
FP
TELin
TV
W/D$c
MW
F-F
INS
£198-512
S 6

Contact Cornish Traditional Cottages, Lostwithiel, Cornwall PL22 0HT
TEL 01144-1208-872-559 or FAX 01144-1208-873-548

BOSANNETH

Nr Truro

Generally we are not inclined to review modern bungalows for *Cottage Holidaying in Britain*. Our feeling is that most North American travellers are looking for a bit of the *olde world* in their European holiday. However, Bosanneth is exceptional, not least its dramatic setting, and deserves to be an exception. Here is an ultra-modern accommodation right at the water's edge on Restronguet Point, with superior interior appointments. Bathroom with jacuzzi, kitchen with Aga, wraparound view over the River Fal Estuary...just a wonderful place to stay.

Nearby Truro is an interesting cathedral city and the administrative center for Cornwall. The Art Gallery and Museum are well worth a visit and, for the architectural enthusiasts, Lemon Street is one of the best Georgian streetscapes in all Britain.

I. B-t [2]
F-3 [2]
II.B-d
F-3
E   H$
FP$
LT
TELc
TV
W/D
DW MW
C-   P-
S-S
INS
£288-642
S 6

Contact Classic Cottages, Leslie House, Lady Street, Helston, Cornwall TR13 8NA
TEL 01144-1326-565-656 or FAX 01144-1326-565-554

MERMAID COTTAGE Nr Zennor

*The place is rather splendid. It is just under the moors, on the edge of
a few rough stoney fields that go to the sea. It is quite alone, as a little
colony....*

So wrote D. H. Lawrence as he and Frieda moved into one side of Mermaid
Cottage in March 1916. The Lawrences' retreat to this far corner of the Motherland
was not, strictly speaking, a holiday. His anti-war posture and Frieda's German
nationality were not very fashionable in Hampstead Heath, and when his novel, *The
Rainbow,* was suppressed as obscene in November of 1915 the Lawrences planned
their emigration to Florida. Their dream was to form a colony of like-minded spirits
far away from staid and self destructing Europe. But Florida did not materialize, and
by the new year their enthusiasm turned to self imposed exile on the Cornish coast.
They came to Zennor and stayed at the Tinners Arms while searching for a cottage.

*What we have found is a two-roomed cottage, one room up, one down,
with a long scullery. But the rooms are big and light, and the rent
won't be more than 4 pounds....*

Apparently being "quite alone" in Mermaid Cottage agreed with D.H.
Lawrence, for it was here that he wrote *Women in Love*, while the obscenity of the
European slaughter proceeded with equal vigor. However, the Lawrences still
longed for a colony of like minds and D.H. wrote glowingly of Mermaid Cottage and
Zennor to colleagues in Hampstead Heath, hoping they would join him.

*There is a little grassy terrace outside, and at the back the moor tum-
bles down, great enormous grey boulders and gorse. It could be so
wonderful...(we) gladly await you, if you feel like coming. It would be
so splendid if it could but come off: such a lovely place....*

Mermaid Cottage and its surrounds are no less inviting today than in

Lawrence's time. Indeed, the accommodations have improved greatly, while the broader scene remains virtually unchanged. The cottage is still semi-detached and sits about a mile from Zennor, undisturbed at the foot of the moor in an endless sea of lush summer greenness. It is comprised of a ground floor kitchen, with all the modern conveniences, and a slate-floored dining room with a rustic pine table and an interesting set of chapel chairs. The Rayburn heater here would have been much appreciated by the Lawrences in the winter of 1917! The small sitting room is comfortably furnished and has a large open fire...a cozy spot to pen a bit of immortality or a fraternal letter inviting comrades to share Mermaid Cottage with you next year. Upstairs there are two comfortable bedrooms with views looking out to sea, toward America where Lawrence did eventually go.

  As it came to pass, the Lawrences did finally receive visitors at Mermaid Cottage, though not the like-minded comrades they wanted. Amidst local suspicions that the bearded writer was a German spy, the police arrived in October, 1917 and put the non-conformists to flight.

ETB 4 Keys; Highly Commended

| I. F-2 |
| II.B-d |
| B-b+s |
| E$c |
| H |
| FP |
| LT |
| TV |
| W/D |
| DW |
| P- |
| S-S   MS |
| TA |
| £250-420 |
| S 5 |

TREVEGLOS FARMHOUSE
Zennor

  Granite on granite; this is the little village of Zennor by the sea; neatly cut blocks of stone mortared to the rock of ages. Let it blow; Zennor poses unflappable against the elements as it has since Irish missionaries arrived in the sixth century with a message of spiritual tenacity. The granite and the faith are welded into one in the Church of St. Sennara (from which *Zennor* is derived) and more of that record of tenacity can be seen in the nearby Wayside Museum.

  Treveglos Farmhouse sits detached within the village, a Grade II Listed building on a dairy farm with a herd of Guernsey cows. It has a large kitchen/diner with parquet floors, and an all-in kitchen. There is a cozy living room with slate floors, exposed beams and an open fire. Nearby there is a cove for swimming and fishing, or if you prefer a more public beach, St. Ives is only five miles away. Pony trekking is available, and the moorland and coastal walks are as inspiring as they were in Lawrence's day.

ETB 4 Keys; Highly Commended

| I. F-1 |
| II.B-d |
| B-t |
| B-b+s |
| E$c |
| H |
| FPS |
| LT |
| TV |
| W/D |
| DW   MW |
| P- |
| S-S   MS |
| TA |
| £250-480 |
| S 7 |

Contact Mr & Mrs Peter Cattran, Tregarthen Farmhouse, Zennor, St. Ives, Cornwall, TR26 3BP
TEL 01144-1736-796-977

REDLANDS
on Trevose Head

Trevose Head is a traditional holiday spot, not to say *resort* area. It reminds me somewhat of Cape Cod, with its expansive sandy beaches, high dunes and summertime beach culture. I should hasten to say that I mean Cape Cod a generation or so ago, for, while Trevose's popularity is self-evident, there is no *start Friday afternoon to get off the Cape by Sunday night* problem here.

This is a large Edwardian house built by one of the first generation of holiday makers to discover the area. Its positioning today is as exciting as it was at the beginning of the century; just off the headlands trail with panoramic views out over Mother Ivey's Bay, which is only a couple hundred yards away. The house sits in two acres of shrubbery and lawn, with croquet, badminton and barbecue facilities, and across the lane is a golf course. It must also be said that there is an adjacent trailer park, which is gratefully in a secluded position and, at any rate, not really in the view plane.

Redlands is an upside down house, as it were, with a huge living room (37 ft.) on the second floor, offering northerly and easterly views of the sea through picture windows. There is a telescope *in situ* and plenty to see...line-ups should be anticipated! The open fireplace will bring extra coziness for spring and autumn visitors. It should be noted for those of us somewhat past the beach bunny age, that these beaches are a pleasure to walk during all but the most inclement seasons...better in the off season in some respects.

There are four bedrooms; two upstairs, one of which has a kingsize bed and both with marvelous views, and two twin rooms downstairs. Also downstairs is the well equipped kitchen with a gas Aga as well as electric stove, and a slate slabbed walk-in larder that you will want to take home with you.

The nearby country club offers temporary memberships with golf, tennis, swimming, as well as socializing privileges in their very pleasant club house.   ETB 5 Keys; Highly Commended

I. B-t [2]
F-3
II.B-t/q
B-d
F-2
E$m
H$m
FP
LT
TEL-BA
TVV
W/D
DW MW
F-F MS
INS
BK$
£351-943
S 8

Contact Helpful Holidays, Coombe, Chagford, Devon TQ13 8DF
TEL 01144-1647-433-593 or FAX 01144-1647-433-694

ASHBURNE COTTAGE Ambleside

This handsome 17th century cottage near the steamer pier in historic Ambleside is a real charmer, but with a split personality. Entering through the kitchen one has the impression that the cottage has been carefully restored in a rustic idiom. Note features like the impressive fireplace with the time-worn timber lintel, and the exposed beams *cottaged-up* with some pretty stencil work. The furnishings here include three inviting wing backs, and this combination kitchen/family room has an easy laid-back feel. A good place to flop for a bracing libation after a day cruising on Windermere or chasing the ball around eighteen challenging holes on one of the excellent local courses. In the living room the flavor changes to one of considerable formality, with pretty floral fabrics in soft furnishings and drapery marking this as the *ladies' room*. Both rooms work to a tee (or tea). Upstairs, you will find three comfortable bedrooms, one with a half tester bed and another with lovely views through original oak mullioned windows. ETB 5 Keys; Highly Commended

I. F-1
II.B-d [2]
B-t
F-3 [2]
E$m   H
FPG
LT$
TELc
TV
W/D
DW   MW
NS   P-
BA
S-S
INS
£220-500
S 6

BORRANS COURT Ambleside

This two-story stone mansion sits on nearly five acres of wooded promontory at Waterhead, within two minutes' walk of Lake Windermere. The property is approached up a long private drive through grounds frequented by deer. The old mansion has been carefully subdivided and condominiumized. Several of the apartments are available for holiday let; each reflecting the taste and personalities of their owners. The most handsomely done unit is BETAMERE, which is located on the ground floor with large casement windows facing out onto the meticulously landscaped grounds and gardens. Betamere has its own exterior front door and private perspective. The open plan living/dining room is impressively proportioned, with high ceilings and a light and airy pastel decor. The same brightness is carried throughout the kitchen area where the newly fitted cabinets are done in limed oak, with new built-in appliances. Betamere is exceptionally well furnished with a commodious floral living room suite, a round dining table and elegant fabricked chairs in the French style. The same high standard of furnishing will be found in the double bedroom with generous views of the lake, and a separate bathroom featuring a corner tub, in addition to the en-suite facilities for the bedroom. ETB 4 Keys; Deluxe

I.B-d
F-1
F-3
E$
H$
LT$
TV
W/D
DW   MW
NS   P-
S-S
INS
£197-264
S 2

Contact Heart of the Lakes, Rydal Holme, Rydal, Ambleside, Cumbria LA22 9LR TEL 01144-1539-432-321

THE OLD COACH HOUSE

Clappersgate

The Old Coach House is less than a mile from Ambleside at Clappersgate, the ancient Roman crossing of the River Brathay. One could not be more central to the sights and activities of the Lake District, with the literary shrines of Rydal and Grasmere just up the road, and the sheer magnificence of Lake Windermere just out the window. The Grade II Listed Coach House, which dates from the reign of Queen Anne, is built on the slope of Loughrigg Fell cascading down to the river, with the entrance (drawing) on the high side and elevated views over the Lake from the back windows. There is a shared garden below, with steps down to water where a boat can be moored for those wishing to explore Windermere afloat. The cottage is furnished to a very high standard, with characterful old pine, rich Sanderson fabrics, and a handsome four-poster bed.

ETB 5 Keys; Highly Commended

I.B-d
B-t
F-3
E$c H$c
FPE
LT$
TELc
TV
W/D
DW MW
NS P-
TA
£306-510
S 4

Contact V.R. Vyner-Brooks, Esq., Middle Barrows Green, Kendal, Cumbria LA8 0JG
TEL 01144-1539-560-242 or 01144-1515-269-321 or FAX 01144-1515-261-331

BRIDGE END FARM COTTAGES Boot

England's highest mountain, deepest lake, and steepest road...these are the western moors of the Lake District National Park. Here is nature in *Panorama Vision* which is no less imposing than the Lakes "Proper", just a whole lot less crowded. All around you there is evidence of the ancient attraction of this area: Stone Age circles, the Roman Fort at Hardknott, even a Viking Cross.

Bridge End Farm offers five cottages, sleeping 2-9, for the contemporary explorer. Set in the quiet little hamlet of Boot, once a mining camp, the cottages are along a quaint cob-bled lane by the river. The Pooles have done a nice job converting these Grade II Listed Tudor barns to holiday occupancy, and have won the England for Excellence Silver Award for their effort. There is a wealth of exposed beams and pretty pink granite stonework, and each cottage is comfortably furnished, with especially nice kitchens done in honey oak.

ETB 4 Keys; Highly Commended

E$
H$
LT$
TV
W/Ds
DW MW
S-S; OPEN
MS
TA
£175-850
S 2-9

Contact Mr. Greg Poole, Bridge End Farm, Boot, Eskdale, Cumbria CA19 1TG TEL/FAX 01144-1946-723-100

LONGLANDS AT CARTMEL

Several years ago we arrived in the Lake District during the busy school holidays with high hopes of a week of glorious walking. It was an impromptu jaunt and we hadn't made reservations for a cottage. "Cartmel," said the agent, "is the best we can do." ....We misunderstood. "Cartmel is not on any of the lakes," we protested. Cartmel is away from it all...away from Windermere, Ambleside, Rydal, Grasmere! Away from the frenetic path of literary pilgrims seeking out the footprints of Wordsworth, Ruskin and Beatrix Potter...."Exactly!" said the agent. All of the above are easily accessible from Cartmel, which is within a pleasant half hour's drive, but the historic village of Cartmel offers sanity and civility...even during the high season rush! Cartmel is where Wordsworth, Ruskin and Potter would live today.

We didn't stay at Longlands on that holiday, though we admired the handsome Georgian building from across the road, not knowing it offered accommodation. Frankly, it looked too perfect to take in guests. Later in the week, while dining in the excellent village pub next to the ancient Priory, we heard about the gourmet dinners and Champagne breakfasts prepared for guests by Robert Johnson, the Squire of Longlands. Served in the elegant house dining room, or, for weary hikers or lake sailors, even delivered to the cottage door!

There are eight cottages, all attached to the main house around a lawned courtyard. Their names indicate original usages: Laundrymaid's Cottage, Groom's Quarters, Huntsman's Cottage, etc. Each is individually and impeccably decorated. These are crafted rooms with English country pastel tones and rich waxed pine furnishings. The kitchens reflect the culinary priorities of the man in the big house, and guests are invited to partake of the herbs in the garden. Private game and coarse fishing is available to guests; the Johnsons will even lend experienced guests their sailing dinghy. That's hospitality!

ETB 5 Keys Deluxe; Winner of 1993 England for Excellence Award.

E$m
H$m
FPG*
LT
TELm
TV
W/Ds
DW* MW
P-BA
E/HC*
S-S MS
INS
TA
£190-690
S 2-6

Contact Robert & Judy Johnson, Longlands, Cartmel, Cumbria LA11 6HG
TEL 01144-1539-536-475 or FAX 01144-1539-536-172

CROSSLANDS HOUSE COTTAGE

Crosslands

Snugged in between activity oriented Lake Windermere and tranquil Coniston Water; just at the edge of walk-filled Grizedale Forest Park; in its own quiet hamlet...this cottage puts you in a perfect spot to do it all, or to do nothing at all!

The cottage is part of a 16th century Listed farmstead and sits in its own secluded courtyard. This is another of the *upside down* cottages, with the open plan living room/kitchen area upstairs, offering generous views over the lakeland fells, while the spacious sleeping accommodations and shower facilities are downstairs. Modernization, carefully designed by the artist owner, has not robbed Crosslands of its historic vernacular character; exposed wall timbers and beams, deep stone casement windows, stone floored entrance, and an open fire that will take coal, wood or peat (mood fuels!)...just a wonderful den to curl up in after a bracing day on the Lakeland trails or waterways. Water enthusiasts, by the way, will find both sailing and motor craft, as well as kayaks and canoes, available for rent on Coniston Water. Also not to be overlooked are the theatrical and concert performances at the Theater in the Forest in nearby Grizedale during the summer months.

I.B-d
F-3
E&H
FP
LT
TV
S-S   MS
INS
TA
£208-300
S 2

Contact The Lakeland Cottage Co., Waterside House, Newby Bridge, Ulverston, Cumbria LA12 8AN
TEL 01144-1539-530-024

HAZELWOOD COURT   Grange-Over-Sands

Hazelwood Court is one of the most recognizable, dowager sort of Lakeland country mansions; a mountain of sturdy and statuesque grey stone, decorated with bright red quoinwork and brick framed windows, set into the side of a green promontory with her perspective set firmly on the vista of Morecambe Bay. Immediately below "Hazel" is a carpet of manicured greenery, eighteen expansive holes of golf links. There are only six apartments for let in Hazelwood Court, furnished with a mix of antiques and contemporary styles. The sitting rooms are typically period in their proportions and retain the Victorian corniced ceilings. The bedrooms, some of which are en-suite, have mahogany or Stag Minstrel furnishings. Each apartment is fitted out to sleep four to five people. Fresh flowers, as well as tea and biscuits, welcome guests.

F-3
W/Ds
DW* MW
C-BA
OPEN
MS
$430-1080
S 4-5

Grange-Over-Sands, a Victorian resort town with immaculate public gardens and interesting shops, is within walking distance, and the lovely historic village of Cartmel is nearby.

ETB 4 Keys; Highly Commended

Contact Mary McCanna, Westminster Lodgings, 160 Westminster Dr., W.E., Jamestown, NY 14701
TEL 800-699-0744 or 716-484-0744

SAWREY KNOTTS   Far Sawrey

Far Sawrey is a must-visit village in the Lake District; indeed, it is a good home base to explore the whole region. The village center consists of an inn/restaurant, small Post Office, general store and a cluster of quaint, white-washed cottages. On the outskirts is the former manor house of the village, Sawrey Knotts. *[Knotts, incidentally, is Cumbrian for hill]* This 1861 house is built of Lakeland stone 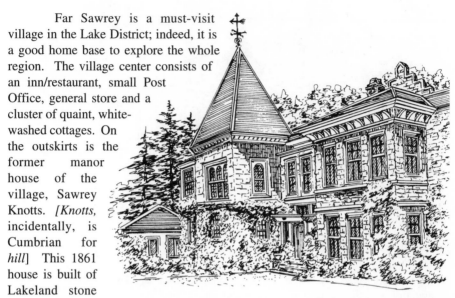 (now largely vine covered) with a rather unusual castellated roof and a tall pointed tower. Early recreational Gothic; impressive in the Victorian estimation, and delightfully curious to the modern eye.

Sawrey Knotts has been divided into six apartments. Because the house is built "up the hill", the upper floor is larger, having four of the flats. There is a central entrance into a spacious hall with wood block flooring and a cozy wood stove. *Rydal* was formed out of the original dining room and enjoys large bay windows and a huge wood paneled inglenook fireplace. The bed is framed by original display cabinets, now containing an extensive collection of old crockery. Rydal's bathroom has a double corner whirlpool. *Loweswater* (the original library, plus lessor rooms) has a double en-suite bedroom, plus a children's bunk room and an additional shower. Small print papers and pink soft furnishings lend a light airy quality to *Loweswater*. Up the paneled stairwell to the other apartments with fine lake views and, in the case of *Grasmere*, access to the upper garden. Sawrey Knotts is furnished with a mix of antiques and contemporary pieces, and all kitchens are fitted with modern units.

The literary "shrine" of Far Sawrey (every Lake District village must have one!) is Beatrix Potter's Hill Top Farm, where she divided her time between raising her beloved Hardwick sheep and penning the endearing stories that may be the last bridge between the generations. Go early to Hill Top when the dew is still on the spiderwebs in Beatrix's garden. It can be a magic place, be you literary pilgrim or just a kid at heart.
ETB 4 Keys; Commended

E$c	H$c
FP*	PS*
L	
TELc	
TV	
W/Ds	
MW	
F-F	
OPEN	
MS	
£120-395	
S 2-6	

Contact Stephanie & Mike Barnes, Sawrey Knotts, Far Sawrey, Hawkshead, Cumbria LA22 0LG
TEL 01144-1539-488-625

HOWTHWAITE Grasmere

They who would holiday in quiet solitude with a book of Wordsworth verse to hand will be thrilled at the prospect of a stay in Howthwaite. This relatively new dwelling (built in 1926 in the sturdy Cumbrian style) is situated directly behind and above William & Dorothy's Dove Cottage. Indeed, the great poet often climbed up to this place for a spot of quiet verse reading and inspired composition, himself.

The house is very spacious, with a wide verandah and long views. As with all the Landmark Trust houses, interior decoration is carefully done to set a mood. In this case a kind of late Edwardian aestheticism seems to prevail; how absolutely appropriate! This is, indeed, a place for long reflective walks and quiet inspiring reads. This cottage knows full well that nature, not man, is the grand thing in these parts.

Contact The Landmark Trust, Shottesbrook, Maidenhead, Berkshire SL6 3SW
TEL 01144-1628-825-925 or FAX 01144-1628-825-417

I. F-1
II.B-d [2]
B-t
B-s
F-2 [2]
E&H
FP
LT
F-F   MS
INS
£485-1147
S 7

GOODY BRIDGE COTTAGE Grasmere

Grasmere has been a rusticators' destination for well over a century, and, despite the considerable summer traffic, modern transient tourism can't seem to put a dent in the utter charm of this village.

Goody Bridge Farm is a half mile away, just a pleasant walk, as it was for William Wordsworth when he trekked here to buy his milk. Today's owners live in the farmhouse across the courtyard and have done an excellent job preparing the old cottage and barn for holiday visitors. The cottage (sleeps 2) has a spacious living/dining room with gas fireplace under a beamed ceiling, and is furnished pleasantly in a contemporary style. The 300-year-old barn

E&H
LT$
TELc
TV
W/D
DW MW
NS
S-S   MS
£185-420
S 2-4

(sleeps 4) was built with Lakeland stone and huge ship-timbers, both having been put to good effect in the renovations. The living/dining areas and the en-suite master bedroom are on the second floor, with beautiful views down the valley to Grasmere. There is, as well, a ground floor en-suite twin bedroom. Both cottages are carpeted and centrally heated.

ETB 5 Keys; Highly Commended

Contact Heart of the Lakes, Rydal Holme, Rydal, Ambleside, Cumbria LA22 9LR
TEL 01144-1539-432-321

THE OLD FARMHOUSE   Nr Hawkshead

Hawkshead dates from Norse times, which is to say that some very farseeing folks staked out this wonderful ground roughly a thousand years ago, give or take a generation. The Viking stock made their mark on the place with the name *Haakr* (which we will assume was a start on *Hawkshead*) and over the centuries a succession of notables have left their marks on this idyllic crossroads in the Vale of Esthwaite. Esthwaite Water, which is one of the District's smaller lakes, was a prize in its own right and is still entirely owned by the Sandys family, late of the 16th century Archbishop of York with the same name, who was responsible for establishing the Grammar School here in 1585. William Wordsworth left his mark here as a boy; that is to say he carved his name on his desk while a student at the Grammar School, and this precocious literary achievement is viewable in the summer when the ancient Grammar School is open to the public.

About a half mile from the village, along a single lane through the woods, is the hamlet known as Keen Ground. More good nomenclature! The Old Farmhouse here dates from the 17th century and is built in the vernacular style of the Lake District. From the handsome oak paneling in several rooms, the oak stairwell, and the carved oak court cupboard, we can assume that the Old Farm at Keen Ground knew periods of considerable prosperity. Today's owners have very effectively used these historic *qualities* as a backdrop for some equally tasteful furnishing and decoration. Comfortable chairs and a settee arranged around an open fireplace in the living room, a separate little dining room with period furnishings, a compact kitchen fitted with everything from quality china to the most modern appliances...all the makings of a distinctly gentrified sojourn in the country. Up the wooden stairs one finds more pretty fabrics and furnishings, not to mention inviting views of the garden across the lane, all enclosed in a beech hedge. There is a master bedroom with a luxurious en-suite shower facility, and two more bedrooms along with another full bath.

II.B-d [2]	
B-3	
B-b	
F-2	
E&H	
FP$	
LT	
TEL	
TV	
W/D	
DW	MW
S-S	MS
INS	
£334-618	
S 6	

Contact The Lakeland Cottage Co., Waterside House, Newby Bridge, Ulverston, Cumbria LA12 8AN
TEL 01144-1539-530-024

MINSTRELS' GALLERY Hawkshead

In days of yore minstrels played in the Crown & Mitre Inn from a screened gallery above the open-to-the-roof convivial Hall. That was a while back, say 500 years or so! These days, all the minstrels have big recording contracts and play in little sound proof cubicles, and tea has come to be served on the lower premises of the old Crown & Mitre Inn.

Towering convivial halls also fell out of fashion, so a floor was laid across, sealing off the minstrels' gallery from the floor below, and, incidentally, providing a new word for the English vocabulary...*ceiling*. Upstairs, above the present owners quaint little tea shop and in the gallery where once plucked ye olde minstrels, there is now a cozy holiday accommodation for four (with or without lutes and flutes). The minstrel screen, along with lots of old character beams and wavy walls, provide a fitting backdrop for some nice decoration and comfy cottage style furnishings. There is a separate entrance to the cottage, up some appropriately ancient stone steps.

What more could one ask for? Well, how about a nice village. Fair enough; you've got it! Hawkshead, lying mid-way between Windermere and Coniston Water, is one of the Lake District's most handsome villages, and, unlike the others, Hawkshead has taken defensive measures against the ye old gasified carts. Parking is on the perimeter of the village, though you will be allowed to drive in for loading purposes. ETB 4 Keys; Highly Commended.

II.B-d
B-t
F-3
E   H$m
FPG
LT$
TV
W/D
MW
NS   P-
S-S   MS
INS
£184-320
S 4

Contact Heart of the Lakes, Rydal Holme, Rydal, Ambleside, Cumbria LA22 9LR   TEL 01144-1539-432-321

THE COURTYARD High Lorton

Exquisite accommodations on an exquisite 19th century estate in an exquisite Lake District setting...it would be sheer avarice to ask for anything more! We have written pleasurably about the Vale of Lorton before; suffice it to say that this is a most attractive corner of the National Park for all the walking and gawking attractions of the Lake District, *sans* some of the people congestion of the Windermere axis.

I. F-3
II.B-d
B-t [2]
F-3
E&H
FPS
LT
TVV
W/D
DW MW
P-
OPEN MS
INS
£450-640
S 6

Mrs. Park's Lorton estate offers two holiday steads, gilt mirror images of each other, occupying the Georgian styled former stables. You will find these cottages spacious and fitted out to an exceptionally high standard, with cushy soft furnishings, carpeted and tiled floors overlaid with oriental rugs, pretty decoratives and plants. Guests are invited to share in the games room for ping pong and snooker, or to wander freely over the forty acres of parkland.   ETB 5 Keys; Highly Commended

Contact Rural Retreats, Station Road, Blockley, Moreton-in-Marsh, Gloucestershire, GL56 9DZ
TEL 01144-1386-701-177 or FAX 01144-1386-701-178

BEANLANDS PARK   Irthington

Beyond the occasionally maddening crowd of the Lake District is the tranquil solitude of the Borderlands. To be sure, there is plenty to do and see up here, history and nature have made this a rich venue for the visitor. But, up here there is a liberating sense of space and time; no line-ups for photo opportunities, no parking problems to solve before taking a simple walk. Here on the Anglo-Scots frontier, it's pull over and ramble at will. And, if you are suddenly hit by an overwhelming urge to join the Legions at Windermere or pay your respects to the Legends of Grasmere and Rydal, you need only drive an hour south (not counting the bottleneck traffic in Ambleside, itself, or the jam of gawkers around Dove Cottage).

Beanlands Park is a handsome Victorian estate sitting proudly on a rise overlooking the River Irthing. The Irthing has risen with surging promise in the Black Fells of the Border National Park, spent itself breaching the ancient Roman Walls of Hadrian and become little more than a gentle brook as it passes at the feet of Beanlands Park. There are lovely garden benches sited around the seven acres of grounds, places to sit among the daffodils and shrubbery for a quiet read or an absorbing gaze at the valley below and the Pennines in the distance.

The principal holiday accommodation at Beanlands Park actually comprises the major part of the house, itself, with four en-suite bedrooms upstairs (one with a splendid balcony), and drawing room, dining room and kitchen downstairs. These are generously proportioned Victorian rooms with high ceilings, handsome mouldings, expansive bay windows, and broad arched entries. The creme and white decor makes for a light and airy atmosphere, actually more Georgian than Victorian. Furnishings are eclectic and colorful.

In addition, there is a small apartment wing, called the *Short Suite,* with a four-poster bed and a wood burning stove. Down the lane is the *The Lodge,* formerly the gate house, full of Gothic character and all the modern amenities.

MAIN
I. F-1
II.B-d [2]
B-t [2]
F-4
F-3 [3]
TV [4]
DW MW
P-
OPEN
£340-674
S 8
SHORT
S.
I.B-d
F-3
FP
S-S OPEN
£194-294
S 2
LODGE
I. F-2
II.B-d
F-3
B-t
W/D
DW   MW
S-S OPEN
£246-400
S4
ALL
E&H
LT
TELin TV
MS

Contact British Travel International, P.O. Box 299, Elkton VA 22827 USA
TEL 800-327-6097 or FAX 703-298-2347

CROSBY HOUSE
High Crosby

We are back in the borderlands, this frontier where Hadrian built his Wall and successive generations of Saxons and Normans fortified themselves against the rugged northern tribes. Later the civilization disparity diminished but the relentless bloodletting continued in the guise of various dynastic and patriotic causes. Nearby at Brampton, Bonny Prince Charlie set up his headquarters before the awaiting doom at Culloden. One doesn't have to be interested in all this history to have a quiet holiday here in the borderlands, but there is such a wealth of museums and archeological digs in Carlisle and the surrounds that historic consciousness is tremendously rewarding.

Crosby House is a perfect base for exploring this region. Michael and Deirdre Dickson provide two beautifully designed and meticulously kept cottages facing onto the private courtyard of their Georgian country house. Woodside Cottage sleeps six and is entered through stable doors and down a few steps into a character den with open beams and a cozy wood fire. There is a modern kitchen with terracotta floors, and upstairs three nicely fitted bedrooms. Across the way is Courtyard Cottage, with two prettily decorated bedrooms downstairs and a spacious living room, brightened by a large arched window and sky-lighting upstairs.   ETB 4 Keys; Highly Commended

WOODSIDE
I. F-3
II.B-d
B-t
B-b
F-2
COURTY
I.B-d
B-t
F-3
BOTH
E$m H$m
FPS
LT
TELc   TV
W/D
MW
P-
OPEN MS
INS TA
£233-445
S 4-6

Contact Mrs. Deirdre Dickson, Crosby House, Crosby-on-Eden, Carlisle, Cumbria CA6 4OZ
TEL 01144-1288-573-239

CHURCH BROW COTTAGE   Kirkby Lonsdale

Turner came to this fine Georgian garden pavilion in 1818 to paint the panoramic scene across the Lune River Valley. Ruskin came later to walk along the avenue of trees below the cottage and proclaimed it "one of the loveliest scenes in England". More recently, Prince Charles came here to announce completion of Vivat Trust's restoration of Church Brow Cottage.

I. F-1
F-3
III.B-d
E&H
FP
TV
W/D
MW
S-S
INS
$580-765
S 2

The Cottage is a full three stories (top story only in drawing) and is approached from below by steep steps to the lower terrace. One enters the kitchen dining area through a pair of French doors and proceeds up a narrow spiral stairs to the sitting room with fireplace, built-in period cabinets, and French doors exiting to yet another terrace with unsurpassable views. Further up the spiral staircase we have the bedroom, furnished in the peerless taste of the Vivat Trust decorating department. All this and the charming town of Kirkby Lonsdale too!

Contact Haywood Cottage Holidays, P.O. Box 878, Eufaula, Alabama 36072
TEL 205-687-9800 or FAX 205-687-5324

THE BIELD
Little Langdale

Little Langdale is scarcely six miles from the ever popular Ambleside, where the traffic can be bumper to bumper at the height of the season. Yet at The Bield, snuggled up in Lingmore Fell, one feels lost in nature, with miles of inspiring walks, up on to the higher fells or down along the river and over the ancient pack horse bridge.

The Bield must be one of the oldest houses in the district, dating from the 1600's, with many vernacular features that one won't find in comparably sized Victorian homes of the Lake District, which were typically architect designed. The living room has a beamed ceiling and original oak paneling, which carries on up the stairwell. There is a carved spice cupboard and a court cupboard bearing the date 1635, and an open fireplace. Furnishings are comfortable and homey, with fitted carpets or flagstone flooring. Upstairs, the master bedroom features a painted landscape frieze and a spacious wardrobe developed from an old wool loft. The main bathroom has a bidet, and there is another full bath/shower room to go with a pair of twin bedrooms (one entered through the other).

Indoors meets outdoors in the all-season glazed garden room, which has comfortable furnishings and lovely views out over the grounds, where you will find a pretty little stream wending its way among the trees. And, if all this peace and quiet finally gets the best of you, do take a drive into Ambleside; traffic or no traffic, there is always something going on, such as the Lake District Summer Music Festival which lasts for two weeks in August with master classes and performances by top ranking players. There are, as well, cruises on Windermere, Coniston, Ullswater and Derwentwater that always render up an eyeful of the grandeur of nature, which up here is especially *grand* during the autumn color that can last well into November.

ETB 5 Keys; Highly Commended

II.B-d
F-4
B-t [2]
F-1
F-3
B-s+s
E$
H$
FP$
L T$
TELc
TVV
W/D
DW MW
P-
F-F
INS
£300-900
S 10

Contact Cottage Life, Rydal Holme, Rydal, Ambleside, Cumbria LA22 9LR TEL 01144-1539-432-321

SOUTHWAITE MILL

Lorton Valley

Below the Lakeland fells the Cocker River cuts a gentle path through the Vale of Lorton. In the last century the mill at Southwaite exploited the rush of energy flowing down from Loweswater, Buttermere and Crummock Water. These days the Mill plays host to a steady flow of tourists trekking up to these same lakes.

The old mill has been attractively redesigned for its new role, and offers six accommodations in the old Mill House, as well as the Granary, Barn, and Mill proper. Throughout, the emphasis is on bright airy space (plenty of it vertical!), with cheerful pine furnishings and all appliance kitchens. There is an indoor heated pool and good fishing in the Cocker, particularly for visitors arriving during the late sea trout run. Wordsworth pilgrims will want a day in nearby Cockermouth where it all began for William and Dorothy, and where much of it is collected now for our curiosity and respect.

ETB 5 Keys; Commended-Highly Commended

E$m
H$m
FPG
LT
TEL
TVV
W/D
DW MW
S-S
MS
INS
$675-2350
S 4-8

Contact Meta Voyage, 1945 Pauline Plaza, Suite 14, Ann Arbor, MI 48103-5047
TEL 800-771-4771 (East) 800-538-6881 (West) or FAX 313-995-3464

BECK HOUSE

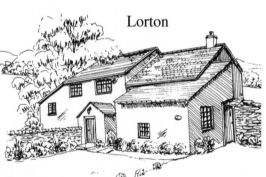

Lorton

This charming whitewashed 17th century cottage lies in the Vale of Lorton, beside scenic Liza Beck. Beck House now has central heating and wall-to-wall carpeting, but still retains its old oak beams and the original built-in bread oven. The new kitchen has lovely pine furnishings and all the modern utilities. The lounge is spacious enough to accommodate a piano and there is an old black leaded open fire for the chilly Cumbrian evenings. Up the original curved stairs, made from local slate, there are three bedrooms; all have beamed ceilings and wonderful views of the countryside. Outside, one may enjoy the large gardens surrounded by a substantial stone wall. All around there are marvelous panoramic views of the surrounding fells. Nearby Scafell Pike is England's highest point and absolutely not to be missed by hiking enthusiasts. There is so much in the Lake District to see and do in the cultural idiom, but up here around Buttermere I recommend that you just surrender yourself to the bold landscape...walk in it, doze in it, dream in it; let it soak in and it will never leave your soul!

I. F-3
II.F-2
B-d [2]
B-t
FP
TEL
W/D
DW MW
$760-1190
S 6

Contact Mary McCanna, Westminster Lodgings, 160 Westminster Dr., W.E., Jamestown, NY 14701
TEL 800-699-0744 or 716-484-0744

CONEGLIANO Newby Bridge

This pretty cottage is situated at the lower end of Windermere where the lake meets the River Leven above the stone arches of Newby Bridge, dating from the 1500's. The property has extensive grounds which go right to the water's edge where a boat can be pulled up on the grass. Mountain bikes are also available locally for hire to explore the shoreline and forests of these beautiful lakelands. Conegliano shares its seclusion with two other cottages, but is within minutes of all the activities and conveniences of Windermere and Bowness.

The cottage is nicely laid out, with two spacious en-suite bedrooms downstairs and a large "L" shaped living/dining room up. French doors open from the living room onto a small balcony which is fitted out for alfresco pleasures. Furnishings throughout the cottage are very handsome, indeed, with coordinated fabrics, nice lighting and plenty of decoratives for a homey feeling. The kitchen is nicely done up in oak cabinetry and is stocked with good quality china and glassware.

```
I. B-d [2]
F-3
F-2
E&H
LT
TELc
TVV
MW
P-
S-S
INS
£275-490
S 4
```

Contact The Lakeland Cottage Co., Waterside House, Newby Bridge, Ulverston, Cumbria LA12 8AN TEL 01144-1539-530-024

HERON CRAG Langdale

The Lake District is, of course, famed for its lakes, but its mountain views and walks are no less inspiring. Heron Crag offers a good measure of both, combined with luxurious accommodation in an imaginatively designed expansion of a traditional fellside cottage.

The architectural aim, to make the home an integral part of the landscape, is fulfilled by the dramatic use of glass and stone, and *tricks* like incorporating a natural rock outcrop into the living room and embellishing it with all sorts of greenery. One enters an expansive marble hallway leading to the 40 ft. living/dining room with its sweeping curved glass wall. Domestic and natural environments are merged and one passes freely through large openings on to the terrace. The furnishing of Heron Crag is elegant and tastefully understated. Large leather chesterfields, which would dominate a smaller or more cluttered room, reside here with subtle dignity. On the other hand, the master bathroom wants to show-off a bit, with its luxurious corner tub, bidet and coordinated fixtures. Well, why not? There is nothing understated about Heron Crag's compact kitchen either; here you will find a showcase of Poggenpohl and Neff fixtures.   ETB 5 Keys; Deluxe

```
I.B-d
F-4
B-t
F-3
E$m H$m
FPS
LT$
TV
W/D
DW MW
NS
C-BA  P-
S-S
INS
£350-580
S 4
```

Contact Cottage Life, Rydal Holme, Rydal, Ambleside, Cumbria LA22 9LR TEL 01144-1539-432-321

KIRKLAND HALL COTTAGES

Nr Penrith

Ian Howes is a photographer by profession and wanted the conversion of Kirkland Hall's barns to be nothing less than *picture perfect*. There is no doubt that he and wife Lesley have done just that, winning the Country Landowner's Award in 1989 for their effort and imagination. For added inspiration in the picture perfect department they only had to look outside to the Pennine foothills and the lush Eden Valley. We are away from the hustle and bustle of Lake District tourism up here in the open fells where the sound of gurgling brooks replaces the sound of the internal combustion engine; horns here come mounted on four legs, rather than four wheels. There are endless great walks, a wealth of fishing opportunities, and plenty of quaint sandstone villages with convivial pubs and caloric tea shops to visit.

The Howes have created four cottages for our pleasure and enjoyment. The largest is called Haybarn (see drawing) and sleeps six. As the Tower of London *features* the Crown Jewels, Haybarn *features* the largest inglenook fireplace I've seen outside a castle! With its honey stone masonry, back lighting and arching timber lintel, this fireplace puts the rest of the room on notice. And, the challenge is answered by one of the prettiest interior decorating jobs you'll see in any old haybarn around your neighborhood...or any old minor palace, for that matter. Luxurious soft furnishings, plush drapery, and richly grained occasional pieces, all framed by gorgeous stone walls and timbered ceilings, and brightly lit by an open conservatory. Above, there is a gallery accessing the master en-suite bedroom, as well as twin bedrooms and another bath.

Your other choices are Shearers and Stable Cottages, sleeping four; and Beck Cottage, alongside the gurgling stream, which sleeps two. You will find the furnishings and utilities in each comparable with Haybarn and very modestly priced from £140-305.

ETB 4 Keys; Highly Commended

II.B-d
B-t [2]
F-3 [2]
E&H
FPS
L; T$
TV
W/D$s
DW MW
P-BA
S-S MS
TA
£210-415
S 6

Contact Ian Howes, Kirkland Hall, Kirkland Nr Penrith, Cumbria CA10 1RN TEL 01144-1768-88295

RYDAL MOUNT COTTAGE

Rydal

Rydal Mount is a calendar perfect English cottage with a Wordsworthian perspective over the Vale of Rydal down to Lake Windermere. In fact, the great poet's home for thirty-seven years, which is now a revered museum, is just above Rydal Mount Cottage.

| II.B-d |
| F-1 |
| B-t |
| B-s |
| F-4 |
| E$m |
| H$m |
| FPS |
| LT$ |
| TV |
| W/D |
| DW |
| S-S |
| INS |
| £201-495 |
| S 5 |

This holiday property is encompassed by pretty lawns and a garden that climbs right up the whitewashed walls of the cottage.

Inside, Rydal Mount is a cozy den with beamed ceilings and a woodburning stove in the sitting room. The large fully fitted kitchen opens into a nice conservatory. Upstairs, you will find double and twin bedrooms, with built in furnishings. The master bedroom has its own WC & basin, and there is a large bathroom (no shower) with bidet. The cottage is centrally heated and has wall-to-wall carpeting throughout.

4 Keys; Highly Commended

Contact Cottage Life, Rydal Holme, Rydal, Ambleside, Cumbria LA22 9LR TEL 01144-1539-432-321

HOWSCALES Kirkoswald Nr Penrith

Kirkoswald is situated in the fertile Eden Valley, where Raven Beck tumbles down from the Pennines. In the 11th century the Normans built a formidable castle here, which is today but a ruin, though the plundered masonry of the old stronghold was conveniently recycled in later construction of the market town of Kirkoswald. Alas, even this wild and woolly frontier town, has gracefully downsized into a peaceful village, with a couple pubs and an ancient inn featuring the old bull baiting rings in the cobbles of its forecourt. A mile or so from the village is the 17th century farmstead of Howscales, sturdily constructed from the redstone that once secured Norman ambitions against the Scots.

Howscales has been handsomely done-up by Elaine and Colin Eade. They offer four generously proportioned cottages in the old barn and byres, all grouped around a pretty cobbled courtyard. Three of the cottages are "upside down", with living rooms upstairs giving long views over the pastoral expanse, with the Pennine Hills in the background. The cottages are bright and airy, with freshly painted over stone walls, lots of original touches, honey pine furnishings, and quality kitchens. All four cottages have showers with seats, and one unit is all ground floor. All in all, Howscales is a very convenient base for exploring this fascinating region from Hadrian's Wall to the Lakes.   ETB 3-4 Keys; Highly Commended

| E$m |
| H$m |
| LT |
| TELc TV |
| W/D$s |
| MW |
| NS C-BA |
| S-S MS |
| INS |
| £140-420 |
| S 2-4 |

Contact Elaine & Colin Eade, Howscales, Kirkoswald, Penrith, Cumbria CA10 1JG
TEL 01144-1768-898-666 or FAX 01144-1768-898-710

RIVERSIDE COTTAGES

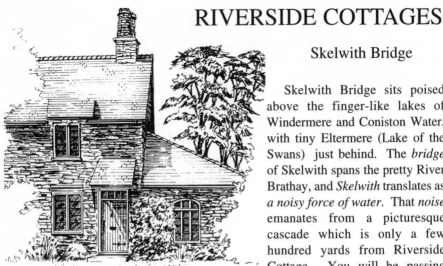

Skelwith Bridge

Skelwith Bridge sits poised above the finger-like lakes of Windermere and Coniston Water, with tiny Eltermere (Lake of the Swans) just behind. The *bridge* of Skelwith spans the pretty River Brathay, and *Skelwith* translates as *a noisy force of water*. That *noise* emanates from a picturesque cascade which is only a few hundred yards from Riverside Cottage. You will be passing these cascades on your walk to the beautiful village of Elterwater. This delightful ramble, right from your cottage door, is just a *warmer-upper*. Beyond Elterwater you'll want to carry on to Chapel Stile, and then you must choose between the rigors of the Langdale Pikes or cutting across and making the circle around Grasmere and Rydal Water. This is the Lake District...**thou shalt walk!** And, just about the time you think you can't go another ten feet (usually accompanied by a sudden awareness of yet another extraordinary photo opportunity) some eighty-five year old dowager with an equally eager West Highland terrier will march past you without so much as a bead of perspiration showing. Might as well be philosophical about it; pause a bit longer to put on your telephoto lens and wait for the artful long shot of her frail silhouette as it crests against the setting sun on the distant hill.

Well, it has been a hard first day on the trail, but you're in luck because pure luxury awaits your sore muscles back at Riverside Cottage. Riverside Cottage (and the attached Garden Cottage) were architect designed in 1872, with character chimneys in the mode of witches' hats. The larger cottage (really a house) is situated on three floors with superb views of the river and mountains. The sitting room features exposed beams and an open fire in the inglenook fireplace. Mr. & Mrs. Vyner-Brooks have won the top accolade *(Deluxe* status) from the English Tourist Board for the complete amenities and tasteful furnishing of these cottages. Among other wonderful surprises, you will find a Victorian style bathroom with bidet, and an absolutely delicious master bedroom featuring a mahogany four-poster bed with the canopy richly pleated into a center medallion.

Adjoining is the romantic Garden Cottage, with an interesting stone and lattice porch entering off the well tended garden. The garden theme, in fact, runs right through the whole cottage to the lovely bedroom with its prettily draped Corona bed.

ETB 5 Keys; Deluxe

RIVER S.	
II. B-d	
B-t	
F-4	
III.B-t	
FP$	
£367-786	
S 6	
GARDEN	
I.B-d	
F-3	
£295-466	
S 2	
BOTH	
E$c	
LT$	
TELc	TV
W/D	
DW	MW
NS	P-
TA	

Contact Mr. V.R. Vyner-Brooks, Esq., Middle Barrows Green, Kendal, Cumbria LA8 0JG
TEL 01144-1539-560-242 or 01144-1515-269-321 or FAX 01144-1515-261-331

LAKEFIELD   On Ullswater

Lakefield is an extraordinary holiday property! Down a private drive, in five acres of woods and clearings filled with daffodils and rhododendrons, to a 1930's retreat built of Lakeland stone and wood right on 500 feet of boulder spotted beach. The single-story "L" shaped home, with an integral boat house, was no doubt a radical design before the war. What stands out now, architecturally, is how much interesting complexity (arches, mouldings, etc.) was incorporated into *early* modern architecture, before *modern* became another word for characterless. Lakefield must have been a bit remote in that earlier day, and some of that campy atmosphere is sustained by the fact that the cottage is still run on electricity supplied by its own generator. However, this is not a rustic camp in the bush; on the contrary, from its paneled walls to its fitted carpeting and comfortable soft furnishings, Lakefield is a home away from home...except this home happens to come with a lake, rowboat and fish!   ETB 3 Keys; Commended

I.B-k
B-d
B-t [2]
F-3
E   H$m
FP
LT$
TV
P-
S-S
INS
£255-685
S 8

BETTY'S COTTAGE   Troubeck

Here we have a character cottage of the first order...thick stone walls and deep set windows, low ceilings with roughly hewn and blackened beams, and an inglenook fireplace with the proportions to remind us that in the 17th century, when Betty's Cottage was built, keeping warm was a necessary preoccupation. Today's guests will also want to strike up a cozy coal fire on the raised hearth, just to set the mood for relaxing in the aesthetically pleasing living room, with its cushy soft furnishings and pretty decoratives. Autumn and winter guests will find another kind of cozy warmth from the Aga in the farmhouse kitchen, but, of course, there is central heating year round for folks who want their heat *plain,* without character.

In the recent renovation of this traditional farm cottage, the owners have wisely preserved the slate floors which were an essential part of the vernacular style and dress so nicely these days with colorful rugs. The characterful Lakeland slate appears again in the staircase and even in the kitchen, where it has been used for the counter tops. There are three bedrooms upstairs, with a bidet in the bathroom and a separate shower cubicle. Exterior amenities include a handsome rock garden and a patio fitted nicely for alfresco dining. One comes to the Lake District to walk, and there are some wonderful rambles that begin right at the door of Betty's Cottage.   5 Keys; Highly Commended.

I. F-1
II.B-d
B-t
B-b
F-4
E$m H$m
FP
LT$
TELc TV
W/D
DW   MW
S-S
INS
£250-550
S 6

Contact Cottage Life, Rydal Holme, Rydal, Ambleside, Cumbria LA22 9LR TEL 01144-1539-432-321

Yeldersley Hall

YELDERSLEY HALL Nr Ashbourne

No faded elegance here! For understandable reasons, many North American visitors to the "old country", including yours truly, occasionally want to have a taste of the gentry life, however vicariously. Let's face it, it's more than just the pursuit of luxury, it's a thirst for the historic. Of course, history was full of hovels, too, but it's rather difficult to work up a _to the manor born_ feeling in a hovel. Over the past couple decades we have stayed on quite a number of Britain's ancient and noble estates, more often than not as a paying guest, self catering and otherwise. The experiences have not been uniformly pleasant. Suffice it to say that there is, in fact, a lot of faded elegance in the noble realm; reduced circumstances eating away at the physical, as well as the spiritual, life of the gentry. Dowdy and depressing; definitely not the makings of a vicarious experience! But not so with Yeldersley Hall.

Yeldersley Hall is quite simply an exquisite Georgian estate, physically and spiritually. Rex and Penelope Sevier would have it no other way. They have done a remarkable job of restoring the East Wing of the Hall and renovating the stables to create three (only three!) peerless holiday accommodations. The work done on the East Wing flat is a restoration, in the proper sense; that is a renewal, both in terms of the infrastructure (plumbing, electrical, plaster & woodwork) and the decorative. The result is not one of museum re-creation, but rather it is a freshening-up within historic proportions and perimeters...as, no doubt, this fine Georgian mansion was freshened-up in earlier generations by house proud and prosperous owners. There is a difference, and one senses it in the highly personalized choices in wallpaper patterns and fabrics for soft furnishings and drapery. The apartment is replete with fine antiques, _objets d'art,_ and all sorts of pretty particulars, which have a feel of being _family property,_ not simply _furnishings,_ however fashionable. But, of course, this apartment is more than _homey,_ it is truly elegant...some people's homes are! That elegance is enhanced, and I should say _elevated,_ by virtue of the apartment being on the second floor (entrance via an external spiral staircase), which, in the best Georgian tradition, unites the life inside with the grandness of nature outside.

ETB 5 Keys; Deluxe

II.B-d
F-2
B-t/q
F-3
E&H
FPG
LT
TELc TV
W/D
DW MW
C-BA P-
S-S
TA
UK265-395
S 4

Contact Rex & Penelope Sevier, Yeldersley Hall, Ashbourne, Derbyshire DE6 1LS TEL 01144-1335-343-432

The YEW TREE GARDEN APARTMENTS

have been fashioned by the Seviers out of a portion of the stable block at Yeldersley. The decorative idiom in these apartments is distinctly *country*, with rush-seat ladder back chairs, gingham tableclothes and pine cabinetry. Both apartments are fully carpeted and open plan, with some of the old architecturals, notably the Victorian iron pillars, worked into the contemporary design.

B-q
F-2
E&H
FPG
LT
TELc
TV
W/Ds
MW
P-
S-S
TA
£140-240
S 2

Whether one stays in the East Wing of the Hall or the Yew Tree Apartments, there are twelve acres of beautifully landscaped gardens to enjoy. You will find plenty of little tuck-away spots to have a private picnic or a quiet read. Perhaps a game of croquet on the front lawn or a stroll by the paddock...all part of the many vicarious opportunities at Yeldersley. Of course, if one feels an urge to be a *common* tourist for a few hours, one can always escape to the spectacular Peak District National Park, just down the road.

ETB 4 Keys; Commended & Highly Commended

Contact Rex & Penelope Sevier, Yeldersley Hall, Ashbourne, Derbyshire DE6 ILS TEL 01144-1335-343-432

KITTY'S COTTAGE

Ashford-in-the-Water

Ashford-in-the-Water, so named for is positioning on the River Wye, is an ancient village, dating back to *Domesday Book* times. The village has come down through the centuries virtually unspoiled, with its much photographed old Sheep Wash Bridge, built for packhorses, and its six wells dressed out with pictures in flowers in the old Derbyshire tradition. Kitty's Cottage is, itself, only a few yards from the river bank, and is situated on the corner of a quiet lane. The Grade II Listed building dates from the 18th century and is in the vernacular style of roughly cut stone with sandstone lintels. To the rear of the cottage there is a flagstone patio and barbeque. Inside, the cottage offers a comfortable sitting/dining room with a coal effect gas fire and a number of older pine furnishings and antiques.

Nearby is the famous pudding town, Bakewell, with all sorts of tourist amenities and comprehensive guidance for touring the Peak District National Park. The spectacular cascading waterfalls of Monsal Dale are only about a mile from Kitty's Cottage.   ETB 3 Keys; Commended

II.B-k	
B-t	
F-3	
E&H	
FPG	
LT	
TELc	
TV	
F-F	MS
INS	
£187-332	
S 4	

Contact Derbyshire Country Cottages, Rosemount, 90 Cavendish Rd. Matlock, Derbyshire DE4 3HD
TEL 01144-1629-583-545

DAIRY HOUSE FARM Nr Ashbourne

It's a line you might want to offer your envious friends back home after you've returned from a holiday in England. "We stayed in a pigsty." You can whelm them further with the curiosity that in England, where virtually every building is protected and preserved under government authority, even pigsties can't be razed and are deemed suitable for domestic conversion. I recommend that you show your chums the pictures of your holiday steads immediately at this juncture.

Andy and Dorothy Harris have done wonders with their Pigsty! Likewise with Looseboxes, formerly a calving pen. Actually, even in Victorian times these were quite handsome accommodations for critters and had more than enough architectural character to merit early conversion for more upright species. Each cottage has its own grounds amidst a quite unusual (for England) stone lawn with tubs (troughs, buckets, urns, etc) of flowers. Blink twice and you might think you were in Bermuda! Beyond that there are regular gardens; the Harris' do it up grand: a thousand daffodils, forty rose bushes, all sorts of flowering trees, geraniums, trailing aubretia and much much more.

PIGSTY
I. B-b
F-1
II.B-q
F-4
£175-300
S 4
LOOSBOX
I.B-d
F-4
£145-250
S 2
BOTH
E&H
FPE
LT
TELc
TV
W/D   MW
NS
E/HC*
S-S   MS
INS

Pigsty sleeps four and is geared particularly well for children, with a ground floor bunk bedroom and the queen-size upstairs under the vaulted ceiling and skylights. Furnishings in both cottages are strictly modern; three piece English cottage suites covered in cream moquette with a russet floral design, pine tables and bedsteads, brick-backed electric fires. The kitchens are nicely fitted, with good working space and interesting arched windows over the sinks. Looseboxes, which has one large double bedroom, is all on one floor, with an open beam ceiling throughout. There is a ramp entry and this cottage is well designed for elderly or disabled visitors.

One could easily fill a week touring within an hour of the Dairy House Farm base: Nottingham and Sherwood Forest, Tutbury Castle ruins where Mary Queen of Scots was imprisoned, Chatsworth House, Shugborough Hall, the Wedgewood and Royal Doulton potteries, and more.   ETB 4 Keys; Highly Commended

Contact Andy & Dorothy Harris at Dairy House Farm, Alkmonton, Longford, Ashbourne, Derbyshire DE6 3DG   TEL/FAX 01144-1335-330-359

OXTON RAKES HALL FARM   Barlow

Oxton Rakes Hall Farm is situated down a long lane just outside the Peak District National Park. The area is rich in touring opportunities, from the bold natural wonders of the Peaks, themselves, to the historic industrial city of Sheffield, just fourteen miles distant. This is also a region full of literary history, *Jane Eyre* country, as it were. In addition, there are a number of stately homes in the "neighborhood" worth visiting, including the magnificent Chatsworth House, home of the Dukes of Devonshire.

Jane Hill has underscored the *lost in nature* feel of her little thirty acre farm by assigning ornithological names to each of her distinctive cottages: Swallow, Owl, Heron, Pheasant, and Jay. On the grounds you will find a heated outdoor pool and a fully fitted games room. Swallow Cottage (sleeps 4) occupies ground floor space, with wide doors and ramps to accommodate partially disabled guests. Typical of all the Oxton Rakes Hall cottages, Swallow is exceptionally bright and airy, with fitted carpets, nice soft furnishings covered in floral blues, and polished pine chairs and tables. Owl Cottage (sleeps 4), which is upstairs, is similarly furnished and has a log effect electric fire. Pheasant Croft, which was opened in 1994 by none other than the Duke of Devonshire, is quite understandably the Hill family's pride and joy. It features a very romantically decorated king-size bedded room, in addition to a twin room, and many extras, not least in the kitchen.

Finally there is Heron Lodge, a modern timber cabin which sits on its own by the lake, looking a bit more North Wood-*ish* than English. It is open plan, with a large stone fireplace at one end and a double brass bed at the other end. A second, twin bedroom, with pretty patchwork quilts and gingham curtains, is located upstairs and the bathroom features a whirlpool bath. Across the front is a wide verandah, a nice place to sit of an evening and watch some of the real life ornithological world come to your doorstep.

All the kitchens are more than adequately equipped, and, indeed, the Hill's farm shop will supply home grown free range chickens and eggs, as well as organically grown produce. In the critter department you will also meet with Ebb and Flo, the Hills' pair of wallabies, who contribute nothing to the "produce" of the farm, but do add a certain *Aus elan* to the holiday venue.

ETB 3-5 Keys; Highly Commended

E&H
LT
TV
W/Ds
DW*
MW*
P-BA
E/HC*
S-S   MS
INS
£210-275
S 2-4

Contact Mrs J.S. Hill, Oxton Rakes Hall Farm, Barlow Nr Sheffield S18 5SE
TEL 01144-1742-890-268 or FAX 01144-1742-891-471

CRESSBROOK HALL COTTAGES Nr Buxton

Back in 1835 the promise of industrial Derbyshire seemed limitless. It was in this spirit that the owner of the Cressbrook Mill went about the proud business of building his residence high above a limestone gorge carved out by the River Wye. Today the Hall and its dependencies make up a small secluded resort, set amidst the bold landscape of the Peak District, catering to all ages of the family. In the spa tradition of nearby Buxton, one may even partake of massage, aromatherapy and various other beauty treatments in the Cressbrook facilities.

There are five interesting cottages including the converted toll house, *Cressbrook Cottage* (pictured above). This cottage sleeps five and adjoins the village green. Other cottages sleep up to six, and Hidesaway has been specially outfitted for the partially handicapped. Cressbrook Hall will be equally enjoyable as a retreat or as a base to explore this most beautiful part of England. ETB 3-4 Keys; Commended

E$m
H$m
FP*
LT
TV
W/Ds
OPEN
MS
$240-1070
S 2-6

Contact Mary McCanna, Westminster Lodgings, 160 Westminster Dr., W.E., Jamestown, NY 14701
TEL 800-699-0744 or 716-484-0744

BLORE HALL COTTAGES Blore Nr Ashbourne

Here we are in the most peaceful corner of the Peak District National Park, full of natural wonders and colorful history. Nearby is Dove Dale, known for obvious reasons as *Little Switzerland.* The Dove is a river which was well known to Izaak Walton, and modern day IW's will do well to follow the master's footsteps. Want some advice on the rich history of the locale or where to drop your hook? Ivan Cope can tell you the whole tale, preferably

E$	H$
LT	
TELc	
TV;	V*
W/D$s	
DW*	MW*
E/HC*	
S-S	MS
TA	
£216-866	
S 2-8	

over a tankard of real ale in his cozy Tudor period pub at Blore Hall. Ivan and Cherry Cope own this expansive 14th century fortified farm, which they have converted into eighteen nicely fitted holiday accommodations. Blore Hall has all sorts of family amenities, from heated pool to games facilities, as well as a bit of a menagerie to amuse the youngsters. There is a restaurant, which will serve to the cottages, and B & B accommodation is offered in the Hall, itself. ETB 3 Keys; Commended

Contact Blore Hall, Nr Ashbourne, Derbyshire DE6 2BS TEL 01144-1335-29525

WHARF COTTAGE   Cromford

Thanks be to Richard Arkwright, Esq. for giving us this handsome structure, which he built as a part of his garden facilities fronting on his Cromford Canal towpath. Also thanks be to Richard Arkwright for giving us the now fascinating little purpose built village of Cromford. It is probably worth mentioning that old Richard Arkwright gave us something else, as well...we call it the *industrial revolution*, and I suppose on balance we thank him for that, too. Alas, however, most of us have forgotten that Richard Arkwright was the father of the modern factory, having built here at Cromford the first successful water powered spinning mill, while most eyes were fixed on the fracas over in the American Colonies. But the Arkwright model was not lost on the generation of industrial entrepreneurs that followed, and Cromford replicas were soon springing up all over New, as well as old, England.

The present owners of Arkwright's Wharf Cottage have spent literally hundreds of hours restoring all the woodwork to its former glory, and have carefully and lovingly furnished the cottage in a traditional style whilst incorporating many modern conveniences. Every picture, ornament, and piece of furniture has been meticulously chosen. The cottage has two entrances; one into the central ground floor hallway, and the other into the beautiful joiner built kitchen/dining room. On entering the kitchen you will see a pretty circular stripped pine dining table, and beyond that the original inglenook fireplace featuring an attractive stove. The kitchen furniture is carefully planned and built to look very traditional, with workmanship second to none. In the living room you will find more beautiful furnishings in toning shades of pinks and greens, with subtle lighting adding to the character of this truly beautiful room. Upstairs the bedrooms are furnished and decorated in a traditional idiom with pretty bedding and a Victorian style bathroom suite featuring hand painted florals on the fixtures.

This Grade II Listed cottage has its own lovely walled garden with the old canal towpath literally at the doorstep. It is truly an idyllic setting and is surrounded by an historic conservation area with an elaborate restoration program being spearheaded by the Arkwright Society... they of long memories.

II.B-d		
B-t		
F-3		
E		H$m
FPG		
L		
TV		
W		
MW		
C-		
F-F	MS	
INS		
$570-1035		
S 4		

Contact British Travel International, P.O. Box 299, Elkton VA 22827 USA TEL 800-327-6097

SYCAMORE COTTAGE

Edale

Sycamore Cottage is a truly unique holiday property. You will find a great number of carefully restored properties in the pages of this book. *Restored,* of course, generally means modernized with a preservationist sense of architectural integrity. In fact, any building with a measure of antiquity has undoubtedly undergone a number of such restorations over the course of its lifetime, at least keeping up with the revolutions in plumbing and heating. Purity of architectural form has not generally been regarded as a substitute for up-to-date facilities, whether it was a Georgian proprietor *restoring* the old Tudor steads or a present day homeowner installing indoor facilities in a period cottage; which, incidentally, is exactly what American owners Nancy and Tony Evans had to do in this mid-18th century cottage. Sycamore Cottage had apparently skipped a few of the aforementioned plumbing revolutions. However, the Evanses aimed to preserve more than some visual historical detail. They wanted a feeling of the experience of how centuries of people have lived in the small villages of rural England. They did their homework, consulting various historians and reference books, as well as the National Trust. The result is more than a live-in museum; in some aspects it approaches a simulation.

As you step through the solid oak front door, it is a bit like stepping back in time. You are standing on flagstone floors with rush matting; the windows have oak shutters with cast iron fasteners; the walls are bare of pictures or the quaint decoratives which we so often imagine as *period.* Instead, the *decoratives* are real functional artifacts, crafts of the time, just as the furnishings are functional pieces of the time, now regarded with a different kind of esteem as *antiques.*

In the kitchen you will find a pot sink with a pine drain board and a very early Rayburn coal burning stove, which cooperates with the coal fireplace in the living room in heating Sycamore Cottage. There is a refrigerator and modern stove, but they've been purposefully concealed, presumably in the same spirit that led the Evanses to install a very *period* Victorian roll top bathtub where other proprietors might have come the whole way to contemporary plumbing. (Personally, I think the apogee of luxurious bathing was probably reached by the Victorians anyway!) Upstairs, the original floorboards have been restored and are scattered with rugs, but one can still see through the cracks to the downstairs. But whoa...you're wondering about the bed; a sack of heather on hard planks? Relax; here the Evanses have made very acceptable compromises with a handsome Victorian brass double bed, nicely covered in a fabric to match the window seat and drapery.

Edale village has much of the same period interest as Sycamore Cottage and is situated at the beginning of the ever popular Pennine Way.

| I. F-2 |
| II.B-d |
| E$c |
| H |
| FP |
| LT |
| TV |
| NS |
| C-BA P- |
| S-S MS |
| INS |
| $475-695 |
| S 2 |

Contact British Travel International, P.O. Box 299, Elkton VA 22827 USA TEL 800-327-6097

NORTH LEES HALL

Hathersage

The Peak District was set aside as Britain's first National Park and it is not hard to see why! The grand sweep of moor and dale, the thrilling cliffs and crags of the escarpment; this is a paradise for climbers, walkers and just plain gawkers.

Charlotte Bronte was a tourist, of sorts, when she came to Hathersage in 1845 to stay with her friend at the vicarage. Among the church memorials, the name Eyre was featured prominently; the Eyres of North Lees Hall. And so it was that *Jane Eyre* was inspired and the image of North Lees Hall entered the literary record as *Thornfield Hall.* It is worth noting that this impressive tower house was already two and a half centuries old when Charlotte Bronte *discovered* it. North Lees Hall has since been declared a Grade II* Listed building, and, thanks to the good works of the Vivat Trust, completely restored.

North Lees Hall has been divided into two truly outstanding holiday accommodations. Both are rich in period(s) character and creature comforts. The first is a studio apartment on the ground floor. I must say that it is just as well that the bed is in the living room, as you will never want it out of sight. Quite simply this is one of the most beautiful sleeping conveyances I have ever seen...a feathery altar! Four poster and canopy, draped from ceiling to floor, ballon curtained and festooned with heavy turquoise frogged cording...colors from every corner of the romantic palette. Sweet dreams are made in this. And that is just the beginning of the baroque charm of this apartment. On the functional side, there is a very spacious kitchen/dining room and a beautifully decorated 3 piece bathroom.

The second apartment is more of the same...more floors! One enters through the original Elizabethan front door to an oak spiral staircase. The apartment occupies the second and third floors with private access to the sitting area on the castellated roof. The drawing room is marvelously large with a richly patterned Elizabethan plaster ceiling and a massive stone linteled fireplace (now harboring a wood stove). The furnishings cross periods from Jacobean to contemporary, but serve the highest standard of decor possible under these circumstances. Highest marks also to the lighting coordinator for achieving just the right saturation point of mellowness in what could have been a stone cold castle. There are two bedrooms, one with a four-poster bed and a separate divan-bed; plus a double.

North Lees Hall sits on the slope amidst gentle pastures and wooded valleys. There is so much to see in the area (the spas at Buxton and the caverns are musts), but frankly, you may never want to leave North Lees Hall.

I. B-d
F-2
$515-685
S 2
II.B-d+s
B-d
F-2
$660-900
S 4-5
BOTH
E&H
FPS
LT
W/D
MW
S-S
INS

Contact Haywood Cottage Holidays, P.O. Box 878, Eufaula, Alabama 36072
Tel 334-687-9800 or Fax 334-687-5324

COTTAGE BY THE POND at Beechenhill Farm Ilam

The Cottage by the Pond is a south-facing, warm, converted barn, which until recently was Terry Prince's milking parlor. Terry and the holsteins moved out and artist wife, Sue, moved in with imagination and a sense of humor. Today, guests enter the cottage through a wide level doorway (one of many features designed for handicapped patrons) into a hallway decorated in a chicken motif...if only the cows could see it now! Sue is an accomplished stencilist and stained glass maker and has rendered the flora, fauna and fowl of the barnyard in both mediums. Through half glass doors there is an uncluttered large sitting room with the dining area at one end, an old pine sideboard, table and folding dining chairs. A pair of dark floral wingbacks are grouped near the coal stove, and above the mantel are hung bundles of dried flowers and herbs...or so it seems at first glance. Actually this is more of Sue's clever stencil work and one must watch out for bits of *trompe l'oeil* throughout the house. A huge patio window offers views over the walled pond area and beyond to the fields of grazing cattle and sheep.

There are three bedrooms in the Cottage by the Pond; two are on the ground floor to accommodate handicapped visitors. The polished pine furniture has been specially designed to allow wheel-chairs up close. The twin bedroom is finished in pink bed linen with floral curtains coordinated to a wide band of stencilling around the whole room. Next door is a second bedroom, with yellow linen and special zip and link beds which can be either two singles or a queen. Between the bedrooms is a tiny en-suite shower room, WC and wash basin. The main bathroom is off the hallway and features a flat floor shower, elevated WC, and a low bath, all carefully designed for handicap access. Up a narrow flight of stairs there is a third bedroom under the rafters with a stencilled ceiling.

The Princes offer a second cottage for two, with a pretty double bed arrangement, a small sitting room and galley kitchen. Best selling author William Horwood stayed here while writing the *Duncton Wood Trilogy*. In fact, Horwood named his saviour of Moledom, *Beechen.*

Beechenhill Farm is in the Peak District National Park, with a great variety of entertaining diversions nearby: caves, cable cars, cycling trails, and stately homes to visit (Chatsworth and Haddon Hall). Ilam, itself, is a famously picturesque village, having been razed and rebuilt all of a piece in 1820 by a somewhat eccentric Lord of the Manor.

ETB 4 Keys; Highly Commended

POND
I. B-t/q
B-t
F-3 [2]
II.B-t
E$m H$m
FPS
LT
TEL   TV
W/D
MW
E/HC
S-S MS
INS
£170-385
S 6
COT-TAGE
I.B-d
F-2
£110-230
S 2

Contact Sue & Terry Prince, Beechenhill Farm, Ilam, Ashbourne, Derbyshire DE6 2BD
TEL 01144-1335-310-274

BANK COTTAGE

Mickleover

Bank Cottage has much more to recommend it than the fact that it is undoubtedly one of the most economical accommodations we have decided to include in this book. Just for the record, the cottage was never a financial institution (no sleeping in an old vault here!). In fact, this 18th century building was the long time home of the village milkman, fondly remembered for his deliveries by pony and trap, and has been in Pamela Pym's family since Christmas Eve of 1889. Though located on the periphery of the industrial city of Derby, the cottage is well situated for touring the Peak District and the Dales, and, for that matter, historic Derby, home of Rolls Royce and Crown Derby, as well as a wealth of museums, galleries and historic sites.

The two bedrooms are comfortably furnished as is the beam ceilinged living room, which has a nice dining area under the bow fronted window. There are lovely views down The Hollow from both upstairs and down. Outside, there is a quiet sitting area amid pretty summertime flower baskets.   ETB 3 Keys; Highly Commended

II.B-d
B-t
F-2
E&H
H
LT
TV
P-
S-S
OPEN
£170
S 4

Contact Mrs P.K. Pym, 2 The Hollow, Mickleover, Derby DE3 5DG TEL 01144-1332-515-607

ROSE COTTAGE   Lullington

Lullington is a small picturesque village amidst the quiet pastoral lands of South Derbyshire. The Village Hall proudly displays awards for *Best Kept Village* and *Britain in Bloom*. Rose Cottage is situated in the center of the village, the middle one of three workers' cottages built in 1831, as recorded in the date-stone mortared into the gable. The cottage remained virtually unchanged until completely renovated by Dr. & Mrs. Ingles a couple years ago. Much of the architectural character (exposed beams, plank doors, etc) were retained and complemented with comfort features like wall-to-wall carpeting and central heating. Curtains, cushions and dining chairs are all done in a deep pink roses fabric, and there is a particularly handsome pine hutch in the kitchen with appropriate country crockery on display. Upstairs via a small galleried landing, one finds more interesting Victorian cottage furnishings. All very cozy and modest...and extraordinarily underpriced!
ETB 4 Keys; Highly Commended

I. F-1	
II.B-t	
F-3	
E$c	H$c
FPE	
LT	
TV	
W/Ds	
MW	
NS	P-
S-S	MS
TA	
£95-130	
S 2-3	

Contact Mrs. Ingles, Victoria Cottage, Lullington, Swadlincote, Derbyshire DE12 8ED
TEL 01144-1827-373-452 or FAX 01144-1827-373-603

SWARKESTONE PAVILION   Nr Ticknall

All sorts of functional and even industrial architecture has been reborn with renewed appreciation. Not so with bowling alley architecture. It's a pity that the aesthetic qualities incorporated into Swarkeston Pavilion, which was most likely built (circa 1632) as a gallery for viewing lawn bowling, didn't set the model for later development of the genre. Now, here's an old bowling alley worth *hanging around!*

The Landmark Trust had their work cut out for them, not only in restoring the building from a mere shell, but in redesigning the compact pavilion for holiday domesticity. The first challenge was aided by the Trust artisans' knowledge and deep appreciation of the craft and fashion of the period. As for the later challenge, I think it can be fairly said that the Trust architects had to *wing it*. The tower (left in drawing) is occupied by a three level flight of stairs; the other tower is comprised of a second floor kitchen and third floor bathroom. The second floor "bridge", with it's magnificent wall of mullioned windows, is the studio living room. Access to the bathroom is across the star covered roof terrace. Umbrella recommended.

II. CS	
III.F-2	
E&H	
LT	
S-S	MS
INS	
£221-304	
S 2	

Contact The Landmark Trust, Shottesbrook, Maidenhead, Berkshire SL6 3SW
TEL 01144-1628-825-925 or FAX 01144-1628-825-417

OLDFIELD HOUSE STABLE WING   Snelston

Snelston is a quiet little Victorian Gothic village marked by its handsome Flemish brickwork and ornate chimney stacks. Squire John Harrison commissioned the design and building of Snelston as an estate village in the mid 1800's, and the proud brick manor,

II.B-d	
B-t	
F-2	
E$m	
H$m	
FP	
L	
TV	
W/D	
S-S	MS
INS	
£163-269	
S4	

Oldfield House, sits at the edge of the village with a tall stone monument in front and the sweep of open countryside to the rear. The coach & stable wing of this Grade II Listed building is attached (on the right in the drawing), and the holiday accommodation is situated on the second floor, above the old coach room. The apartment is comfortably furnished, with some antiques and a welcoming old open fireplace in the living room.

Nearby is historic Ashbourne and a host of worthy sights and activities; Dovedale with its steps across the river; Alton Towers, the noted theme park; and fine walks over the extraordinary Derbyshire landscape.

Contact Derbyshire Country Cottages, Rosemount, 90 Cavendish Rd. Matlock, Derbyshire DE4 3HD
TEL 01144-1629-583-545

WISTERIA COTTAGE   Wirksworth

We are right at the edge of the Peak District National Park, up on the hill above the historic town of Wirksworth. Dating from Roman times and once the center of lead mining industry, Wirksworth is a fascinating place, with its winding alleys and narrow zig-zag streets. The town is renowned for its historic preservation policies, and for its civic pride. Every Whitsun bank holiday thousands turn out to watch the town's *well-dressing* ceremonies, a thanksgiving for fresh water dating back many centuries. George Eliot set her novel, *Adam Bede*, in the Wirksworth area, and later D.H. Lawrence came to live in Mountain Cottage a short walk away at Middleton. Perhaps some of the same attraction brought the present owners, a graphic designer and his French wife, to live part-time in Wisteria Cottage, dividing their time with other homes in Nottingham and in France. Certainly their house pride and enthusiasm for the venue is reflected in the exceptional furnishings and decoration you will find in Wisteria Cottage.

II. B-d
F-3
E&H
FPS
L
TV
P-BA
S-S   MS
INS
£118-197
S 2

Contact Derbyshire Country Cottages, Rosemount, 90 Cavendish Rd. Matlock, Derbyshire DE4 3HD
TEL 01144-1629-583-545

WILLOW COTTAGE

Abbotskerswell

Abbotskerswell is a most pleasant little traditional Devon village just outside the all services town of Newton Abbot. The latter has a very extensive indoor market complex, a number of fine shops, and good antiquing, as well. Ten minutes' drive in the other direction delivers you to the beaches of the *English Riviera* and the busy holiday center of Torquay.

Willow Cottage began life as a cider barn and has been very skillfully redesigned for contemporary domestic use. It is actually a very pretty cottage, with its colorful stone facade carrying on into the garden wall, and its handsome thatch *chapeau*. The same can be said for the interior, which is furnished comfortably in a contemporary style, within a frame of exposed beams and pristine white plaster. There is an open stairwell and gallery, as well as an ultra modern bathroom suite including bidet. Kitchen oriented guests will not be disappointed with the completeness of the facilities at Willow.   ETB 4 Keys; Highly Commended

II.B-d[2]
B-t
F-3
F-4
E$m
H$
FPE
LT$
TV
W/D
DW   MW
P-
S-S   MS
INS
BK$
£207-495
S 6

Contact West Country Cottages, The Geminids, Priory Rd, Abbotskerswell, Devon TQ12 5PP
TEL 01144-1626-333-678 or FAX 01144-1626-336-678

COURT COTTAGE Bigbury

Court Cottage hugs the road as it has for centuries, while the land around the ancient whitewashed cottage seems to have risen, as if to peek at the sea. The *sea* here is Bigbury Bay, a wide open half moon with the mystical little Burgh Island guarding the mouth of the Avon River, appearing as a worn away bump in the grand wash...a St. Michael's Mount with a character tavern.

Court Cottage has been expertly renovated and all the character of exposed beams and stonework have been carefully retained. The furnishings range from the comfortable contemporary living room suite to some very handsome mahogany pieces. Downstairs there are window seats deeply set in the thick stone walls, and fireplaces in both the living and dining rooms. The kitchen is nicely fitted out and has a breakfast bar. Upstairs there is a spacious master bedroom under the open beams with wonderful views over the farmland and sea, and another double bedroom with a brass bedstead. Outside there is a secluded patio with garden furniture and a barbeque, and access to the elevated lawn. For immediate recreation we can recommend the antique dens of nearby Modbury. You will find a golf course a mile away along the Avon; the beach is just a bit further and, of course, there is the ritual of having a drink on Burgh Island.

II.B-d [2]	
B-b	
F-3	
E$	H$
FP$	FPS
LT$	
TV	
W	
MW	
P-	
S-S	MS
INS	
£164-400	
S 6	

Contact Toad Hall Cottages, Union Road, Kingsbridge, South Devon TQ7 1EF
TEL 01144-1548-853-089 or FAX 01144-1548-853-086

SHUTE GATEHOUSE

Axminster

If you count active young knights among your entourage give some thought to this 16th century gatehouse, with its open green, mystery woods, and separate bunk room for sleepy jousters (far left in drawing). In the center tower you will find somewhat more courtly bedrooms and bath facilities on the second floor, with a spiral stone stairs carrying on to the upper floor living room. This room features a very handsome Jacobean plaster ceiling and views to the wooded area in the rear, where the National Trust-owned Shute Barton is located. The Gatehouse is comfortably furnished, albeit more rustic than many Landmark Trust houses.

Axminster, noted for its carpet industry, is an all services town and a good base for exploring the south coast of Devon. Nearby Honiton is a must for antique hunters.

II.B-d	
B-s	
F-2	
B-b	
E & H	
LT	
S-S	MS
INS	
£288-613	
S 5	

Contact The Landmark Trust, Shottesbrook, Maidenhead, Berkshire SL6 3SW
TEL 01144-1628-825-925 or FAX 01144-1628-825-417

SHEPLEGH COURT   Blackawton

As a youngster I lived in a small midwestern town where there was a modest home known to all as the *Lincoln Slept Here House.* In those days every town in the South had a *Robert E. Lee Slept Here House* and sometimes a *Jefferson* or *Washington Slept Here House,* to boot! Nowadays, I suppose we don't like to think of our heroes sleeping at all (though considerable attention is paid to their sleeping around). Well, I see nothing wrong with admitting that even giants need forty winks now and then. Thus, for me at least, Sheplegh Court will always be the *Ike Slept Here House.* I really can't document this claim, but, since this fine old manor house was Allied HQ leading up to D-Day, it seems reasonable to assume that Ike must have at least nodded off at some point (probably when Monty was running on a bit).

One thing is for sure, Sheplegh Court offers more reposeful accommodations today than in those tense days and nights back fifty years ago. In more recent years Sheplegh Court has been converted to condominium apartments, most of them residential, rather than holiday rentals. What was once the frenetic launching pad for invasion has come to gentler times as the peaceful destination for retreat. In this sense, perhaps Sheplegh Court has come full cycle, because in a much earlier time it was a monastery. (No; there is no record of any saints having slept here.)

Rosecourt apartment is a delightfully decorated and furnished ground floor apartment for two with French doors opening onto the fountain courtyard. In the bedroom you will be greeted by a handsome pine four-poster bed. Sheplegh Court definitely has a romantic aspect at night, with the illumination of the courtyard fountain and conservatory, as well as the outdoor heated pool which is situated below the house at the foot of the valley. There is also an indoor splash pool, sauna, and billiard facilities, as well as good all weather tennis courts and a charming little summerhouse.

Blackawton is an equidistant ten minutes from the historic beaches of Start Bay, the glorious Tudor market town of Totnes, and the fine shops and dining of Dartmouth.   ETB 4 Keys; Commended

I.B-d
F-2
E$m
H$m
LT
TV
W/Ds
DW
P-
S-S MS
INS
BK$
£135-378
S 2

Contact West Country Cottages, The Geminids, Priory Rd, Abbotskerswell, Devon TQ12 5PP
TEL 01144-1626-333-678 or FAX 01144-1626-336-678

THE ANCHORAGE

Bolt Head

There is a *top of the world, lost in nature* feel about this house, with its commanding views of the English Channel and secluded position among its own mature semi-tropical gardens.

The Anchorage is a stucco over stone gambrel roofed home with unsurpassed views from the ground floor rooms, as well as the bedroom dormers. A delightful vine covered balcony off the master bedroom enables you to step right into the view. Ditto the French windows leading off from the sitting room. The sitting room furnishings bring the garden inside with nicely coordinated florals and rattan. The kitchen is fully equipped and very workable, and is joined to a dining arrangement seating eight. The Anchorage sits next to the National Trust's Sharpitor, with immediate access to the spectacular cliff walk to Bolt Head.

I. F-3
II.B-d
B-t
B-b
F-3
E&H
FP
LT
TELm
TV
W/D
DW MW
F-F
$840-1610
S 6

RINGRONE Bolt Head

This is a ground floor flat, one of seven in the historic marine property known as Ringrone. Every ship, every fishing boat, every grand sailing yacht going up the busy Kingsbury Estuary must come across your bow at Ringrone. The views across to Prawle Point, Devon's southernmost promontory, and up the mouth of the estuary are nothing short of breathtaking, day and night. It is a short drive back into Salcombe for shopping, but you may prefer to take the ferry at South Sands Beach, which is only a short walk down the hill. The property is adjacent to the sub-tropical gardens at Overbecks and the National Trust's spectacular Courtenay Walk out to Bolt Head.

Flat Four is entered through a glass door into a traditional small pane window sun porch, with pleasant rattan furnishings and bamboo drop curtains. The sunroom flows into the living room through a broad plastered arch with cinnamon velvet drapes, all satin lined and tied back. The living room, which is uncluttered and comfortable, features a three piece suite in a cheerful cabbage rose fabric with cinnamon piping and matching throw pillows. There is an exceptionally large kitchen, with breakfast bar and adjoining dining area. The master bedroom features a queen size bed and modern vanity unit, with a French door to the terrace. A second twin bedroom can be supplemented with Z-beds or a cot for expanded parties.

I.B-q
B-t
F-3 [2]
E&H
FPE [2]
LT
TEL TV
W/D
DW MW
F-F
$575-1080
S 4-6

Contact British Vacation Rentals, Box 227, 154 Chadwick Court, North Vancouver, B.C. V7M 3KI, Canada Tel 1-800-663-6330 (US & Canada)

LEWORTHY MILL
Nr Clovelly

Attention skinny readers! It has come to my attention that there are individuals out there who have yet to experience the *udder* joy of Devon cream...thick, rich, clotted...gooey, yummy, delectable; by spoon or shovel a sure cure for the cruel affliction of emaciation. If your jealous friends make disparaging remarks behind your back about your figure, whispering about *narrowing* dietary discipline and the *thin* line between vanity and obsession, it is time to take a bold stroke to rejoin the *well rounded* majority by spending a week with the Price family at Leworthy Mill. Where else will you find a dozen amiable Jersey cows dedicated to your enhancement! And, unlike other dairy operations I have known, there is no early morning clatter and bang, moo and shoo in the milking parlor here. No sir; these *Girls* like to sleep in too, just like the guests, and, since their milk is all processed into clotted cream (and ice cream!) right here on the farm, there is no rushing to meet the dairy tanker rolling in before even the rooster gets up a good voice. Cream tea, after all, is an afternoon ritual!

Leworthy Mill dates from the 13th century and is mentioned in the Domesday Book. The present Grade II Listed buildings date from the 18th century and have been very handsomely restored by the present owners, with part of the wheel apparatus to be seen through the arched window overlooking the mill stream to the back. The interior decor is airy and bright, with country style furnishings, making good use of country pine and pretty floral fabrics. There is wall sconce lighting, and exposed beam ceilings for extra character. Upstairs, one bedroom features a four-poster bed covered with a rich ivory lace bedspread and matching drapes...all very romantic. The bathroom is large and has a jacuzzi. There are fine views of the wild flowers along the bank of the mill stream and over hill and dale with grazing sheep and a line of oaks following the path of the stream, which incidentally bears the name *Dipple Water* (just the sort of water a lovely old Jersey wants to make her best clotted cream!). Doves in the dovecote, hens in the orchard, sweet brown eyed Jersey calves in the meadow...if you can't take all this bucolic bliss you can drive down the road a couple miles to Clovelly and have a nice Devon cream tea on the picturesque pier.

II.B-d
B-d+s
F-4
E$c
H$c
L
TV
W
MW
S-S   MS
INS
£182-395
S 5

Contact Farm & Cottage Holidays, Victoria House, 12 Fore Street, Northam, Bideford, Devon EX39 1AW   TEL 01144-1237-479-698   or   FAX 01144-1237-421-512

FURSDON   Cadbury

We first came upon Fursdon quite by accident a number of years ago. It was a crisp autumn day and we had just finished harvesting the wine grapes from Gillian Pearkes' vineyard at nearby Bickleigh. There was a bit of a picnic left from the copious communal spread laid out at noon by Gillian, and, as we just happened to have a bottle of her fine Yearlstone wine still in the boot, we decided to take the back road home and find a pleasant place to finish our repast. The little road that meanders along the hillside from Cadbury to Thorverton is scarcely more than a lane wide. We were poking along looking for a wide spot when, suddenly, Fursdon loomed above us on the hill. The low autumn light cast the whole scene in a kaleidoscope of color and shadow. The perfectly proportioned Georgian manor was itself dressed out in the most wonderful coat of burnt red vinery. It was truly stunning, like a painting by an eighteenth century master; the Age of Reason with an ethereal glow; like reading Rousseau with a flagon of port at one's side. We had our picnic right there along side the lane and drooled vicariously over our find until the last light of day had disappeared.

PARK WING
II.B-t [3]
F-2
E$ H
W/Ds
P-
£170-330
S 6

GARDEN WING
II.B-t/k
B-b
F-2
E$c H
W/DS
P-
£130-245
S 4

Fursdon is, in fact, a small country estate which has been the family home of the Fursdons since 1259. That's quite a long tenure, but then what fool would ever leave such a perfect place? The estate of seven hundred acres encompasses not only the manor house, with its well kept gardens and lawns that just fade away into pasture and forest, but also traditional thatched farmhouses and cottages. Lying between the market towns of Tiverton and Crediton, Fursdon is a short distance from several National Trust properties, which is a reminder that securing a family presence in the ancestral steads can be a challenge in the 20th century.

There are two self contained apartments in Fursdon House which are approached via a cobbled courtyard and up a wide oak staircase to the second floor. The Park Wing has magnificent views over the grand landscape where we once picnicked. During the 18th century, when Fursdon was *Georgianized,* The Park Wing sitting room was created out of part of the medieval Great Hall. Right in the middle of the house, and with an open fire and three wide south facing windows, with casement shutters, it makes the perfect sitting room for all seasons. More Rousseau; more port, *s'il vous plaît!*

LIME-HOUSE	
I. B-s	
F-3	
II.B-s	
B-t [2]	
B-k	
F-2	
E$C	
H$M	
W	
£210-430	
S 8	
ALL	
FP	
LT$	
TELc (s)	
TV	
F-F MS	
INS	
TA	

The Garden Wing is smaller and has one spacious bedroom with a king sized bed which can divide into twins if desired. A second, very small bedroom has a set of bunks for the children. The paneled sitting room of The Garden Wing was at one time the family schoolroom, and has an open fire and a window seat overlooking the garden to the rear.

The Limehouse, which is on the grounds of the manor house, was converted from a granary and mason's store, and, with its own secluded garden, has almost total privacy. It has a large, kitchen/dining room with a big pine table for moving the family picnic inside. The sitting room provides good views to the south, and, again, there are window seats and lots of books to while away the indoor hours. One of the bedrooms has a south facing balcony with a view that goes for miles. On the ground floor there is also a single bedroom. The cottage is ideal for a family, but cozy enough for a couple.

Contact Mrs. Catriona Fursdon, Fursdon House, Cadbury, Exeter, Devon EX5 5JS
TEL 01144-1392-860-860

PIGWIGS PLACE
Nr Cornwood

A nice cottage by any standard, Pigwigs Place will be especially appreciated by children. Set amid the park-like scene of the former National Gardens Trust, there are a hundred acres of adventure explorations to be had; also a boat and canoe for excursions and fishing on the pond, and a hard tennis court. The cottage, which is a converted shippen, is still attached to a very large stone barn (empty) and has its own private court yard. The interior features many of the old architecturals (exposed beams, etc.) but is outstanding for its primary color modern furnishings. There is a wood stove and a nice long pine dining table. Upstairs you will find three bedrooms, including one with a king-size bed and an open ceiling to the peak, as well as a children's playroom lined with an Egyptian tent. As for things to do in the neighborhood, Dartmoor is practically out the back door and invites a lifetime of exploring for its unique flora, fauna, and geological formations. Eight miles in the other direction and you are at the seashore.

II.B-q	
B-t [2]	
F-2	
E$	
H$	
FPS	
LT	
TV	
W/D	
MW	
P-BA	
F-F MS	
INS	
BK$	
£209-472	
S 6	

ETB 4 Keys; Highly Commended

Contact Helpful Holidays, Coombe, Chagford, Devon TQ13 8DF
TEL 01144-1647-433-593 or FAX 01144-1647-433-694

PASSAGE HOUSE Dittisham

It wouldn't take a lot of imagination to invent a pretty colorful or risque history for Passage House, right here on the quay of old Dittisham. Grisly old salts up from the sea and poor transported country lads in desperate flight from the naval bureaucracy a couple miles down stream at Dartmouth. And *ladies* too...well, female persons, the bosomy and ribald Miss Pollys of Robert Louis Stevenson novels. All characters in some kind of *passage* and welcomed here in the house of the same name, as, indeed, modern guests have found this a welcoming venue.

The cottage is laid out on three view-filled floors, with a large open room at the water's edge serving as both living and dining room. The kitchen is situated at one end, partially screened off by a high-back wooden settle. There is a red tile floor under foot and the furnishings are a mix of sturdy traditional pieces all gathered up in front of the fireplace. No fashion designer awards here, but a special campy atmosphere that is easy to relax in. There is a nice garden behind, with garden furnishings and a barbeque, and parking is just up the beach, three to ten minutes walk away, depending on the tide. How far to a character pub, you ask? The Ferry Boat Inn is just two doors down the quay.

II. B-t
B-t+s
F-3
III.B-d
B-t
F-2+bidet
E   H$
FPS
TELc
TV
W/D
DW   MW
S-S   MS
INS
£256-397
S 9

Contact Toad Hall Cottages, Union Road, Kingsbridge, South Devon TQ7 1EF   TEL 01144-1548-853-089

KINGSWEAR CASTLE Nr Dartmouth

If a holiday in Kingswear Castle doesn't bring out the kid in you, then you can put in for social security benefits in good conscience. This late 15th century fortress was built to protect Dartmouth, and is every inch a thrill, from its textured stone walls and passages, to its gun port lighting and perspectives over the River Dart.

We begin at grade level of the square tower, and ascend the circular stone stairs to a huge double bedroom on the second level, and a view-filled living/dining/kitchen area on the third floor, with a parapet sun deck above. A second level passage takes us off to the round tower twin bedroom, very compact and private. Fifty yards along the craggy shore is a WW II blockhouse, now offering spartan berths for two and a slit-window panorama of all the river traffic. Across the way, reached by car ferry, is the beautiful town of Dartmouth, all safe and sound thanks to your vigilant occupancy of the Castle. A memorable holiday is in store for the family that does duty at Kingswear Castle!

II. B-d
B-t
IV.F-2
E&H
LT
S-S   MS
INS
£623-1175
S 6

Contact The Landmark Trust, Shottesbrook, Maidenhead, Berkshire SL6 3SW
TEL 01144-1628-825-925 or FAX 01144-1628-825-417

SMUGGLERS COTTAGE   Dittisham

More Robert Louis Stevenson! Four-hundred-year-old thatch and stone Smugglers Cottage is banked up against the tide, safe atop its own rock quay, a silent witness to the lazy ebb and flow of the River Dart. In fact, at low tide there is enough stone beach in front of the quay to park your car, and, in the outlaw traditions of Smuggler's Cove, there'll be no meter maid to tell you when you've over stayed your time. Today's wary smugglers tend to leave their vehicles in the village car park after unloading their holiday booty. There is a steep access path behind the cottage for scowless inhabitants of these environs.

The cottage is snugly backed up into the hill with all eyes fixed on the river; and what an eyeful it is, from every room, save the kitchen! There must have been some kind of understanding, the King's tax man never cometh at supper time. From the kitchen one descends a few steps on the ancient slate floors into the dining room, all cozy with undulating bare stone walls and the blazing wood stove. Further along there is a study (much used by plotting smugglers, who apparently also practiced their piano here), and thence into the sitting room with its big inglenook fireplace. Doors from the study and dining room put one on to the quay terrace, the traditional spot for smugglers to take cocktails, work on their tan, or just sit with their sketch books and capture the ever changing watery scene (but never to snooze!). Plenty of room upstairs for forty winks, with pretty windows in every bedroom peeking out from under the thatch brow. The captain's en-suite quarters even have a back exit directly into the elevated garden, there no doubt to bury contraband amongst his posies.

II.B-d [2]
F-2 [2]
B-t [2]
E$
H
FP
FPS
LT$
TELc
W/D
MW
S-S   MS
INS
£256-697
S 8

Contact Toad Hall Cottages, Union Road, Kingsbridge, South Devon TQ7 1EF
TEL 01144-1548-853-089 or FAX 01144-1548-853-086

GIBHOUSE
Nr Drewsteignton

From childhood I can remember drooling over the colorful hunting prints that adorned my grandmother's hallway.   The swarm of baying hounds, the pell-mell dash of beautiful horses over the hedges, those gallant red coated riders tooting pretzel shaped horns and holding on for dear life. Tally Ho! Later, when I reached the age of conscience, I collected some hunt prints of my own done by a certain Regency artist. My artist was definitely no friend of the bilious wastrels in red and made the huntsmen the sport of cruel caricature. "Hooray for the fox!" I proclaimed, having by then sworn off any appreciation whatsoever for this ancient and brutal pageant. Then, one morning a number of years ago, we were taking pictures of an absolutely idyllic street scene in the quaint village of Drewsteignton when, suddenly, from around the corner came that swarm of fox hounds and the bobbing sea of red coats aboard high stepping steeds; a bit of parade before the chase! The moment was charged and my reaction involuntary; I swung the camera into action, capturing all those thrilling and colorful images from my Granny's hall. It was the perfect *Merry Ole England* scene...well, anyway, Drewsteignton is undeniably a perfect *Merry Ole England* village!

In a peaceful combe close to the village, sitting sweetly by its own pond, is the thatch and granite cottage called Gibhouse...another perfect scene of *Merry Ole England*! The name derives from "Glebe House", which the cottage was at some time during its three hundred years.   It was also the gardener's cottage for Castle Drogo, which is perched high on the hill above. The gardener's wife used to climb 400 feet up to the Castle each morning with the milk supply! The current owners, Su and Euan Bowater, who in their capacity as the proprietors of Helpful Holidays have seen all the very best in holiday accommodations, set out to make their own rental cottage nothing less than picture perfect. It is no coincidence that they've earned the English Tourist Board's very highest accolade. Enter through the granite pillared porch to a warm and friendly combination living/dining room with granite open fire and bread oven. Character is only ever achieved by merging decorative detail and architectural peculiarities, and this is a *character* cottage par excellence! There is an en-suite twin bedroom (wheelchair accessible) on the ground floor with delightful views.   Ascend the gentle spiral staircase to a sitting room/library and a double bedroom with a combination bathroom/dressing room. Yes, my Granny would have approved; this is her *Merry Ole England*; for sure!   ETB 5 Keys; DeLuxe

I. B-t
F-3
II.B-d
F-2
E$m
H$
FP
LT
TEL
TV
W/D
DW MW
C-BA
E/HC
F-F   MS
INS
BK$
£233-612
S 4

Contact Helpful Holidays, Coombe, Chagford, Devon TQ13 8DF
TEL 01144-1647-433-593 or FAX 01144-1647-433-694

TOWN'S END COTTAGE Hartland

Town's End Cottage was until recently the home of the late Mary Norton, the noted children's writer. The cottage interior, with its nicely proportioned Georgian mantel fireplace, pretty display alcoves, comfortable chintz soft furnishings, and assorted mahogany antiques, bespeaks a graciousness quite rare in holiday fare. There are spacious sitting rooms both downstairs and up, the latter providing a good panorama over the rolling farmland and distant views of the sea. The kitchen is in the farmhouse style, and has every modern convenience. To the rear of the cottage you will find a very pleasant garden that catches all the sun. The cottage also features a quite separate annex, sleeping two, which might appeal to certain travel groupings, and a sun & games room which will certainly appeal to the younger set.

Hartland, itself, is a rather plain village, but you are only a couple miles from some of the most spectacular coastal scenery and walks in all of England. Golf, trout fishing, swimming, and a host of other recreational attractions, aquatic and otherwise, are nearby.

I. F-1
B-d
F-3
II.B-t
F-2
CS
E   H$
FP & FPG
LT$
TELc TV
W
DW MW
S-S   MS
INS   BK$
£149-409
S 6-8

Contact North Devon Holiday Homes, 19 Cross St., Barnstaple, Devon EX31 1BD
TEL 01144-1271-76322 or FAX 01144-1271-46544

THE LIBRARY

Nr Great Torrington

If you (like me) fancy you might have been more suited to the 18th century, and long to slip quietly into the Age of Reason, then may I suggest a week of thoughtful seclusion in The Library. Here we have modest elegance, rather than opulence; a venue for vicarious time walking of a *realistic* sort.

The Library is paired off with the Orangery (sleeping two in the summer) and has been restored to its 1710 purity by the Landmark Trust. We enter via the loggia to find a ground floor twin bedroom and bath and a kitchen of ample proportions. A graceful circular stairwell takes us up to the room of my dreams, wide open and airy, with handsome wainscotting and an immaculate plaster ceiling with just the right amount of ornamentation. Broken pedimented fireplace, paneled shutters, wide board floor with antique rugs, period furnishings, and fine gilt frame portraits (yes, I definitely see my family likeness!). Only one thing is missing...the telephone to call the Trust and extend my stay...for life!

I. B-t
F-2
I. B-t
E & H
FP
LT
P-
S-S   MS
INS
£302-655
S 2-4

Contact The Landmark Trust, Shottesbrook, Maidenhead, Berkshire SL6 3SW
TEL 01144-1628-825-925 or FAX 01144-1628-825-417

EXMANSWORTHY FARMHOUSE

Nr Hartland

Flanked by spectacular Hartland Point and the famous picturesque village of Clovelly, and only a short walk off the breathtaking Coastal Footpath, Exmansworthy Farmhouse is an ideal base for holidayers who want to get right *into* the peerless scenery of the Devon Coast. The beaches of Westward Ho! and the surfers' paradise at Bude are minutes away, as are the colorful pannier markets of Bideford and Barnstaple.

This is a big house made cozy by careful attention to decorative details and an unparsimonious approach to furnishings. Paired families holidaying together might value the fact that there are two large living rooms, complete with separate fireplaces, televisions and other electronic entertainments. Both are character rooms, with beamed ceilings, exposed stone and plaster walls, plenty of pictures, dried flowers, nice carpets, good lighting, etc. Sleeping arrangements are equally commodious with five bedrooms featuring pretty floral linen, and plenty of bathrooms in the right places. There is also a very welcoming kitchen with many homey touches, such as terracotta spice jars, plants, and, of course, all the most modern equipment. A lovely home in a lovely location!

I. CS
F-1
II.B-d [3]
F-3
B-t
B-b
F-2 [2]
E   H$
FP
FPS
L
TVV
W/D
DW   MW
P-BA
S-S   MS
INS
£400-970
S 10-12

*Contact Farm & Cottage Holidays, Victoria House, 12 Fore Street, Northam, Bideford,
Devon EX39 1AW   TEL 01144-1237-479-698 or FAX 01144-1237-421-512*

SOUTHOLE Nr Hartland

The predominant images of Devon as either a lush green patchwork quilt or a dramatic moonscape moorland evaporate when one approaches the County's west coast. Here, spectacular crags and cliffs meet a surging sea to provide a rugged and unforget-

HELIGAN
I.B-d
B-t
F-3
EMBURY
I.B-d
B-t
F-3
E&H
FPS$
TELc   TV
W/Ds
MW
P-
S-S   MS
INS
£201-384
S 4

table panorama. It is impossible to stand on the cliffs of Hartland Point, looking out toward Lundy Island, with anything like a normal pulse rate. Set back a quarter of a mile from the coastal path is Southole with the two cottages which Ray and Valentine Sabin have brilliantly fashioned from old farm buildings. St. Heligan and Embury Cottages are delightfully decorated, with unusual painted furnishings, good country antiques, and warm colors. I can't think of a more cozy space to return to after an inspiring hike along the cliffs or a busy day photographing nearby Clovelly, which for good reason is probably England's most photographed village. And, if we are really smart we will have asked Valentine, who is a *Cordon Bleu* chef, to prepare one of her specialties for our return.

*Contact Classic Cottages, Leslie House, Lady Street, Helston, Cornwall TR13 8NA
TEL 01144-1326-565-656 or FAX 01144-1326-565-554*

NYMET   King's Nympton

Just off the main road linking Barnstaple and Exeter, Kings Nympton is a pretty little village with a notable pub/restaurant (The Grove). The cottage, Nymet, (which means *sacred grove*) is a Civil War vintage thatch and cob, sitting peacefully behind an old stone wall.

II.B-d [2]
B-t
F-2
FPS
LT
TELc   TV
W/D
C-
F-F;
OPEN
INS
BK$
TA
£200-360
S 6

This is a typical Devon *character cottage,* with those lovely crooked old beams and whitewashed walls of a similar dis-orientation, a big inglenook fireplace with bread oven (and in this case a small wood stove), and a flagstone hearth with bits of copper and basketry...the time tested formula for *cozy.*

Both Dartmoor and Exmoor are close by, and even the immediate area has supplied us with many simple pleasures over the years. Stop for tea at the Eggesford Garden Center along the River Taw, and be sure to pickup an apricot and pork pie from the pie man in Lapford just ten minutes down the road.

Contact Mary Spivey, The Independent Traveller, Thorverton, Exeter EX5 5NT
TEL 01144-1392-860-807 or FAX 01144-1392-860-552

COLLACOTT FARM

King's Nympton

Does your dream holiday want a horse in it? Do you envision yourself taking early morning rides along an endless maze of hedgerow lanes in the lush patchwork of the rolling North Devon countryside? Or perhaps your dream holiday has the children safely off pony trekking on Trigger, enabling you to relax by the pool and vicariously peruse the real estate offerings in *Country Life.* In either case, Collacott Farm is a good place to take your dream.

Collacott Farm has seven very pleasant terraced (attached) cottages artfully resurrected from the workings of an old farmstead. Indeed, Collacott is still a working farm focused on all manner of equestrian activity. Yes, the proprietors do run scheduled riding camps for young people. No, the accommodations definitely do not look like summer camp kid-proof barracks. The decor says *House & Garden,* not *Camp & Corral.* Living rooms have lovely contemporary soft furnishings ranging from airy florals to festive plaids. There are exposed native wood timbers in the construction and pine is the wood of choice for occasional pieces and dining sets. Throw rugs over fitted carpets lend a cozy feeling, and real warmth is ensured by woodburning fires in each cottage. Bedrooms have fitted carpets, electric radiators, and are supplied with pretty bed linen and duvets. Pictures on the walls, books on the shelves, plants in windows...call it home (horse camp was never like this!).   ETB 4

E   H$c
FPS$
LT
TELc TV
W/Ds
DW MW
F-F;
OPEN
MS INS
£135-775
S 2-12

Contact Mrs. Susan Francis at Collacott Farm Cottages, King's Nympton, Umberleigh,
Devon EX37 9TP   TEL 01144-1769-572-491

MALSTON MILL FARM Nr Kingsbridge

Malston Mill Farm is comprised of a half dozen (only) cottages skillfully fashioned out of a grist mill dating from the middle of the eighteenth century. *Fashioned* is just the right word, for these truly are fashionable accommodations, fully deserving the English Tourist Board *Deluxe* status, which most of the cottages have been awarded.

We will come back to the cottages below, but first a few words about the collective amenities at Malston Mill Farm. I think it fair to say that, in general, the British offer far more extra amenities per unit of accommodation than we are accustomed to in North America. In our tourist industry the rule of thumb seems to be multiplication...ten cottages deserve a pool; fifteen units gets the pool heated; twenty makes for a tennis court; thirty might justify a sauna or whirlpool...if you want a horse, go to a dude ranch! This particularly cold commercial logic has made us a continent of motels; even many of our resorts are developed on a motel philosophy and multiplication accounting. Corporately speaking, I suppose it really doesn't make much sense to put in an expensive tennis court unless there are the number of users to justify the capital expense. But this is precisely the difference. The motel is almost nonexistent in Britain. Family operators, not corporate accountants, have established the dominant modes of tourist facilities. Six cottages may well justify an expensive hard surface tennis court if the owner's family happens to like a game of tennis now and then, or if the owners are inclined to see their guests as part of their family, returning with annual regularity like distant cousins. The general tendency then is for quite personalized mini-resorts to emerge from tourist operations with relatively few beds. More toys per person...and better ones, as well.

Malston Mill Farm has taken this very pleasant tendency to the limit. There are only twenty one guest beds on the farm, but, by North American standards, the recreational amenities here could easily serve many times that number of guests. There is, of course, a pool...and not an oversize kidney bean bathtub either! This is 50 x 25 ft., heated and surrounded by a spacious patio, beyond which is a lovely rose garden. There is a very cleverly laid out leisure center with billiard and snooker tables, as well as skittles, table tennis and a host of other games on the mezzanine above the chess court. Chess *court?* Yes, chess *court;* a walk on, *get in among the troops*, proportioned chess game. (Standing up, I may even have a chance of beating our ten-year-old chess whiz when he accompanies us to Malston Mill!). You will also find a solarium for all season sunning, and a well equipped fitness room. Over by the pool there is a summerhouse and a covered barbeque area. On Thursday evenings your host likes to fire things up for a collective grill...that is, for the *extended family*. Other times the barbeque is there for your private enjoyment. You might even want to make it a fish fry, and you won't have to go far to cast your line. The one acre mill pond is stocked with Brownies, as well as Rainbow trout, tench and carp. Golfers will have to go up the road a bit to the Dartmouth Country Club, but Malston Mill Farm has arranged reduced greens fees for its guests.

The cottages are nicely distributed around the old mill buildings and barns...none of that *all in a row* feeling here. Each has an architectural personality of its own, though in all cases good effect has been obtained from old timbers and stonework; even the old mill stones have even been aesthetically exploited. Each cottage has a masonry fireplace, and all the master bedrooms feature "character beds", four-posters or testers. Lakeside and Waterfall Cottages only sleep two; Dairy Cottage accommodates three; Riverside and Courtyard Cottages will take four; and my favorite, Mill Cottage, which has incorporated the old mill workings in its decor, will sleep up to six.

E$c	H$c
FP$	
LT	
TV	
W/Ds	
MW	
P-	
S-S	MS
INS	
BK$	
£156-636	
S 2-6	

ETB 4 Keys; Highly Commended & Deluxe

Contact West Country Cottages, The Geminids, Priory Rd, Abbotskerswell, Devon TQ12 5PP
TEL 01144-1626-333-678 or FAX 01144-1626-336-678

BOLT HOUSE
Nr Kingsbridge

Bolt House is part of a handsome small development with dramatic views over Bigbury Bay. On the ground floor are three bedrooms, all en-suite and pleasantly decorated. Upstairs, divided by a spectacular galleried landing, there is a kitchen/dining area and a nicely furnished lounge...all very spacious and wonderfully bright under the skylights and vaulted ceiling. The kitchen is beautifully fitted out in oak against an exposed stone wall, and there is a open fire in the living area.

Nearby is the village of Bigbury-on-Sea where one can walk across to Burgh Island or take the elevated tractor at high tide. The bar at the Inn is an interesting place to have a drink in the afternoon; very art deco and *Agatha Christie*...keep an eye out for the furtive looking portly gentleman with the white fedora who always seems to be nursing a cup of espresso behind the potted plants when we stop in.

I.B-t
F-3 [2]
B-d
B-b
F-2
E   H$
FP$
LT
TV
W/D
MW
P-
S-S
INS
£276-609
S 6

Contact Classic Cottages, Leslie House, Lady Street, Helston, Cornwall TR13 8NA
TEL 01144-1326-565-656 or FAX 01144-1326-565-554

LUSTLEIGH MILL

Lustleigh

It has occurred to us that Jan & Mike Rowe are among a handful of the luckiest people in the world, who by some odd coincidence all happen to live in the idyllic village of Lustleigh. Set in the Dartmoor National Park, Lustleigh is an historic village with thatched cottages and a village pub clustered around the 12th century church. The village is nestled in a picturesque valley carved out by the tiny River Wrey which wends a twisty course between the ancient Devon longhouses of the village and the adjacent hamlet of Wreyland.

No matter which way you strike out, this is superb walking country...up the mysterious wooded Cleave, out on to the open moorland, or down stream following the rushing Wrey to the broader River Bovey and then on to the lovely market town of Bovey Tracy. If you leave the village in the direction of Higher Hisley and follow the old mill leat, built in the 14th century, you will soon come to Lustleigh Mill, which until a few years ago ground the corn for the surrounding villages. The leat still pours over the precipice at the side of the house and now drives the Rowe's water turbine. As always, the welcome mat is out; let's go in.

In older times the grain was brought in through what is now the entrance to the *Old Granary*, the name Jan & Mike have given to the compact self catering quarters of the Mill. [They also do B&B in the house.] You will notice the antiques everywhere; the Rowe's are in the business, and they have an exceptional eye for quality pieces, as is evident from the furnishings in The Granary. In the entrance hall you will find an 18th century oak chest and a handsome corner cupboard displaying a collection of blue and white plates, bowls and figures. A short staircase leads us up among exposed beams bearing the marks of hauling ropes long used in lifting grain for milling. Into the bedroom area; more fine antiques, a 19th century double bed in rosewood, and by its side a mirror-fronted period mahogany wardrobe. The sitting room, with its pristine whitewashed stone walls and blackened beams is a perfect backdrop for more character furnishings, including an amply proportioned antique settee, and a pair of Victorian easy chairs, as well as Georgian wavy back dining chairs, a dresser of the same period and a military chest. The kitchen is a compact affair, under the rafters, but is adequate for holiday purposes. On all sides, and from low positioned skylights, there are wonderful views: over the river below where we have seen the foxes come to water so many times; across the orchard, where Jan & Mike's cows graze. Did I mention, these are the luckiest cows in the world! And the same goes for the foxes!   ETB 3 Keys; Commended

III.B-d
F-3
E&H
LT
TELm
TV
W/Ds
MW
NS P-BA
S-S   MS
INS
TA
£140-250
S 2-3

Contact Mike & Jan Rowe, Lustleigh Mill, Lustleigh, Newton Abbot, Devon TQ13 9SS
TEL 01144-0647-7357 or 01144-1647-277-357

STOCKADON FARM

Loddiswell

Fern Cottage (in the drawing) and Chestnut Cottage are both located on Stockadon Farm. Each is set off on its own in wooded areas and surrounded by its own pretty garden. Fern Cottage has a storybook entry past a veil of roses into a charmingly decorated sitting room with a cozy fireplace. Chestnut is a larger hip-roofed house, with pretty pink washed exterior walls and an equally soothing color scheme of peach and pink on the inside. Both cottages are comfortably furnished and have adequate kitchens. Fern Cottage features an oil fired Aga, and Chestnut has a Rayburn heater, in addition to a conventional stove.

These cottages are strategically located for touring the many sights of the South Hams. The nearby tunneled vineyards, which brought me to Loddiswell the first time on a journalistic mission, are a must to visit for anyone with an interest in grapes or their most notable derivative libation. ETB 3 & 4 Keys; Commended

FERN
II.B-d
B-t
F-2
FPS$
£156-378
S 4
CHEST N.
I. F-1
II.B-d
B-t [2]
F-2
W/D
£207-495
S 6
BOTH
E&H
LT$
TV
NS P-
F-F   MS
INS
BK$

THE GARDEN APARTMENT   Ivybridge

Ivybridge is on the most southerly tip of Dartmoor; in fact it is the point at which the open high moor and semi-tropical sea shore come the closest together. If you were about to say this would be the optimum place for a retiring Colonial Governor of Ceylon to settle, I must congratulate you on your percipience! This quite statuesque late eighteenth century stone house, with its precisely cut quoin work, was, indeed, built for just such a gentleman. Quite clearly the Governor brought back a lesser rajah's taste for opulence, a good measure of which has been passed along to subsequent owners. The Governor's experience in the Southern Hemisphere no doubt inclined him to bright rooms with high airy ceilings and well tended grounds filled with exotic flora to mark off his regal presence from the oppressive climate and jungle. That tradition continues here in Ivybridge, as well. In short, the Garden Apartment in this stately old home offers a very pleasant base for exploring the Devon moor and shore.
ETB 4 Keys; Highly Commended

I.B-d
B-t
F-2
E$m
H$m
LT$
TV
W/D
DW MW
NS
C-BA   P-
S-S   MS
INS
BK$
£135-324
S 4

Contact West Country Cottages, The Geminids, Priory Rd, Abbotskerswell, Devon TQ12 5PP
TEL 01144-1626-333-678 or FAX 01144-1626-336-678

LUNDY ISLAND   Off Bideford

We board the supply ship, *MS Oldenburg*, at Bideford on the North Devon coast, a town we have heretofore visited periodically to watch the hustle & bustle of activity along its mile long quay, after filling every available basket at the exceptional pannier market in nearby Barnstaple. But it is a sea adventure before us now, a voyage to a place about as far as one can get from the elbow bumping, banter & buy of market day shopping. A little over two hours out into the Atlantic waters that form the Bristol Channel is Lundy Island, the quintessential *get away from it all* holiday venue!   No cars and no crowds, except of course for the bit of human compacting necessary to lighter us off the *Oldenburg* into the launch that will beach us on Lundy, the way all our predecessors through time have arrived on this cliff bound Island.

Lundy is presently under the dominion of The National Trust and has been architecturally restored and put in an enterprising way by the Landmark Trust, whose brilliant preservation work can not be over praised. Lundy Island has had a number of previous landlords, going back to the Norse, who gave this three square miles of rock its name (*Lund ey*, meaning puffin island). Later proprietors have included Queen Elizabeth's famous admiral, Sir Richard Grenville, and a host of unsavory characters. In the 13th century Henry III took possession and built a castle here to put the island to rights; in the 19th century, the Reverend Hudson Heaven (obviously born with a *calling*) arrived to build a church and put the islanders to rights.   His church, dubbed *The Kingdom of Heaven*, still holds to its original mission, while the Castle of Henry has found a new life as holiday accommodations.

The Castle is just one of a number of unique historic berths for the the special breed of holiday-makers who come to Lundy for more than a turn-around day trip. In addition to a number of self-catering dwellings, there is a small hostel facility and

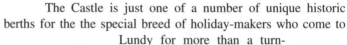
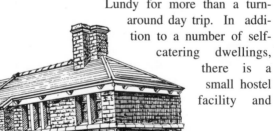

TRINITY
I.B-t
B-s [2]
F-3
£205-495
S 4
VENTURER
II.B-t [2]
B-s
F-3
£220-624
S 5
BOTH
E&H
FPS
LT
P-
S-S   MS
INS

camping is also allowed. The Trust limits occupancy to about a hundred people at any one time, and there are about twenty year-round residents, all in the service of the Landmark Trust. About the only place you will bump elbows is in the Marisco Tavern, the island's convivial center for bending elbows and getting an earful of your co-habitants' daily discoveries. Indeed, discovery is what Lundy Island is all about. If your interests run to geology (caves & an earthquake chasm), plant life (a tunnel of rhododendrons), birds (280 species), rock climbing (400 ft. cliffs), diving (10 accessible shipwrecks), photography, or just taking vista-filled walks, there won't be a dull moment in a week spent on Lundy Island. As for the children, the Island is theirs for the roaming, along with the free ranging sheep & ponies, mountain goats & and an amazing array of wildlife, from rabbits to Sika deer. Conservation officers are on hand to give guidance on nature walks, be it the high heather lands, the shore, or underwater. There is even a boat for the piscatorially inclined.

Many of the accommodations on the Island are rather on the *rustic* side. This is not for want of taste and refinement on the part of the Trustees, who have spent a fortune rendering Lundy Island in a form that allows us to step back into the past and into the pure boldness of nature at the same time. The fact is that the inhabitants of Lundy have always lived with the elements, and there is a degree of that feeling in today's experience, albeit with more of the vital conveniences in place. However, even the last caveat begs exception. Take for example Admiralty Lookout, a tiny granite structure ringed in a circle of granite, like a Neolithic shrine, which was built in 1909 to house four hearties with good eyes in the service of HMG. It is said that fourteen lights can be seen from the cottage (and an incalculable number of stars), though to be sure the occupants of Admiralty Lookout enjoy absolute privacy of their own, being over a mile from the village. Here you will find the *bare* necessities; a cozy, paneled all purpose room with a galley kitchen, and a bunk room with

the original four berths. Such an atmosphere would be ruined by electricity and indoor plumbing, which is to say it isn't!

Atmospheric privation ceases, but certainly not the atmosphere, in the two original light-keeper flats attached to The Old Light. You don't have to be a kid to admit to a thrill at the prospect of living in a lighthouse. This lighthouse (one of three on the island) was designed by the architect who gave his King Dartmoor Prison to accommodate Napoleonic POWs. *Sturdy* is the word! Not counting the shower and modern kitchen fixtures, the Lighthouse flats are pretty much *as it were* (after much restoration); a spartan life comforted by the kind of meaningfulness which most of us would like to experience in our own existence. Well, for a week...

Spartan ceases, but still not at the expense of atmosphere, as we move *up* to Millcombe House, which was built in 1835 to house the Reverend Heaven and his angelic (and large!) brood. The good reverend must have thought he had arrived in heaven when the launch prowed up on the sand to deposit him on Lundy Island. His

lovely classical home sits like a white monument in a gorgeous wooded valley looking down to the beach where he arrived. This home, with its seven bedrooms, is rich in 18th century interior detail and contains some very handsome 19th century furnishings, as well as some nice artwork. In his own way, the Reverend Heaven, like the lighthouse keepers, lived according to the comforts of his mission!

There are other equally generous accommodations on the Island, but on a scale more suited to the contemporary sized family. Sir John Borlase Warren's Old House, dating from the late 18th century, has been restored to period elegance for a party of five. Square Cottage, a pretty granite hip-roofed building adjacent to Marisco Tavern, offers very comfortable accommodations for three. Government House, once the home of the Island manager, is another beautifully furnished period abode with three bedrooms. All in all, the Landmark Trust offers 23 fully restored homes for self catered occupancy. And, by no means does holiday just mean summer out here; serious birders will want to be on hand in the spring and fall, and, since the climate is somewhat milder than on the mainland, many of Lundy Island's attractions can be enjoyed in the winter months as well.

MILL
COMBE
I.F-2 [2]
F-1
II.B-d [2]
B-t [3]
B-s [2]
F-1
E&H
LT
P-
S-S   MS
INS
£390-1296
S 12

Contact The Landmark Trust, Shottesbrook, Maidenhead, Berkshire SL6 3SW
TEL 01144-1628-825-925 or FAX 01144-1628-825-417

CHURCH FORD COTTAGE   Little Torrington

Little Torrington is a pleasant hideaway on the River Torridge, within minutes of the sand beaches of Westward Ho! and the famous postcard village of Clovelly. The little thatched cottage (right in drawing) at Church Ford adjoins the 17th

COT-TAGE
I. F-2
II.B-d+s
B-t
E$ H$
FP
L-BA$
TV
W
MW
S-S   MS
INS
BK$
£107-271
S 5

century farmhouse in an acre of grounds and is entered via a rose covered verandah. The cottage is nicely furnished in a cottage style and features an inglenook fireplace with the old bread oven, beamed ceilings, and quarry tiled floors in the kitchen.

The Church Ford Farmhouse, itself, is available for holiday occupancy during a six week period in the late summer when the owners are on their own holiday.

Contact North Devon Holiday Homes, 19 Cross St., Barnstaple, Devon EX31 1BD
TEL 01144-1271-76322 or FAX 01144-1271-46544

UPPER HALL   Nr Manaton

We first heard about Upper Hall Farm several years ago from a neighbor in our "home" village of Lustleigh. Knowing of our fascination with the vernacular architecture of Devon, he pointed us to this rare structure which had recently been restored, but was not then a rental property. "Besides, it is just a bit beyond your regular ramble up the Lustleigh Cleave," he coaxed. He was right; the prospect of approaching this prize through that great mystery forest, rather than by road from the far side, was all the more exciting....in truth we had never gone to the end of the Cleave and we felt a bit like Columbus going to the edge in search of rare treasure. So off we set, lunch packed, walking sticks in hand; across the Mighty Wrey (actually a rock-hopper of a dear little stream) and up through High Hisley farm; then down the forested trail to the River Bovey which has carved out the deep valley over the past million years or so. Here the pretty moss on the rocks of the rushing stream have occasioned many a pause for some quick sketching (also a good spot to chill the wine)...thence up the Cleave under a darkening canopy of high foliage, Hansel and Gretel, but this time armed with a detailed Ordnance Survey map. Past Houndtor Wood which takes a tangent up to the famous Becka Falls. Past the climb up to Pethybridge, where the mushrooming is sensational in August and September; past the side trails to Nut Crackers and Raven's Tor...past the heart of romantic darkness and on to the light at the end of the green tunnel. Veer off at Neadon Cleave; suddenly we find ourselves in an open pasture and there it is...Upper Hall! Through the time-warp of Lustleigh Cleave we have discovered the Old World...positively *Pre-Columbian!*

Upper Hall is now a Grade I Listed medieval *hall house* with direct links through the Normans to the architecture of Brittany...indeed, far from being vernacular Devon, it is almost without comparison in all England. Constructed from large cut granite blocks, one enters on the second floor through an oaken arch and stable door. In the ante-room there are views of the Lustleigh Cleave through 13th century tracery. The "hall" is the whole second floor, now with an open plan kitchen/dining area and a gallery bedroom at one end, which is reached by a marvelous set of chestnut stairs. There are great oaken beams and joists, a massive granite mantel, and many archeologically fascinating features, like the *piscina* (not what you think) and the *garde robe,* a tiny alcove cut into the thick stone wall which **does** have a plumbing hole (for the finicky, thoroughly modern facilities are presently situated off the ante-room). The owner's son (who manages the farm) and his wife (who sculpts) were the first modern tenants, and Upper Hall was furnished and decorated with tremendous sensitivity to both history and comfort.
ETB 4 Keys; Highly Commended

II. F-2	
III.B-d	
E$m	
H$m	
FPS$	
LT	
TELc	
TV	
W/D	
S-S	MS
INS	
BK$	
£153-346	
S 2	

Contact Helpful Holidays, Coombe, Chagford, Devon TQ13 8DF
TEL 01144-1647-433-593 or FAX 01144-1647-433-694

HOE MEWS   Lynton

Lynton & Lynmouth are sister towns; one poised high on the cliffs of the North Devon coast, and the other nestled below, where the Rivers Lyn gush into the sea. Like so many tourist towns on the South Coast, these enclaves were created by the Victorian passion for escaping to a place *by-the-sea*. But the Bristol Channel cuts a more rugged coast and, despite immense popularity and some remarkable sand beaches, the "L"s have not been flooded with tourists and *carnivalized* like so many of the English Channel holiday towns. True, the great natural *flood* of 1952 pretty nearly washed Lynmouth to oblivion.

Hoe Mews is situated just below the foot path, with sweeping views across the Bristol Channel. A bit further along the footpath is the famous Valley of the Rocks, much favored by wild eyed poets and not quite so wild goats, who seem to find a common aesthetic quality in this moonscape terrain. Hoe Mews is very commodious and exceptionally well furnished. All the comforts and mechanical conveniences are here for a most enjoyable holiday.

II.B-d [2]
B-t
F-2
E&H
LT $
TV
W/D
MW
S-S   MS
INS
BK $
£152-426
S 6

Contact North Devon Holiday Homes, 19 Cross St., Barnstaple, Devon EX31 1BD
TEL 01144-1271-76322 or FAX 01144-1271-46544

CIDER ROOM COTTAGE   Nr Membury

Cider Room Cottage is part of a quintessential Devon longhouse farm complex, in this case the old apple storage rooms. This is cider country and, in fact, the cottage overlooks the old orchard. There is also a pond with chatty ducks and a couple gregarious Vietnamese potbellied pigs.

The cottage is entered via a passage off the cobbled yard, down flagstone steps into the main living/kitchen room. The kitchen is divided from the sitting room by a low stone wall, capped by darkly stained oak to match the ancient posts and beams. The kitchen is fully fitted, with nice china and glassware, and the dining area features a really fine Queen Anne style mahogany dining table and chairs. The cottage has Laura Ashley fabrics in the curtains and blinds, comfy home-style soft furnishings, and is carpeted throughout. Mrs. Steele will also provide wonderful country style meals of salmon & trout, pheasant, lamb, etc, at very reasonable prices.

II.B-d
B-t
F-3
E$m
H$m
FPE
LT$
TV
MW
P-BA
OPEN TA
£130-250
S 4

Cider Room Cottage is within ten miles of all the sights and amenities of the Devon/Dorset coast, including Lyme Regis, and even closer to the antique hunter's happy hunting ground at Honiton.

Contact David & Pat Steele, Hasland Farm, Membury, Axminster, Devon EX13 7JF TEL 01144-1404-881-558

THE BARNS AT CHURCHILL FARM

Nr Marlborough

Marlborough literally means the *meeting place,* and, indeed, the Barns at Churchill Farm put you right in the middle of a holiday triangle of marine highlights in Salcombe, Kingsbridge and Hope Cove. Everything is within two or three miles. The focal point of this hilltop village is the Church of All Saints, whose tall spire will guide you home after a busy day of sightseeing or marathon walking. The two friendly pubs along Marlborough's old street might do likewise.

Churchill is still a working farm, but the holiday cottages are at some distance from the agricultural activity. Three cottages have been created out of a very large old stone and shingle barn. The layout is "L" shaped with a communal lawn and picnic tables in front. There is an outdoor pool (fenced and unheated). The complex faces southeast, down the North Sands Valley toward the sea. May and Oak Cottages (to the right in the drawing) each sleep four with open plan sitting, kitchen, dining areas. These are exceptionally neat and tidy cottages, tastefully, if somewhat sparsely, furnished. The kitchens are fitted with all the modern conveniences, including oven/grills, and offer plenty of working counter tops. There are two bedrooms upstairs; a double and a twin.

Chestnut is the larger end-wing cottage, sleeping up to eight. The very spacious sitting room is dominated by a massive stone wall into which a flush fire box has been built...really quite an impressive piece of masonry. High ceilings and full glass doors make for a bright airy feeling. The rose pattern three piece suite is nicely matched to the oriental throw rug over the neutral green wall to wall carpeting. There are four bedrooms upstairs, all en-suite, and the master bedroom is en-suite with bidet.

Nearby Hope Cove, once a smugglers entrepot, is the beginning of an absolutely super footpath back along the cliffs to Bolt Head. Also not to be missed is Kingsbridge's busy 16th century market arcade, called *Shambles.* Golf enthusiasts will find a nice course at Thurlestone, 4 miles away.

OAK&MAY
II.B-d
B-t
F-3
E&H
LT
TV
W
F-F
$385-815
S 4
CHESTNUT
I. F-1
II.B-q [2]
B-t [2]
F-4
F-3 [3]
E&H
LT
TELm
TV
W/D
DW MW
F-F
$875-1670
S 8

Contact British Vacation Rentals, Box 227, 154 Chadwick Court, North Vancouver, B.C. V7M 3KI, Canada TEL 1-800-663-6330 (US & Canada)

THE ROUND HOUSE   Noss Mayo

Dartmoor, which can get a pretty substantial snow cover in winter, is the mother of many rivers whose distant mouths came to be settled as the principle coastal towns of Devon: Dart-mouth, Ex-mouth, Teign-mouth, etc. Eventually it enters the mind of most serious moor ramblers to track down the humble moorland origins of these famous river ports. Three of my personal favorites are the *mmm* rivers of the southern moor, the Rivers Plym, Erme & Yealm. These three rise in close proximity above Shell Tor and thence trickle away independently in search of a seabound place to *make a name for themselves*: Plym-mouth, Erme-mouth, and *Noss Mayo*. Poor River Yealm; it seems that a community well up stream grabbed its name in a vain unpronounceable conglomeration of consonants (Yealmpton) and the true mouth of the noble little River Yealm had to settle for Noss Mayo (an ancient Celtic phrase meaning *hold the mayonnaise, please!*).

No matter, Noss Mayo is a wonderful village, painted picturesquely on the hillside as it tumbles into Yealm Estuary. A particularly scenic part of the Coastal Foot Path ends here, joining the little switch-back road zig-zagging its way down the hill to Bridgend and thence through Newton Ferrers on the opposite side. At the water's edge there are several pubs with sunny patios to pass a leisurely hour or two watching the boats and birds. The Round House property also comes down to the water's edge, with a steeply terraced garden leading to a little private quay with a hirable row boat hauled up and a mooring off.

The cottage is comprised of a very well equipped kitchen and a spacious combination sitting/dining room with a view-filled picture window overlooking the estuary. There is another, more traditional, sitting room with character beams and an original open fireplace. The sofa in this room converts to a double bed for larger parties. The sleeping quarters, all with nice views over the water, are paired off upstairs and arrived at by separate stairwells.

I. CS
II.B-s
B-t
B-d
F-3
E$
H$
FP
L
TV
W/D
MW
C-BA
P-BA
F-F   MS
INS
£215-559
S 5-7

Contact Toad Hall Cottages, Union Road, Kingsbridge, South Devon TQ7 1EF
TEL 01144-1548-853-089 or FAX 01144-1548-853-086

STILLMEADOW COTTAGE · Ottery St. Mary

Stillmeadow is the middle of three cottages situated in this 16th century thatch row. Though facing on the street, it has a secluded rear garden, nicely furnished with patio equipment and landscaped with urns and a dolphin fountain under the magnolia and apple trees. Ottery St. Mary, itself, is noted for its 14th century church (rather ambitiously modeled on Exeter Cathedral) and as the birthplace of Samuel Taylor Coleridge in the vicarage during that rebellion over in America.

This is classic Devon, architecturally, and has profited greatly from the sensitive decoration by its owner, an American antique enthusiast. One enters into a center hall with color-washed terracotta walls and an old walnut chest, then moves through a passage conservatory planted with flowering vines. The sitting room features a huge fireplace with lovely pieces of antique porcelain on the mantle. Soft furnishings are done in harmonizing print fabrics of terracotta, soft greens, apricot, with plum and turquoise accents. There are good oils and watercolors throughout, and this room exudes the sophisticated taste of its owner.

The kitchen has all the essentials and is prettily decorated with deep green tiles, William Morris fabric blinds, colorful pots and pans, lithographs and an antique white ironstone dinner service. There is a sunny dining room with an old pine table and dresser displaying the owner's collection of antique blue and white china. French doors lead to the garden.

Upstairs we find a wide hall, having good pictures, bookshelves and a mahogany desk. Off this is a very large master bedroom, done in a delicious deep rose, with a four-poster bed, painted with griffins, unicorns and dragons...a one of a kind cottage piece for sure! Redoute rose prints, soft green carpet patterned with ribbons and roses, and a fine Georgian chest of drawers are all part of the atmospheric meld. There is a second twin room with Bill Blass fabric quilts and ballon blinds. Again, lots of books and pretty prints, and, as with all rooms except the kitchen, pleasing views of the garden.

There is much to see in this neighborhood: Cadhay, the Tudor mansion, is nearby...Honiton for antiques...Budleigh Salterton for a whiff of the sea.

I. F-2
II.B-q
B-t
FP
LT
TELm TV
W/D
C-BA
OPEN
INS
BK$ TA
£170-330
S 4

Contact Mary Spivey, The Independent Traveller, Thorverton, Exeter EX5 5NT
TEL 01144-1392-860-807 or FAX 01144-1392-860-552

LOWER MILL

Peter Tavy

The Lower Mill in its present form owes its existence to Olive Eggleston, who has brought this Grade II Listed building back from the shambles. It is one thing to have the courage to take on a reclamation project of this magnitude, and quite another to bring it to a successful completion, preserving the rich detail of early industrial architecture in characterful domesticized forms. For example, the corner[less]stone (sorry; just couldn't resist!) of any mill is, of course, its grindstone (most often carted off these days to become pavers in the garden). At the Lower Mill one of the grindstones has been carpeted and cushioned to make a seat. Likewise, the backbone of the mill, its working spindle, has been retained and reaches from the kitchen up to the living room. These clever touches make the Lower Mill a continuously interesting venue for memorable holidaying.

Architectural curiosity is not the whole story of Lower Mill. Much has been made of space and natural light in the design of the multi-leveled living areas. Exposed beams are common enough in the preservation architecture of Britain, but here we have very substantial load bearing timbers resting on very thick outer stone walls...old utilities very dramatically shaped into new aesthetics. Luxury standards have been observed in every thing from the lighting to the furnishings. There are some fine antiques here, amidst handsome contemporary soft furnishings. Lower Mill is large, but has been thoughtfully designed with two kitchens and a division plan that will accommodate the privacy requirements of disparate traveling groups or generations within the family.

As one might expect, the situation of the Mill is pretty spectacular in its own right. There is a sun-trap garden with attractive shrubbery and the old leat. Down a rather steep drop one finds the old wheel works and the river. Nearby is an ancient humpback bridge, which is, itself, designated as a national architectural treasure. It should be noted that some of the "perpendicular" aspects of both the Mill and its grounds require a measure of vigilance with small children among guests.

Peter Tavey is a small character village on the quiet fringe of Dartmoor National Park. The handsome town of Tavistock is four miles away.

| I. F-1 |
| B-2 |
| F-2 |
| II. B-t |
| F-2 |
| B-d |
| F-3 |
| III.B-d [3] |
| F-3 [3] |
| E&H |
| LT |
| TELin |
| TVV |
| W/D |
| DW MW |
| S-S MS |
| INS |
| £390-936 |
| S 12 |

Contact Classic Cottages, Leslie House, Lady Street, Helston, Cornwall TR13 8NA
TEL 01144-1326-565-656 or FAX 01144-1326-565-554

UPPER COTTONWOOD COTTAGE

Nr Riddlecombe

Cottonwood is an old hamlet settled by charcoal burners in the seemingly remote middle of Devon, more or less equidistant from Exmoor, Dartmoor, the "metropolis" of Exeter and the busy north coast market town of Barnstaple. Everything is accessible (there is even a golf course five miles away), yet if one wants to shut the world out this is a lovely place to do it. Salmon stalkers will note that the River Taw (which we have enjoyed fishing on two occasions without seriously depleting stocks) runs nearby and day privileges may be purchased at pubs along the road. The cottage, itself, is a traditional thatch and cob dwelling, about 300 years old and sited nicely overlooking the coombe. It has a large inglenook fireplace with bread oven and wood stove in the cozy sitting room. This is a simple cottage, neat and tidy, with homey floral patterned soft furnishings and waxed pine tables and chairs. There is a compact downstairs bedroom with built in bed and drawers, and two interconnecting bedrooms upstairs.

I. F-2
B-s
II.B-s
B-d
E H$
FPS$
LT
TELc
TV
W
MW
NS P-
S-S
INS
$450-785
S 4

Contact Chapel House Cottages, P.O. Box 878, Eufaula, Alabama 36072 TEL 334-687-9800 or FAX 334-687-5324

CABLE COTTAGE

North Sands Beach

If your idea of a holiday is rising early for a long walk along the shore, poking about in the sand for tidal treasures, then give Cable Cottage a thought. This is an eccentric little Gothic cottage situated directly across the road from North Sands Beach. There isn't a straight line in the place, and happily none were forced on it in the recent renovations. There are two sitting rooms, both with good views of the water and one with a sturdy Victorian stone fireplace. Furnishings are modest but comfortable. There are two twin bedrooms and two singles. The cottage sits on its own, behind a roadside stone wall with patio gardens fore and aft. The name, incidentally, derives from the fact that the first transatlantic cable to this region entered here.

I. F-3
II.B-t [2]
B-s [2]
E&H
FP
LT
TV
W/D
F-F
$915-1610
S 6

Contact British Vacation Rentals, Box 227, 154 Chadwick Court, North Vancouver, B.C. V7M 3KI, Canada TEL 1-800-663-6330 (US & Canada)

THE STUMBLES

Salcombe

Salcombe has long been one of our favorite coastal destinations...reminiscent of another favorite, Sausalito in California... towns that cascade down the heavily wooded hills in a maze of narrow characterful streets to meet busy little boat harbors. We are eternally grateful that Salcombe has not become overcrowded like Sausalito, nor has it slipped toward the sad destiny of many once lovely English coastal resorts...that is, row upon row of threadbare utility hotels, the *Fawlty Towers* towns. Salcombe has remained up-market, without at the same time becoming a snob hole...you can eat, drink, shop or sail in Salcombe without courtier attire or hasty bank financing. Despite its almost tropical climate, which has led many a comparable Mediterranean village down the road to debauchery, Salcombe has retained balance and common sense...one would never say it's *a nice place to visit*, without going on to say it would be *an even better place to live.* To see what I mean, go during the Town Regatta, held since 1857. The sailing races are, of course, spectacular to watch (or to participate in), but Salcom(b)ites put as much enthusiasm into the crab competition off Victoria Quay, or the songfest, or the family treasure hunts. Afloat or ashore you've never been among a better bunch of folks. In fact, Salcombe's only drawback is that it is surrounded by the South Hams, which are plain and simply irresistible for touring. Just once, I'd like for us to spend a whole week strolling the streets of Salcombe from a comfy little tuck-away cottage in the center of town.

Such a place is The Stumbles. Situated on a street that a midget could straddle, this 19th century fisherman's rowhouse has recently undergone complete renovation. Knotty pine and bright white new plaster make this an exceptionally light and airy accommodation. The ground floor begins with a combination kitchen/dining/living room. Compact, yes; but very workable. The kitchen is galley size, but amazingly everything is there (including dishwasher and microwave). There is an equally compact dining arrangement served by nicely cut pine benches. The old coal fireplace has been preserved and prettily framed in pine. The master bedroom is upstairs amidst a geometric puzzle of roof and dormer angles, and is...surprise...huge! Queen size bed, large wardrobe, dresser, bed tables (naturally, all in honey pine) and still lots of wide open spaces. Believe it or not, there's another queen size bedroom!

I. B-q
B-t
F-2
II.B-q
F-3
E&H
FPG
LT
TELc
TV
W/D
DW MW
NS
S-S
$660-1335
S 6

Contact British Vacation Rentals, Box 227, 154 Chadwick Court, North Vancouver, B.C., V7M 3KI, Canada TEL 1-800-663-6330

LA BARANCA
Salcombe

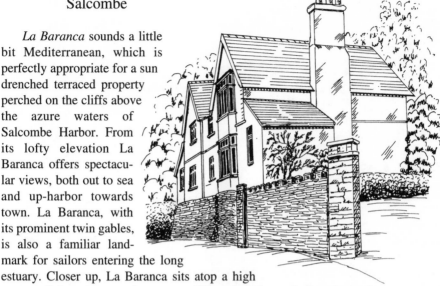

La Baranca sounds a little bit Mediterranean, which is perfectly appropriate for a sun drenched terraced property perched on the cliffs above the azure waters of Salcombe Harbor. From its lofty elevation La Baranca offers spectacular views, both out to sea and up-harbor towards town. La Baranca, with its prominent twin gables, is also a familiar landmark for sailors entering the long estuary. Closer up, La Baranca sits atop a high stone wall, hanging over the narrow cliff road, with a walled garden and flagstone patio peeking over the hedge. Total privacy is insured by the forest on three sides of the house, yet it is only a few minutes' walk to the North Sands Beach.

Inside, La Baranca is furnished with a comfortable mix of antiques and older style sofas and chairs. There is a large cove moulded living room (20'x28') with a particularly handsome natural wood, pilastered mantel framing an open fire. There are fitted carpets throughout, with assorted accent rugs, and lovely bay windows overlooking the water. Dried flowers and cozy table lamps add substantially to the atmosphere.

La Baranca will be a definite treat for the culinary spirit, and the Devon coast is a great piscatory larder. The kitchen is expansive, with oodles of good working counter space, and all the modern conveniences. In fact, in addition to a good Bosch (electric) ceramic hob and oven, La Baranca has the pride of the finest English home, an Aga cooker. (A true Brit will hock the family portraits before he'd part with the Aga!) There is a good sized dining area within the kitchen and a handy service window from the kitchen into the study.

Upstairs there is a gable-end master bedroom, done in small pink prints and with quite lovely floor-to-ceiling floral drapes framing the bay window views. A second (twin) and third (double) bedroom share another bathroom.

Salcombe is all about water. Whether your passion is sailing or swimming, fishing or just mingling with the marine crowd, Salcombe is the place to be.

I. F-1
II. B-t [2]
F-4
B-d
F-3
E&H
FP
LT
TELm
TV
W/D
DW MW
C-BA
S-S
$930-1755
S 5-6

Contact British Vacation Rentals, Box 227, 154 Chadwick Court, North Vancouver, BC V7M 3KI, Canada TEL 1-800-663-6330 (US & Canada)

8 ST. ELMO COURT   Salcombe

This is a ground floor unit in a recent development of seventeen luxury apartments. If you're thinking standardized rental condo fixtures, *chi chi* catalogue furnishings, up market motel; Don't! Number Eight sparkles with individuality and the owner's outstanding taste.   First of all, the Elmo Court complex as a whole was not designed by the early obsolescence box folks. These apartments have wonderful cove mouldings, arched doorways, discrete balconies (not cages hanging off obscene perpendicular towers); in other words, much character was built in before the interior decoration even began.

Number Eight accommodates four in outstanding comfort, with plenty of space to entertain in style if necessary. The living room, cast in shades of *creme brulee,* with art deco wall lighting, features three lovely sofas, commanding pictures and Imari-type plates ganged around a starkly modern log effect gas fireplace.

I.B-d
B-t
F-3 [2]
E&H
FPG
LT
TELm
TVV
W/D
DW MW
NS
C-BA
F-F
$830-1650
S 4-5

Occasional tables carry an interesting array of candlestick lamps, pottery and literature; and, since this is the English *tropics,* there is a respectable bit of indoor greenery. Through the arch into a dining room...furnishings here are more uniformly antique with a Victorian chandelier and matching wall sconce.   Note the clever adaptation of an old press into a contemporary drinks stand. Richly swagged drapes, matching the fabric in the dining chair seats, frame the doors to the south facing courtyard which is fully fitted for alfresco pleasures. One bedroom is a double en-suite with an archway adjoined dressing room; the other a twin. There is a heated outdoor pool and it is only a short walk down the hill to the North Sands Beach.

Contact British Vacation Rentals, Box 227-154 Chadwick Court, North Vancouver, B.C. V7M 3KI, Canada
TEL 1-800-663-6330 (US & Canada)

CAROLINE COTTAGE
Salcombe

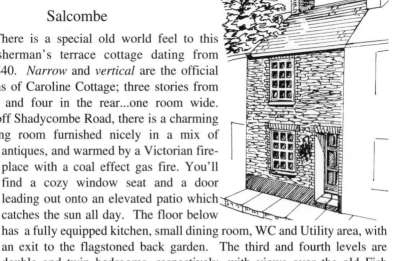

There is a special old world feel to this quaint fisherman's terrace cottage dating from around 1840. *Narrow* and *vertical* are the official dimensions of Caroline Cottage; three stories from the street and four in the rear...one room wide. Entering off Shadycombe Road, there is a charming little sitting room furnished nicely in a mix of antiques, and warmed by a Victorian fireplace with a coal effect gas fire. You'll find a cozy window seat and a door leading out onto an elevated patio which catches the sun all day. The floor below has a fully equipped kitchen, small dining room, WC and Utility area, with an exit to the flagstoned back garden. The third and fourth levels are double and twin bedrooms, respectively, with views over the old Fish Quay. Ample patio furnishings and a barbeque are provided. Caroline Cottage is particularly convenient for day sailors, being only a short walk to the boatyards and dinghy park, as well as the busy town center.

I. F-1
III. B-d
F-3
IV. B-t
E&H
FPG
LT
TELm
TV
W
DW MW
NS
S-S
$465-925
S 4

Contact British Vacation Rentals, Box 227, 154 Chadwick Court, North Vancouver, B.C. V7M 3KI, Canada
TEL 1-800-663-6330 (US & Canada)

BADGER & KINGFISHER
Sherford

Here are two extremely spacious barn conversion cottages, where others might have carved out a half dozen units. You will find them well furnished, with wood stoves in living rooms and smartly fitted kitchen/dining areas. The upstairs are open to the peak and have three large bedrooms; a double en-suite, plus two twins with a bathroom and shower to share. In front there is an expansive raised patio with barbeque and lawn furniture and a separate (heated) pool house, with sauna, solarium and change rooms. Fishermen can wet their line in the pay-for-catch trout pond, with all the gear supplied to guests. The cottages are ideally situated in the tranquil South Hams, only three miles to the sea at Torcross and a mile or so from the ancient market and sights of Kingsbridge.
ETB 5 Keys; Highly Commended

II.B-d
B-t [2]
F-3 [2]
E$c   H$c
FPS
LT
TELc
TV
W/D
DW MW
S-S   MS
INS
BK$
£225-733
S 6

Contact Helpful Holidays, Coombe, Chagford, Devon TQ13 8DF
TEL 01144-1647-433-593 or FAX 01144-1647-433-694

STANCOMBE MANOR

Sherford

Situated just north of the village of Sherford, nestling in a secluded valley and surrounded by rolling farmland, Stancombe is steeped in history. Former owners include the Earls of Devon and Sir Francis Drake, who was given the hamlet of Sherford, of which Stancombe was the Manor, by Queen Elizabeth in recognition of his circumnavigational voyage.

The present Manor is somewhat unique for a Georgian country house in these parts. Indeed, the *tropical* colonial style of Stancombe Manor is far more typical of the 18th century *mansions* one finds in Bermuda and the far flung Empire plantation islands of the period. The house was built in stages between 1750 and 1780, with all due attention to classical detail and symmetry, but with a paved and covered verandah, which might have put off a Robert Adam, but which is really quite fetching today. One thing is for sure, the siting of Stancombe, with breathtaking views over the undulating valley, is pure Georgian. This is cider country, and the present owners have restored the traditional orchards, which would have been very much a part of the 18th century perspective, just as the heady cider was an integral part of the good life...and is again in the produce of the Stancombe Manor cider works.

The Manor is rented as a whole. One enters via an impressive entrance hall with a fine Victorian mosaic floor. By no means is this a huge mansion, but the reception rooms are wonderfully proportioned, lending a sense of generous space. And, the refined detail is here as well: classical cornice work, natural wood doors, window shutters folding into the deep casements. There are open fireplaces in the dining and withdrawing rooms. At mezzanine level and to the side of the house there is a spacious conservatory, which is approached via an internal staircase. The original wine cellar, with its gargantuan slates, has been converted into a cloakroom and shower room. Furnishings are a combination of contemporary pieces and period styles, tastefully chosen and, like the Manor itself, somewhat understated. Upstairs there are three bedrooms, sleeping eight, including one with a very handsome four-poster bed.

In addition to the Manor House, there are eleven holiday cottages available in the detached stables and farm buildings. Stancombe also offers a wide variety of outdoor and recreational amenities, including an indoor pool and badminton facility, sauna, snooker, hard court tennis, croquet, boules and an adventure playground for the younger set. The beach, incidentally, is only three miles away at Slapton Sands of D-Day fame.   ETB 3-5 Keys; Highly Commended

I. F-3
II.B-d+s
B-t+s [2]
F-4
E   H$
FP$
L
TV
W
P-
OPEN MS
INS
TA
£540-1146
S 8

Contact Stancombe Manor Country Holidays, Sherford, Kingsbridge, Devon TQ7 2BE
TEL 01144-1548-531-634 or FAX 01144-1548-531-012

RINGMORE TOWERS   Shaldon

Ringmore Towers is a castellated folly built out into the River Teign where the estuary meets the sea at Shaldon. Though Ringmore is a Grade II Listed building dating back three centuries, most of what exists today is the product of a late Victorian restoration. Follies should bring out the kid in us (or the romantic), and Ringmore is just that kind of a delight with its castellated walls, Rapunzelesque towers, plank doors, cobbled courtyards...you can even fish off your private balcony or beach your dinghy alongside.

There are five apartments in this mock castle, each with a personality all its own...and a sense of humor. The grandest is *West Towers* (sleeps 8-10), with expansive leaded windows overlooking the estuary, parquet floors, French windows to the courtyard where there is a barbeque and patio furniture, and beyond that a waterfront balcony. *West Towers* has two staircases; one leading to the three "regular" bedrooms, including the master en-suite bedroom and a large twin with brass beds and stained glass windows. The other staircase will definitely tease out the kids and romantics in the party. This spiral stone stairs leads up to the 17th century tower room, with a vaulted painted ceiling, convertible sofa, and a door out onto a castellated bridge overlooking the estuary and courtyard. *The Round Tower* apartment begins with its own ground floor entrance, up a spiral stairwell to the living room with Victorian stained glass windows and a marble fireplace (gas fires). There are two bedrooms, sleeping up to six, on the same floor. Another spiral stone stairs takes one up to the   castellated roof terrace, with furnishings for alfresco lunches, snoozing or the endless pleasures of watching the estuary activity. *The Snug* (sleeps 4-6), *The Cobbles* (4-6) and *The Coachhouse* (6-8) all have marvelous estuary views and special delights for kids of all ages.

Contact Helpful Holidays, Coombe, Chagford, Devon TQ13 8DF
TEL 01144-1647-433-593 or FAX 01144-1647-433-694

E$m H$m
FPG*
L
TV
W/Ds
DW
MW*
P-
E/HC*
S-S & F-F
MS
INS
BK$
£190-819
S 4-10

Old Cotmore Farm Stokenham

Old Cotmore Farm has an interesting history, having been part of Stokenham Manor, which was given to Catherine Parr by her betrothed, Henry VIII, as a wedding present. The old manor house has disappeared into history, but the character buildings of Old Cotmore Farm have enjoyed continued use and recent conversion into two exceptional holiday rentals. The larger accommodation, Catherine's Cottage, sleeps up to nine persons and is in the best tradition of Devon character cottages, with a wall sized inglenook fireplace, gnarly old darkened beams and pristine whitewashed stone walls. The inglenook fireplace, with its two ancient bake ovens, is, in fact, so huge that today it accommodates a good sized wood burning stove, the television, and an extensive collection of decorative pottery and china. These proportions appear again in the 36 ft. long en-suite master bedroom, with a queen size bed as well as a commodious sofa bed. Catherine's cottage is clad on the exterior with clematis vines, and outfitted on the inside with very comfortable contemporary furnishings. The rose clad Gamekeeper's Cottage is adjacent and sleeps five in a comparable fashion.

I. F-1
II.B-q [2]
B-d
B-s
CS
F-3 [3]
E$ H$
FPS
LT
TVV
W/D
DW MW
P-
S-S   MS
INS
£242-589
S 7-9

ROUNDHOUSE Nr South Pool

Architect/owner at work! Result: an exceptionally well designed barn conversion right on the estuary, a mile or so up from Salcombe Harbor. The renovations have cleverly taken advantage of the various levels of the old barn and incorporated a variety of the vernacular features

B-t [2]
F-3
B-d
F-1
E$ H$
LT
TELc
TV
W
C-BA
P-BA
S-S   MS
INS
£225-732
S 6

(beams, crucks, and stonework). The accommodation is laid out on three levels, with a large, glass fronted "D" shaped living/dining room on the ground floor. This bright room is prettily furnished, with colorful rugs over the red tile floors. There are a pair of twin bedded rooms with access to the terrace, and a narrow staircase leads to a double bedded gallery overlooking the living room.

Across the walled courtyard is the old stone, pillar fronted linhay, now containing a fine indoor lap pool. Boats, which can be rented in Salcombe, may be beached on the property.

Contact Fulford Holiday Cottages, 7 Fore Street, Kingsbridge, Devon TQ7 1PG
TEL 01144-1548-856-552 or FAX 01144-1548-854-285

HINGSTON COTTAGE
South Milton

This is a traditional Devon *fairy tale* house, with its ancient undulating walls and pretty thatch, snugged back into the rolling hills of the beautiful South Hams. Isn't it amazing how they knew three centuries back just what the essence of *quaint* would look like today! I should hasten to add that the semi-detached Hingston Cottage is not just some figurine salt shaker or a backdrop for a BBC production of *Great Expectations;* it is very real with an equally characterful interior. There you will find the mandatory cavernous fireplace, the window sills cut deeply into the stone and cob, the darkened beams and the serpentine walls...quainter than quaint! There is a wonderfully terraced lawn and garden and a games room in the house which will delight young and old. South Milton Beach is just a couple miles away; boating on the Kingsbridge Estuary, people-watching in Salcombe...a holiday filled with sights and activities...and a fairy tale cottage to call home. ETB 4 Keys; Commended

I. F-1	
II.B-d	
F-1	
B-t	
B-s	
F-2	
E$m	
H$m	
FP$	
LT$	
TV	
W/D	
P-	
S-S	MS
INS	
BK$	
£186-447	
S 5	

Contact West Country Cottages, The Geminids, Priory Rd, Abbotskerswell, Devon TQ12 5PP
TEL 01144-1626-333-678 or FAX 01144-1626-336-678

ENDSLEIGH Nr Tavistock

Mark Girouard reminds us that the Victorian passion for the picturesque in architecture has its roots in Georgian aesthetics, and the Dutchess of Bedford's picturesque estate, Endsleigh, built during the Regency, is an important bridge between the two aesthetic regimes. An immense amount of money and professional imagination went into the creation of these *simple* dwellings; mock vernacular stages in/and upon which the nobility played at the *simple life.* And what a life it must have been here in the Swiss Cottage perched in the wooded Tamar gorge, with a window on nature that was as inspirational for the painter Turner as for us today. *Charming* doesn't really do it justice; *sublime* is the word!

This Alpine cottage is amazingly roomy, in the Victorian sense of many little rooms, distributed over three floors and encompassed within a spectacular wraparound balcony. I have a particular affection for day & night properties and many an evening of enchantment could be spent sitting on the Swiss Cottage balcony just listening to the night sounds and feeling the breeze. The ground floor kitchen lends itself to picnicking on the sloping lawn...call it getting right into the picturesque!

I. B-b	
III.F-2	
B-t	
E&H	
LT	
S-S	
MS	
INS	
£337-637	
S 4	

Contact The Landmark Trust, Shottesbrook, Maidenhead, Berkshire SL6 3SW
TEL 01144-1628-825-925 or FAX 01144-1628-825-417

THE DUCHESS Topsham

Begin with a characterful old three story inn and situate it in an ancient port town on what was once a Roman waterway. Divide the inn in two and call one part *The Duchess* and the other *The Duke*. Then amass and install a collection of antiques, *objet d'art*, statuary, original paintings, and fascinating collectibles. Put it all together with a walloping big measure of humor, albeit sometimes a bit macabre. We are not talking about a Howard Johnson motel room here! Character heaped on character!

What is more, there is a *plot* to The Duchess; a mystery, as it were. It may be important for you to know that, prior to the Monmouth Rebellion in the mid seventeenth century, the Duke & Duchess of Monmouth stayed at this inn in Topsham and the Duke addressed the crowd from the upper window of the inn. The present owner, who is an historian, lives in The Duke and is responsible for the unique storybook restoration of both cottages. Each has its own cobbled courtyard and they share the garden, which is laid out in the seventeenth century style. The plot thickens a bit when you see that The Duchess has a theme of *Alice Through the Looking Glass*. Tenants who solve the puzzles which are placed around the cottage can discover one of the cottage's secrets. You may want to have a quiet drink out in the courtyard and compare notes with Humpty Dumpty on the wall.

The owner has many famous friends and in both cottages are mementoes from the likes of the Beatles, Robert Lindsay and a host of other noted artists and designers. In the garden there is a replica set from *The Sword in the Stone*, where you will also find one of the actual swords used by Kevin Costner in *Robin Hood: Prince of Thieves*.

If you get bored at home, which is highly unlikely, the beautiful and enriching city of Exeter is just up river four miles.

ETB 2 Keys; Highly Commended

I. Kitchen
II. CS
F-3
III.B-d
E$ H$
FP
LT$
TV
C-BA P-
S-S   MS
INS
BK$
£135-324
S 2-4

Contact West Country Cottages, The Geminids, Priory Rd, Abbotskerswell, Devon TQ12 5PP
TEL 01144-1626-333-678 or FAX 01144-1626-336-678

OLD BEER HOUSE

Throwleigh

Like stepping into a calendar, this quintessential 15th century Devon long-house was once the Royal Oak Beer House. Quaint cottage at the center of quaint

II. B-q
B-s
B-d
F-2
F-3
E$m
H$
FP
LT
TELc
TVV
W/D
DW MW
NS P-BA
S-S MS
INS
BK$
£187-400
S 5

village, all within Dartmoor National Park, with shaggy ponies and sheep wandering about...here is the recipe for a memorable holiday!

The Old Beer House has been nicely restored without imposing too much rude modernity on its character interior. One enters through a stable door (remembering, of course, that the critters once shared the premises) to low ceilings, dark old beams, a big inglenook open fireplace and bread oven. There are some wonderful antiques here and lots of little things to inspect; games to play, books to read (even a small video library). The kitchen is modern and has an oil-fired Rayburn as well as gas stove. Upstairs there are three bedrooms, one an en-suite queen, and another up a few character steps. ETB 4 Keys; Commended

Contact Helpful Holidays, Coombe, Chagford, Devon TQ13 8DF
TEL 01144-1647-433-593 or FAX 01144-1647-433-694

LEMPRICE FARM

Lemprice Farm dates back 300 years and sits on the old Roman road to Exeter (12 miles away). The neighboring farm was the birthplace of Sir

Yettington
Nr
Budleigh Salterton

Walter Raleigh. There are five cottages here; among the most spacious barn conversion holiday accommodations one will ever find. Indeed, these amazing spans are created by a fascinating converging and pyramiding network of beams that will keep you looking up. The pine furnishings were specially crafted for the Coates from timbers rescued from the Devonport Dockyard clearance. There are fitted carpets throughout, plants, and interesting lighting taking advantage of the vaulted ceilings. The gardens have herbs for your kitchen, and beyond that a small pond with swans and ducks (not for your kitchen!). Lemprice is ideally situated to day trip all along the Devon coast and up to Dartmoor. ETB 3 & 4 Keys; Highly Commended.

E
H$
LT
TELc
TV
W/Ds
MW
NS P-BA
E/HC
OPEN
MS

Contact Mrs Hanneke Coates, Lemprice Farm, Yettington, Budleigh Salterton, Devon EX9 7BW
TEL 01144-1395-567-037

KINGSTON COTTAGES   Nr Totnes

The Kingston Estate is pretty nearly perfect! A proud Georgian country house built with a rationalist passion for classical symmetry. A fine array of character "out buildings" assembled around a cobbled courtyard. A marvelous situation in the beautiful South Hams, just four miles from the peerless Elizabethan market town of Totnes, which I've written so much about in the past. No; Kingston is not Chatsworth or Longleat; it's *home!* The *perfect* home of Elizabeth, Michael & Piers Corfield and, happily for us, their guests. Shall I confess the depth of my envy of the Corfields? Well, yes, of course I must acknowledge that such absolute perfection does engender a certain greenness. But perfection doesn't fall out of the sky, and it has taken the Corfields nine years of ceaseless energy and aesthetic imagination to create what appears now to simply be a blessed (e)state. Let's have a look at the results:

Walnut Cottage was built around 1789 to accommodate the house servants, and continues to be adjacent to the main house kitchen. The entrance hall to Walnut is painted a chalky white and is carpeted in a rich corn hue, but the dominating feature to the eye is a nineteenth century mahogany hall table and a large Victorian milk churn used for umbrellas (yes, it does occasionally rain in Devon). In the kitchen you will be impressed with the old slate floors solidly under foot, and notice the ceiling hooks, once used for hanging game and now for drying herbs and flowers. There are nice antique pine furnishings here and plenty of natural light provided by a central window overlooking the countryside to the west. There is also a traditional dresser (hutch) bearing a handsome display of blue and white willow pattern china. Down the hall, and down a step, is the sitting room...all light and

E$m
H$m
FPS*
FPE*
TELm
TVV
W/D
DW MW
P-
E/HC*
S-S   MS
£169-715
S 2-6

airy in the summer and snug with a wood stove in the winter. French doors provide a wonderful view, as well as access to the terrace, where white reproduction Victorian furniture is installed for the summer pleasures. A timber staircase takes us to a landing hung with rustic pictures, and on to the master bedroom with its   impressive four-poster bed hung with glazed chintz...all very spring like. In the   en-suite bathroom you will find nice touches, like Adams reproduction taps and mahogany paneling. Two other bright cottage style bedrooms make Walnut a   wonderful venue for six.

Bull and Shippen Cottages are the smallest at Kingston. Both are arranged in long rectangular barns which, though single story, are nevertheless capacious and open to the roof beams. Entrance to both cottages is through an attractive little quad which offers pavement cafe style seating during the summer. Wrought iron porch lamps and stable door entries invite the guests into an open plan sitting room and kitchen. Furnishings here have a country house in miniature feel. All of the cottages have fireplaces, however those that were formally farm buildings have electric fires in place of wood burning stoves. A double bedroom with en-suite bathroom is located beyond the kitchen and offers nice views of the countryside.

Coach and Stable Cottages, which sleep four, are in the classic eighteenth century break fronted coach house with its clock tower and weather vane, depicting a sailing ship in hot pursuit of the Leviathan.   Double doors, through which the

coaches once rolled, now provide entry to a large area common to the two cottages. Note the medieval ceiling beam with faces carved into it, which pre-dates this building by a couple hundred years. Upon entering The Old Stables the visitor will round the staircase before finding themselves in a lofty room full of light, polished wood and exposed beams. The kitchen is neatly defined by a stone arch...subtle lighting and a character checkered floor set the tone for pleasant culinary endeavors. Each of the cottages is filled with a unique collection of antiques, pictures, china and small decoratives. The carpets are a rich gold ascending the staircases which, far from being tucked away in some corner to save space, have been cast in leading roles as pieces of furniture in the open plan interiors. On the upper floor of both Coach and Stables are master bedrooms with mahogany four-poster beds nicely draped in chintz, as well as cleverly concealed vanity units. Austrian balloon blinds on the windows are both decorative and warming in the winter.

The Corfields also offer three bedroom suites in the mansion, and fine dinners by prior arrangement. The outdoor amenities at Kingston House include an impressive 48 x 18 foot heated indoor pool, sauna, solarium, steam room, mini-gym and games room. The other outdoor amenities include Devon! Need I say more?

Contact Kingston House, Staverton, Totnes, Devon TQ9 6AR   TEL 01144-1803-762-235 or FAX 01144-1803-762-444

STABLE COTTAGE   Tuckenhay

It is with a considerable measure of embarrassment that I confess to having only belatedly "discovered" the idyllic hamlet of Tuckenhay on the Dart Estuary. This oversight is all the more perplexing since we had been coming regularly to the Friday market at Totnes (just 5 miles away!) for a couple years. In this case, the oversight was corrected by the magazine editor who dispatched us to interview and photograph the culinary celebrity, Mr. Keith Floyd. Floyd, whose life on and off television reads a bit like a cork at sea, was far more shrewd than ourselves (then or now), having finally discovered and then settled in to this heaven sent spot. With his famous eatery now just up the lane, nobody at Stable Cottage need fear starvation, though bank overdrafts are a distinct possibility if one gets too deeply into Keith's wine list. Actually, the area has always been long on gastric bliss, with the Waterman's Arms practically across the street and a wonderful pub, where we have enjoyed a number of good meals and chatty evenings, just a short trek up the hill in Ashprington.

Stable Cottage sits right on the banks of the Dart, with a private south facing waterside terrace where the swans cruise in for scraps, having already wolfed back some pricey hors d'oeuvres down stream at Keith's. (Other places have gulls; Tuckenhay comes with swans...what more can I say!) Inside you will find an attractively decorated and furnished living room with an open fireplace, and a combination kitchen/dining room with French doors to the terrace.

II.B-d	
F-2	
B-t/q	
F-3	
E$	H
FP	
L	
TELin	
TV	
W	
DW	MW
P-	
S-S	MS
INS	
£174-420	
S 4	

Contact Toad Hall Cottages, Union Road, Kingsbridge, South Devon TQ7 1EF
TEL 01144-1548-853-089 or FAX 01144-1548-853-086

HIGHER WELL   Ugborough

I. F-1	
II.B-d [2]	
B-t	
B-s	
F-3	
E	H$
FP$	
LT$	
TVV	
W/D	
DW	MW
P-	
S-S	MS
INS	
BK$	
£264-636	
S 7	

I distinctly remember my first visit to Ugborough. We were on our way to the nearby Shire Horse Farm, and as we drove into the hilly little village I had a *deja vu* sense of being in Tuscany. Close by is Higher Well.

Formerly a working farm, it is now a country house set among bucolic fields of cows and sheep, with various types of cluckers and quackers strutting about (local foxes permitting). The original 17th century farmhouse is now the holiday let and has been renovated to an exceptionally high standard. There is a substantial stone fireplace to make things cozy on a winter's night, and a handsome conservatory to enjoy during the bright *chianti days* of spring and autumn. Kitchen type people, such as myself, will be thrilled by Higher Well's large, completely equipped kitchen, with its quarry tile floors and beamed ceiling, and its monument to culinary excellence...the Aga.   ETB 4 Keys; Deluxe

Contact West Country Cottages, The Geminids, Priory Rd, Abbotskerswell, Devon TQ12 5PP
TEL 01144-1626-333-678 or FAX 01144-1626-336-678

ROSE COTTAGE
Woolfardisworthy

Novitiates to the Devon scene will no doubt be amused, and perhaps relieved, to know that the natives of Woolfardisworthy long ago gave up twisting their tongues around the extraordinary name of their village. Just say *Woolsery* and you'll pass for a local...well, sort of...but whether you stumble through *Woolfardisworthy* or let *Woolsery* roll off your tongue, you will be warmly welcomed in this neighborhood.

However, that isn't quite the end of the problem, because you must also determine which Woolfardisworthy is your destination. Yes indeed, there are two Woolfardisworthys in Devon (when you've got a good thing...). Just remember, Rose Cottage is to be found near the Woolfardisworthy which is down the lane from the hamlet of Black Dog (pronounced *Black Dog*), which, speaking personally, has always been an easy way for us to remember that this is the Woolfardisworthy with the veterinarian. Perhaps you won't be needing a vet during your sojourn, in which case you might also choose to locate your Woolfardisworthy on the map just north of the busy market town of Crediton. Crediton doesn't have a vet, or at least it didn't back when we needed one, but it does have just about everything else. I mention this because it is possible that you may want to load up at the green grocer and the butcher, pick up a jug of wine at the off license and a few fresh loaves from the baker, and head up to Woolfardisworthy with the intention of getting away from it all. Well, if that's your pleasure, you couldn't pick a more glorious place to do it!

Rose Cottage is simply the picture perfect thatch cottage, with ancient thick cob walls covered by climbing roses and clematis. Inside, carefully preserved amidst all the modern conveniences, are all the makings of a character cottage, par excellence. Your reclusive mood will be no less sated by the wonderful rolling lawn and garden out back where you can sit and read to your heart's content or just listen to the brook tumbling over the little waterfall. However, if you suddenly get an itchy foot, there's only about a million things to see and do within a thirty mile radius.

ETB 5 Keys; Highly Commended

I. B-s
II.B-d
F-3
B-t
F-2
E$c   H$c
FP
LT$
TELc
TVV
W/D
DW MW
P-
S-S   MS
INS BK$
£186-447
S 5

Contact West Country Cottages, The Geminids, Priory Rd, Abbotskerswell, Devon TQ12 5PP
TEL 01144-1626-333-678 or FAX 01144-1626-336-678

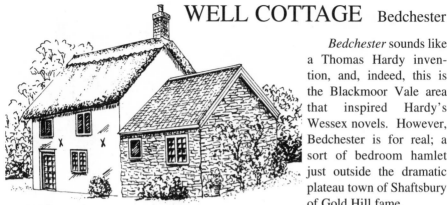

WELL COTTAGE   Bedchester

Bedchester sounds like a Thomas Hardy invention, and, indeed, this is the Blackmoor Vale area that inspired Hardy's Wessex novels. However, Bedchester is for real; a sort of bedroom hamlet just outside the dramatic plateau town of Shaftsbury of Gold Hill fame.

Well Cottage is a little whitewashed Tudor period house lost in a sea of mown lawn. Inside you will find a cavernous brick fireplace with a bread oven and pretty brasses mounted to its timber lintel. The downstairs gets a flood of light through pretty leaded windows, while upstairs the windows are set low, peeking out from under the thatch. The cottage is comfortably furnished with contemporary pieces.

ETB 3 Keys; Commended

I. F-2
II.B-d [2]
B-s
E$m H$m
FP
LT$
TELc
S-S   MS
INS
BK$
£144-342
S 5

Contact West Country Cottages, The Geminids, Priory Rd, Abbotskerswell, Devon TQ12 5PP
TEL 01144-1626-333-678 or FAX 01144-1626-336-678

THE CHANTRY
Bridport

Bridport is an essentially Georgian town, with its broad streets, which were at one time used to dry the locally made rope. Yet Bridport's location on Lyme Bay has always been strategic and the Norman conquerors of this land wasted no time building their fortifications here. The Chantry, or parts of it, almost certainly began as a Norman lighthouse and battlements. Later this stonework found its place in the ecclesiastical enterprise (hence the name), and now, thanks to the saving works of the Vivat Trust, it has been transformed into a holiday cottage and an income earner to save other deserving historic properties.

III.B-d
B-b
F-2
E&H
FPS
LT
TV
W/D
MW
S-S
INS
$515-735
S 2/4

Typical of all the Vivat Trust restorations, The Chantry is something of a masterpiece. The stone spiral staircase, stone casement windows, wall paintings, and medieval arches speak to The Chantry's history. The deep colors, rich fabrics, exquisite furnishings, and ingenious lighting speak to The Chantry's present, as a superb holiday let. All this and the Dorset coast too!

Contact Haywood Cottage Holidays, P.O. Box 878, Eufaula, Alabama 36072
TEL 334-687-9800 or FAX 334-687-5324

ROSE COTTAGE

Burton Bradstock

Here is the quintessential thatched cottage in an equally quaint English village. Burton Bradstock is noted for its 15th century church with the embattled central tower, now monumentally floodlit

I. F-1
II. B-d
B-t
B-s
F-3
E&H
FPG
LT
TV
W
DW MW
NS
OPEN
MS
INS
£290-530
S 5

at night and situated just across from Rose Cottage. Nearby is the ancient swannery at Abbotsbury and the still thriving, though no less steeped in history, town of Bridport.

The Cottage, itself, dates from the 1600s, with lovely wall sconce lighting, a *watch your head* ceiling in the upper landing, a splendid inglenook fireplace, and oodles of Merry Ole England character. Great effort has gone into the decor and furnishing, with plenty of nice homey touches, and, of course, first rate appliances and cozy central heating. Though the cottage exterior is dressed with pretty climbers and shrubbery, there is no garden, aside from a small patio.

DAWN COTTAGE Chideock

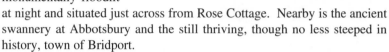

II. B-d
F-3
II.B-d
B-t
F-3
E&H
FPG
LT
TV
W
DW MW
E/HC
F-F MS
INS
£360-615
S 6

Situated between historic Bridport and fashionable Lyme Regis, Dawn Cottage is just a ten minute walk from the sea and is an ideal base for exploring this dramatic stretch of the Dorset coast. Golden Cap, the *cliff of cliffs*, is nearby on the coastal footpath. Literary pilgrims can readily see many of the sights through the eyes of Jane Austen, Thomas Hardy, and the still-in-residence John Fowles.

This spacious thatched home sits among manicured lawns and gardens, with handsome French doors rendering an airy feel to the downstairs public rooms. There is a cheerful bedroom suite, also located at garden level. You will find pretty floral soft furnishings, tasteful accent pieces and decoratives, and cozy wall sconce lighting. Also, as with all the Rural Retreats cottages, you will be welcomed with a basket of victuals and a nice bottle of vino.

Contact Rural Retreats, Station Road, Blockley, Moreton-in-Marsh, Gloucestershire, GL56 9DZ
TEL 01144-1386-701-177 or FAX 01144-1386-701-178

KNOWLE BARN

Nr Corfe Castle

Mr. Noel Freer of Church Farm is very proud of his barn, also called Knowle ...as well he should be, for here is one of the most imaginative barn conversions anywhere in Britain. In fact, there seems to something approaching a personal relationship between Noel Freer and his barn, Knowle. I'm tempted to call it an *old friendship,* and it is for sure that Noel Freer knows all about the history of his friend and will happily tell the whole story; how Knowle was built with extra thick walls in the early 19th century; how Knowle was granted a highfalutin stone roof rather than a common thatch *chapeau;* how Knowle was graced with ancient ship's timbers bearing the seal of the Royal Admiralty itself; and how the slates for Knowle came all the way from Wales on the new railway...all the sort of ancestral insights we are likely to collect about our life long confrere.

Nor is all this esteem necessarily just in the eye of the beholder. The pride of this statuesque cow palace was particularly invested in its flagstone floors...call it a bit of vanity on Knowle's part, for common barns with muddy feet have always looked up to the superiority of a stone floored neighbor. Knowing his friend's feelings in this regard, Mr. Noel Freer took extra pains to retain and spruce up Knowle's old flagstone floors when it came time to give his old chum a major facelift. Which actually brings us to the point of this little backgrounder. As we all know, old friends can also sometimes be old protagonists. It is a delicate matter, but it would appear that Knowle Barn was feeling just a bit of ire about Noel Freer back a few years ago; a sense of neglect, perhaps, though I'm sure there are two sides to that story. At any rate, it all came to a head during the hurricane of 1987, when in a fit of pique, Knowle Barn flung off one of its roof slates...they that came all the way from Wales on the

I. CS	
F-1	
F-3	
II.B-t [2]	
F-3	
B-b	
E$m	
H	
FPS$	
LT	
TELc	
TV	
W/D	
DW	MW
NS	
F-F	MS
INS	
£220-550	
S 8	

new railroad...and popped Noel Freer square on the head. Never was fraternity more put to the test. Did Noel Freer bring in the wrecking ball? No sir! Noel Freer brought in the best craftsmen from all around (that is, after pleading poor old Knowle Barn's case for a reprieve before the local authority for five years!), and, as the story most deservedly goes, the two old friends are proudfully reunited and have opened their doors for everybody to come for a visit. Suffice it to say, Church Farm is a very friendly place. And, if you come to the conclusion that Knowle Barn is one of the prettiest, most spacious, most handsomely furnished holiday cottages you've ever stayed in...well you won't get any argument from Noel or Knowle...or me.

ETB 4 Keys; Highly Commended.

Contact G.E.N. Freer, Church Farm, Church Knowle, Wareham, Dorset BH20 5NG
TEL 01144-1929-480-228

SCOLES MANOR BARNS

Corfe Castle

Corfe Castle is a beautiful village that wears its history on its sleeve...or perhaps I should say Corfe Castle wears its history like a crown. The *crown*, of course, is the Castle ruin, which dominates every perspective, giving visitors a memorable visual thrill and residents a deeply ingrained sense of identity. In this regard, Corfe Castle is much like my favorite French provincial town, Chinon on the Loire, though the former is really only a village in proportions. Like Chinon, the cast of characters who left their often bloody mark on Corfe Castle is legendary. King Edward the Martyr was murdered here in 988 and six hundred-fifty years later the Royalist garrison withstood Cromwell's troops for two years before surrendering. Parliament then ordered the complete destruction of the Castle, thereby providing us with this dramatic ruin of today.

Scoles Manor is long on history, as well. Originally built as a hall-house around 1300, it was subsequently enlarged into a small Jacobean manor in 1620. It is the oldest continuously inhabited dwelling in the parish of Corfe Castle and was named after the Norman knight, William de Scoville. The present owners, Peter and Belinda Bell, tell me that the clan Scoville in America trace themselves to an immigrant from here who decamped for Boston in 1662.

The three holiday accommodations are located in the 18th century stone threshing barn and attached dairy, which is about fifty yards from the manor, peacefully situated in their own courtyard with ethereal views of the Castle in the distance. These were converted in 1990, taking care to incorporate many of the old architectural features, while installing central heating and all the modern facilities. Within the very statuesque barn are two cottages, one with two bedrooms and the other with three. In both, the bedrooms are downstairs, with living areas and kitchens upstairs. The Dairy has four bedrooms with a large window in the living room, offering breathtaking views. All three cottages have new pine furniture and pleasant pictures of local sights.

Beach and golfing are nearby and the Purbeck Hills are wonderful for walks filled with amazing vistas. Our walking in these hills has generally been in the autumn, followed by a steaming bowl of Blue Vinny Soup, a unique specialty of the friendly pub in nearby Church Knowle. ETB 5 Keys; Highly Commended

E$m
H$m
LT
TELc
TV
W/D
DW   MW
NS
E/HC*
P-$
F-F   MS
TA
£175-775
S 4-8

Contact Peter & Belinda Bell, Scoles Manor, Kingston, Corfe Castle, Dorset BH20 5LG
TEL 01144-1929-480-312 or FAX 01144-1929-481-237

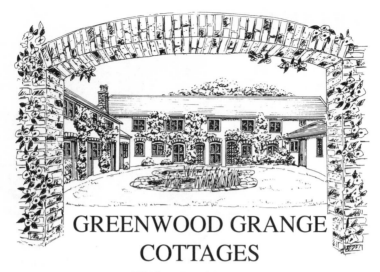

GREENWOOD GRANGE COTTAGES

Higher Bockhampton

Thomas Hardy pilgrims are almost at the *heart* of their quest here at Greenwood Grange in Higher Bockhampton. The novelist was born nearby in a thatch cottage, and Hardy's father built this impressive block of barns in 1849. Alas, however, for the real *heart* of Hardy one must take the pretty walk to the next village, Stinsford, where his heart was actually interred. This is but one of the many mandatory Hardy rambles to take in these parts, where all the place names have their Hardy doppelgangers. From *Upper Mellstock* (Higher Bockhampton) it is only a couple miles walk to *Casterbridge* (Dorchester), a simultaneous meander through some of England's most poignant pages of literature and beautiful rolling country.

Denise and David Hedges of Greenwood Grange offer fifteen very handsome cottages fashioned out of the old Hardy barns. Accommodating from two to six persons, the cottages are focused on a large, neatly landscaped, center court. Even as built by Hardy Senior, these stone buildings were very impressive, with decorative lintels over broad arched doors, now glassed to maximize the light and airy feeling in each cottage. Old and new architectural achievement has been complemented by a fine hand in interior design and decoration. By the standards of selection in this book, Greenwood Grange is a large holiday complex; yet the decoration of these cottages seems very personal. Each cottage comes alive with rich colors in paint and fabric, as well as pretty particulars: flowers, bows, pieces of china. There are welcoming furnishings throughout, from pretty floral living room suites to romantically draped canopy beds and honey pine chests.

Amidst all this Hardy interest, let us not forget that Dorchester was also a prominent Roman town and the area still abounds in associated sites. It is for sure that the Hedges haven't forgotten the Latin element, as evidenced by their flight of fancy in designing the indoor swimming/sauna /gym facilities around a Roman bath motif. What a good place to cool out after a long trek in pursuit of the *heart* of Hardy country!

ETB 4 Keys; Commended

E$m	H
FP*	
L;	T$
TV	
W/D$s	
MW	
P-*	
E/HC*	
S-S;	F-F
MS	TA
£208-715	
S 2-6	

Contact Greenwood Grange Farm Cottages, Higher Bockhampton, Dorset DT2 8QH   TEL 01144-1305-268-874

GATE LODGE

Longburton

The village of Longburton sits on the main road between Sherborne, with its Raleigh castle ruins and the "modern" castle packed with art treasures, and Dorchester, the gateway to Thomas Hardy Country and site of fascinating Roman digs. Nearby is the 1500-year-old Naked Giant of Cerne Abbas, and, at Abbotsbury may be your one chance ever to visit a swannery.

Gate Lodge began life as the Victorian gatehouse for the nearby Tudor mansion and was expanded recently into a very sizable...house size...cottage. The very modern interior decor is also very classy, with darkly stained maple ceilings and fitted maple cabinetry, contrasting with starkly white walls glowing under indirect light. Good books, interesting watercolors and a stone archway going to the dining room. The en-suite master bedroom and another twin downstairs effectively make this an all-on-one-level domicile for those who prefer to avoid steps.

I. B-q
F-4
B-t
F-3
II.B-t
F-4
E&H
FP
LT
TELin
TV
W/D
DW MW
S-S
INS
$620-1290
S 6

Contact Chapel House Cottages, P.O. Box 878, Eufaula, Alabama 36072
TEL 334-687-9800 or FAX 334-687-5324

ARMADA HOUSE Lyme Regis

Lyme Regis is a town deep in dramatic moods. For the past couple centuries Lyme has been a seaside resort, courting fashionable sun seekers. Yet, for me, it has always been the drizzly days when Lyme's unique atmosphere has emerged. In the mist and damp a stroll along its cobble streets or braving a walk out the long curving harbor wall known as *The Cobb* is sure to inspire the romantic imagination. It did for Jane Austen (*Persuasion*) and it still does for John Fowles (*French Lieutenant's Woman*), who continues to prowl these streets, sun and rain.

Armada House is the end property in a row of adjoining cottages on what was once the main road into Lyme Regis. This might well have been the lodgings of a character from one of these Gothic novels. Next door is the Ship Inn, and it is only a short walk down to the water. Even the name, *Armada House*, evokes history and romance, and is derived from the oak paneling in the sitting room that was reputedly salvaged from one of the tragic ships of the Armada debacle. There are other nautical bits and pieces to keep you in the mood and a four-poster *admiral's bed* to transport the imagination into slumber. Adjoining is Drake's Cabin, with a ground floor bedroom and an open plan living/kitchenette area upstairs. Drake's Cabin is only rented in conjunction with Armada House, though the latter may be taken alone.

ETB 4 Keys; Commended

ARMADA
II..B-d
B-t
B-s
F-3
DRAKES
B-d
F-3
CS
E$m
H$
FP$
LT$
TV
W/D
MW
NS P-
S-S   MS
INS
BK$
£168-636
S 6-10

Contact West Country Cottages, The Geminids, Priory Rd, Abbotskerswell, Devon TQ12 5PP
TEL 01144-1626-333-678 or FAX 01144-1626-336-678

OLD CHAPEL COTTAGE
Milton Abbas

Here in the peaceful heathland sits what has been called the model 18th century thatch village. The Old Chapel is not that old (b 1895), but it too adds character to this scenic place. In its conversion, the brick *Gothicized* chapel offers very spacious accommodation for a family, with separate rooms for living and dining and plenty of lawn and woods for run arounds. The beamed living room has a woodburning stove and a mix of older and modern furnishings. There are four bedrooms upstairs; a double with en-suite shower, two singles and another double.

This is Hardy Country, of course, and has something for everyone; *novel sights* for the Hardyites (*Casterbridge, Kingsbere, Weatherbury*), historic homes of various periods, and even a Tank Museum for young commandos and old soldiers.

I. F-1
B-s
II.B-d [2]
B-s
F-2
F-3
E&H
FPS
LT
TV
W
S-S
INS
$395-875
S 6

Contact Haywood Cottage Holidays, P.O. Box 878, Eufaula, Alabama 36072
TEL 334-687-9800 or FAX 334-687-5324

HIGHER WATERSTON FARM COTTAGES
Puddletown

This row of flint and brick stables has been converted into four exceptionally well designed cottages, open and spacious, yet with many character nooks and angles, as well as exposed posts and beams. Romney and Barn Cottages offer three bedrooms; Lleyn and Texel Cottages have two bedrooms. Texel has been carefully laid out for the disabled. Each cottage is furnished with a sparing but tasteful hand, rendering an airy and uncluttered feeling. There are nice teak tables and chairs, bright pine doors and fitted carpets throughout. Each cottage has a woodburning stove and first rate kitchen facilities. The exterior amenities include a tennis court and the limitless pleasure of walking the rolling pastures of the Hammicks' sheep farm... this is the heart of Hardy Country!

ETB 4-5 Keys; Commended

E$m
H$m
FPS
TELc
TVV
W/D
DW MW
E/HC*
TA
£215-410
S 2-6

Contact Carol Hammick, Higher Waterston Farm, Puddletown Nr Dorchester, Dorset DT2 7SW
TEL 01144-1305-848-208 or FAX 01144-1305-848-894

MARSH COURT Nr Sherborne

Marsh Court is a stone roofed manor house flanked by one of the most handsome stable yards in the region. Coach House Cottage forms one arm of the courtyard and backs onto an expansive lawn enclosed by a beech hedge. The cottage is all ground level and was historically the groom's quarters and tack room. The latter area now serves as the living room, with high ceilings, a big fireplace, a huge convertible sofa, and other commodious soft furnishings. There is a spacious master bedroom and a smaller twin. The kitchen is well equipped and has French doors opening on to the terrace and lawn, beyond which is the tennis court.

In addition, a completely independent wing of the Manor House, itself, is available for holiday accommodation. It sleeps four and is furnished with comparable good taste and at the same price.

ETB 3 Keys

COACH	
I.B-d	
B-t	
CS	
F-2	
E$	H$
LT$	
TELc	TV
W/D	
MW	
S-S	OPEN
MS	TA
£100-240	
S 4-5	

Contact Mrs. M. Fox-Pitt, Knowlton Court, Nr. Canterbury, Kent CT3 1PT
TEL 01144-1304-842-402 or FAX 01144-1304-842-403

PEEL TOWER Staindrop

There are the castles that were Gothic follies inspired by romantic imagination; then there are the castles that were all about the grim business of survival. Raby Castle, the 14th century fortress home of the Nevilles, is of the latter type and still looms huge and foreboding on the Durham landscape. Durham, it seems, has always been under assault, hardened by its position on the frontier with Scotland, then on the resource frontier of industrialization. Still, the rugged landscape of Durham, moor and mountain, has survived these man-made trials.

The Peel Tower cottage is fascinating in its historic venue and amazingly comfortable in its refurbishments. On the ground floor there is a spacious kitchen, as well as dining and lounge area with a large inglenook fireplace. There are en-suite twin bedrooms (brass beds) on the ground and middle floors; bathrooms with bidets. In good baronial fashion, the third floor is reserved for an impressive living room, with stone faced walls, open beamed ceiling, polished soft wood floors with colorful rugs, and yet another big inglenook fireplace. The immediate grounds of the Peel Tower include a patio/garden with lawn furnishings and a small stream. Raby Castle, itself, is open on a limited basis through the summer.

I. B-t	
F-4	
II. B-t	
F-3	
F-1	
III.B-s	
E	
H$m	
FP[2]	
LT	
TV	
DW	
S-S	
INS	
$530-1225	
S 5	

Contact Haywood Cottage Holidays, P.O. Box 878, Eufaula, Alabama 36072
TEL 334-687-9800 or FAX 334-687-5324

BERROW FARM · Ashleworth

Ashleworth sits midway along the meandering course of the lower Severn; and, ecclesiastically speaking, midway in the converging shadows of the Abbey Tower in Tewkesbury and the Cathedral Tower in Gloucester. This is the Severn Valley, with agricultural traditions going back to Roman times...*five horse land,* deep clay soils that required horse power in that number simply to pull a plow, but with the assurance of bounty that has also made this the land of huge tithe barns. Its bountiful rusticity is also evident in the pleasures and pastimes of the hardworking men of the Valley...cider and skittles, the former in good measure, the latter with a passion unequalled in all Britain.

Berrow Farm House is down a winding lane about a mile from the village and was once the bailiff's home for a large working estate. The honey gold Cotswold stone verily glows in the long light of afternoon. The accommodation is all on the second floor of a building adjoining the house; what was two hundred years ago built as a hayloft, the larder for the aforementioned horse power. The ground level entrance is to a hall with stairs leading up to the kitchen. This is a very complete kitchen right down to the spices in the rack, and there are two lovely sunny windows with views down to a pretty garden of lavender and roses. Through a glazed door we are into the sitting room. Not to be confused by a few exposed beams, this is no bare-utilities barn-conversion. Furnishings are a bit of everything, no design particularly, other than genuine homeyness and good quality. There is a rather elegant pine fireplace with tile panels which nearly match the Liberty print covers on the sofa and armchairs. A mahogany dining suite, small grandfather's clock, drop front secretary, pictures in ornate frames, plenty of books...a very pleasant home to return to after a day of touring.

Berrow Farm is ideally situated for visiting all of the highlights of both the Cotswolds and South Wales: Broadway and the Forest of Dean are within a half hour and bibliophiles won't want to miss nearby Ross-on-Wye. ETB 4 Keys; Highly Commended

II.F-2
B-t
E$m
H$m
FPE
LT
TEL   TV
W/D
P-BA
S-S
INS
TA
£160-225
S 2

Contact Cottage Holidays, Forest Gate, Frog Lane, Milton-U-Wychwood, Oxford OX7 6JZ
TEL 01144-1993-831-495 or FAX 01144-1993-831-095

LITTLE MANOR

Ashleworth

Ashleworth village is built on Saxon foundations along the banks of the River Severn. Until the dissolution of monasteries, Ashleworth Manor was occupied as a summer residence by the Lord Abbot of St. Augustine's Abbey at Bristol. The half-timbered house is thought to predate the 15th century, at which time considerable improvements were made, including the insertion of chimneys and intervening floors over the earlier *great hall* plan. Further building was carried out in keeping with the original style during the last two centuries.

Little Manor is a self contained wing of the manor house and is screened from the main house by a private garden. The whole property is surrounded by delightful gardens, including herbaceous borders, a formal rose garden, a *wild* area, as well as a grass tennis court. One enters the holiday accommodation through a small hall with access to the kitchen/dining room. The traditional kitchen features a pine hutch, and in the dining area there is a fine antique oak corner cupboard and gate-leg table. Leading off is the sitting room, with beamed fireplace, comfortable chairs, grandfather clock and a handsome 18th century mahogany bureau. From here one enters a small hallway with an antique oak bureau/bookcase.

Upstairs under the sloping beamed ceiling there is a master bedroom in beige and cream colors, with period oak furnishings and splendid views of the garden. Bath and shower facilities are separate. A second staircase leads to a landing with a single bedroom and a twin. All the beds have dual-weight duvets in pretty florals.

A tour of this historic region might as well begin with a short walk across the field to the medieval tithe barn and Court House...and then (purely for *historical* interest, of course) go another couple hundred yards to the riverside pub which has been owned and run by the same family since the 16th century.

Contact Cottage Holidays, Forest Gate, Frog Lane, Milton-U-Wychwood, Oxford OX7 6JZ
TEL 01144-1993-831-495 or FAX 01144-1993-831-095

I. F-1
II.B-d
F-3
F-1
III.B-t
B-s
E$m
H$m
LT
TEL
TV
W/D
P-BA
S-S
INS
TA
£165-300
S 5

THE LODGE Broadwell

Broadwell is a pretty little village with a handsome green, a Norman church harboring some remarkable grave stones from the early 1600s, and a convivial pub. The Lodge is situated just outside the village on the way up the hill toward Stow-on-the-Wold. From the outside, The Lodge is dressed out in the traditional Cotswold honey stone with broad modern windows. On the inside, The Lodge is dressed out with exceptional furnishings, including a very impressive canopied four-poster bed and many fine decoratives. Enthroned in the kitchen is the Rolls Royce of cooking conveyances...to wit the Aga, of which we have written much before. All in all, a most pleasant venue for a touring holiday of the Cotswolds.

I. F-1
II.B-q
B-t
F-2 [2]
E&H
FP
LT
TV
W/D
DW MW
P-
OPEN MS
INS
£450-640
S 4

NORTHWICK PARK Blockley

I suppose one runs the risk of understatement to say that the tiny village of Blockley is much the same as its neighbors...but then we must remember that the neighbors are the Campdens & the Bourtons, with the Swells and the Slaughters residing just down the road. But we need not judge Northwick Park by the company it keeps. Here is a fine old estate, with extremely attractive holiday accommodation offered in The Gallery, adjacent to the mansion.

In the Gallery you will find a sunken living room, flooded with light and filled with exquisite soft furnishings and bright pine accent pieces. The dining area is framed by a Palladian window with long views across the cobbled courtyard into the pastoral surrounds, of which there are thirty five acres designated for leisurely strolls by guests. The Gallery is a perfect venue for a couple traveling with a small child, as it has a proper nursery room adjacent to the master bedroom. Country Club membership is available for guests, and that Rural Retreats trademark, the basket of victuals and wine, will be there to greet you.

I. F-1
II.B-q
B-n
F-3
E&H
FPG
LT
TV
W/D
MW
P-
OPEN MS
INS
£320-485
S 2+

Contact Rural Retreats, Station Road, Blockley, Moreton-in-Marsh, Gloucestershire, GL56 9DZ
TEL 01144-1386-701-177 or FAX 01144-1386-701-178

ULLENWOOD COURT Nr Cheltenham

Approached along an avenue of red-twigged limes bordered by landscaped gardens, Ullenwood Court is a 100-acre hilltop property situated in the famous *Royal County* of Gloucestershire.

The area itself is nationally designated as one of *Outstanding Beauty* and the Cuttell family seem to have taken the designation as a royal command in their monumental reclamation of what was, during the war, the site of the 110th U.S. General Hospital. Where 3,000 servicemen once resided and healed in ninety hastily constructed buildings, Michael Cuttell began thirty-five years ago planting trees and shrubs...over 7000 of them! Today Ullenwood is a delightful country park which incorporates Neolithic sites as well as small monuments to that more recent conflict, such as the wartime mess with its painted wall murals depicting American history. Tucked away in the maze of lawns and gardens expect to find other little surprises: Victorian ornamental lamp posts, artifacts of a cider mill, and even a historic red telephone kiosk (in full working order!).

In 1977 the Cuttells converted a single building into three delightful holiday cottages. The gentle serenity felt amidst the Cuttells' landscape is carried into the design and decor of the cottages. Neat, uncluttered, bright and airy best describe these accommodations. Cider Mill Cottage is the largest with three bedrooms. The living room offers a soothing fusion of bright white walls and rose colored soft furnishings. The neutral fitted carpet acts as a cozy underlay for colorful occasional rugs.

Staddle Stones Cottage and Pine Trees Cottage each have two bedrooms. All the cottages have color coordinated modern kitchens, with pristine white counter tops. Windows in most rooms of all three cottages offer sweeping views across the lawns and gardens and flood the rooms with splendid natural light.

Recreationally, Ullenwood Court does not attempt to be a resort. However, there is a riding school on the estate and the first tee of the Cotswold Hills Golf Club is only 500 yards from the front door of your cottage. And, if you'd prefer to "play" the nags rather than ride them, the famous Cheltenham Race Course is nearby.

ETB 3 Keys; Highly Commended

E&H
FGP
LT
TELc TV
W/D
MW
S-S
INS
TA
£150-335
S 4-6

Contact: Mr & Mrs Michael Cuttell, Ullenwood Court, Ullenwood nr Cheltenham Spa, Gloucestershire GL53 9QS Tele 01144-1242-236-770; fax 01144-1242-254-680

EAST BANQUETING HOUSE
Chipping Campden

The ruins of Campden Manor have caught my eye for years, but little did I realize that lodgings were actually offered in the spectacular outbuildings of this tragic estate. In 1613 Sir Baptist Hicks built his mogul's palace at the edge of Chipping Campden. Thirty years later the Royalist forces spitefully *unbuilt* it, though gratefully they overlooked some of Sir Baptist's architectural *toys,* including this magnificent three story banqueting house. Hicks' descendants still own the ruins and have leased the Banqueting House to Landmark Trust for restoration and holiday rental.

This fascinating Jacobean miniature has two different faces; one side is a full three stories high, while from Sir Baptist's garden promenade the banqueting room appears to be single story shrine. Inside and out, the Banqueting House is rich in perspectives...the kind that hold you to long gazes; *entrancing!* The Trust has done its usual superb job of furnishing to make the mood. High marks also go to the Trust designers for locating the kitchen on the middle floor, rather than spoiling the ethereal space of banqueting room with an *open-plan* design. In addition to the double & twin bedrooms in the Banqueting House, itself, there is another en-suite twin located in a separate garden building, if required.

I. B-d	
	F-2
II. B-t	
E&H	
FPS	
LT	
S-S	MS
P-	
INS	
£563-935	
S 4-6	

Contact The Landmark Trust, Shottesbrook, Maidenhead, Berkshire SL6 3SW
TEL 01144-1628-825-925 or FAX 01144-1628-825-417

ORCHARD RISE
Chipping Campden

Chipping Campden is one of the great unspoiled villages of the Cotswolds, thanks to the protectionist Campden Trust, established sixty-five years ago. Orchard Rise is one of a set of three modern attached cottages which has been allowed to *rise* in this preservation area, which attests to its design character and

I. B-d	
	F-3
III.B-t+s	
	F-3
	B-d
	F-2
E&H	
FP	
LT	
TV	
DW	
	P-BA
S-S	
INS	TA
£285-450	
S 7	

quality. Orchard Rise is to the reader's left in the drawing; a three-storied cottage with pretty views over the rolling countryside and rooftops of the village. The ground level has the entrance hall with a reproduction dresser, stairs, and an en-suite double bedroom furnished in nice honey pine. The middle floor has the kitchen with fitted cabinets done in French limed oak and tiled counters. Off the kitchen is a small patio and garden area. The living room contains a three piece suite in floral fabrics and some nice reproduction pieces. Up another flight of stairs is a large twin bedroom, en-suite, with separate shower and a marble washstand, as well as a third bedroom, a double with en-suite luxury tub.

Contact Cottage Holidays, Forest Gate, Frog Lane, Milton-U-Wychwood, Oxford OX7 6JZ
TEL 01144-1993-831-495 or FAX 01144-1993-831-095

YEW TREE & OAKWOOD COTTAGES Ebrington

Master Kyte, a man of great power,
Lent 'em a cart to muck the tower
And when the muck began to sink
They swore the tower had grown an inch.

Back in the 14th century, Master Kyte was apparently among the townsmen of Ebrington who were upset by the showy height of the newly constructed church tower in neighboring Chipping Campden, then enjoying the prosperity of the wool trade. In a fit of rivalry the penurious citizenry of Ebrington conspired to have their own rather outdated church tower raised by natural means...to wit, the perpendicular Norman edifice was thoroughly manured in hopes that it might grow. While there is no evidence that this innovative technique was effective in this particular instance, it could be argued that a school of architecture, which *bloomed* in the 20th century, may have had its origins in medieval Ebrington.

Gratefully, a couple hundred years later when this farmhouse came to be constructed, the Ebrington builders had returned to traditional methods. The result is a thoroughly handsome bit of vernacular architecture, much in keeping with this delightful village of thatched roofs and vine covered walls. More recently the farmhouse has been subdivided into two holiday homes, Yew Tree and Oakwood Cottages. This latter transformation has been accompanied by a most careful renovation, preserving a wealth of historic detail (inglenook fireplaces, exposed beams, ancient stone kitchen floors, and much more) and enriching it with decorative charm which is surely the equal of anything offered in Chipping Campden.

As with all the Rural Retreat properties in the Cotswolds, Yew Tree & Oakwood guests enjoy privileges at the Walton Hall Country Club near Stratford-upon-Avon.

YEW
II.B-q
F-2
B-t [3]
F-3
£585-935
S 8
OAK-WOOD
II.B-q
F-2
B-t
B-s [2]
F-3
£450-640
S 6
BOTH
E &H
FP
LT
TV
W/D
DW MW
F-F MS
INS

Contact Rural Retreats, Station Road, Blockley, Moreton-in-Marsh, Gloucestershire, GL56 9DZ
TEL 01144-1386-701-177 or FAX 01144-1386-701-178

OWLPEN MANOR   Nr Dursley

Prince Charles calls Owlpen Manor *the epitome of the English village!* This is not only a golden testimonial, but also a pretty good clue as to the special quality of Owlpen Manor as a holiday destination. The Owlpen Estate does not appear as a resort complex at all, but rather as a sleepy hamlet...an ancient small village offering quiet accommodations in historic buildings, some grand, some quite modest (at least on the outside) tucked away discretely in idyllic situations within this romantic little out of the way valley.

The valley (the *Pen* of Owl*pen*) is uniquely private and is contained, *pen-like*, by steeply rising hills forested in beech. A stream meanders along the base; watering hole for the deer and badger, home for fish and fowl. Having trouble remembering exactly who you are in the big world back home? Try wandering over to the Owlpen mill pond with your fly rod around dusk; or take a sunrise walk up through the beech woods to the ridge and cast your eyes down on the wisps of smoke and mist in the *pen* below. **Here you are!** You're bound to be alone up here on the ridge, except perhaps for the ghost of the Saxon chieftain, Olla, who brought his flock to this *pen* about twelve centuries ago! Later inhabitants took the place name as their surname (*Olepenne*) and began building the present Manor House in the 15th century. By the early 20th century, however, the Manor House had been an uninhabited ruin for nearly a hundred years. Enter the noted Cotswold architect, Norman Jewson, who restored the Manor in the inter-war years, and then the Mander family, who began twenty years ago creating the holiday retreat we know today.

The accommodations at Owlpen begin in the Tudor Manor House, which is home for the Manders, but with two bedrooms set aside for B&B guests. Both rooms are museum quality in their sumptuous antique furnishings. The Queen Margaret Room is believed to have hosted Henry VI's bride during the War of the Roses, though not in the fine latter-day

ALL	
E	H$c
FP*	
FPS*	
LT	
TELc	
TV	
DW*	
MW*	
OPEN	MS
TA	
£145-670	
S 2-9	

Chippendale style four-poster bed which now graces this room. The Manor also has a sumptuous dining room and elegant drawing rooms for special occasion bookings.

Self catering guests have their choice of nine cottages dispersed around the Estate. Smallest is the split level studio apartment, framed characterfully within the giant crucks of the 15th century Tithe Barn. This apartment, as with all the Owlpen accommodations, may be rented by the night as well as week, and at rates which are quite simply among the very best values in Britain (far less than American brand name hotel rates!).

There are other romantic cottages for two at Owlpen. Summerfield Cottage is a prettily furnished accommodation set on its own across the brook. Because it is all on one level, Summerfield is much favored by older guests. Peter's Nest Cottage is the furthest afield from the Manor, set by a woodland spring. The cottage has a soothing decor and a modern woodburning stove, with a double bedroom upstairs. Manor Farm Cottage is, in fact, a modern cottage built in the traditional Cotswold style with mullioned windows and peaked gables. The interior is, as well, very historic, with a grand Hepplewhite four-poster bed, as well as another handsomely decorated twin room. Attached is Over Court, which can sleep five in three bedrooms or be joined with Manor Farm for a large house effect.

Very special is The Court House, dating from Stuart times and Grade I Listed. Really a banqueting house set in the formal garden amongst the giant yew trees, Court House doubled as a venue for the periodic dispensing of justice by the Lord of the Manor. With kitchen and facilities on the ground floor, one ascends a spiral staircase to bedrooms sleeping up to five on the two floors above, and wonderful views from the bull's eye windows in the peaked rooms atop.

Finally we come to the historic mill, dating perhaps from the 13th century, but in its present form since 1726, when the handsomely ostentatious leaded cupola and weathervane were added to attest to the prosperity of the Lord of the Manor. The Mill, with its wheel intact and the water still tumbling by, sets deep in the valley with the mill pond dammed up at the second story level behind. An open plan kitchen/living/dining room stretches out across the thirty foot ground floor under massive beams. The atmosphere here is warm and comfy, good quality furnishings that aren't trying to be elegant. On the second floor one finds cheerful bedrooms including one with a canopied four-poster bed and all season views through leaded glass panes. Up the wooden stairs there are two more tastefully furnished bedrooms, and above this the gantry cat-walk and mill workings of yesteryear. ETB 4 & 5 Keys; Highly Commended

GRIST M.	
II. B-q	
B-t	
F-2	
III.B-q	
B-t	
CS	
F-2	
E	H$c
FPS	
LT	
TELc	TV
DW	MW
OPEN	MS
TA	
£390-770	
S 6-9	

Contact Nicholas & Karin Mander, Owlpen Manor, Nr Dursley, Gloucestershire GL11 5BZ
TEL 01144-1453-860-261 or FAX 01144-1453-860-819

POUND COTTAGE   Kings Stanley

Kings Stanley is on the southern edge of the Cotswolds and is mentioned in the *Domesday Book*. The prosperity of the Stroud Valley was based on the wool trade and there is a unique heritage of mills alongside the network of rivers and the (now partly restored) Stroudwater canal system, dating from 1779.

Pound Cottage is on the edge of the village and overlooks what has traditionally been called *The Pound*, a triangle of grass where, historically, livestock which had strayed from the common land was impounded until a fine was paid at Court Farm opposite, dating from the 17th century.   Adjacent to this is a contemporary recreation park, formerly the Hanging Close for human stock that had *strayed,* but didn't get off so easily as Bosy and Fleecy. Pound Cottage is newly (re)constructed from Cotswold iron stone, with curious windows (rounds & half rounds) and an assemblage of interesting materials salvaged from local demolitions.

One enters through a coach-house door to a hall with terracotta floors. Off this lies a kitchen, nicely done in custom fitted pine, with a flagstone floor, black slate counter tops, and a china sink with old polished brass taps. There is a lovely pine hutch containing a collection of Blue Willow china, and the woodstove accesses both the living room and kitchen, making for a cozy atmosphere in each.

Into the living room...the ceiling stops short at the front windows of the cottage to provide a balustraded gallery to the main bedroom, with light spilling into both levels. This is a surprisingly spacious room, made all the more so by a huge pine framed mirror over the wall recess containing the wood stove. There is a handsome oval oriental carpet on the maple floors, and furnishings include a 1920's ball footed settee and side chairs recovered in pink and black Liberty fabric, several cane pieces and a pine-book case with reading for all tastes: English classics, Royals-lit, children's, etc. Upstairs, under oak purlins and a multiple angled ceiling, there is the galleried double, as well as a twin single bedroom. Inveterate tub readers will be thrilled by the old ball-footed Victorian in the upstairs bathroom.

ETB 4 Keys; Commended

I. F-1
II.B-d
B-t
F-2
E&H
FPS
LT
TV
W
DW
S-S
INS
TA
£185-295
S 4

Contact Cottage Holidays, Forest Gate, Frog Lane, Milton-U-Wychwood, Oxford OX7 6JZ
TEL 01144-1993-831-495 or FAX 01144-1993-831-095

SUNNYSIDE COTTAGE

Lower Swell

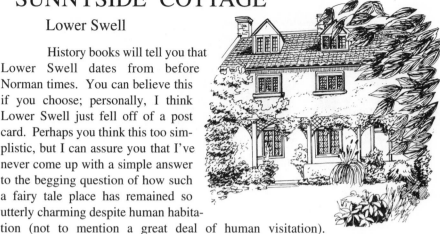

History books will tell you that Lower Swell dates from before Norman times. You can believe this if you choose; personally, I think Lower Swell just fell off of a post card. Perhaps you think this too simplistic, but I can assure you that I've never come up with a simple answer to the begging question of how such a fairy tale place has remained so utterly charming despite human habitation (not to mention a great deal of human visitation).

However, upon reflection, I must confess that everybody I've met in this village seems to have tumbled from the same colorful post card. Quite simply this is a magical place.

Sunnyside Cottage fits the picture in every way. Set it a picturesque garden, we enter under a veil of lattice and vinery to rooms done in primary colors and polished pine. You will find very comfy furnishings and open fires in both the living and dining rooms. There are dual stairs, making Sunnyside Cottage particularly well suited for the privacy requirements of companion parties.

II.B-q
B-q+s
F-3 [2]
III.B-t [2]
E&H
FP [2]
LT
TV
W/D
DW MW
OPEN MS
INS
£450-640
S 6-8

Contact Rural Retreats, Station Road, Blockley, Moreton-in-Marsh, Gloucestershire, GL56 9DZ
TEL 01144-1386-701-177 or FAX 01144-1386-701-178

FOLLY FARM COTTAGES Tetbury

Folly Farm is only a short walk from the center of the Cotswold character town of Tetbury, an Elizabethan market town made rich and famous by the wool trade. Today, however, the Bentons of Folly Farm milk Friesian cattle, rather than woolies, and offer ten very well done holiday cottages fashioned out of the old barns. The long and varied history of agrarian enterprise here is indicated by the cottage names: *Churn, Kiln, Cowbyres, Weigh House, Wheelwrights, Cider Loft* and *Bull Pen*. Whichever you choose, from those suited for couples to Bull Pen, which sleeps ten, you will find it very well appointed in a country style with all the modern amenities. All are carpeted and have central heating, and some are suitable for the partially disabled. In addition, the Bentons offer Folly Cottage, an 18th century detached house lost in its own sweet garden, which sleeps nine.

ETB 3 & 4 Keys; Commended

E&H
FPS*
LT
TV
W/D$s
DW* MW
E/HC*
F-F MS
£140-640
S 2-10

Contact Julian Benton, Folly Farm Cottages, Tetbury, Gloucestershire GL8 8XA
TEL 01144-1666-502-475 or FAX 01144-1666-502-358

TEWKESBURY HOLIDAY COTTAGES

Tewkesbury

Margaret Lucas and her husband have been collecting historic Tewkesbury houses and renovating them for holiday accommodations for the past twenty years. I'd say that their pride in Tewkesbury, itself, is about equal to their pride in their house projects. In both cases it is completely justified.

The old market town of Tewkesbury, one of England's twelve *Gem* Towns, has been settled since pre-Roman times. The town lies at the confluence of the Rivers Avon and Severn in the lush Vale of Evesham, sheltered by the Malvern Hills to the north and the Cotswolds about ten miles to the south. Rich in medieval, Tudor and Georgian architecture, the little town is dominated by the magnificent 12th century Abbey which has the most massive Norman tower in Europe. Surrounded by fertile meadows and streams, this rich manor often belonged directly to the early kings of England. Today, glorious Tewkesbury is an architect's and historian's dream. The magnificent Abbey notwithstanding, Tewkesbury is not a heavily *touristed* town; indeed, as I have related elsewhere in this book, a visitor is far more likely to be adopted by the locals than ignored. Mrs. Lucas' affection for her town is quite wide spread, and that affection seems to apply to any visitor who shows an interest in Tewkesbury's amazing landmarks.

Tewkesbury Holiday Cottages are all quietly situated in the most picturesque part of town, a stone's throw from the Abbey and thirty yards from the River Avon. The exception is Apple Tree Cottage, which is located in the little village of Tredington, three miles south of Tewkesbury. The town houses were originally craftsmen's work buildings, built during the 18th century. Stonemason's House (pictured next page) has its own private little paved garden with traditional English

APPLE
I. B-t [2]
F-3
II.B-t
B-d [2]
B-s
F-2
F-3
E$ H$
L; T$
TELm
TV
W/D
DW MW
F-F
OPEN
MS TA
£200-600
S 12

plantings: snowdrops, daffodils, mint, thyme, sage, native geraniums, Canterbury bells, etc. One enters Stonemason's House through a wide old Georgian door, opening into a square hall with tile floor. To the right is the kitchen, clean white walls and cabinetry, all very neat and tidy. Off the hall to the left is the sitting room, with a pair of large old sofas, polished pine floors and a large Hamadan rug. French windows open out onto the scented garden. Stairs curve up out of the sitting room to the upper floor bedrooms which have Berber wool carpeting throughout.

Apple Tree Cottage (pictured above) is superb; a richly timbered 16th century yeoman's house, fully restored, with Laura Ashley decor and furnished mostly in solid oak. All the modern conveniences are present, but discreetly inconspicuous. This is a big house, sleeping up to a dozen guests, and has a large garden as well. Apple Tree is much in demand and tends to be let for several weeks at a time.

The Lucases are expanding their offerings as we go to print. The Monk's Barn will be available in 1995. This handsome 13th century monastery barn, which has served English kings, as well as the Benedictine monks, looks straight across to the Abbey and its fine old grounds (which are floodlit at night ...and flooded with music quite often, as well).

| STONE |
| MASON |
| I. F-1 |
| II.B-t |
| B-s |
| B-d |
| F-3 |
| E$m H$m |
| L; T$ |
| TELm |
| TV |
| W/D |
| MW |
| OPEN MS |
| TA |
| £150-325 |
| S 5 |

It should be noted that the Lucases have a somewhat unique pricing policy, charging by the person in such a fashion as to make the larger houses available to couples and small parties at rates that are comparable to renting a one bedroom cottage. Indeed, a couple will look far and long for rates as generous as £195 for Stonemason's in high season; or £260 for Apple Tree, also in high season! ETB 4 Keys; Highly Commended

Contact Margaret Lucas, Tewkesbury Holiday Cottages, The Manor House, Mitton, Tewkesbury GL20 7EA   TEL/FAX 01144-1684-293-794

TYTHE BARN COTTAGES
Winchcombe

Winchcombe, population 5000, is set in the rolling Cotswold Hills Country and was the historic capital of the ancient kingdom of Mercia. Nearby is Sudeley Castle, the final resting place of Queen Catherine Parr. Stratford-upon-Avon, Oxford, and all of the picturesque gem villages of the Cotswolds are within a thirty-minute radius. Tythe Barn patrons also enjoy recreational privileges at the nearby Hotel DeLa Bere, including heated pool, tennis, and sauna facilities.

Tythe Barn Cottages, four in number, began life in the 18th century as stone barns. They have been sympathetically converted to holiday use, and very handsomely furnished. Forge Cottage is the largest, sleeping six in three bedrooms, including two doubles and two bathrooms. The soft furnishings here, as with all the cottages, are especially noteworthy for their pretty floral fabrics, with bright piping, all color coordinated to the drapery. Blacksmith Cottage also sleeps six and features interesting exposed stone walls, with upstairs bedrooms tucked under the beamed eaves. Horseshoe Cottage will accommodate five, and Anvil is a sweet little hideaway for two, with pretty tie back drapes pulling across the archway separating kitchen and sitting room.   ETB 5 Keys; Highly Commended

| E&H |
| FPE* |
| LT |
| TELc |
| TVV |
| W/Ds |
| DW MW |
| S-S MS |
| INS |
| £160-500 |
| S 2-6 |

Contact Geoff and Hazel Bourne, Tythe Cottage, Cowl Lane, Winchcombe, Glos. GL54 5RA
TEL 01144-1242-603-855 or FAX 01144-1242-604-149

PAX COTTAGE   Stanton

From an architectural perspective these huge Cotswold barns are simply amazing; monuments to the productivity of the heart of England and to the tax and tithing system that filled them with grain and all sorts of produce. They were, in fact, great feudal warehouses, not to be confused with cow sheds. The Grade II Listed barn that once served Stanton Manor has been converted into three cottages, including Pax. The barn dates from 1640 and the one time mistress of this estate was none other than Catherine Parr, the lucky wife...that is the surviving one...of Henry VIII.

Driving past the riding school and cricket field along the horseshoe lane that serves as main street in the picturesque tiny village of Stanton, one is not likely to notice that the three story thatched structure is anything but a great Tudor barn. What one notices are the massive plank doors facing the lane, skirted by a high foundation of golden Cotswold stone upon which rests the exposed timbers of perpendicular Tudor framing. Only from behind does the Stanton Manor Barn admit its domesticity; three very carefully designed cottage fronts coiffured in thatch finery. Cotswold stone walls make for individual front garden entrances, all nicely landscaped.

The ground floor arrangement could as well be in a modern bungalow; two bedrooms, a queen and twin, with some quite interesting 19th century furnishings looking like they wanted to be in more characterful premises. Up a flight of stairs and the picture changes dramatically. Vertical! Here is that great barn you saw from the outside; here are the great crucks and beams you knew had to be. This is wonderful bold space with fabulous light and views of the Cotswold escarpment. There is a lovely older sofa suite and dark green carpets and nice decoratives. Up amongst the web of beams there is a balustraded gallery with a double bed, and beneath it a very serviceable galley kitchen. This may be the best bargain in the Cotswolds.

ETB 3 Keys; Commended

| I. B-q |
| B-t |
| F-4 |
| III.B-d |
| IV.F-4 |
| E&H |
| L-BA |
| TELc |
| TV |
| MW |
| P-BA |
| £180-300 |
| S 6 |

Contact Mrs. D. Smoothy, North Lodge, Home Farm, Havering-atte-Bower, Essex RM4 1QB
TTEL/FAX 01144-1708-340-635

SUDELEY CASTLE COTTAGES Winchcombe

Sudeley Castle is certainly one of the most visited historic properties in England, and deservedly so. Perhaps Sudeley can not be counted among the nation's very grandest, nor its most architecturally treasured, but on both scales this castle is not without significance. Rather, it is to its continuous royal associations that we must turn to explain Sudeley Castle's fascination. During Sir Thomas Seymour's tenure, Henry VIII and Anne Boleyn stayed here, and, of course, the good Sir Thomas subsequently took in the widow Queen Katherine Parr and made her his wife. With Katherine came the little Princess Elizabeth and the ill-fated Lady Jane Grey. Later, another doomed *head* of state, Charles I, took up residency during the Civil War. This did not endear the Castle to the spiteful Mr. Cromwell, who ordered that the much used royal retreat be *slighted!* Slighted it was, and left in ruin for a couple centuries until its restoration became the mission of the Dent family. The Dents still reside at Sudeley Castle, in the persons of Lord and Lady Ashcombe.

There are a total of seventeen holiday accommodations around the periphery of the Estate. For the most part these delightful old Cotswold stone buildings have always been human domiciles, presumably housing retainers and villagers associated with the castle enterprise. Today's guests have complete access to the extraordinary grounds and eight beautiful garden areas around the Castle. Being part of the contemporary Castle *village*, guests also have free access to Sudeley Castle, itself, during the regular visiting hours.

The cottages vary immensely in design and decor, though they are consistently well furnished and prettily decorated. Considerable effort has been put to carrying through interesting interior themes: a nautical motif for the Lord High Admiral Flat; a Victorian dowager theme in the Emma Dent Cottage; Georgian touches in the George III Apartment; Tudor furnishings in the Anne Boleyn Gatehouse Cottage, etc. The cottages accommodate from two to seven guests.

ETB 4 Keys; Commended

E&H	
LT	
TELc	
TV	
S-S	
MS	
TA	
£153-495	
S 2-7	

Contact The Cottage Secretary, Sudeley Castle, Winchcombe, Gloucestershire GL54 5JD
TEL 01144-1242-602-308 or FAX 01144-1242-602-959

FOREST GLADE COTTAGE

Bartley

This peaceful little cottage sits back with a rail fenced paddock in front. To the rear there is the open heathland of the New Forest, with ponies and cattle ranging freely as they do in the moorlands of the West Country. The grounds around Forest Glade Cottage and its parent house, where the owners live, are a bucolic picture of lush green pasturage dotted by pretty flowering cherries and chestnuts, silver birch and oak. The cottage dates from the turn of the century and offers *neat as a pin* convenience as a base for   touring the south coast or for just relaxing with a bit of golf at the numerous courses in and around the New Forest. Downstairs there is a sitting/dining room, comfortably furnished with an old rose design cottage suite and a good log burning stove in the fireplace. The kitchen is newly fitted and has pretty views through the Dutch doors. Upstairs there are two bedrooms, and the garden amenities include a brick built barbeque.

II.B-d	
B-t	
F-3	
E&H	
FPS	
LT	
TELin	
TV	W
F-F	MS
INS	TA
£250-370	
S 4	

Contact Foxhills Properties, The Old Vicarage, Netley Marsh, Southampton, Hants SO4 2GX
TEL/FAX 01144-1703-660-177

POND COTTAGE

Droxford

Ah! to be a storybook English hedgehog and live in a charming little snug over the pixie bridge between the ancient garden wall and the romantically fenced pond of lilies; there among the pretty flowers to bask in the bliss of privacy bordering on invisibility...erh, that is, with one other lucky little hedgehog. Pond Cottage is, indeed, hedgehog heaven, with its sunny spacious open plan, including a double bed and a convertible sofa, as well as a fully fitted kitchenette and separate shower room.

E$	H$
LT	
TV	
W-BA	
MW	
P-BA	
S-S	INS
$305-525	
S 2-3	

And what would a pair of lucky little hedgehogs do on the other-side of this blissful sanctuary. For sure, they would join the Wayfarers Walk right at the cottage wall. Then they would take in a play or two at the famous Chichester Festival Theatre (30 minutes away), and along the way they might do as we always do when in this neighborhood; that is, have a romantic lunch at Hambledon's Bat and Ball country pub, the birthplace of cricket.   ETB 3 Keys; Commended.

Contact Chapel House Cottages, P.O. Box 878, Eufaula, Alabama 36072 TEL 334-687-9800 or FAX 334-687-5324

LADYCROSS ESTATE   Beaulieu

The proprietors of the Ladycross Estate invite you to leave your humdrum existence behind and have a fantasy holiday. They've provided several quite marvelous thematic stage sets for you to step through the looking glass. The Estate, itself, is in reality a piece of *the otherside*...established by William the Conqueror in 1067 as a hunting retreat; just a little place for an invasion-weary Norman king to escape from the humdrum routine of conquest...conquest...conquest! William thought big in the hideaway mode (as in all else) and the result of his fantasy retreat is what we now call the New Forest, 150 square miles of wild deer and free range ponies. In the middle of it all, at the pretty village of Beaulieu (deNormanized pronunciation: *Bulee*), is the Ladycross Estate, which belonged to the Crown until 1971. The Lodge remains a family home, but the servants quarter mews have been reborn as luxury accommodations of very particular sorts. The *sort* is in the *name*.

THE ROYCE takes its theme from the Rolls of the same name, and was no doubt inspired by Ladycross friend and neighbor, Lord Montagu of Beaulieu, who has developed one of the world's premier vehicular museums just down the road. The otherside of the looking glass in this instance is all grey, silver and pink (your traditional RR colors), with all manner of Rolls memorabilia. Even the TV, video and stereo are hidden behind a cabinet door fashioned as a RR grill. *THE ROYCE* is a one bedroom romantic *trip,* with a four-poster bed and dreamy fabrics of white and pink in the French bow motif. Romance gives nothing to mere functionality in the *toilette,* where one is greeted by a large corner tub, dual basins, and bidet in your traditional RR spend a penny colors of pink and silver.

UPSTAIRS DOWNSTAIRS is dedicated to Mrs. Bridges...who actually probably never dreamed of stepping through the upstairs looking glass (traditionally, a green baize door), but if she had...! Both levels of Edwardian life are in this up & down two bedroom cottage. If you think Mrs. Bridges' labors were all too grueling, you never cooked on an Aga, the Rolls Royce of English kitchens. Some Aga models were roughly the size of a Silver Ghost, with as many "extras", but the one in this cottage is of more modest proportions...leaving room for an enormous open fireplace. Yes, there are all the modern utilities tucked away among Mrs Bridges late-Victorian implements, gadgets and cookbooks. Upstairs you will find two delicious bedrooms (twin or double, as you wish), one done in Jade green, the other in crimson with coronet beds.

FISHERMAN'S TALES (sleeps 4-6), *POOP DECK* (sleeps 4), *COACHMAN'S HALT* (for two), or *ROYAL BOX* (for two); all offer an instant new persona for a single night, weekend, or the week. Incidentally, one doesn't have to be Chancellor of the Exchequer to afford a Ladycross cottage. For example, a one night stay for a couple in *THE ROYCE* (with breakfast hamper) costs about as much as a plain room at the Boston Sheraton!

E$c
H$c
FP*
FPS*
LT
TELc
TVV
W/D
DW
F-F MS
INS
VAT$
TA
£199-630
S 2-6

Contact the Ladycross Estate Office, Beaulieu, Hampshire SO4 27QL
TEL 01144-1590-22973 or FAX 01144-1590-22860

LUTTRELL'S TOWER

Eaglehurst

It is believed that Mssr Luttrell was something of a smuggler, despite his seat in the Parliament of Westminster. If so, this splendid tower, with its crow's nest view of all navigational movement on The Solent and its secret tunnel down to the beach, might have served him well. A bit showy, perhaps, but by all accounts Temple Luttrell had a penchant for being in the thick of things...which may explain his premature demise in Paris during the French Revolution. The Tower has never ceased to attract attention; Queen Victoria fancied buying it, but then opted for Osborne across the water on the Isle of Wight. Marconi moved in with his wireless at one point, and the Welsh genius architect, Sir Clough Williams-Ellis, enhanced the noticeability of Luttrell's Tower considerably by the addition of a monumental staircase down to the beach. Well, what good is a folly, anyway, if not for a bit of exhibitionism!

Luttrell's Tower may be bold, but it is not brash, less still crass. In fact, inside and out, the Tower is a masterpiece of design and refined detail, with lovely Georgian plaster and wood work. Landmark Trust's decorative department has skillfully exploited the streams of light flowing through The Tower and filled it with an array of interesting period furnishings. A turnpike stairs spirals from the basement to the look-off. The third floor room is reserved for living and dining, with a tiny kitchenette tucked in a corner.

I. B-t
F-1
II.B-d
F-2
E&H
LT
F-F
MS
INS
£578-954
S 4

Contact The Landmark Trust, Shottesbrook, Maidenhead, Berkshire SL6 3SW
TEL 01144-1628-825-925 or FAX 01144-1628-825-417

HAWTHORN COTTAGE

Emery Down

This little Victorian cottage stands in a pretty garden of camellias and lilacs, and is surrounded by the open heath of the Crown-owned New Forest. Emery Down is just a mile or so from Lyndhurst, the principal village of the National Park, while the beaches of Bournemouth and the yachting center at Lymington are only a short drive away. Hawthorn Cottage also provides a convenient base for day tripping to the Isle of Wight.

The cottage has undergone complete refurbishment in 1992 and has a fresh and airy feel, from the new fitted carpeting under foot to the pristine white walls. There are some handsome pieces of traditional furnishing: the oak sideboard, a dark oak dining suite, and in the living room a comfortable wood framed three piece suite.

I. F-3	
II.B-d	
B-t	
B-s	
F-2	
E&H	
LT	
TELin	
TV	
W	MW
F-F	MS
INS	
£270-410	
S 5	

Contact Foxhills Properties, The Old Vicarage, Netley Marsh, Southampton, Hants SO4 2GX
TEL/FAX 01144-1703-660-177

ROSE COTTAGE Lymington

Want to summer in England and winter in Madeira this year, but only have a week's holiday? God knows, it's a common enough predicament! But take heart, there's a solution: Rose Cottage in sunny Lymington...by all exterior appearances merely a modest fisherman's row house, but you'll be sending me lots of *obrigados* for this one!

To describe Rose Cottage as a bijou among cottage interiors would not be misplaced. The ground floor has been conceived in the Jacobean style, complemented by an eclectic assortment of beautiful furnishings and amazing curiosity pieces. Upstairs slips into a more Victorian mode, albeit, again with acquisitive curiosity and even humor, rather than period discipline. One might guess all this is the work of a clever professional designer out to tilt some fashion windmills....one would be right!

Back to the living/dining room. Here's the picture: large hand hewn blackened oak center beam with interesting knees braced against the pristine whitewashed walls...an ornate open fireplace...hand carved oak staircase...more oak carving in the doors...French windows with a hand painted roller blind...an ornate darkly varnished chair rail around the entire room...an intricately cut lintel panel over the doors to the garden, affecting the roof line of a Moorish palace...rich hanging tapestries, an ancient mariner map, plate rails with china treasures in flowing blue hues, all sorts of bric-a-brac from Aladdin's cupboard...on and on it goes.

It's lucky I'm telling you all about these things, because you probably won't notice. No, your eyes are going to be glued to the wainscotting...HOLY VINHO VERDE, Isabella!...the place is completely plastered in 17th century hand painted (Wedgwood blue and porcelain white) Portuguese tiles. You're suddenly in a tropical floral jungle on the mountain terrace of a *quinta* high above Funchal...you're gazing out onto an azure blue sea and salivating for *pao doce* and chilled *vinho verde*. "This can't be real," you say. You look through the Moorish arch out onto this Lymington patio...by god, it *is* a tropical floral jungle! You step outside into the tiny walled garden with the pretty hand painted tile mural; there *is* a sea breeze (it *is* the same ocean, after all!)....Later that evening, after a repast of *bacalhau* washed down with a sturdy *Dao,* you decide to take your little glasses of sweet Malmsey and investigate the upper environs...the "Victorian bit."

Up the Porto-Jacobean staircase observing the hand painted cornices and dado rails with wallpaper from the Holly Hill collection. First a master bedroom in restful lavender colors, and a fitted cupboard with hand-painted panels and lined lace curtains. Along further is a single bedroom (for child or chaperon) with more pretty hand-painted furniture. But have we lost our Portuguese dream world? Not on your life...step into the bathroom! More Portuguese tile murals, and solid brass fittings throughout...even the toilet brush has a brass handle (which reminds me of an incident in a *quinta* up the Duoro some years back...but, well, that's another story....

I. CS
II.B-d
B-s
F-2
E
H
FP
LT
TEL
TV
W
P-
S-S
INS
$490-855
S 3-5

Contact Chapel House Cottages, P.O. Box 878, Eufaula, Alabama 36072 Tel 334-687-9800 or Fax 334-687-5324

FOREST BANK COTTAGE

Lyndhurst

This 18th century cottage was built as a home for the gardener at the Countess Errol's Forest Bank House here in the ancient capital of the New Forest. Today the cottage sits amidst its own pretty garden, with a wide variety of ornamental trees and flowering shrubs, plus plenty of lawn to enjoy a ball game or tea on the green. Lyndhurst, itself, is an attractive setting, and the cottage is but a three minute stroll from the village teashops, passing Queens House, the village church, and the Verderers Hall, where the King's agent held court over the centuries. Turning the other direction from the cottage, our walk takes us to the open forest at Swan Green and the ancient beech woods beyond, or along Pinkney Lane to the hamlets of Bank and Gritnam.

The owners of Forest Bank Cottage have carefully renovated the property to reveal some truly remarkable historic features. The low oak beamed ceilings, the crooked door frames, and the steep & winding polished oak staircase give the cottage its old world atmosphere. In fact, several rooms show off the original oaken frame-work of the cottage, with plenty of exposed brick and plaster panels to enhance the historic feel. One enters from a quaint porchway directly into the dining room which features a traditional large inglenook fireplace with a bread oven. This room is furnished in dark oak, more or less in a Jacobean style with heavy turned legs on the dining table and a matching sideboard. There is an assortment of decoratives and rustic antique pieces, such as the old butter churn, as well as books and games for evening relaxation. The sitting room is fashioned in a more modern idiom, with a small brick fireplace featured in the corner and a picture window overlooking the attractive garden. The cottage has central heating.

The sleeping arrangements are comprised of a double bedded room, decorated in lilac and pale green, with a Victorian fireplace; a larger twin bedded room with the original 18th century fireplace and exposed beams; and a cosy twin room on the ground floor with low ceilings, making it the "children's room". The positioning of the bathroom, which is off a landing midway up the oak stairwell, lends yet more character to Forest Bank Cottage.

I. B-t
F-3
II.B-d
B-t
E&H
LT
TELin
TV
W
MW
F-F
MS
TA
£220-410
S 6

Contact Foxhills Properties, The Old Vicarage, Netley Marsh, Southampton, Hants SO4 2GX
TEL/FAX 01144-1703-660-177

WISTERIA COTTAGE

Nr Rockbourne

Wisteria, the vine, has always evoked granny memories for me, and this cottage fits the picture perfectly. Lost in a wild little garden with a trickling brook flowing through it, Wisteria Cottage and its attached twin (on left) are about a mile from the village of Rockbourne. Rockbourne, itself, is very picturesque, with its one long street running parallel to the stream that is bridged for each house on the north side. Wisteria Cottage is comfortably furnished with plenty of granny charm downstairs and three bedrooms upstairs peeking out from under thatched brows.

ETB 3 Keys; Commended

I. F-1
II.B-d
B-t
B-s
F-2
E
H$
FPE
LT$
TELc
TV
W/D
S-S
MS
INS
BK$
£144-342
S 5

Contact West Country Cottages, The Geminids, Priory Rd, Abbotskerswell, Devon TQ12 5PP
TEL 01144-626-333-678 or FAX 01144-1626-336-678

1 KINGS HUTS   Nr Lymington

Lymington is a yachtsmen's paradise; great sailing, great boat watching, and great people watching. One doesn't want to miss Saturday market on the main street of this ancient town! This cottage is half way between the beach and cultural pleasures of Bournemouth, and the historic maritime city of Southampton on The Solent, with its curious four tides per day. At Lymington you are also in a privileged position for the ferry line-up to day trip on the Isle of Wight.

Grade II Listed, No. 1 Kings Huts is an exceptionally cozy berth for the mariner or landlubber...simple, laid back soft furnishings with odd decorative bits (including some wonderful Caribbean shells) and a Baxi open fire. There are two bedrooms, a double and twin, and an enclosed garden with barbeque. The cottage is very accessible to golf, fishing, and equestrian activities; and, for the car buff, Lord Montagu's National Motor Museum at Beaulieu is a *must-see*.

I. F-3
II.B-d
B-t
E&H
FP
LT
TELc
TVV
W/D
MW
NS
$305-525
S 4

Contact Chapel House Cottages, P.O. Box 878, Eufaula, Alabama 36072 TEL 334-687-9800 or FAX 334-687-5324

OLD STABLE COTTAGE   Rockbourne

This is an exceptionally pretty cottage, inside and out, sitting in an interesting location, which is at the same time strategically positioned for a holiday of mixed coastal and interior pleasures. You are at the edge of William the Conqueror's old play-ground, the New Forest, where the ponies range freely, except, that is, on the several golf courses. Serious marine enthusiasts (and marina gawkers, like myself) are only a few minutes away from the best in British boating. The Isle of Wight is a short ferry hop away, the symphony in Bournemouth is an easy after-hours drive, and the spire of Salisbury Cathedral is (practically) in sight. And, if fishing is your pleasure, our young son would highly recommend a nearby reservoir where he hooked a 5 pound Rainbow a couple years ago. So much to do and see, and such a charming home to return to after each excursion.

The Old Stable is a 17th century exposed timber frame and brick nogging building; a real character structure that has not been abused in conversion to domestic occupancy. The thatch is deep and decorative, the bricks as mellow as very old Burgundy, the exposed timbers, inside and out, beg reflections on antiquity. There is a modest brick fireplace with an interesting undulating flu and a handsome oak lintel; not original, but a reasonable likeness of a fixture that might have warmed the grooms' quarters. The interior walls are cleanly white-washed and work with the latticed windows to make the cottage airy and bright. There are very interesting pictures and equally handsome framing, a prized old sampler, and some unique brass decoratives. The furnishings are a mix of comfortable wingbacks and good quality antique occasional pieces. The kitchen is fitted and furnished in warm honey pine, with an antique pine hanging cupboard, bulls-eye mirror, and brass lighting.

Exterior amenities include a detached conservatory, lawned garden and immediate access to the public footpath behind the owner's paddock.

I. F-3
II.B-d
B-t
F-3
E   H$
FP
LT
TELin
TV
W/D-BA
S-S
INS
$490-855
S 4

Contact Chapel House Cottages, P.O. Box 878, Eufaula, Alabama 36072
TEL 334-687-9800 or FAX 334-687-5324

HORSEBRIDGE STATION

Nr Stockbridge

Calling all Railroad buffs! A holiday on the old Sprat & Winkle Line is in the offing. In days of yore you might have traveled up from Southampton in this Sprat & Winkle carriage; these days you'll enjoy a stationary *trip* on the idyllic rural siding of the wonderfully restored Horsebridge Station. Your berth is strictly first class! Living/dining room, complete galley kitchen, and two (yes, two!) bedrooms, both (yes, both!) en-suite. Toot! Toot!

Late arriving passengers may book the Parcels Office, now a cosy cottage for two along the Station Walkway. The Station, itself, is packed with RR memorabilia and is the home of the owner, a fellow of very definite *Iron Horse* passions. This is also a delightful venue for walkers, with strolls along the River Test just across the tracks and the ancient Roman Winchester Road (now a public path) practically at the carriage door. This is also big time fishing country...ask where to wet your line at the Grosvenor Hotel bar in Stockbridge.

S&W
B-d
B-t
F-2 [2]
E$m
P-
$570-855
S 4
PARCELS
B-t/q
F-2
E
$475-695
S 2
BOTH
H$m L$
TV
S-S
INS

Contact British Travel International, P.O. Box 299, Elkton VA 22827 USA
TEL 800-327-6097 or FAX 703-298-2347

SWISS COTTAGE

Canon Frome

This cottage is an utterly charming Swiss-style timber lodge set amidst five acres of wilderness streams and gardens. Built in 1838 (the Age of Romance!) and recently renovated, Swiss Cottage features a wrap-around balcony on the second floor that overhangs the idyllic River Frome just below a charming little waterfall. Kingfishers and otters may be seen along its banks. The cottage comprises a small bedroom on the ground floor, with ascent via a kind of ship's ladder to an open-beam, open-plan living room and full kitchen upstairs. There are windows with lovely views all around and French doors leading to the balcony. Honeymoons, first or second, are made of this!

ETB 3 Keys; Highly Commended

I. B-d
F-2
E$m
LT
TEL
TV
MW
C-   P-
$275-575
S 2

Contact Mary McCanna, Westminster Lodgings, 160 Westminster Dr., W.E., Jamestown, NY 14701
TEL 800-699-0744 or 716-484-0744

BREDON HILL   Nr Bredon

The gentle flowing River Avon, meandering its way along through blossomy orchards and a lush green countryside dotted with perfect little villages cut from honey-yellow stone...now that's a picture; the Cotswold picture. It's enough to take away the breath of even the most ardent Devonite!

Bredon is a large village, but no less pretty for that, with notable historic landmarks, like its 14th century tithe barn, and good facilities, including a friendly pub. The major local attraction, of course, is Bredon Hill with its Gothic folly and panoramic views. The Romans came here, as did their predecessors even into prehistory, though, to be sure, not on missions of idle tourism.

Within hiking distance of Bredon Hill, the promontory, is Bredon Hill, the estate. The American, Victoria Woodhull, once lived here and was known to have entertained the future King Edward VII and Prime Minister Balfour. Today the great manor house, with its many gabled bays and mullioned windows, operates as an up-market bed and breakfast. In addition, Bredon Hill has four self-catering accommodations with newly fitted kitchens and a mix of contemporary and older furnishings.

The vine covered *Coach House* (drawing above) is, as the name indicates, part of the former stable block. It has been domesticized in the upside down manner; this time with the kitchen and laundry facilities down, and the drawing room, with nicely exposed beams and dormer views, upstairs. There are three bedrooms with an additional single on the landing. *Stable Cottage* is similar in size, with the bedrooms at ground level and living room upstairs. The *Pool House* also offers accommoda-

E
H$
LT
TELc
TV
W
DW MW
S-S
INS
$530-1485
S 5-6

tion for six with an en-suite double downstairs and two more twins upstairs, along with the living room. Finally, there is a very large wing available in the main house, having a 32 ft. living room upstairs and a ground floor entertainment room with piano and snooker table. A covered walkway joins the main house to the pool house where there are also sauna and jacuzzi facilities. The heated pool, incidentally, may be booked privately by guests on an hourly basis.

Contact Haywood Cottage Holidays, P.O. Box 878, Eufaula, Alabama 36072
TEL 334-687-9800 or FAX 334-687-5324

WYE LEA COUNTRY MANOR   Bridstow

For all practical purposes, Wye Lea is a complete country hotel, but with a self catering dimension that the country hotels lack. Britain has, of course, made a high art form out of the country hotel business, particularly in the last couple decades. Those Bertie Wooster, *pop down to the country* holidays for a spot of (shooting, fishing, golfing, riding, tennis, swimming, partying, gourmet eating, tippling, or all of the above) once enjoyed at the expense of their chums or country aunties, are now available for us all at our own expense...usually in the aunties' grand old country manors, gone commercial, and *sans* the aunties. In place of Aunt Dahlia, Wye Lea now has owners Sally & Colin Bateman and a professional staff that would give Jeeves a run for his money in the business of making life easy for us latter-day Berties, Tuppys, Bingoes and Madeleine Bassetts. As for recreational diversions, all of the above and more await you at Wye Lea.

Wye Lea offers accommodations (13 in total) ranging from suites in the Manor House, to a detached house, to the row of attached modern cottages developed from the old stables. There is a very pleasant and expansive atmosphere here, largely because the accommodations, restaurant, and recreational facilities are widely dispersed over the 17 acres of grounds on the estate. (This is not a barn conversion *out back* of the house; but rather a stable conversion *way over there*). And, of course, nature as well as estate planning makes its contribution to the charm of Wye Lea, most particularly because one side of the property is banked by the pretty River Wye. Nor is the river there just to photograph, as this is one of England's best salmon rivers and offers exceptional coarse fishing as well. The Estate owns a mile of fishing rights on the Wye, and offers four salmon rods per day to guests on a first booking basis. A boat, and even a ghillie to advise, are also available.

As for the accommodations, they are uniformly superb in fashion and facilities, though individual in layout. These are very much *designer* rooms, very stylish in country and period idioms, quality furnishings and decoratives, and plenty of them. There is nothing rustic about Wye Lea; this is *Country Life*, without the dowdy overlooked corners at Aunt Dahlia's.

E&H
FPG & E
L;   T$
TVV
DW   MW
E/HC*
F-F; S-S
MS
INS
£234-865
S 2-8

Contact Wye Lea Country Manor, Wye Lea, Bridstow, Ross-on Wye, Herefordshire HR9 6PZ
TEL 01144-1989-562880 or FAX 01144-1989-768-881

BROADWAY COURT COTTAGES

Broadway

The Cotswolds have a character all their own...an indelible image of yellow cream stone architecture in a sea of lushgreenness.

Cotswold villages are the most distinctive in all Britain; calendar quaint, yet incredibly dignified and mannered even when overrun by tourist hordes; at peace with themselves in all seasons. More than unspoilt, these villages are virtually unspoilable. Cotswold villages are classics, like Burgundian wines, and have their own hierarchy...the *petite villages,* the *premier villages,* and the *grand villages.* Broadway, along with the Slaughters, Bourton-on-the-Water and and a few others, is definitely a *grand village.*

Graham & Rita Smith know where they are. Their three cottages (four, counting Barn Cottage which is reserved for B&B) had to be top drawer, and they are. *Swallow Cottage,* in the quiet back of the court, oozes genteel character from its polished parquet floors to its exposed stone and plaster white walls. The sitting room is not large, but its charm and dignity is whelming; luxurious soft furnishings in floral fabrics, with well chosen mahogany occasional pieces, dried flowers, antique clock....and much more. The stairs are richly paneled with a graceful turned newell. Upstairs there are a brace of spacious double bedrooms and a bathroom with shower.

Woodpecker Cottage greets you with a spacious exposed beam hallway and a starkly contemporary open tread stairwell. The furnishings in the hallway, alone, would put many a "deluxe" cottage to shame. Stable doors take you into a splendid sitting room (note the King Charles spaniel portrait over the brass hooded electric fire) with Welsh dresser and another designer perfect (convertible) sofa. Through the kitchen and another stable door there is a private suntrap patio. Upstairs there are two bedrooms under wooded ceilings.

Dove Cottage, fronting on the street, is the largest. This is the Elizabethan part of the Court, though the interior treatment has a vaguely Victorian flavor with a white-framed mantle mirror and red oriental throw rug over the fitted carpets. One hesitates to assign such generic labels because the key here is not genre, so much as just good taste. Again a switch, a country kitchen with pine table and gay checked wall paper. You will find a double and twin bedroom upstairs, with heritage blue snowflake patch quilts and small print country curtains.

ETB 4 Keys; Commended

SWALLOW	
II.B-d [2]	
F-3	
DOVE	
II.B-d	
B-t	
F-3	
WOOD P.	
II.B-d	
B-t	
F-3	
ALL	
TV	W/Ds
MS	
£260-385	
S 2-4	

Contact Graham & Rita Smith, 89/93 High Street, Broadway, Worcestershire WR12 7AL TEL 01144-1386-852-237

STANTON COURT COTTAGES Nr Broadway

These delightful ancient stone cottages are grouped around the courtyard of Stanton Court, built in the 16th century by Queen Elizabeth's Chamberlain. Surrounded by five acres of manicured lawns and beautiful gardens, the carefully converted barns and granaries combine country charm with modern amenities. Stanton Court has a certain majesty about it, yet there is a friendly in-scale feel about the estate as well. Perhaps it's that soothing Cotswold color, all creamy and golden, the comforting hues of sweet dreams. Stanton Court also has an aura of maturity about it, yet in the spring the estate explodes with the youthful colors of blossoming fruit trees and daffodils. Simply, this is a nice place to be, and that is the beginnings of a memorable holiday.

The cottages range in size from intimate accommodations for honeymooners to ample quarters for growing families. Peach Cottage, with a three level open plan reaching playfully up into the rafters, sleeps two in a galleried double bedroom. At mid-level is a nicely fitted out kitchen and dining area, stepping down into a sunken living room with a large fireplace of Cotswold stone. Everywhere in Peach Cottage, as with all the others, there is visual interest; wonderful rich masonry and wood work, bold geometry in rafters and beams, lots of perpendicular space and architectural curiosities. For couples traveling together, Peach Cottage has the advantage of opening into Paddock Cottage, which fronts onto a delightful Victorian kitchen garden. Paddock Cottage, as well as Shenberrow (sleeps four), have been rendered wheelchair accessible without the slightest compromise to either the luxury furnishings and fittings or the period character.

Larger parties will favor Rosemary Cottage (for six) which was for generations the home of Stanton Court's gardeners and their families. Kitchen and dining spaces are downstairs; upstairs are the bedrooms and the large sitting room, framed by a tent of heavy oak rafters and furnished with pretty wingbacks and a pair of floral print sofas. Garden Cottage is a bit larger yet, with lovely furnishings, including a grandfather's clock and an antique pine refectory table. Granary Cottage sleeps seven and offers splendid views through stone mullioned windows. Stanton Court, for all its historic dignity, is very much a family place; there is swimming and tennis, as well as play facilities for children, and baby sitting can be arranged, as well.
ETB 4 Keys; Commended

TV
W/Ds
MW*
MS
$485-1320
S 2-7

Contact Mary McCanna, Westminster Lodgings, 160 Westminster Dr., W.E., Jamestown, NY 14701
TEL 800-699-0744 or 716-484-0744

COWARNE HALL   Much Cowarne

Miniature High Gothic. Miniature GRAND High Gothic! Architecture can be such fun and every generation of British builder from the Elizabethans on has revelled in the construction of imaginative follies. The Victorian builder of Cowarne Hall was, of course, not out for a folly. Quite the contrary, he wanted a right and proper school hall...right & proper in the eyes of God and contemporary temporal authority. And he succeeded. Even the bible of English historic buildings, Pevsner's *Buildings of England*, singles out and tips it's hat to Cowarne Hall. Still, good humour will out, and in its recent conversion to holiday cottages, Cowarne Hall has become a real fanciful tickler.

It is hard to say whether there are three, four, or five cottages here. The imaginative design allows for a closing of this door and opening of that to create different size accommodations. We begin with Meadow Cottage, with three bedrooms facing south over its own garden and out to the Malvern Peaks. The living room has open beams and a pleasant open hearth fireplace. There are double doors onto the patio and suitable outdoor furnishings for a picnic, etc....But what you really want to do here is go to bed, or at least go sit in bed and look out. The master bedroom frames the world for you in a glorious high-arched, floor to ceiling, stone mullioned window. Snoozing in church was never quite like this!

Orchard Cottage at the other end of the hall is the yin to the yang of Meadow, though the view (not to say the "view hole") is less interesting. Rose Cottage is a hideaway for two. Furnishings are not luxurious, but are homey and comfortable.

Much Cowarne village has been around since the *Domesday Book* and is noted for its 13th century church and medieval dovecote. This village is conveniently located within a mile or two of all the main roads, without being subjected to the

E&H	
FP*	
FPS*	
LT	
W/Ds	
MW	
P-	
S-S MS	
£180-575	
S 2-8	

traffic of any of them. The village is spread out and has lovely lanes with fine views of the Welsh Mountains and the Malvern Hills. Fromes Hill lies at the end of the village and offers a vista over five counties and the Welsh border. As an added attraction, Mrs. Bradbury's straw crafts studio is on the property and guests may arrange for demonstrations or tutorials. Margaret Bradbury is a delightful host; don't be surprised if she runs up the Stars & Stripes in honor of your arrival.
ETB 4 Keys; Highly Commended

Contact: Mrs. R. Bradbury, Much Cowarne, Herefordshire HR7 4JQ   Tel 01144-1432-820-317

THE COTTAGES at Crowle

They don't come much more picturesque than this 16th century timber frame and thatch Grade II Listed building, which contains two cottages. Situated in the village amidst pretty gardens of roses, geraniums, and all sorts of spring bulb flowers, the cottages are full of character features: low beamed ceilings, inglenook fireplace with bread oven, narrow winding staircase, etc. The cottages are modestly furnished in more or less a Victorian mode, and have modern kitchens.

Crowle is wonderfully situated for touring: Worcester's Dyson Perrins Museum is a must for porcelain admirers; Spetchley Park is practically next door for the gardeners; and Stratford-upon-Avon is just down the road a half hour. Also in the neighborhood is the Queen Anne Hanbury Hall, with the Orangerie that we have photographed and sketched so often that it has probably become our favorite building in all England.

Contact Cottage Holidays, Forest Gate, Frog Lane, Milton-U-Wychwood, Oxford OX7 6JZ
TEL 01144-1993-831-495 or FAX 01144-1993-831-095

FRONT
I. F-3
II.B-d
B-s
£132-204
S 3
BACK
II.B-t
B-d
F-2
£155-240
S 4
BOTH
E$m
H$m
FPE*
LT
TELc TV
W
P-
S-S
INS TA

GHORST FARM COTTAGE

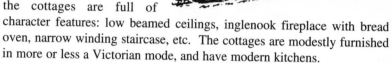

Pudleston Nr Leominster

This is the gentle land of sweet-faced Hereford cattle and sweet-*squeezin'* cider apples. In fact, Ghorst Farm was once a part of the famous Bulmer cider family estate. The 17th century cottage was derelict until recently, but has been brought back to life in traditional Herefordshire architectural style. The black beam and white plaster interior includes a large fieldstone inglenook fireplace with a glass fronted wood stove under a huge timber lintel. Chintz soft furnishings, fitted carpets with pretty throw rugs...all very comfy. The kitchen is galley style with a ceramic counter-top stove and all the essentials, under low character beams. The upstairs bedrooms, also framed in exposed timbers, are prettily decorated and have pastoral views. Worth noting is a seated shower, suitable for the partially disabled.

I. F-3
II.B-t/q
B-t
F-2
E&H
FPS
LT
TV
W/D
MW
C- P-
E/HC
F-F
INS
TA
£306-326
S 4

Contact Cottage Holidays, Forest Gate, Frog Lane, Milton-U-Wychwood, Oxford OX7 6JZ
TEL 01144-1993-831-495 or FAX 01144-1993-831-095

ABBOTS COURT COTTAGES

Vale of Evesham

Allan and Anne Umbers are not ones to rest on their laurels. In 1989 they received the England for Excellence Award, which is *the* Academy Award in the English tourist industry. This, in a nation with upwards of 70,000 self-catering holiday accommodations! In 1991 they did it again! Justifiably, they are as proud of the many Conservation Awards they've received for the architectural restoration work that has gone into making Abbots Court such a gem. Suffice it to say that the trophy room in the Umbers' home might look a bit like Anthony Hopkins' these days. But the measure of success which Allan and Anne are most enthusiastic about doesn't hang on their wall; it is registered in the mountains of guest commentary books.

Having been in this business and having interviewed hundreds upon hundreds of tourist industry professionals who genuinely aspire to the kind of success the Umbers enjoy, I can assure you that the astronomical success of Abbots Court is not accidental. It takes more than ambition, good intentions and hard work, though all of those are essential in large measure. The difference between the winners and the near misses comes down to two elements: Location (yes, all the cliches about *location...location...location* are absolutely true) & Strategy. The Umbers' strategy is very clear in their own heads and in their property. Plain and simply it is to respond to the individuality of their guests. There are no cookie cutter accommodations at Abbots Court. There is no hollow, *have a nice day sir*, service. Each of the twelve cottages at Abbots Court is distinctive and individual, common to each other only in the measure of taste and imagination that went into their design. Allan Umbers is given to saying *we have something for everyone*, which may be a bit optimistic, since the fact is that most of the tourist market is perfectly content with photocopy accommodations and agnostic service. However, if you are one of the distinct individuals in Anne and Allan's rather special *everybody*, consider this cross section of Abbots Court, in some of *their own* words, as well as a few of my own.

E&H
FPE*
LT
TELc*
TV V*
W/Ds
DW MW
P-
E/HC*
OPEN
MS
TA
£155-1395
S 2-6

POND: *Situated adjacent to the village pond, this elegant and tastefully furnished cottage has a distinct Regency flavor; tall arched windows with* beautiful tie-back drapes in a delicious apricot *and very high ceilings* highlighted by subtle wall sconce lighting...a classically pilastered fireplace with an ornate gilt mirror over the mantel...*gracious living room views over the garden* and no shortage of strategically placed greenery within...*character farm house kitchen with old pine table, chairs and dresser. The period staircase leads to a romantic bedroom with queen size four-poster bed, en-suite bathroom...*

OLD YEW: *The ivy clad walls around the front door welcome you...Living room has a distinct Victorian ambience...high ceilings and cast iron fireplace...creamy yellow hues...comfy* deep blue sitting room suite with red piping and a collector's mix of antiques: dressers, tables, chairs, mirrors and frameables. *The kitchen and dining area has a stone flagged floor surrounded by turned Victorian style balustrades...*

EASTER HILL: *Quietly situated...constructed of old mellow bricks with hand made roof tiles...accommodation all on one level...living room tastefully furnished* with spring color floral suite, grandfather clock, pine occasional pieces, *exposed brick wall*, in a herringbone pattern laid within exposed timbers...*inglenook style fireplace...French doors to secluded private garden....*

Yes, there is something here for all the right *everybodies,* in combinations of two, four and six; young and old. Two cottages are wheelchair accessible. Golf, tennis, even rowing, are nearby and all arranged by the Umbers. Which brings us to the other question: *Location.* Answer: the Vale of Evesham is the essence of tranquility itself, just as some have argued that nearby Stratford-on-Avon is the heartland of British culture. Oxford, Bath and Cheltenham are all within an hour's drive, and London is just over two hours away. I think we can definitely call this an *England for Excellence Location!*   ETB 4-5 Keys; Deluxe

Contact Allan & Anne Umbers, Abbots Court Cottages, Abbots Lench, Worcestershire WR11 4UP
TEL & FAX 01144-1386-870-520

HALL FARM COTTAGES
Sedgeberrow

Daphne Stow and her husband bought this expansive Georgian farmstead in 1980 and have devoted themselves to the development of each of the cottages, one by one, over the years. They were rewarded this year with the District award for the best conversion of farm buildings. Part of their devotion has been combing the auctions and shops for interesting Victorian and Edwardian pieces of furnishing, light fixtures, pictures, etc. There is great variety in accommodation: Pippin, Greengage, Russet, and Bramley are delightful apartments in the big house (perhaps you can guess what they grow at Hall farm!); the *Highly Commended* Moat Path and Stable Yard cottages were converted from the Victorian period barn; Coopers, with beautifully exposed cruck and beams was once the stable. Exterior amenities include two acres of gardens, tennis, bicycles, a heated outdoor pool and summertime fishing in the River Isbourne which crosses the farm. Hall Farm is strategically sited for *doing* the Cotswolds, without being dead center in the heavily trafficked postcard villages.   ETB 4 Keys; Commended to Highly Commended

E&H	
LT	
TELm	
TV	
W/Ds	MW
P-	
F-F	S-S
INS	TA
£115-430	
S 2-6	

Contact Daphne Stow at Hall Farm, Sedgeberrow, Evesham, Worcestershire WR11 6UB
TEL 01144-1386-881-298

THE COTTAGES AT WESTWOOD
West Malvern

In an area designated for "outstanding natural beauty", an hour from Shakespeare's Stratford, the Cottages at Westwood House nestle on the western slope of the 600 million year-old Malvern Hills. You are very near the summit here, where the Victorians came in good spirited pilgrimages to cast their eyes on 18 counties at one time. The counties may have changed, but the view is still the one that inspired the likes of Sir Edward Elgar and the Chaucerian poet, Langland. Malvern is also the home to the world-famous spa water which holds the Royal Warrant.

There are three cottages on the grounds of this late Regency home built for a clergyman with the delightful Dickensian name, *The Reverend Scarlet Vale*. Ostlers & Coachmans have been converted from the Reverend's coach house, and Westwood Cottage was the original gardener's cottage. Westwood Cottage, which sleeps up to six, was the national winner of the Holiday Home of the Year Award. Standing snugly in its own Malvern stone walled garden, with a small lawn, climbing roses, and hedges of yew, laurel, holly and lilac, you enter Westwood Cottage through a bright little porch-way with its profusion of scented honeysuckle. Warmth and detail (Carl Larsson prints abound) characterize this peaceful three bedroom hideaway with panoramic views of the Welsh sunset.

Ostlers and Coachmans each sleep four. Again, native pine is the wood of choice in architectural detail (stripped pine doors & natural pine staircase) and in the furnishings (wardrobes and chests). There is fitted green carpeting throughout, and the walls are adorned with an interesting array of prints and country-style porcelain. In Coachmans there is a twin-bedded room and a double bunked room; Ostlers offers a twin bedded and double bedded option.

ETB 3 & 4 Keys; Highly Commended

OSTLERS
II.B-t
B-q
F-3
COACHMAN
II.B-t
B-b
F-3
WESTWOOD
I. B-q
B-t
F-3
II.B-t
E&H
LT
TELc TV
W/D-BA
P-
S-S; OPEN
MS TA
£210-520
S 4-6

Contact Jill Wright: Cottages at Westwood House, West Malvern, Worcestershire WR14 3DS
TEL 01144-1684-892-308 or FAX 01144-1684-892-882

BRISSENDEN COURT

Bethersden

Brissenden Court is a charming development of converted traditional Kent estate buildings, including an oasthouse. Red clay bricks and equally red peg-tile roofs against a sweeping panorama of pastoral green; all providing a nice *get away from it all* feeling. Of course, in this part of southern England one is not really away from it all, but rather in the middle of a wealth of historic sites and contemporary activities. The medieval weavers' village of Biddenden (also home of an award winning vineyard), the Cinque Port of Tenterden, historic Rye, *more* historic Hastings...all within a short drive.

E&H
FPS
LT
TELc TV
W/Ds
DW* MW
E/HC
S-S MS
TA
£175-950
S 2-10

There are eleven accommodation units at Brissenden Court, all comfortably furnished in a contemporary idiom, with a host of recreational amenities from the indoor heated pool to the tennis and floodlit shuffleboard courts.   ETB 4 Keys; Deluxe

Contact Jean & Richard Bishop, Brissenden Court, Bethersden, Kent TN26 3BE
TEL 01144-1233-820-746 or FAX 01144-1233-820-213

DOVE COTE   Boughton Monchelsea

Boughton Monchelsea is a small village on the outskirts of Maidstone, the county town of Kent. Greater London is within an hour's drive. This area is known for its fruit orchards and hop gardens, and for the famous ragstone quarries which supplied the stone for Westminster Abbey, as well as the Beveridges' old Dove Cote, recently converted to a handsome holiday let adjacent to their home in the converted oast. The cottage is peacefully situated down a quiet country lane and up on a south facing rise with four acres of grounds. There is just the one cottage and the Beveridges have proudly preserved the ancient dove nesting boxes in the gable. The inside decor works within a very pretty magnolia and green color scheme, with coordinated drapery. The sitting room has a comfy convertible sofa and french doors leading to a pleasant patio overlooking the gentle rolling countryside. The Beveridges are most amiable hosts, and you will likely find one of Gill Beveridge's delicious fruit cakes or her fresh cut flowers awaiting your arrival, or, in autumn a large bowl of Spartan apples from their garden. The pool and hard tennis court are available for Dove Cote guests. All in all, the Dove Cote promises to be most pleasant steads for touring the multitude of sites in Kent, as well as reaching into the capital scene of London.
ETB 4 Keys; Highly Commended

I.B-d
CS
F-2
E&H
LT
TELc TV
W
MW
NS
E/HC
S-S
OPEN
TA
£175-250
S 4

Contact Gill Beveridge, Wierton Oast, Wierton Hill, Boughton Monchelsea, Maidstone, Kent ME17 4JT
TEL 01144-1622-741-935

KNOWLTON COURT Nr Canterbury

Knowlton Court is a Grade I Listed mansion and has a long and proud history. The Saxon church beside Knowlton Court is in the *Domesday Book,* and Bishop Odo of Bayeux, brother of William the Conqueror, was the first inhabitant of Knowlton Court, itself. Many great families have lived at Knowlton and owned/ruled vast areas of Kent from this manor. Sir Thomas Peyton of Knowlton Court led the failed Kentish Rising in 1648 which sought to restore Charles I, and, as a consequence, his daughters, impoverished by the fines imposed by the Commonwealth Government, finally sold the estate. Admiral Sir John Narborough bought the estate in 1685 and commissioned the Grinling Gibbons monument in the Church to honor Sir Cloudesley Shovel and the Admiral's own sons-in-law who were all lost at sea off the Scilly Isles in 1707.

Later Lords of the Manor were the Speed family, who undertook a major remodeling at the turn of this century, embellishing the house and garden with the help of such luminaries as Sir Edwin Lutyens and Sir Reginald Bloomfield. Lutyens was a giant in the architectural world, with a range of creativity spanning colossal monuments, such as the Parliament Buildings in New Delhi, to stables, such as those he designed at Knowlton Court. His own home in Devon, the ersatz Castle Drogo discussed earlier, was the culmination of his romantic antiquarian vision, which is much in evidence in his work at Knowlton Court. During the 1900 remodeling more Grinling Gibbons carvings were introduced to the magnificent drawing room. Also, the avenue of lime trees were planted at this time, though after the hurricane damage of 1987 many of the lime trees had to be lifted and replanted.

Suffice it to say that a holiday at Knowlton Court is an invitation to step back into a telescope of time incorporating fascinating periods of cultural genius and social ambition. There are nine holiday accommodations on the estate. Stable Cottage, sleeping 4/5, forms the end of the still working stable yard. It has its own secluded garden surrounded by a high

THE FLAT
III.B-d
B-t [2]
F-2
E&H
LT$
TV
MW
S-S OPEN
MS
TA
£160-290
S 6

LODGE C.
B-t [2]
B-t+s
CS [2]
F-1 F-2
F-3
W/D
£150-325
S 7/9
STABLE C.
B-q
B-s [2]
F-2
F-1
£95-225
S 4/5
BOTH
E$ H$
LT$
TELc
TV
MW
S-S OPEN
MS
TA

hedge and overlooks the ancient pigeon house, which was built by the Lords of the Manor to house thousands of pigeons which once foraged voraciously on the crops of the tenants. The repeal of the Corn Laws in 1846 put a stop to this callous inequity, and since then the Pigeon House has just been another of Knowlton Court's endearing architectural curiosities.

The Lodge is the gate house to Knowlton Court, which sleeps up to nine, and was also designed by Lutyens. Manicured yew hedges surround the front of the garden, and the lawn at the rear is carpeted with daffodils in the Spring. Inside, the hall is overlooked by the oak staircase and off each side are sitting rooms, with the dining room at the back. In the kitchen you will still find the arches which contained bread ovens. Upstairs, leaded windows offer a grand perspective up the avenue of lime trees to the mansion. If you'd prefer to look out from, rather than at, the mansion, there is a third floor flat in Knowlton Court, itself.

ETB 3-4 Keys; Commended

The Dower House (drawing below) is a superb Elizabethan home, built for the comfort of the widows of the Lords of the Manor when the sons and heirs rose to their positions. The most recent dowager occupant

was Enid Speed, granddaughter of Frederick Leyland, noted patron of the artists Whistler and Rosetti. This Grade II Listed house has seven main double/twin bedrooms (plus others), yet the Dower House is so thoroughly homey that smaller parties will not be lost in its expanse. It has just been completely refurbished and restored. You will find the furnishings utterly delicious, mostly "older" in style, with Colefax & Fowler and Marvic fabrics much in evidence. Old Persian rugs are laid over newly fitted carpeting, and leaded pane windows fill the rooms with light as well as offer grand views. Two of the bedrooms even have large open timbered fireplaces. Outdoor amenities include tennis on the estate, riding in the area, and golf at any of six courses within a thirty minutes' drive.   ETB 5 Keys; Highly Commended

DOWER H.
B-q [2]
B-t/q [2]
B-t [4]
B-t+s
F-2/3 [7]
E&H
H
FP
LT
TELc
TV
W/D
DW MW
P-BA
F-F; OPEN
MS TA
£575-1100
S 19

Contact Mrs. M.M. Fox-Pitt, Knowlton Court, Nr Canterbury, Kent CT3 1PT
TEL 01144-1304-842-402 or FAX 01144-1304-842-403

HOLE COTTAGE   Cowden

The Weald of West Kent and Sussex is a place to come and see things...an area of many attractions, as it were. Within minutes of Hole Cottage you will find Hever Castle; also Penhurst, Chartwell, Royal Tunbridge Wells, and on it goes; an itinerary that requires much stamina and plenty of Kodak film.

However, there may be a problem. Hole Cottage is not really a place to dump your bags and run. This is a *Hansel and Gretel* place, lost in the woods, lost from time. I am told that, in fact, many of the guests come down from the City by train, hike through the woods from the Cowden Station, put a log on the fire, open a book, and aren't seen until they arrive back at the stationmaster's wicket a week later. I can believe it, because this is a truly charming little cottage, full of medieval character, with just enough modern conveniences to close the door on the outside world.

II. B-d
B-b
F-2
E&H
FP
LT
F-F
MS
INS
£408-600
S 4

PROSPECT TOWER   Nr Canterbury

One doesn't have to tour England long to find the birthplace of cricket... several birthplaces, in fact. Certainly cricket has many hallowed grounds, and the pitch adjacent to Prospect Tower on the Belmont Park estate can very definitely claim sacred association. Lord Harris, one of the game's founding fathers, used the Tower as a dressing room for his players. If you're thinking clanking lockers and slippery floors under the bleachers, forget it.

Today, this pristine Georgian folly is a wonderful nest for two while touring the many attractions of the Southeast. The Landmark Trust interior decorators have incorporated some handsome cricket memorabilia amongst the impeccable period furnishings. The Tower is laid out with the sitting room, kitchen and dining areas above to take advantage of the views, while sleeping quarters are situated below, where once Pimms may have been spilled on the cobble floor during celebrations of victory. Perhaps I have *mixed* my drinks? Well, what ever the libation, we can raise my glasses to yet another fine restoration property from the folks at Landmark Trust.

I. B-t	
F-3	
E&H	
FP	
LT	
P-	
F-F	MS
INS	
£289-340	
S 2	

Contact The Landmark Trust, Shottesbrook, Maidenhead, Berkshire SL6 3SW
TEL 01144-1628-825-925 or FAX 01144-1628-825-417

CIDERPRESS & WALNUT TREE COTTAGES

Goldhill Mill

Goldhill Mill was already in existence at the time of the Norman Conquest, and corn was milled here until 1918. The present buildings, part Tudor, part Georgian, are set round a cobbled courtyard beside the millstream. It is an extremely peaceful and idyllic situation, with sheep grazing in the meadows and swans cruising in the river.

Vernon and Shirley Cole have recently created two absolutely marvelous cottages out of the Mill's old outbuildings: Ciderpress and Walnut Tree. Ciderpress has two en-suite bedrooms and is all on one floor, apart from an apple loft reached by a ladder from the living room. The living room and master bedroom are both open to the eaves with spectacular Tudor beams. There is an inglenook fireplace with a large open wood burning stove, fitted neutral carpets, and a host of decorative touches that testify to Shirley's professional expertise as an interior designer. The detail here, from carefully coordinated floral fabrics to interesting old paintings, is something to behold. And, the best place to *behold* it is probably the comfy sofas in front of the cozy fire.

Walnut Tree Cottage has three bedrooms, also all en-suite. Two of the bedrooms are reached by an iron spiral staircase, and again the rooms rise to fine old open beams. The dormer windows look out over the red tile roofs of the Tudor barn next door. There is very tasteful dusky pink carpeting throughout. The superbly equipped kitchen, with chestnut cabinetry, opens through a glazed door onto a little private garden beside the river. The cottages are surrounded by a country garden with a veritable hedge of sweet peas marking off the vegetable garden. Tennis and croquet facilities are also available for guests.

Goldhill Mill is only four miles from Tunbridge Wells with exceptional shopping. Day tripping to London is merely a forty minute train ride away. Goldhill Mill is also ideally placed in relation to an exceptional number of historic castles, stately homes and gardens: Leeds, Hever (Anne Boleyn's home), and Sissinghurst (for Vita Sackville-West fans) Castles; and Chartwell, of course, to catch a glimpse of Churchill's home life. The wonderful vineyards of Kent have, of course, come along since Churchill's day, but he would have insisted on your having a visit, and a taste, of them as well.

ETB 5 Keys; Deluxe

Contact Vernon & Shirley Cole, Goldhill Mill, Golden Green, Tonbridge, Kent TN11 0BA
TEL 01144-1732-851-626 or FAX 01144-1732-851-881

CIDER P.
I.B-q [2]
F-3
F-4
£275-525
S 4
WALNUT T.
I. B-q
F-4
II.B-q
B-t
F-2
£325-625
S 6
BOTH
FPS
LT
TELm
W/D
TVV
DW MW
NS C-BA
E/HC
S-S INS
TA

THREE CHIMNEYS FARM

Nr Goudhurst

Three Chimneys Farm is a small working estate located in a quiet hamlet at the end of a mile long private track. These lovely old oast houses are on top of a hill with outstanding views across the farmland to Goudhurst village to the north and over Bedgebury Great Lake to the south. We have spent many wonderful days in the vineyards that have sprung up in these rolling Kent hills: *Tenterden, Biddenden, Lamberhurst*; all within minutes of the bygone old hop mill of Three Chimneys. Sometimes, I guess, one good thing **does** follow another.

Until ten years ago Three Chimneys Farm was part of the Crown Estates, and the old buildings, because of the identity of their former owner, are extremely well built and preserved. Marion Fuller, who is an architectural designer, and her husband have converted the distinctive buildings into four holiday cottages, in addition to their own home. Though they've not been working with quite the number of figures in their budget as their predecessors, they've done a remarkable job.

Each cottage is completely unique and much has been made out of the unusual spatial proportions of these character buildings. There are interesting floor textures as well: bold red terracotta here, fitted seagrass matting there, bare wood, and scatter rugs in a multitude of colorful designs. The kitchens tend to be rather Scandinavian, clean line & no clutter, though the challenge of installing a kitchen in a round room was taken up with verve. It turns out that a round kitchen is not only fun to look at, but fun to work in, which is no surprise to those of us who think that kitchens are really supposed to be adult playgrounds.

Sheepwash sleeps four and is all on the ground level, making it particularly suitable for elderly guests. *Spoonlets* has accommodation for four or five and features a wonderful gallery bedroom. *Starvegoose* is a detached single bedroom cottage, and *Ironlatch,* which sleeps five, has the much sought after bedroom in the round under the glass topped oast cone.

E$m	
H$m	
FPS	
L	T$
TELc	TV
W	D*
DW*	MW
P$	
E*	
S-S	
MS	
TA	
£171-501	
S 2-6	

Contact Marion Fuller, Three Chimneys Oast, Goudhurst, Kent TN17 2RA
TEL 01144-1580-212-175

LAMBARDS OAST Nr Sevenoaks

This picturesque cottage adjoins a converted twin-kiln oast dating from the 17th century. The brick and stone cottage sits in two acres of peaceful gardens and is next to the well known garden of Great Comp. The cottage consists of a very pretty sitting room, nicely furnished with antiques, two lovely bedrooms and a fully fitted kitchen. You have the option of full English breakfast or a three course evening meal in Mrs. Russell's elegant round dining room for an additional charge. Lambards Cottage also has its own private garden with suitable furnishings. Guests may use the Russell's floodlit tennis court, as well as the games room with snooker and ping pong.

B-d
B-t
F-3
E$m
H$m
LT
TV
W/D
INS
$555-605
S 2

Sevenoaks is really a bedroom town, with train service to London on the half hour. Facing the other direction, this is the land of hops and great country houses. In fact, there are more famous houses concentrated here than anywhere in Britain, many of them open for visitation. And, of course, there is also Royal Tunbridge Wells, second only to Bath as the historic spa town of England.   ETB 4 Keys; Highly Commended.

Contact Mary McCanna, Westminster Lodgings, 160 Westminster Dr., W.E., Jamestown, NY 14701
TEL 800-699-0744 or 716-484-0744

THREE GATES STABLE COTTAGES
Nr Fawkham

These five cottages are arranged around a central courtyard, nicely landscaped with clematis and wisteria covered arbors setting off quiet areas to relax and read, with a little pond and barbeque common. There are one and two bedroom cottages in this converted stable court; all are carpeted throughout and each has a fully tiled shower room. The living-dining-kitchens are open plan, with pristinely white kitchen units and pretty floral covered soft furnishings. Bedroom colors run to peach and rose hues, with lovely floral duvets and nice prints on the walls. These are modest cottages, neat and tidy to a fault, and very good value. London is only forty minutes away by car or train, as is historic Canterbury and an endless array of tourist sites and family activities. Nearby is Brands Hatch, the well known auto racing track. ETB 3 Keys; Highly Commended.

E$c H$c
LT
TELc
TV
W/D$s
MW
TA
£180-300
S 2-5

Contact Mr. & Mrs. Tom Cramer, Three Gates Stables Holiday Cottages, Speedgate Hill, Fawkham,
Kent DA3 8NJ TEL 01144-1474-827-739

ST JOHN'S COTTAGES   Sandwich

The St. John's Almshouse was originally built for paupers, but today a stay in the Maxtone Grahams' delightful cottages will go far to preserve you from being pauperized by your holiday. Set in the very heart of the fascinating medieval town of Sandwich, these cottages have an inspiring tale to tell, right up to the modern story of their condemnation by a demolition minded municipal council and a harrowing thirteen year struggle to save them.

There are six cottages in the row, small and simple; in fact they are the same size and configuration as when built in 1805 on the razed remains of the preceding almshouse built in 1287. This is a restoration, not a conversion, and all the more interesting for the scale and historic detail. On the ground floor you will find a cozy living room with a coal burning open fire and fitted carpets. The furnishings are an eclectic mix of antiques for the most part (the proprietors are in the business) with interesting prints, watercolors and bric-a-brac. Also on the ground floor of each cottage is a tiny kitchen and a door to a private garden. Up a winding staircase there is a twin bedded room (joined to make a double if you prefer) with chest of drawers, dressing and bedside tables. The living room sofa converts to a bed for the sprouts or a foursome.

Though in the middle of a busy historic town, crowded by commerce and sightseers, the St. John's Cottages enjoy tranquil seclusion tucked in behind the church amidst some extremely creative landscaping. In fact, if a guest shows the slightest green orientation, the Maxtone Grahams will provide a detailed map of the gardens, flower by flower, shrub by shrub, herb by herb...by my count, 263 horticultural varieties. However, don't spend your whole holiday in the garden. Sandwich is an ancient and absorbing port town, one of the Cinque Ports, with its narrow streets, half-timbered buildings and overhanging houses.   Don't miss Thursday morning market!

```
I. CS
  F-2
II.B-t/q
  E$m
  H
  FP$
  LT$
  TV
  MS
  £155-195
  S 2-4
```

Contact: Claudia & Robert Maxtone Graham, 6 Moat Sole, Sandwich, Kent CT13 9AU
TEL 01144-1304-613-270 or FAX 01144-1304-615-436

MARTIN LANE FARMHOUSE COTTAGES

Burscough

Burscough is a small rural community nestled in the rich farmland of the West Lancashire Plain. These cottages are an equidistant hour's drive from the tourist meccas of Northern Wales and the Lake District, as well as historic Liverpool.

Elaine and Alan Stubbs have been very much hands-on in the conversion of these traditional farm buildings into two spacious holiday accommodations. To the rear is a cobbled courtyard, large garden and paddock where guests are welcome to relax, play, and barbeque. The Stubbs' hens are truly free-range and love to be fed tidbits by children, as does their small flock of friendly sheep. The Leeds/Liverpool canal cuts across the end of the lane and makes for a very pleasant walk to one of the many canal-side inns along the route.

The Shippon is the smaller of the two cottages, sleeping 4/5. The ground floor is open plan, and in the construction Alan took pains to retain all of the original beams. Elaine has decorated it a farmhouse style, with a solid pine Welsh dresser and matching table and chairs. The living room features a contemporary rose pink, dralon suite, with pretty floral curtains and cushions. Upstairs, the Shippon has two bedrooms, one with a double bed, which can also take an extra single if required. The other bedroom is a twin. Furnishings here are contemporary pine, with nicely color-coordinated floral fabrics and duvets.

The Granary is the larger of the two cottages and will accommodate up to seven people. The main feature is its impressive picture window; barn door size, in fact! There is a staircase leading from the living room to a gallery landing, off which there are twin and double bedrooms, as well as a bathroom and separate shower. The third bedroom is located downstairs and contains a single bed, as well as adult size bunks. As with the Shippon, decor runs to florals with contemporary soft furnishings and polished pine. Both cottages feature a knotty pine accent wall, with plenty of pictures, frameables and display plates. The Granary has an interesting collection of tankards. Both are centrally heated and have fitted carpets.

The village of Burscough is home to the noted Martin Mere Wildfowl Sanctuary. Nearby is the seaside resort, Southport, with its grand Victorian shopping arcades.   ETB 4 Keys; Highly Commended

SHIPPON
II.B-q
B-t
F-3
UK200-299
S 4
GRANARY
I. B-S+B
II.B-q
B-t
F-3
UK250-350
S 7
BOTH
E&H
LT
TELc   TV
MW
W
S-S   OPEN
MS   INS
TA

Contact Mrs. Elaine Stubbs, Martin Lane Farmhouse Cottages, Burscough, Lancs. L40 8JH
TEL/FAX 01144-1704-893-527

ROCKINGHAM CASTLE   Rockingham

   To say that Rockingham is a venerable old castle is something of an understatement. For the past 450 years the Castle has been the family seat of the Watsons, they who were much favored by King Henry VIII. However, for the 450 preceding years Rockingham belonged to the Crown, itself. William the Conqueror positioned his fortress atop this hill with long views over five present-day counties. When vigilance was not the order of the day revelry was, and Rockingham was much used by the   succeeding Royals for the Hunt and associated convivialities. Conviviality was also the mark of Rockingham Castle during Victorian times. Charles Dickens came often to visit his friends, the Watsons, and favored the Castle with many of his amateur theatricals. Rockingham Castle was immortalized as "Chesney Wold" in *Bleak House*, and Dickens dedicated *David Copperfield* to his Rockingham hosts.

   Street House is a castle-proportioned apartment within the walls of Rockingham Castle (left of the twin towers gate in drawing). It is, in fact, the only rental accommodation in the Castle, which is the principle residence of the Watson family, as it has been since the reign of Henry VIII. The accommodations are approached from a narrow cobbled walkway which leads to the bell tower. Though Rockingham Castle is a popular tourist attraction and stages summertime re-enactments of the battle between the Roundheads and Cavaliers, the Street House apartment enjoys complete privacy and tranquility.

   One enters through a spacious foyer, with the original flagstones underfoot and ascends the staircase into the long hallway which forms the spine of the quarters. The hallway has windows overlooking an inner courtyard of the Castle and all of the rooms lead off from this hall. The living room has enormous mullioned windows overlooking the busy central courtyard and thence to views over the Castle walls and down the Welland Valley toward the Fens. Furnishings range from contemporary to antique and the walls are adorned with some appropriately handsome paintings. The three bedrooms are furnished in a traditional style, again with a number of antiques. There is a separate dining room and a modernized Mrs. Bridges style kitchen. Away from the maddening crowd at Rockingham means a private interior garden, which is shared with the Watsons, as is the outdoor swimming pool for summertime guests.

I. F-1
II.B-d
B-t [2]
F-2
E$m
H$
LT
TV
W
DW
P-
F-F   MS
INS
$750-1565
S 6

Contact British Travel International, P.O. Box 299, Elkton VA 22827 USA TEL 800-327-6097

RUTLAND WATER COTTAGES
Edith Weston

To say that the British have a great deal of pride in place is a gross understatement. The test of that pride is when some government agency declares an ancient district a *non-place*, as in the 1970's when local government reformers tried to lose England's smallest county, Rutland, in the indeterminate landscape of Leicestershire.... Nothing doing! Rutlanders are still Rutlanders; *what King John hath given let no bureaucratic nimrod take away!* Actually, the *giving* of Rutland happened even before King John; that is, when Edward the Confessor gave the whole County to his wife. For most of the centuries that followed the tiny province remained a sort of kingdom within the kingdom, which helps to explain the wealth of listed buildings and the historic record associated with Rutland. Edward's wife, incidentally, was named Edith, and she gave her name to the delightful village beside the lake now known as Rutland Water. And, here it is that we find the four delightful stone cottages owned and managed by Tim & Kitty Walmsley.

The cottages are actually quite independent of each other, situated in different parts of this character lake-front village. Well Cross Cottage (above) is located by the ancient village well. One enters via a pretty front garden and up a Victorian stone porch with a veil of climbing roses to greet you. There is a cheerful little living room with a cozy fireplace and comfy soft furnishings covered in florals. As with all of Kitty Walmsley's decors, there are lots of interesting decoratives and frameables. Barn Cottage, adjacent to the Post Office, also sleeps four; in this case all on the ground floor. The decor here runs to peach hues and lovely florals with plenty of light from the French doors leading to the patio. Middle and Corner Cottages each sleep two, with twin bedrooms upstairs, and ground floor living rooms featuring exposed stone walls, handsome open fires and nice antique accent pieces as well as good quality soft furnishings.

In addition to the many recreational pleasures of the lake, this is a great area to tour with many stately homes, such as Burghley House, and historic towns, such as Stamford of *Middlemarch* fame. Stamford is also noted for its summer stock Shakespeare theatre.

Oh yes, I should mention that every one of Kitty's refrigerators comes with a chilled bottle of wine and a bowl of fruit, just to let you know that, though Rutland may not *exist*, it is a very welcoming place.

ETB 4 Keys; Highly Commended

E&H
FP
LT
TV
W
DW*
MW
E/HC*
S-S   MS
INS
£155-350
S 2-4

Contact Kitty & Tim Walmsley, Rutland Water Cottages, Dormer Cottage, Ryhall, Stamford Lincs. PE9 4JA
TEL 01144-1780-64001 or FAX 01144-1780-481-333

HOUSE OF CORRECTION   Folkingham

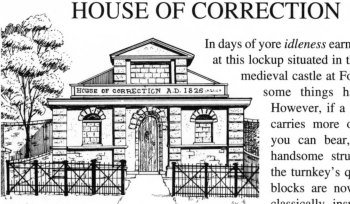

In days of yore *idleness* earned a person a stay at this lockup situated in the grounds of the medieval castle at Folkingham. Well, some things haven't changed! However, if a holiday in a gaol carries more of a stigma than you can bear, take heart...this handsome structure was really the turnkey's quarters. The cell blocks are now gone, and this classically inspired gate house enjoys a place of solitary prominence on the mown lawn of the ancient moat works.

The interior layout is intricate, to say the least, and incorporates three floors of attractive domesticity. The ground floor left and right bays (as in drawing) comprise living room and kitchen/dining rooms, respectively. Two separate stairs take us to the twin bedroom (over living room) and bathroom (over kitchen). Bridging the arched entry is a third floor double bedroom. Comfortable furnishings, interesting decoratives, tranquil views; prison was never like this! Who says idleness doesn't pay?

II. B-t
F-2
III.B-d
E&H
FP
LT
S-S MS
INS
£304-479
S 4

Contact The Landmark Trust, Shottesbrook, Maidenhead, Berkshire SL6 3SW TEL 01144-1628-825-925

CRIFTON FARM   Epperstone

This 17th century granary has been converted into a very pleasant and spacious upside-down cottage. The upstairs living room is nicely vaulted with the original exposed beams and skylights as well as front eyebrow windows. Jenny Esam has done an exceptional job of decorating to create a warm homey feeling, mixing antiques and modern floral soft furnishings. Downstairs is the spacious kitchen/dining area, all pine and well lit, and large enough to accommodate a wing chair for the culinary observer. There are two twin bedrooms nicely made up with billowy duvets and wonderful carved pine headboards. Each bedroom is en-suite.

II.B-t [2]
F-3 [2]
E&H
LT
TEL TV
W/D
MW
P-
OPEN
TA
£265-300
S 4

Guests enjoy a delightful walled garden where there is a barbeque set up and heated swimming pool, and a separate snooker room. As for touring, this is Robin Hood country; only a bow-twang from the Major Oak. Also nearby is Byron's home, Newstead Abbey, which he long pined (and penned) for after losing the family estate to debt. Crifton is very much a working farm and you will find "real people" hospitality in the Esam family.

ETB 4 Keys; Highly Commended

Contact Mrs Jenny Esam at Criftin Farm, Epperstone, Nottingham NG14 6AT
TEL 01144-1602-652-039

WAINGROVE FARMHOUSE   Fulstow

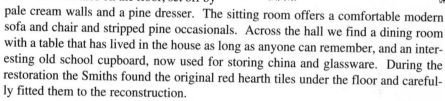

Waingrove Farmhouse is approached over a bridge and down the drive. You will recognize it for the garden seat under the cherry tree in front. It is a traditional Lincolnshire farmstead, built of brick and terracotta pantiles in the first years of young Victoria's reign. Stephanie Smith's husband grew up here and still farms this land. In 1989 they completely restored the homestead for holiday use, and have earned an enviable reputation for their extra special hospitality in the years since.

The entrance hall still has the original Victorian tiles on the floor, set off by pale cream walls and a pine dresser. The sitting room offers a comfortable modern sofa and chair and stripped pine occasionals. Across the hall we find a dining room with a table that has lived in the house as long as anyone can remember, and an interesting old school cupboard, now used for storing china and glassware. During the restoration the Smiths found the original red hearth tiles under the floor and carefully fitted them to the reconstruction.

The kitchen is a mix of up-to-date fittings with some old timers left for decorative effect, eg. the meat hooks on the ceiling (now hung with dried flowers) and an old range (purely for show). Upstairs there are four bedrooms, including an *eaves bedroom,* all pale cream with a sloping ceiling under the beam. The double bedroom is furnished in a pink and clover idiom. There is also a nursery in navy and white with a cot, nursing chair, and stairgate.

Fulstow is a small country village on the fertile land between the Lincolnshire Wolds (Tennyson Country!) and the Coast. Nearby Horncastle is a must for antique enthusiasts. The Lincoln Cathedral towers over the landscape for miles around, but the spire of St. James Church in Louth is the local favorite...*Princess of the Wolds*, they say. Louth, incidentally, is a wonderfully preserved Georgian town and an absolute must-visit on market day.

ETB 4 Keys; Highly Commended

I. F-1
II.B-d
B-t [2]
F-3
E$c   H$
FP   FPE
LT
TV
W/D
MW
P-
OPEN MS
INS   TA
£175-375
S 6

Contact Mrs. Stephanie Smith at Waingrove Farm, Fulstow, Louth, Lincolnshire LN11 0XQ
TEL 01144-1507-363-704

ASHWATER HOLIDAY HOMES Louth

Yvonne and David Mapletoft have created three exceptional modern holiday accommodations on two acres of country gardens at the edge of a private fishing lake. To top it off, this little island of serenity is situated in Louth, one of the best preserved Georgian towns in all of England, here in the rolling Lincolnshire Wolds within sight of the sea.

Pond Cottage is a large wing of the owner's handsome red brick and tile roofed home, Ashwater House. Pictured to the left in the drawing, the accommodation has a ground floor living room with lovely views over the pond through leaded pane windows. There is a distinctive fireplace, fashioned from old bricks and inset with some of the antiquities found during the excavations. The cottage is very cozy, with richly patterned Axminster wool carpeting, a mix of tasteful furnishings, including some notable antiques, such as the George III Windsor chair and a handsome Welsh dresser. Upstairs there are two caringly furnished double bedrooms, with yet more views of the endless parade of wildlife that shares the pond with the Mapletofts.

Crows Nest Cottage sits in a detached position across the patio from Ashwater House, surrounded by the elaborate and colorful garden and arbor. There is a bathroom shower facility on the ground floor, with living room and a small twin bedroom upstairs, offering a picturesque vista over the adjacent paddock and pasturage. This little nest is prettily decorated in coordinated floral fabrics for curtains, duvet and pillows.

Kingfisher is a new Scandinavian style cedar lodge sitting at the edge of the pond; very merry steads, indeed, albeit perhaps not merry ole England. There are pretty floral covered soft furnishings, all the more handsome in this carefully rusticated environment.

ETB3 & 4 Keys; Commended

POND
II.B-d
B-t
F-2
CS
£250-310
S 5
CROWS
II. B-s [2]
CS
F-3
£190-220
S 2-4
KINGFISHER
I. B-d
B-b
F-3
£200-275
S 4
ALL
E&H
FPG
LT
TV
W/Ds MW
NS
S-S OPEN
MS TA

Contact Mrs. Yvonne Mapletoft, Ashwater House, Willow Drive, Louth, Lincolnshire LN11 0AH
TEL 01144-507-609-295

APPLETREE COTTAGE

Ropsley

It doesn't get much more quaint than this! What is more, it never gets more economical than this...indeed, Appletree Cottage may be the most cottage for the least money in this book.

This sweet little stone cottage was built in 1717 as the first village school. It is light and bright, with white walls and dark oak beams, and is surprisingly spacious.

The entrance porch opens into an absolutely charming open plan lounge area, with soft furnishings in pastel pinks, blues and greens, and colorful flowers in season...all very country cottage*ish*. Especially noteworthy here is a handsome old Dutch wheel-back dresser, laden with showy pieces of old china; reminding us that we are, after all, on the periphery of the *Holland of England*, the Lincolnshire Fens. There are other interesting articles of pottery and wall hangings reflecting the owners' travels abroad. The cottage is made all the more cozy by an open fire and character lamps with fringed shades, and by wall sconces on either side of the fireplace.

The kitchen opens directly on to the sitting area and is galley style, with fitted oak units and quarry tile worktops.   At the garden window there is an octagonal mahogany dining table and a pair of leather back chairs. Upstairs, the bath-room decor is in black, white and red. An arched doorway from the landing leads into the bedroom, with furnishings in green, cream and brown. There are twin beds and a handsome antique mahogany wardrobe providing generous storage space.

Appletree Cottage is filled with wonderful colors...and surrounded by yet more wonderful colors! There definitely appears to be a passionate green thumb lurking about here, though Elizabeth Hogan proclaims disdain for the whole garden-ing enterprise! Praise be to the elves who have filled the cottage's private garden with such a wonderful mix of formal and informal landscape features including archways, an ancient gnarled apple tree (naturally!), English country garden shrubs and a multitude of flowers. There is also a lawn and a private little patio.

The cottage, which is adjacent to the owner's property, is situated right in the award winning village of Ropsley, next to St. Peters Church. Nearby is the historic city of Lincoln and the pretty towns of Stamford (alias *Middlemarch*), Spalding (alias *Tulipland*) and Boston (the original one, that is).   ETB 4 Keys; Highly Commended

I. F-1
II.B-t
F-3
E&H
FP
LT
TV
W/Ds
MW
P-BA
S-S
TA
£130-160
S 2

Contact Martin & Elizabeth Hogan, Appletree Cottage, Stone House, Church Lane, Ropsley, Lincolnshire NF33 4DA   TEL 01144-1476-585-620

KIRKSTEAD OLD MILL COTTAGE

Woodhall Spa

This part of Lincolnshire holds a particular attraction for North American travellers, for here are to be found the roots of conscience and separatism that became the foundation of America. The drama that made Pilgrims of those independent minded souls was played out from the great Cathedral city of Lincoln to the jail cells of Boston on the Wash. Lincoln and Boston are bound by the meandering River Witham, and midway along its course through this bucolic landscape is Kirkstead Old Mill Cottage.

There is a wonderful "separatism" about this cottage as well, which you will begin to sense as you traverse the mile long approach along an untraveled track across quiet pastures beside a lazy little stream that joins the Witham River just beyond the cottage gate. You will find the Hodgkinson's rowboat tied up on the creek bank in front of the cottage. Later you may want to take the boat and some fishing gear out onto the River Witham, which actually resembles a broad gentle canal in this stretch. The local coarse fishermen entrenched along the bank are a good sign that you may be rewarded for wetting a line here. But first let's have a look in the house, itself.

Tony and Barbara Hodgkinson hope to retire here eventually, and they've gone about the renovations and decorations accordingly. By combining two older cottages they have created exceptionally efficient and spacious accommodations for an extended family gathering. The four bow-fronted bay windows lend a nice bright and airy feel to the downstairs public rooms. There are parquet floors in the living room and dining room, and quarry tile floors in the kitchen; all very clean and modern in design. The furnishings are likewise very clean lined: beige Scandinavian convertible settee and side chairs, teak dinette set with seating for ten, tile topped coffee table, and so on. The fireplace is a high efficiency Baxi type, set in a wall of mortar-less appearing stonework. There is also an upright piano (tuned!) for communal sing-songs and plenty of reading material for solitary leisure.

I. F-3
CS
II.B-q
B-t/q
B-b
F-4
E$m H$m
FP FPE
LT$
TELm
TV
W/D
DW MW
NS
S-S MS
£99-350
S 7-10

In addition to the historic sites associated with the Pilgrim Fathers, there is much to see and do in this neighborhood. Walkers will definitely want to take on a bit of the noted Viking Way (perhaps, the easy going course north from Woodhall Spa toward Tennyson's beloved Wolds). And, though taking the waters is no longer fashionable, Woodhall Spa still has much to offer, not least one of England's finest golf courses. Kirkstead Cottage guests may also use the Hodgkinsons' membership in nearby Bainland Country Park for swimming, tennis and golf, as well as children's entertainments. ETB 4 Keys; Highly Commended

Contact Mrs Barbara Hodgkinson, "Hodge's Lodges", 52 Kelso Close, Worth, Crawley, West Sussex RH10 7XH
TEL 01144-1293-882-008 or FAX 01144-1293-883-352

THE CHATEAU   Gate Burton

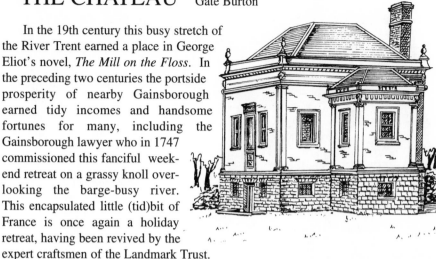

In the 19th century this busy stretch of the River Trent earned a place in George Eliot's novel, *The Mill on the Floss*. In the preceding two centuries the portside prosperity of nearby Gainsborough earned tidy incomes and handsome fortunes for many, including the Gainsborough lawyer who in 1747 commissioned this fanciful week-end retreat on a grassy knoll over-looking the barge-busy river. This encapsulated little (tid)bit of France is once again a holiday retreat, having been revived by the expert craftsmen of the Landmark Trust.

I. B-s
F-2
II.B-d
E&H
FP
LT
S-S MS
INS
£247-426
S 3

The second floor sitting room of The Chateau is spacious enough, with Turner*ish* views over the parkland and river fore and aft, high ceilings with intricate mouldings, and a cosy Georgian framed fireplace. You will find comfy period style furnishings and careful attention to drapery and decorative detail, the hallmark of all Landmark Trust properties. A double bed fully occupies one wing off the sitting room, with a single bedded room in vertical symmetry below. Also on the ground floor is a kitchen alcove and a divided bath and WC.

Contact The Landmark Trust, Shottesbrook, Maidenhead, Berkshire SL6 3SW
TEL 01144-1628-825-925 or FAX 01144-1628-825-417

PENYWERN ROAD
Earl's Court

Just south of the high rent district and Kensington Gardens, this Earl's Court flat offers exceptionally spacious accommodations within easy reach of transportation to all the London attractions. The apartment has a huge garden with a raised patio and plenty of greenery. The large living room features a gas log fireplace against a cheerful *art deco* style decor. The larger bedroom is queen size and prettily furnished with its own sofa and gas log fireplace. Throughout, you will find interesting pictures, attractive drapery, and plenty of little decoratives. French doors exit from both bedrooms directly to the patio. Notably, there are separate shower and bath rooms, and a very modern kitchen with a bright ivory tiled floor.

I. B-q
B-t
F-3
E&H
LT
TELc TV
OPEN
MS
£500
S 4

Contact Rosamond Rose Properties, 22A Upper Addison Gardens, Holland Park, London W14 8AP
TEL 01144-1716-032-704 or FAX 01144-1716-031-710

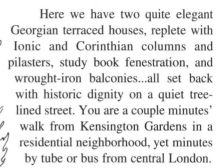

INVERNESS TERRACE
Bayswater

Here we have two quite elegant Georgian terraced houses, replete with Ionic and Corinthian columns and pilasters, study book fenestration, and wrought-iron balconies...all set back with historic dignity on a quiet tree-lined street. You are a couple minutes' walk from Kensington Gardens in a residential neighborhood, yet minutes by tube or bus from central London. This pair of houses has been converted into 2-3 bedroom apartments with spacious rooms of elegant proportions ...the Georgian passion for natural light is everywhere in evidence. Each apartment has a large sitting/dining room and a newly fitted kitchen, with dishwasher, microwave, freezer and, in most cases, a washer/dryer combination.

The apartments are similarly furnished in a stylish manner approaching luxury. To take one as an example: A sitting room with sofa in soft green, piped in yellow; floor-to-ceiling broad French windows; heavy lined drapes with pelmets and tiebacks in blue, green, yellow and peach floral; lemon yellow walls; good quality paintings (more on this later); dried flower arrangements; dining table and chairs (in this case a modern Chinese Chippendale style); colonial style brass chandelier and tasteful table lamps. The bedroom is done in Toile de Jouy style fabric; drapes and ballooned Austrian blinds; a queen size bed with draped pelmet; lots of pillows, a thick richly colored duvet and white dust ruffle; a French provincial occasional chair; and, for late movies in bed, a television amongst all these pretty particulars. While on the functionals, it is worth mentioning that all apartments have phones and some have fax phones. Alas, no elevator.

If your appetite is whetted to make an art purchase, you have only to step down the street to the high fence around Kensington Gardens where hundreds of artists have put up their creations for discovery at generally very reasonable prices. Princess Margaret lives just beyond in Kensington Palace, no doubt because she is also always on the lookout for a good cheap picture...all those walls to decorate!

E&H
LT
TELc TV
W/D
DW MW
OPEN
INS
BK$ TA
£650-950
S 3-6

Contact Mary Spivey, The Independent Traveller, Thorverton, Exeter EX5 5NT
TEL 01144-1392-860-807 or FAX 01144-1392-860-552

LADBROKE SQUARE HOUSE
Holland Park

This is an elegant Georgian house in the midst of a vital older residential neighborhood much favored by aesthetically oriented professionals of all sorts...for example, an Academy Award winning British playwright of my acquaintance occupies a similar apartment directly across the square. You are on the very fringe of Portobello Road, with hundreds of antique shops to explore at your leisure during the week, and probably avoid on the weekends, except perhaps to mingle in the atmosphere of this commercial and recreational bazaar.

Ladbroke Square is a private residential park wholly enclosed behind a wonderful period wrought iron fence. The apartment is on the third floor (with lift) and overlooks the park, which is accessible for guests. There are two bedrooms (double and twin) and bathrooms in equal measure. Furnishings are a blend of modern and traditional, with, for example, a white wicker sofa and chairs upholstered in beige in the living room and nice ladderback chairs in the dining area. There is beige carpeting throughout and plenty of pictures, plants and china ornaments.

| III.B-d |
| B-t |
| F-3 [2] |
| E&H |
| LT |
| TV |
| W |
| E/HC |
| OPEN |
| INS |
| BK$ |
| TA |
| £400-500 |
| S 4 |

BRECHIN PLACE South Kensington

Well situated in an area with good, affordable restaurants and pubs, close to both the Gloucester Road and South Kensington tube stations, this is a large ground floor apartment with a patio in a very handsome Georgian building.

There is an elegant bow-fronted living room with an open fireplace framed by a proper Georgian mantelpiece. The room is decorated in wonderful shades of blue, with beautiful floor-to-ceiling drapes and sheers in the bow front. The sofa and chair suite are covered in blue florals and the room is filled out with assorted antique pieces, including an interesting library globe and some nice occasional rugs. The eat-in kitchen is furnished with a nice pine table and chairs and a pine hutch with interesting china on display.

There are two bedrooms, both very pleasant, indeed. The master bedroom, which has a kingsize bed, is done in cheerful white and peach hues, with very feminine ballon curtains and sheers. The vanity and closets are all of a fitted piece, again very feminine with white with gold trim. The larger bedroom is en-suite, with shower. The second bedroom is also a double and there is an additional bathroom in the apartment.

This is a central area, close to Chelsea shopping and all the museums.

| I.B-k |
| F-3 |
| B-d |
| F-2 |
| E&H |
| FP |
| LT |
| TV |
| W/D |
| MW   DW |
| OPEN |
| INS   BK$ |
| TA |
| £500-600 |
| S 4 |

Contact Mary Spivey, The Independent Traveller, Thorverton, Exeter EX5 5NT
TEL 01144-1392-860-807 or FAX 01144-1392-860-552

STRATFORD ROAD

Kensington

Stratford Road is situated in the heart of the good residential area of Kensington, and this quiet street also benefits from a number of interesting shops and restaurants rendering something of a village atmosphere.

This is a very spacious family apartment on two levels in an elegant, period house. The front door is up one flight of stairs and opens onto a second, shorter flight that leads up to the handsome living room. There is a matching pair of convertible sofas here, with stylish glass top occasional tables and nice prints set off against the soothing blue-grey walls. The living and dining rooms both have fireplaces and fitted carpets.

Upstairs are two bedrooms and bathrooms in equal measure. The twin room is en-suite, and the double bedded room has a French door leading on to a small stone balcony. There is another French door on the stair landing, leading up to a roof terrace.

III.B-t
F-3
B-d
F-3
E&H
FP
LT
TEL
TV
W/D
DW
£1075
S 4-6

DE VERE MEWS   Kensington

De Vere Mews must be one of London's best hidden streets. It is tucked away with a mews entrance off Canning Place, and one could easily not notice it at all. This corner of Kensington, lying between Kensington High Street and Gloucester Road, is a maze of pretty, winding lanes, interspersed with garden squares and grand Victorian mansion blocks. There are a couple appealing boutiques, one highly regarded restaurant (*Launceston Place*) and a popular pub called the *Builders' Arms*. Otherwise, this corner is purely residential of the nicest sort.

The rental flat is on the second floor and can be reached either by the spiral staircase or by the very slow lift! The building has a very amiable porter with whom to pass the time while waiting for the elevator.

Once inside, the entrance hall takes one into a good sized living room with attractive and comfortable furnishings and beige carpeting. The perspective here is due south, overlooking Canning Place. There are three sofas, one of which converts to a double bed. The dining suite accommodates six, and you will find many little pretty particulars and homey touches. The kitchen is smallish, but fully equipped, and the bedroom features a queen size bed with a wall of fitted closets.

II.B-q
F-3
CS
E&H
LT
TV
W/D
DW
£595
S 2-4

Contact In The English Manner, Lancych, Boncath, Pembrokeshire SA37 0LJ
TEL 01144-1239-77444 or FAX 01144-1239-77-686

CHEVAL PLACE
Knightsbridge

It is very hard to find an economical place to stay in London; almost impossible to find such quarters in one of the *preferred* areas. Well, here is a charming little two story cottage tucked away in a quiet mews in the midst of posh Knightsbridge. This is the land of the *Sloane Rangers,* trendy restaurants, fine shopping, and relatively safe walking (keeping in mind that London is a big city with all the associated security problems).

The mews cottage is laid out in the *upside-down* manner, putting the living room upstairs with a little balcony overlooking the interior courtyard. The balcony doors and good front lighting, together with an all white interior, make this a light and

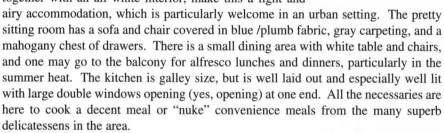

airy accommodation, which is particularly welcome in an urban setting. The pretty sitting room has a sofa and chair covered in blue /plumb fabric, gray carpeting, and a mahogany chest of drawers. There is a small dining area with white table and chairs, and one may go to the balcony for alfresco lunches and dinners, particularly in the summer heat. The kitchen is galley size, but is well laid out and especially well lit with large double windows opening (yes, opening) at one end. All the necessaries are here to cook a decent meal or "nuke" convenience meals from the many superb delicatessens in the area.

Downstairs we find a double bedroom with a nice bedstead of stripped pine and a modern vanity with ample drawers. There are soft green and peach fabrics, and pretty pictures on the walls. The sofa upstairs also makes into a bed, and the two-floor configuration does make this a more livable arrangement for non-family travellers. The shower room and WC are separate, and you will find an extra special treat for the city...a washer and dryer! Another treat: garage available.

Knightsbridge is, for many people, the most elegant area of London. Cheval Place is only a five minute walk from Harrods and the tube, close to Beauchamp Place and its posh shops, as well as a host of cultural venues, such as the Victoria and Albert and Natural History Museums...if travelling with children, buy the long pass at the Science Museum (you will be returning!). For a neighborhood park you have Hyde and Kensington Gardens (roughly the size of Kansas) to stroll in...I highly recommend a walk around the Serpentine very early of a morning for a refreshing gaggle with the Canadian geese and the *bread people*...two very cordial species of city dwellers.

I. B-d
F-1
II.CS
E&H
LT
TV
DW MW
W/D
OPEN
INS
BK$
TA
£400-500
S 3-4

Contact Mary Spivey, The Independent Traveller, Thorverton, Exeter EX5 5NT
TEL 01144-1392-860-807 or FAX 01144-1392-860-552

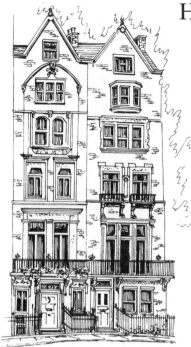

HANS PLACE   Knightsbridge

Hans Place is a very exclusive little garden square in the heart of Knightsbridge, just around the corner from Harrods. There are lovely, private gardens in the center of the square. One of London's finest private schools is across the garden from the flat. The buildings are of red brick in the Victorian style. From here, one can head up to Knightsbridge or easily walk to Sloane Street and down to Sloane Square. There are tube stations at both Sloane Square and Knightsbridge.

The flat, which occupies space on both the ground and first floors (left in drawing), is light, bright and quite elegant. There are two small bedrooms on the ground floor, and between them is a handsome tiled bathroom and shower facility. Upstairs, we find a large drawing room with floor to ceiling windows looking out over the greenery of the Square. The room is decorated in beiges and pretty soft colors and has a fireplace. There are, as well, dining facilities for up to six people and a good sized kitchen, fully fitted with practically every modern convenience.

I.B-d
B-t
F-3
E&H
LT
TV
W/D
DW MW
£975
S 4

MALLORD STREET   Chelsea

Mallord Street...has a nice aristocratic ring to it, *n'est ce pas*?   Well, of course it does! No need to lug around all those republican prejudices when *in Rome!* I expect there are quite a few (younger generation) M'lords and M'ladies bib-and-tuckered away down here in the heart of Chelsea...maybe even on this short smart lane off Old Church Street. However, you can bet they are paying rather more for their steads than is required to rent this very serviceable holiday flat.

Through the main front door of the building, one gains access to the apart-ment, with stairs down to the lower ground floor...what in polite society is called a *garden apartment*. There is a hallway, off which is the living room, comfortably furnished in an older style with a brace of homey sofas in front of an open fire. The shelves are filled with assorted decoratives, and you will find a unique *Early Nero* coffee table fashioned out of the capital of a stone column! One may exit on to the terrace (with its table & chairs) from here or from the bedroom. The bedroom has twin mahogany beds with a matching chest and a fitted wardrobe. This apartment has parquet floors throughout, with good older oriental style carpets. The kitchen is long and narrow, but has all the necessary conveniences.

I.B-t
F-2
E&H
LT
TEL
TV
W/D
DW MW
£525
S 2

Contact In The English Manner, Lancych, Boncath, Pembrokeshire SA37 0LJ
TEL 01144-1239-77444 or FAX 01144-1239-77-686

BEAUFORT GARDENS
Knightsbridge

Beaufort Gardens, a quiet oasis tucked away from the milling crowds and bustle of Knightsbridge, is an attractive rectangular *cul-de-sac* just three minutes' walk from Harrods. The terraced houses are five stories high and have been divided into handsome, high ceilinged flats, or small exclusive hotels.

III.B-q
F-3
B-t
B-s
F-3
E&H
FP
LT
TEL
TV
W/D
DW
£1425
S 5

The lift takes us up to the third floor and, as the saying goes, into the lap of luxury! The apartment has been beautifully designed to offer a large and elegant drawing room with a pillared entry into a good sized dining room. The decor can only be described as sumptuous: big cushy roll arm sofas done in a royal blue floral chintz; color coordinated drapes with fine sheers behind; deep pile fitted carpeting overlaid with oriental rugs; proper botanical prints; and, all this encased in rooms done with bold colors and papers, burnt sienna for the living room, rich small print paper in the dining room. Altogether, this is wonderful space for entertaining or just relaxing in a sea of elegance. Oh yes, we can sleep here, as well! There are three medium sized and handsomely furnished bedrooms. And eat; the kitchen is large and equipped with every possible convenience. But we don't have to clean; the maid is included and comes once a week.

RICHMOND MANSIONS   Earl's Court

This elegant flat is on the second floor of a handsome red brick mansion block, just three minutes walk from the Earl's Court tube station. Gourmands will be happy to know that nearby are two famous London eateries, Pontevecchio and Boswells.

The accommodation comprises a large entrance hall, which also serves as a formal dining room furnished for six. There is a spacious, very elegant living room with a quality queen-size sofa bed, a working fireplace, pretty armchairs in the French style, and a most attractive antique highboy. The apartment is not wanting for the little pretty particulars either; note the oriental pieces, pretty lamps and interesting books. You will find the kitchen is modern, streamlined and well equipped. The sleeping arrangement includes a quiet queen sized bedroom with en-suite bathroom, a twin bedded room, and a single bedded room which doubles as a study. Overall, this apartment is in excellent decorative order, having recently undergone complete refurbishment. The apartment also comes with weekly maid service.

II.CS
B-q
F-3
B-t
B-s
F-2
E&H
FP
LT
TV
W/D
£925
S 5

Contact In The English Manner, Lancych, Boncath, Pembrokeshire SA37 0LJ
TEL 01144-1239-77444 or FAX 01144-1239-77686

BEAUFORT HOUSE   Knightsbridge

Beaufort House is a far cry from a "cottage in the country" and its city venue is the not the sole measure of the difference. This is luxury self-catering in the complete services environment of a first class hotel. However, strictly speaking, Beaufort is not a hotel and the refined intimacy of the apartments veil all the institutional amenities which are discreetly in place to serve and protect their guests. But then, even at one's cottage in the country, the best service is always discreetly veiled.

Beaufort House is nestled in a quiet tree lined square just off the prestigious Brompton Road, a short walk to Harrods and Harvey Nichols stores for the shoppers. For cultural pursuits the Victoria and Albert, Natural History, and Science Museums are just up the street; the Royal College of Music and Royal Albert Hall only a block or two further, and beyond that you have the boundless *countryside* of Hyde Park.

The elegance and style of 19th century England is epitomized in the Regency facade of the building; an image that pervades all twenty-two suites. Apartment sizes range from single bedroom suites to four bedrooms, and in all cases the Beaufort motto is adhered to: maximum comfort and minimum intrusion. Each apartment is individually and sumptuously appointed to reflect traditional high class English tastes in paintings, furnishings, and decor. Number Fourteen is typical of the Beaufort style. It consists of three bedrooms (one en-suite), drawing room, a beautifully fitted kitchen, dining room, bathroom and cloakroom. The apartment is furnished throughout with quality mahogany pieces, Colefax and Fowler sofas grace the drawing room, and Coles wallpapers in warm yellow (drawing room), rich reds (bedrooms) and regal turquoise (dining room).

E&H
LT
TELm
TVV
W/D
DW* MW*
OPEN MS
VAT$
£785-2205
S 2-7

All apartments have a video entry system enabling guests to screen visitors, and direct dial phones for complete privacy in business and family matters. Maid, secretarial, theatre booking, catering, baby sitting, and a host of other services can be provided. Complimentary membership in the exclusive Aquilla Health Club is also offered. Daily rates are on an exact *pro rata* basis of the weekly rate.

Contact Beaufort House, 45 Beaufort Gardens, Knightsbridge, London SW3 1PN
TEL 01144-1715-842-600 or FAX 01144-1715-846-532

ARTESIAN ROAD
Notting Hill

Contrary to what one might expect, London is largely a city of houses, that is, of single family dwellings and family oriented neighborhoods. It is not all highrise and apartment blocks, which is owed, in part, to the fact that London's demography is still largely shaped by pre-industrial patterns of urbanization. There is an amazing continuity in the good neighborhoods of the City, and London is less an apartment culture than any city I know, except perhaps San Francisco, which, of course, is only a fraction of the size of the British capital. Rarely, however, do visitors have an opportunity to rent a family type home, and, indeed, this Artesian Road home is only available during the summers when its owners of the past twenty-five years depart for...you guessed it...the country. Well, that is our good fortune; and speaking of *fortunes,* it doesn't take one to rent this complete *home away from home.*

The house is a side-hall plan, with through access to the back terrace and garden, an amenity sure to be used regularly by summer residents looking for a bit of breeze and a pleasant venue for alfresco dining. Summer absences notwithstanding, the terrace gardens, front and back, are nicely maintained and have pretty flowers and Victorian style wrought iron chairs and table. The kitchen overlooks the back garden and is exceptionally well equipped, as one might expect in a family home. The living room features an open fire with a handsome marble fireplace and a gilt mirror. Artesian Road is adjacent to the Portobello market, London's principal antique district, and it is apparent that the owners of this house have made good use of their fortunate proximity. There is an eclectic mix of furnishings, ranging from a handsome antique pine corner cabinet to a contemporary piano. You will find a very comfy overstuffed sofa in the living room, which converts to a double bed, and lots of characterful decoratives: statuary, china, pictures and all sorts of frameables. The electronic entertainments (TV, video, music systems) are all in place, as well.

Upstairs, there are two bedrooms, one with a Victorian brass bed and a pretty covered side chair of the same period; the other with twin beds and the collected paraphernalia of children who have come of age on the premises. On the third floor there is a self contained loft room with a fridge and washbasin, as well as a double bed and sitting area.

I. CS
F-1
II. B-d
B-t
F-3
III.B-d
E
FP
LT
TEL
TVV
W
DW
OPEN
£500
S 6

Contact Rosamond Rose Properties, 22A Upper Addison Gardens, Holland Park, London W14 8AP
TEL 01144-1716-032-704 or FAX 01144-1716-031-710

STANLEY MANSIONS

Park Walk

Park Walk is a pleasant residential street which runs off of Kings Road. Nearby is the bustle of Fulham Road with its wide selection of good small shops and diverse restaurants. A short bus ride takes you to Knightsbridge for more exclusive shopping and entrancing people-watching.

The flat is accessed across the private mews courtyard to the rear of Stanley Mansions, down a short flight of stairs to a securely gated front entrance. One enters into a spacious kitchen-cum-dining room. The modern fitted units are done in limed oak and there is an octagonal dining table for six. The dining area also features a handsome key-arched corner cupboard with pretty china on display, and some impressive pictures. Through the double doorway is the living room, most agreeably furnished in the English country house style, with a number of pleasant homey touches. There is also a coal effect gas fire.

Sleeping arrangements are comprised of an attractive, en-suite double bedroom with nice furnishings and a fitted wardrobe. In addition, there is a twin bedroom looking out onto a small private courtyard that comes with the apartment. This bedroom is also en-suite, and the bathroom has a small washing machine, along with an unusual fixture for a London flat, to wit, a pulley-operated clothes horse dryer which rises above the bath.

This is a most warm and inviting home away from home for sight seeing and show going in London.

I.B-d
F-3
B-t
F-2
E&H
FPG
LT
TV
W
MW
£795
S 4

HEREFORD MANSIONS   Notting Hill

This is a spacious, light and airy flat on the second floor of a handsome Victorian block just north of Notting Hill Gate. Hereford Road is an attractive residential street with an excellent range of neighborhood shops and one very quaint pub called the *Slug & Lettuce!* The nearest tube station is Notting Hill Gate, which is just a five minute walk.

This apartment is entirely self-contained with its own front door, but is *within* a very large flat owned by one of Britain's most eminent architects, Sir Hugh Casson. The Cassons use the premises as their office; their own home is also in the building. On entering the hallway, the front door to the holiday let is immediately opposite. This leads into a small inner lobby with the immaculately tiled bathroom off to the left. To the right is a large, modern and fully equipped kitchen. Further along we find a large twin bedded room and a spacious living room with wall to wall carpeting and a handsome dining suite situated under the broad bay windows. The apartment is furnished in a nice mix of older style wingbacks and mahogany chests and tables. Arrangements may be made for a child's bed to be installed in the bedroom or sitting room if needed.

II.B-t
F-3
E&H
LT
TV
£595
S 2-3

Contact In The English Manner, Lancych, Boncath, Pembrokeshire SA37 0LJ
TEL 01144-239-77444 or FAX 01144-1239-77686

ABBEY HOUSE

St. John's Wood

A couple of years ago we had the pleasure of spending two months on an assignment in the *Holy Land.* Our residence was, in fact, only a block or so from the *Shrine of Shrines,* that much revered destination point of pilgrims from around the world. Each morning as I walked past the hallowed monument on my way to work, the starry-eyed faithful (usually middle aged) would flock to me, gesticulating and mutely proffering expensive 35mm cameras, begging that I might take their image posed solemnly in front of the Holy Edifice. Their ecstasy at that moment when the camera clicked was a reoccurring challenge to my own cynical agnosticism. How I envied their faith, they who had diligently traveled the long long Abbey Road to worship at the feet (prints) of Saints John, Paul, George & Ringo. I dare not think what a frenzied riot might have resulted if the zealous multitude had known that just next door to their hallowed temple there was a holiday flat for rent!

The apartment in question is situated on the fifth floor of this well maintained block, and consists of a small attractive sitting room, with candy-striped sofa-beds, plus a twin bedded room, bath and kitchen. After the long journey, pilgrims will be relieved to know that this building comes equipped with an elevator, and even a porter, if one needs assistance with the camera bags and incense burners. The apartment is very well equipped and even has a washing machine. There is an assortment of books and a cassette player (for religious observations involving the harmonics of the aforementioned Saints of Abbey Road). Piccadilly is ten minutes away by the tube and the St. John's Wood station is only a short walk from Abbey House. The neighborhood shops can supply everything a pilgrim needs for sustenance or religious service (excellent bakery and wine shop!). In fact, this is a wonderful neighborhood even if one is not drawn to it by blind adoration. There are many attractions here, including Lords, the cricketers' temple; and, definitely not to be forgotten, the home of Sir Thomas Beecham, just around the corner from Abbey House, where I have, myself, posed for a picture...but, of course, only out of intelligent respect for The Genius!

IV. B-t
CS
F-2
E&H
LT
TELc
TV
W
OPEN
MS
£250
S 4

Contact Rosamond Rose Properties, 22A Upper Addison Gardens, Holland Park, London W14 8AP
TEL 01144-1716-032-704 or FAX 01144-1716-031-710

SERVICE SUITES Sloane Square

Service Suites is composed of twelve apartments in three houses which are situated just off Sloane Square. These are quite handsome Victorian mansions, dating from 1886. They were built of brick and Portland stone in an ornate show of urban prosperity which has been assiduously maintained by the present owner, Mrs Kinga Hoyer, who converted and furnished the houses herself. Indeed, the business is very personal to her, and after thirty years she is particularly pleased to welcome a second generation of guests who first stayed with her back in the mid 1960's. Service Suites has a very competent staff, but Mrs. Hoyer lives in one of the houses herself and personally supervises her crew.

The apartments vary in size from studio flats to those with three bedrooms and two reception rooms. All the larger apartments have two bathrooms. The two bedroomed flats with two bathrooms are very popular with paired couples travelling together. The studios meet the needs of business travellers. Each apartment is different. They are furnished in a traditional style, some with antique pieces of furniture, along with good period reproductions. There are original prints and pictures, and even some attractive decorative china to add a homey feeling. Flooring is either wall to wall carpeting or carpets over hardwood.

Typical of the larger flats is Number Nine at 4 Lower Sloane Street, which is practically on the corner of Sloane Square. The entrance foyer of the building is a striking room itself: bold Chinese red walls with whiter-than-white paneled wainscotting and ceiling, and a black and white tiled floor, with a consul style half table prettily decorated with flowers. Number Nine is situated on the second floor, and comprises a reception room on two levels, two bedrooms with bathrooms in equal measure, and a compact kitchen. To the left of an entrance hall are the twin bedded rooms with built-in wardrobes and Florentine cream and gold painted furniture. The larger bedroom can, if desired, have the beds concealed in a wall cupboard and be used in the daytime as a second sitting room or study. The sitting room has a parquet floor, dove-grey wood paneling and a beautiful Georgian style mantel piece. The room is cleverly mirrored to enhance both its proportions and handsomeness. Partly separated by an iron grill from the sitting room and a few steps up from it, is a stage-like gallery which forms a dining room overlooking the sitting room, It commands a view of the garden to the rear of the house.

| E$m H |
| LT |
| TELm |
| TV |
| VAT$ |
| £366-959 |
| S 1-6 |

Mrs. Hoyer's staff will arrange secure parking in the immediate area and the apartments are cleaned six days per week at no extra charge. Service Suites prefer 14-day bookings, but have a daily rate if flats are available. LTB 2-4 Keys

Contact Service Suites, 42 Lower Sloane Street, London SW1W 8BP
TEL 01144-1717-305-766 or FAX 01144-1717-301-261

43 & 45A CLOTH FAIR

Smithfield

Until struck by incurable vegetarianism, I often came in the early mornings to mingle in the bustle and color of the long iron & glass arcade that is recognized as one of the truly great symbols of carnivorism around the globe. In an earlier time, *Smoothfield* was *staked* out for incinerating religious recalcitrants; Queen Mary, alone, dispatched upwards of 300 souls here...a tidy number, to be sure, though not quite up to the weekly flow of 70,000 poor beasts which were driven through the narrow streets of the Old City to *meat* their end here by the late 18th century. One by one, most of the other great character markets (old Covent Garden, Billingsgate) have been run out of old London town, but Smithfield survives in the heart (stomach!) of the City, as does this fine Georgian building and its neighbor, No. 41, on Cloth Fair, which is the only surviving house in the City built before the Great Fire. More recently No. 43 was the home of Sir John Betjeman, whose name continues to grace the banner on the grog shop occupying ground floor premises.

These two flats have been handsomely restored and furnished by the Landmark Trust. The larger, 45A, offers a second floor living room overlooking the street, with an impressive library wall and furnishings in what could be called an 18th century (not to say medieval spartan) ascetic style; very appropriate, indeed, for our own dalliances in the City for library research or theatre recreation. The flat has a reasonably good sized kitchen and a tiny single bedroom to the rear. On the floor above, overlooking the churchyard of St. Bartholomew the Great, is a very spacious en-suite double bedroom, plus another single and complete bathroom.

Next door, with separate ground access, is No. 43. This flat, also occupying second and third floors, enjoys a second level roof terrace in the rear. There is a galley size kitchen off the stairwell, and a good size bathroom and twin bedroom above, with windows framing the ancient church across the way.

A holiday domicile in the heart of the Old City may not be everyone's cup of tea, but for the historically conscious this is an exciting venue, just a couple blocks from the Museum of London, where the fascinating urban story is all laid out, and surrounded by the architecture in which it all happened...St. Paul's, Old Bailey, the Guildhall, and, of course, Smithfield the stomach, perhaps the most poignant metaphor of historic London.

#45A
II. B-s
III.B-d
F-2 [2]
B-s
£497-up
S 4
#43
III.B-t
F-2
£369-up
BOTH
E&H
LT
P-
S-S;
OPEN
MS
INS

Contact The Landmark Trust, Shottesbrook, Maidenhead, Berkshire SL6 3SW
TEL 01144-1628-825-925 or FAX 01144-1628-825-417

FOUNDRY BARN
Burnham Market

With its expansive village green, Burnham Market is one of the prettier towns of north Norfolk. This exceptional conversion of 18th century buildings to holiday condominium use is situated only a short walk from the village green. The buildings are constructed in the Norfolk vernacular tradition of smooth pebble facing, "squared off" in decorative brick work. These properties are individually owned and are therefore furnished and decorated with very distinct personalities. Foundry Barn has a small private courtyard in front and an open view of the countryside to the rear. There are many interesting architectural features (posts, beams, alcoves and polished wood floors) but what really sets the mood of this cottage is the glassed walls on both sides of the living room and a bedroom upstairs. It is said that no wood loves natural light like pine and there are interesting pine pieces here to prove the point. The whole scene is further accented by upstairs ceilings that go to the roof peak and pristine white walls throughout.

I. F-3
II.B-d
B-b
B-t
F-2
E$m
H$
FP$
TV
W
S-S   MS
INS
£250-468
S 6

FOUNDRY COTTAGE

Perhaps it's the sun trap courtyard in front, with tubs of colorful flowers; perhaps it's the parched stone walls and the bright red tile roofs, but this bit of north Norfolk could easily pass for the south of France. Foundry Cottage is at right angles to Foundry Barn, next door. There are exposed beams in this cottage as well, but the charm of this place owes more to the pretty decoration than to the architecturals. The living room features a very comfy floral sofa, a pair of handsome wingbacks, and a number of good quality pine occasional pieces. There is an interesting arched window to the courtyard and a pine framed fireplace, as well as wall to wall carpeting accented by colorful throw rugs.

I. F-3
II.B-d [2]
B-b
F-3
E$m   H$
FP$
TEL
TV
W
S-S   MS
INS
£250-468
S 6

The kitchen/dining room has quarry tile floors and, though fairly compact, there are plenty of working surfaces and all the necessaries in the kitchen to cook up a feast of Norfolk's famous *fruits de mer*. Upstairs you will find three very tidy and spacious bedrooms, basically unadorned except for handsome pine floors polished like the duke's Rolls. There is a wealth of stately homes in the area to visit, including Sandringham, whose grounds are open when the Royals are away. And, of course, there is the sea for sailing, fishing, or just potting along the shore.

Contact North Norfolk Holiday Homes, Lee Warner Avenue, Fakenham, Norfolk NR21 8ER
TEL 01144-1328-855-322 or FAX 01144-1328-851-336

LAMBS COURT Claxton

Half way between the Cathedral city of Norwich, with its famous Norman tower and castle, and the fine sandy beaches of the Norfolk coast is Claxton in the Broads. The Broads, long thought to be a natural geological formation, are, in fact, the result of man's persistent heat-searching dig for peat, going back to prehistory. Today the Broads provide endless aquatic pleasures and great habitat for wildlife.

Lambs Court is approached via a long private drive and looks out over fifty acres of water meadow in a small valley. Built in the middle of the last century on the site of a former clay workings, the house has been extended with east and west wings built in a distinctive Flemish style.

The West Wing (sleeping 8-10) contains the main entrance hall, with a decorative plasterwork fireplace and niches, and a twelve light brass chandelier. The pink drawing room features a canopied fireplace and French windows to a paved terrace. The dining room has a massive table to seat fourteen and a further Louis style fireplace. The original part of the house provides a further sitting room with a canopied inglenook fireplace and beamed ceiling. More open beams are to be found in the kitchen which has been fitted with oak cabinets and nice tiled work surfaces. Upstairs the double height hall gives access to four bedrooms off a pleasant gallery which has comfortable seating. One bedroom features a double half tester bed and shower/bathroom. The others are also en-suite; one with a four-poster bed, and a pair of twin rooms. There is a connecting door at the end of the gallery which accesses the separate East Wing.

The East Wing has two bedrooms, a nice lounge, and dining room, with an open fire. There are boats for hire within a mile; also golf, riding and a friendly pub. And, the entertainments of city and shore are all of fifteen minutes away!

EAST
II.B-d
B-t
F-3
E&H
FP
LT
TVV
W/Ds
MW
S-S
INS
£155-344
S 4
WEST
II.B-d [2]
F-3 [2]
B-t [2]
F-2 [2]
CS
E
FP$
LT
TV
W/D
P-BA
S-S INS
£295-676
S 8-10

Contact Coast & Country Holidays, 15 Town Green, Wymondham, Norfolk NR18 0PN
TEL 01144-1953-604-480 or FAX 01144-1953-606-671

OLD GAMEBIRD COTTAGES Cranworth

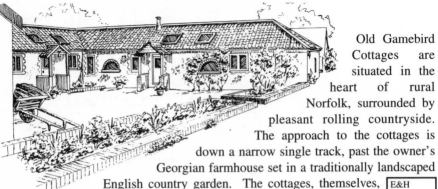

Old Gamebird Cottages are situated in the heart of rural Norfolk, surrounded by pleasant rolling countryside. The approach to the cottages is down a narrow single track, past the owner's Georgian farmhouse set in a traditionally landscaped English country garden. The cottages, themselves, are of traditional unknapped flint and brick construction dating from early Victorian times, and form three sides of a small courtyard. Pheasant Cottage is the largest, with three bedrooms and a nice kitchen fitted in oak. Partridge Cottage has double and twin bedrooms, and little Pigeon Cottage offers a double bedroom and an open plan living room/diner. All three are nicely furnished and have cozy wood-burning stoves in addition to central heating. A tennis court and games room are also on the property for guests. ETB 4 Keys; Highly Commended

E&H
FPS$
L; T$
TELc
TVV
W/Ds
MW
P-BA
F-F
MS
£130-360
S 2-6

Contact Mrs. Jacqui Wigg, The Courtyard, Cranworth, Thetford, Norfolk IP25 7TB
TEL 01144-1362-821-022 or FAX 01144-1362-820-298

HINDRINGHAM HALL COTTAGES

Nr Fakenham

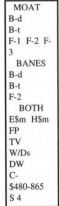

There are two pretty cottages on the grounds of Hindringham Hall, a magnificent moated Tudor country house built in 1495. Hindringham Hall, with its welcoming dependencies, is entirely secluded within its own parkland of moated gardens. Moat House cottage may be approached across a lovely little suspension bridge with tile roofed *tori* ends which double as cable anchors and rose arbors. The bank of the moat is wonderfully wild with flowers and summer life. Moat cottage, itself, is built of flint and brick under a traditional pantile roof. There is a very cozy sitting room with herringbone wood block flooring, a window seat and French doors to the garden. Banes Cottage dates from about the time a local chap named Nelson was making a name for himself at Trafalgar. You will find open fires in both the living room and bedroom in Banes. These are wonderful cottages in a scented land of lavender and salt air.
ETB 4 Keys; Commended

MOAT
B-d
B-t
F-1 F-2 F-3
BANES
B-d
B-t
F-2
BOTH
E$m H$m
FP
TV
W/Ds
DW
C-
$480-865
S 4

Contact Mary McCanna, Westminster Lodgings, 160 Westminster Dr., W.E., Jamestown, NY 14701
TEL 800-699-0744 or 716-484-0744

LEES FARM   Erpingham

This is quite simply one of the most stunning holiday properties anywhere. Looks can be so deceiving, which is not to say that Lees Farm doesn't look quite handsome from the outside. However, behind the (presumably Victorian) brick facade is a timber framed farmhouse that was past the blush of new when Columbus sailed the ocean blue. Here, somewhat paradoxically, is a historic house which has been preserved on the inside and "modernized" on the exterior. Strictly speaking, this is a bit deceiving also, because the interior has had all the modern facilities installed and there have, no doubt, been many *modernizations* since the 15th century. Yet we have here a museum quality dwelling, albeit an architectural exhibition spanning five centuries, sensitively restored and furnished by the contemporary owners.

We begin in the living room with the raised inglenook fireplace encompassing a modern woodburning stove, a cruck-like timber lintel that certainly saw the 15th century, and masonry from some time in-between....effect: stunning!..even before the interesting collection of brasses was affixed to the lintel. Furnishings in this room and all the others: delicious!...even before the original oil paintings, sepia with age and rich framing, were added to the pristine white walls. Speaking of walls, some of the walls here are exhibits in themselves: exposed timber framing, worn and polished to the pinnacle of *character* by time, near black on ultra-white; a melange of post & beam, wattle & daub, ancient brick and plaster...a veritable gallery of ancient construction technology! In the dining room you will admire the old domed bread oven and the lighted mahogany alcove, with table and chairs also in mahogany. Note the grandfather clock and the stone stairs up to a gallery landing. Subtly integrated into this historic environ are all the modern luxuries from the king size bed to the bidet.

Norfolk is much favored by British tourists and overlooked by overseas visitors. We have enjoyed exploring this area of Norfolk a number of times in the past twenty years...the next time I hope Lees Farm will be available as our base...but it's one to book early!

I. B-s
F-1
II.B-k
F-3
B-d
B-t
F-2
E
H$
FPS
TV
W
DW MW
S-S
INS
£196-442
S 6

Contact Coast & Country Holidays, 15 Town Green, Wymondham, Norfolk NR18 0PN
TEL 01144-1953-604-480 or FAX 01144-1953-606-671

THE WHITE HOUSE
Holt

This is certainly one of the best bargains in family holiday accommodation in East Anglia. Situated just at the edge of Holt, which is one of the more interesting Georgian market towns of north Norfolk, it is in an ideal location for pursuing all of the family pleasures offered by nature and commerce along the shore. The house is exceptionally large, being in part a former granary dating from the last century. The "cottage" is also laid out in a family oriented plan, with a spacious kitchen (stools at the counter, as well as a breakfast table) which exits on to the patio and large walled yard, as well as into a huge conservatory, which will no doubt become *the* place to be, possibly engendering some competition between the generations. In addition there is a separate dining room with an exceptionally large table, and some other pleasant features (massive gilt mirror in the hall, arched gothic-style patio doors...even a bidet).

I. B-t
F-1
II.B-t
B-d
F-4
F-1
E$m
H$
LT$
TV
W
DW
S-S MS
INS
£272-510
S 6-8

Contact North Norfolk Holiday Homes, Lee Warner Avenue, Fakenham, Norfolk NR21 8ER
TEL 01144-1328-855-322 or FAX 01144-1328-851-336

OLD CHAPEL COTTAGE
Hickling

This delightful little flint and brick cottage with its red pantile roof sits behind a hedge in a well planned jungle of beautiful flowers and shrubbery...ivy & roses, hollyhocks & poppies, hydrangea & honeysuckle, just for starters! The sitting room has an inglenook fireplace and is

II.B-d
B-t
F-2
E&H
LT
TELc TV
W
DW
C-BA
P-BA
S-S OPEN
MS
£170-210
S 4

furnished in a cozy homey style with an eclectic mix of antiques and collectibles, cheery curtains and pretty pictures. The rooms are cozy, with little secret garden views. Upstairs there are two bedrooms, a twin and a double, and the bathroom has that cleverest of all English amenities, the heated towel rack. You are in the Norfolk Broads and that means wonderful walks for the naturalists and all manner of inland boating for the water enthusiasts. As if that wasn't enough, there are long stretches of sandy beach only a couple miles away.

ETB 3 Keys; Highly Commended

Contact Mrs. Corrine Brown at "Hollingbery", Guilt Cross, Kenninghall, Norwich NR16 2LJ
TEL 01144-1953-813-14

THE FARMHOUSE
Plumstead

This traditional farmhouse has much to offer the large holidaying family, but is also available at reduced rates for smaller parties. You are within minutes of the long sandy beaches of the Norfolk north shore and the summertime culture of the popular old resort towns of Sheringham and Cromer. The house is furnished in a homey style, with some interesting antiques, such as the mahogany breakfront and upright piano in the living room, and Scandinavian style furnishings in the dining area. There are two fireplaces, the principal one being a handsome Victorian framed in pretty tiles, with a gilt mirror over the mantel. You will find wood and original quarry tile floors downstairs with bright rugs, and nice soft lighting in all the rooms. Outside there is an acre of lawn bordered by a holly hedge, and a number of decommissioned farm buildings restricted to children.

I. F-3
II.B-d
B-t [3]
F-2
E   H$
FP [2]
TV
W
MW
P$
S-S MS
INS
£227-425
S 8-10

Contact North Norfolk Holiday Homes, Lee Warner Avenue, Fakenham, Norfolk NR21 8ER
TEL 01144-1328-855-322 or FAX 01144-1328-851-336

GILES COTTAGE
Houghton St. Giles

Houghton St. Giles has been receiving tourists for nearly ten centuries. In the lingo of the travel industry, Houghton St. Giles was not so much a *destination point*, as a *stopover*. What the tourists of yore stopped over for was the Slipper Chapel, last in a chain of ecclesiastical *resting points* on the pilgrimage route to the Shrine of Walsingham, just a mile or so down the road. Having traveled from the far corners of the land, we may wonder why these pilgrims, among whom were the Kings of England themselves, paused just short of their destination. Religious anticipation-cum-ecstasy is probably the answer, but a mile was considerably further then (even a *last* mile), and one shouldn't over-look the fact that Houghton St. Giles is, itself, a very pleasant place.

The same can be said for Giles Cottage, which was built about the time Henry VIII put the whammy on tourism in this area...well, Papally organized tourism, at any rate. Today Giles Cottage sits prettily in its own garden and welcomes visitors of all denominations to enjoy its quaint rusticity. You will find the accommodations quite spacious for two or three persons, with a melange of comfy furnishings and some markedly handsome antiques (note the grandfather's clock).

I. CS
II.B-t
F-3
E&H
FP
LT
TEL   TV
DW   MW
NS
W-W
MS
INS   BK
$460-660
S 2-3

Contact Meta Voyage, 1945 Pauline Plaza, Suite 14, Ann Arbor, MI 48103-5047
TEL 800-771-4771 (East) 800-538-6881 (West) or FAX 313-995-3464

ROSE COTTAGE   Merton

Rose Cottage lies just off the village green in the pleasant hamlet of Merton. It is one of a pair of semi-detached thatched cottages built around 1811 for the estate of Lord Walsingham, who was then the sole landowner in Merton and also owned substantial parts of the surrounding villages.

The cottage is constructed with solid walls of locally dug clay and thatched with reed from Thompson Water, a nearby mere. A gate leads from a small lane to the grassed drive. In front of the cottage is a large garden, well-screened by hedges. At the rear of the house, where there is a barbeque, bench and chairs, the garden backs onto the open fields. Birders will be thrilled to know that over fifty species of birds have been recorded in the garden.

We enter the house via the living room, which has a beamed ceiling, old stripped pine doors and a large inglenook fireplace of Norfolk Red bricks, with a wood-burning stove. On each side of the fireplace are cupboards with the original plank doors, wherein guests will find a supply of logs, books, games, tourist information, and other necessaries such as an iron, etc. The living room is nicely furnished with a floral three-piece suite, an extending dining-table, chairs and occasional tables. The kitchen is very pleasant, with beamed ceiling, and has plenty of working spaces and gas cooking.

Upstairs are two pretty bedrooms with pine doors and some exposed beams. The original staircase leads to a landing bedroom, which has an antique chest and chair. Opening from this room is the main bedroom papered in a nice bright small print pattern, with pine trim. There is a double bed and a large walk-in wardrobe, as well as pine chest and mirror.

I. F-3	Walkers will want to have a go at part of the Peddar's Way which passes near the cottage, and within a few miles are the Great Eastern Pingo Trail and the Nature Reserves at Thompson Common and Wayland Wood (supposedly the setting of the *Babes In the Wood* tale!). Fishing is available by permit at Thompson Water in season.
II.B-s	
B-d	
E H$	
FPS	
LT	
TV	
S-S MS	ETB 4 Keys; Highly Commended
INS	
£132-276	*Contact Coast & Country Holidays, 15 Town Green, Wymondham, Norfolk NR18 0PN*
S 3	*TEL 01144-1953-604-480 or FAX 01144-1953-606-671*

THE LONG BARN

Mulbarton

Historically known as *The Great Barn* at Mulbarton, its Dutch gable stands watching over Mulbarton village common as it has done for hundreds of years. The Barn was originally part of a great farming estate with buildings on this site dating back to the 11th century; in fact, parts of the original structure are still to be seen in The Long Barn. Sections of the original moat remain, as well, although now they are the preserve of waterfowl and migrant birds. The original building here is believed to have been built by the St. Omer family, who came with William the Conqueror.

Adjoining The Barn are the Coach House and The Stable, enjoying beautiful views over the common. They have recently been skillfully converted into two separate holiday accommodations with light airy rooms, *mind-the-head* doorways, and original beams in abundance. The Stable is compact, sleeping two, with a comfy living room and small dining area. Furnishings are a homey assortment of pine, rattan and a contemporary suite. The kitchen is galley style, but large enough to accommodate a small washing machine.

The Coach House is the larger of the two rentals, with a kitchen and dining area on the ground floor and a turned staircase up to the living room. This is a spacious room, nicely furnished with a floral suite and a number of summery rattan pieces under a ceiling that goes to the peak. There is a double en-suite bedroom on this level, with stairs going up to a gallery bedroom with a double sofa bed, and then through to a twin room.

Mulbarton, itself, dates back to Roman times and is mentioned in the *Domesday Book*. Nearby is Hingham, home of many of the Pilgrim fathers, as well as the Lincolns, late of Illinois. However, not all the persons of antiquity removed themselves to foreign lands; in fact, some of the previous occupants of the Long Barn reportedly *drift in* for the occasional visitation...all quite amiable. The present custodian would be happy to relate his experiences with the apparitions over a glass of ale at the nearby Worlds End Pub. The Worlds End, incidentally, is used to playing host to American friends, not least (then) Captain Jimmy Stewart, who relaxed over many a pint here while stationed at Mulbarton.

STABLE
I.B-d
F-3
£104-235
S 2
COACH
II.B-d
F-3
III.CS
B-t
£154-346
S 6
BOTH
E
TELc
TVV
W
MW
S-S   MS
INS

Contact Coast & Country Holidays, 15 Town Green, Wymondham, Norfolk NR18 0PN
TEL 01144-1953-604-480 or FAX 01144-1953-606-671

Worsted Cottage

NORWICH BREAKS
Norwich

Norwich Breaks own and manage five holiday properties situated in and around the famous old city of Norwich. This fascinating city is really the hub of Norfolk and is arguably England's most complete medieval city. The 900-year-old Norman Castle and the famous Cathedral are, of course, major attractions, but there is a life and pulse to Norwich that is worth taking in, as well. A good place to begin is with the open air market.

Typical of the Norwich Breaks offerings is Worsted Cottage, named, of course, for the weaving of worsted cloth for which Norwich was famous. This is a Grade II Listed 16th century flint and timbered cottage situated in the most historic Colegate part of the city. The cottage is in a quiet courtyard with trees and shrubs and forms part of Bacon House, which had associations with Ketts Rebellion after the death of Henry VIII. Entering via a heavy oak door, one is amazed to see the size of the oak ceiling beams. Floral curtains, comfortable soft furnishings, good prints and lighting render a cozy feel in the living room. The upstairs bedroom has undergone modern renovations, altering the wall locations, but the queen size bed is framed by blackened oak posts which testify to the antiquity of Worsted Cottage. This is an exceptionally pretty room, well lit, with an interesting gallery effect over the stairwell. The bathroom is en-suite with champagne colored fixtures. ETB 4 Keys; Highly Commended

II.B-d
F-3
E&H
L; T$
TELc
TV
W/D
P-
S-S OPEN
MS
TA
£220-280
S 3

Another of the Norwich Breaks prizes is Strangers Court. This property literally overlooks the back garden of one of Norwich's most famous museums, the Strangers Hall. The *strangers* were, in fact, the Flemish weavers who lived here in the 16th century and were the backbone of the new industry, if not apparently quite an integral part of the community.

III.B-s [2]
F-3
III.B-d
E&H
L; T$
TELc TV
W
NS
S-S OPEN
MS
TA
£250-320
S 4

You will find the living room of Strangers Court done in a rose pastel, with nice soft furnishings, a Victorian pine dresser, rush covered dining chairs and French doors to the patio garden. The kitchen is done in pine and there is a nice Royal Doulton crockery set. Upstairs, the master bedroom is carpeted in a deep pile cream color, and there are two single rooms with large wardrobes and Victorian pine dressing tables. ETB 4 Keys; Highly Commended

Contact Desmond Wain, Norwich Breaks, 22 Christchurch Rd., Norwich, Norfolk NR2 2AE TEL 01144-1603-453-363 or FAX 01144-1603-259-729

APPLETON WATER TOWER Sandringham

History records that the Princess of Wales, Alexandra, laid the foundation stone for the Appleton Water Tower in 1877. One wonders whether she ever returned to take in the far reaching views when the Tower was completed, views which would have included the Royal country residence of Sandringham, practically at the foot of the Tower. Today, Sandringham is favored by Royal-watchers, as well as Royals, and is the home of the Royal Car Museum among other attractions.

From the beginning, the Appleton Water Tower had a domestic, as well as utilitarian, role. Thanks to careful restoration by the Landmark Trust, the old caretakers quarters on the first three floors are now available for holiday let, and the adjoining stair-tower takes us to the roof terrace for those spectacular views, day or night, and all in private. The interior octagonal rooms are a delight, with Victorian period furnishings and decoratives, and wrap-around views of the surrounding rustic parklands through character gothic windows. Ground floor kitchen and bathroom facilities can be classified as *cubby*, but the third floor double bedroom is spacious enough to accommodate a full size sofa and offers direct access to the stair-tower.

I. F-3
II. B-t
III.B-d
E&H
FP
LT
S-S MS
INS
£352-613
S 4

Contact The Landmark Trust, Shottesbrook, Maidenhead, Berkshire SL6 3SW
TEL 01144-1628-825-925 or FAX 01144-1628-825-417

BECK FARM Sustead

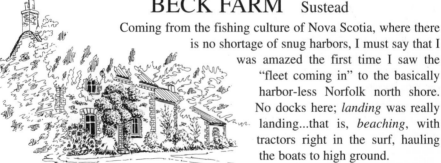

Coming from the fishing culture of Nova Scotia, where there is no shortage of snug harbors, I must say that I was amazed the first time I saw the "fleet coming in" to the basically harbor-less Norfolk north shore. No docks here; *landing* was really landing...that is, *beaching*, with tractors right in the surf, hauling the boats to high ground.

A short drive inland from where I watched those crab boats landing that day is the cottage at Beck Farm. This is a mid-Victorian farmhouse, constructed in the vernacular flint and brick style. The house is surrounded by open fields and natural hedgerows; a wonderful peaceful area for walking and communing with nature. Massive fireplaces dominate both the kitchen and sitting room, though electric fires have been installed. Furnishings are comfortable, with a couple markedly fine antiques, and the bedrooms are bright and airy, albeit with quite low ceilings.

I. F-3
II.B-d [2]
B-s
F-2
E$m H
FPE
L
TV
W
MW
S-S MS
INS
£170-318
S 5

Contact North Norfolk Holiday Homes, Lee Warner Avenue, Fakenham, Norfolk NR21 8ER
TEL 01144-1328-855-322 or FAX 01144-1328-851-336

VERE LODGE
South Raynham

George Bowlby is one of the true veterans in the British tourist industry. He has had his hand in self-catered tourism for a long time...actually, both hands, back, heart and soul! He founded and ran the largest, up-market self-catering agency (by far) in Britain, serving up to 250,000 holiday clients per year, and has, to put it mildly, garnered some real insight into what makes for a happy holiday. Seven years ago George sold the English Country Cottage Agency and retired to the Bowlby family home, Vere Lodge. It had taken the Bowlbys thirty-five years to transform the run-down Georgian estate into an elegant home for themselves, and it seemed the time had arrived to enjoy it. Alas however, within a year George got bored and lonely; it would seem that life without holidaymakers was just no holiday for the Bowlbys. So the building process began again, resulting in the transformation of the Vere estate buildings (and some others on the periphery) into thirteen superb holiday cottages...the kind which are sure to make for a happy holiday (and a happy George Bowlby).

There are luxurious accommodations here for couples, such as Dove Cottage with an elegantly furnished living room upstairs, opening out on to a private roof garden with wonderful views over the gentle Norfolk countryside. Downstairs there is a delightful king sized bedroom, mirrored as if to take a picture of itself. I have used the words *luxurious* and *elegant* in this description, terms used very sparingly in this book; not because these qualities are inappropriate to a number of the properties we've selected, but because over-used superlatives blur, rather than elucidate. Yet several of the Bowlby cottages beg exception, which is not to say the other Vere cottages are anything less that handsome in the extreme. And characterful; take Possum Cottage, named after the Bowlbys' nanny of thirty years. A one time billiard room, Possum has been converted into a gallery bed-loft over a sumptuous blue papered open plan room which features a wall of antique pine cupboards.

Eight of the cottages are family sized, though no less...here's the word again...elegant. Wonderful soft furnishings, fine grains in the occasional pieces whether they be period or contemporary styles, lots of decoratives and lush carpets. Frankly, I am amazed that Vere Lodge doesn't exclude children; these are not sticky finger premises, and even as parents, ourselves, who almost always travel *en famille,* we couldn't blame

E&H
FP*
LT
TELc
TVV
W/Ds
DW MW
P-BA$
E/HC*
F-F S-S
MS OPEN
INS
VAT$
£213-924
S 2-7

the Bowlbys for being a bit protective. But George and Jane Bowlby are not about to child-proof their retirement; in fact, one is almost required to have children to stay at Vere...or at least come with a grandparent. It soon becomes apparent why Vere Lodge invites children. If the kids didn't come, who would accompany George on the parade of the morning feeding? This formal assembly begins when most parents want to be lazing in those aforementioned *luxurious* beds. However, Yang the potbellied pig; Sugar, Spice and Everything Nice, the three miniature Angora goats; Saturday, the Jacob's sheep; Mingo the donkey; Toby the pony; Collies Asher & Blue, and all the bunnies, peacocks, hens and assorted wild hangers-on are very much awake and ready for the ritual. Smart parents will put together their left-over contributions to the fete the night before, and make arrangements for meeting the sprouts later somewhere on the Vere grounds, perhaps in the games room, adjacent to the large indoor pool, or at the tennis court or croquet lawn. There is, incidentally, a comfortable sitting room overlooking the pool with a small bar facility and light lunches during the peak season. In the same building you will find a help yourself freezer with dinners, expertly prepared in the Bowlby kitchen, and, for payment, a *trust you box*. Vere Lodge is that kind of place. ETB 3 & 4 Keys; Highly Commended

Contact George & Jane Bowlby, Vere Lodge, South Raynham, Fakenham, Norfolk NR21 7HE
TEL 01144-1328-838-261 or FAX 01144-1328-838-300

HARPERS COTTAGE
Syderstone

This is a pleasant terraced cottage dating from 1820 and tastefully modernized in 1981. The cottage is constructed of attractive mellowed brick with the original pantiled roof. The interior retains the beamed ceilings and cottage latch doors. As is common in Norfolk, entrance is through the part glass back door into the kitchen/diner. The kitchen is pleasant and airy with an interesting old church pew. In the sitting room there is a large open fireplace with red brick surrounding the chimney breast and a woodburning stove on a quarry tiled hearth. The furnishing is *cottage* style, modest and comfortable. Outside, the front garden is full of climbers and cottage plants, while the back garden is more secluded and grassed, with a good selection of herbs for cooking and outdoor furniture for alfresco lunches.

II.B-d
B-b
F-2
E$m
H$m
FPS
LT
TV
MW
S-S
INS
£124-248
S 4

Contact Coast & Country Holidays, 15 Town Green, Wymondham, Norfolk NR18 0PN
TEL 01144-1953-604-480 or FAX 01144-1953-606-671

STABLE COTTAGE

Wymondham

Stable Cottage is situated two miles from town, within the grounds of the Grade II Listed Wicklewood Hall. The cottage is adjacent to a fenced pond which abounds with wild life. Wicklewood Hall, itself, is a 17th century manor house with distinctive stepped gables.

The stables were converted to holiday accommodation about five years ago, preserving an interesting array of oak and pine timbering which make the exposed roof space an integral part of the living accommodation. The lounge and bedrooms are carpeted, the bathroom has vinyl flooring, and the kitchen Norfolk pamments. Furnishings are mixed in style but pleasant enough to the eye and comfortable.

This is an interesting area to explore, not least for the Abbey in Wymondham with two extraordinary towers, built as a result of a feud between the townspeople and the monks.

I.B-d	
B-t	
F-2	
E	H$
TV	
W	
DW	MW
S-S	
INS	
£132-276	
S 4	

Contact Coast & Country Holidays, 15 Town Green, Wymondham, Norfolk NR18 0PN
TEL 01144-1953-604-480 or FAX 01144-1953-606-671

GOLDEN GOOSE COTTAGE

Wiveton

The name of this village has been a curiosity to me. I wonder if perhaps its origins might be in some ancient maritime tragedy; a village with all its menfolk lost on an ill-fated fishing expedition? Interestingly enough, there is a ceremony of handing out money to pensioners carried out here on the Wiveton Green on Saturday after-

I. F-3	
II.B-d	
B-t	
E$c	
H$c	
FPS	
TV	
NS	
S-S	MS
INS	
£170-318	
S 4	

noons. They've been at it since before Shakespeare was born, which is about when this cottage was built. It's an unassuming little den, with blackened beams, a cozy wood burner in the sitting room, and a sunny dining spot in the bay window. Upstairs you'll find a couple bright and tidy bedrooms under the eaves. A good value cottage in a good location for naturalist excursions to the Blakeney Point Reserve or for sailing out of nearby Blakeney Harbor.

Contact North Norfolk Holiday Homes, Lee Warner Avenue, Fakenham, Norfolk NR21 8ER
TEL 01144-1328-855-322 or FAX 01144-1328-851-336

THE DIRECTORS SALOON

Wymondham Station

The historic Railway Station at Wymondham will be 150 years old in 1995. This Grade II Listed building with a number of cottages (also Grade II Listed) form a delightful square. Even the original 1935 Telephone Kiosk has been listed. The whole scene is being beautifully restored to mint condition, surrounded by flowers and landscaped gardens.

To the right of the Station, standing alongside the main Norwich to Cambridge line, is a 1950's Mark I London South Western Carriage which has been converted for luxurious holiday accommodation or as a meetings venue. It has been dubbed *The Directors Saloon*. The interior is impressively renovated with mahogany and brass throughout, rich blue/grey/rose flame stitch upholstery, deep blue velvet curtains and deep pile gray carpets. The lounge-diner features a collection of beautifully framed steam train pictures and has a color television with video. The former brake room, still with the brakeman's apparatus, is now a convenient telephone and fax room. The snug room, with all the original carriage fittings, is a super place to have morning coffee and imagine yourself clicky-clacking along to Edinburgh...or Istanbul, for that matter; after all, it's your private car!

Nomadic gourmands will not be disappointed. The galley kitchen is fully fitted even down to a washing machine. You will be eating off Royal Duchess china. There are two bedrooms, one with a four foot divan, the other with sleeping car bunks. Outside there is a platform with garden furniture overlooking a landscaped garden.

The coach is completely unique in Britain and was restored to a high standard. All of the works at Wymondham Station are owed to the dedication and hard work of David Ainger-Turner, Baron of Tierragh, Lord of Fundenhall with Hapton. The Directors Saloon may not be everybody's *ticket*, but every railway buff or prospective *choochoophile*, young or old, will have a memorable stay. And, if you get the antique train bug, you will want to have a look at the railway and steam engine collection at nearby Bressingham Hall.

I.B-d
B-b
F-3
E
LT$
TELc
TVV
W
S-S
INS
£132-276
S 4

Contact Coast & Country Holidays, 15 Town Green, Wymondham, Norfolk NR18 0PN
TEL 01144-1953-604-480 or FAX 01144-1953-606-671

THE LODGINGS
at PREBENDAL
MANOR
Nassington

Prebendal Manor House is a Grade I Listed antiquity with a history extending back to the Late Saxon Period. In fact, the original lord of this manor was none other than the Danish King, Canute. The Lodgings was added in the 15th century when feudal prestige necessitated the ability to house a great number of inspecting nobles and visiting clerics, particularly during periods of festivity when grand banquets would be given. The Lodgings, then, was a sort of VIP dormitory. The antiquity of the building is reflected in the wealth of large oak beams and the stone spiral staircase which leads to the two cozy, well appointed bedrooms. Even if you are not a nosy noble or a *come-from-away* Bishop, you will be impressed with the antique furnishings and chintz drapings in these bedrooms, one with fine views extending over the countryside, the other overlooking the old orchard of the manor.

The open plan living arrangement on the ground floor has a fine polished wooden floor overlain with Indian rugs. All the furniture is antique, but of a cottage style very suited to this medieval building. On the walls hang a number of prints depicting past life in rural England.

The use of herbs in medieval England was of prime consideration, a measure of prosperity and hospitality that would have been carefully noted by sojourners from afar. Prebendal Manor continues the tradition of a separate area for useful plants, such as herbs, inside the Lodge grounds, with a later extension of the gardens for ornamental species. All the plants were grown for food, medicinal purposes or to provide sweet fragrances. Likewise, the Manor had (and has) a large fish pond and dovecote, and a tithe barn to accommodate feudal levies.

Nassington is close to the beautiful town of Stamford, familiar to many as the setting for the TV series *Middlemarch*. Cambridge is only forty minutes away, and a number of great naturalist walks (Wakerley Great Wood & Titchmarsh Reserve) and great houses (Kirby Hall and Lyveden New Bield) are in the immediate neighborhood.

II.B-d
B-t
F-2
E&H
LT
TV
W/D
MW
C-BA
P-
S-S
INS
BK$
£230-300
S 4

Contact Discover Britain, Shaw Mews, Shaw Street, Worcester WR1 3QQ
TEL 01144-1905-613-744 or FAX 01144-1905-613-747

OUNDLE COTTAGE BREAKS

Oundle

The historic market town of Oundle lies on the eastern side of Northamptonshire close to the adjoining county of Cambridgeshire. This is an old town, having been a settlement even before Roman times, and having enjoyed great prosperity in Tudor and Georgian times.

Our first experience in Oundle lives as one of my most vivid memories of all our years of travel in Britain. We arrived in the town quite early one morning to inspect a house we were considering buying. Even for a busy market town, there seemed to be an inordinate amount of scurry and bustle on the narrow little streets around the Market Place. As we were early for our appointment with the estate agent, we ducked into a quaint little tea shop on the main street. The place was a sea of newly pressed blue uniforms and freshly scrubbed cherub faces. Nor was it a calm sea; it was first day of the autumn term at Oundle School, a boarding institution of national repute, and the children seemed to boil in a hubbub of renewing comradery, while stiff-upper-lipped parents (also very neatly pressed and scrubbed) queued up for tea and heaped plates of sweets...caloried penitence for sending the little dears off, maybe; sugary *adieus,* for sure.

Near the small Georgian townhouse we had come to see is the pharmacy owned by Richard Simmonds. Indeed, there has been an apothecary here since Dickens' time, and there is more than a little Dickensian flavor to the Market quarter of this fascinating town. The cottages are situated in the walled garden behind, lost, as it were, in an oasis of traditional English plants and shrubs, many of which have medicinal or herbal qualities and found their way into the garden over many generations of apothecary occupation.

There are three brick and stone built cottages in the old stable court: *Grooms, Courtyard* and *Stable,* by name. The first two sleep two, while Stable has a pair of bedrooms. They have exposed beams and carpeting throughout, with pretty pastel decors in bedrooms and nice cottage style soft furnishings in the living rooms. Breakfast is complementary on the first morning, and, indeed, the cottages may be let on a very reasonable B&B basis for any number of days.

ETB 4 Keys; Highly Commended

STABLE
I. F-3
II.B-d
B-t
F-2
E&H
LT
TELm
TV
W/D   DW
NS
OPEN MS
TA
£125-250
S 2- 4

*Contact Richard Simmonds, Oundle Cottage Breaks, 30 Market Place, Oundle Nr Peterborough
PE8 4BE   TEL 01144-1832-273-531 or FAX 01144-1832-274-938*

8 Front Street   Bamburgh

The popular seaside resort town of Bamburgh has grown up around the formidable red sandstone Castle, which towers 150 feet above the sea. This is the ancient home of the Kings of Northumbria. The other great architectural landmark here is St. Aidan's Church, dating from Norman times, and reminding us of the retreat of the sainted Bishop of Lindisfarne, Cuthbert, to the nearby Farne Islands in the 7th century. Today, the boat trip out to the Farnes from Bamburgh is much favored by visitors interested in seeing the bird and seal sanctuary, and the Holy Island of Lindisfarne may be reached over the causeway at low tide. One does want to mind the tide chart very carefully, however, or one may be spending the night dancing with the shadows of Viking ghosts!

Angela Moore's holiday cottage is only about 250 yards from the towering silhouette of Bamburgh Castle. The cottage is, itself, a Grade II Listed building, with the front dating from the 17th century, while the rear is late Victorian. There is a pretty courtyard garden and beyond that a lawned area with herbaceous borders.

One enters the cottage to an oak beamed side hall with a wide, inviting staircase leading up, and a pair of spacious living rooms on the ground floor. The front room has an unusual inglenook fireplace, with a stone arch rather than the more typical timber or stone lintel. The inglenook easily accommodates a good sized woodburning stove. There are some very handsome pieces of furnishing here, including a fine highboy chest and a pretty floral suite with pink piping. An even larger living/dining room combination, with adjoining kitchen, is at the back of the house. There is another open fireplace here, though the house is centrally heated. The stairs have a middle landing, off which there is a double bedded room looking onto the Grove across the street and the church beyond. To reach the fully tiled bathroom and two further bedrooms overlooking the garden one climbs a further three steps. Furnishings, excepting the beds, are mainly late Victorian. ETB 4 Keys; Highly Commended

I. F-2
II.B-d [2]
  B-t
  F-3
E$m
H$
FP$
FPS$
LT$
TEL$m
TV
W/D
MW
P-BA
S-S
£150-450
S 6

Contact Mrs. A.D. Moore, 79 Cookridge Lane, Leeds LS16 7NE TEL 01144-1532-679-332

GIBBS HILL FARM COTTAGES
Nr Hexham

Turn north at the sign posted for Once Brewed; when you get to Hadrian's Wall, go just a bit further. How's that for a distinctive address!

Actually, as you approach Gibbs Hill Farm it appears like some kind of a stone-built oasis in a billowing sea of greenness rolling on for miles around. There is something positively *Australian* about this traditional hill farm in the grand open-ness of Northumberland. There is also an extraordinary opportunity to stand in a place and look out over a scene that has not changed measurably since Roman times. It doesn't take much imagination to put yourself in a Roman legionaire's shoes... make that *sandals*...to sense his exhilaration of being a sentinel at the absolute rim of the civilized world. The rim held for 250 years; a seventy-three mile long stone neck-lace across the throat of Britain, studded with watch towers, mile castles, and seventeen forts stationed by legions a thousand strong.

But wait a minute. From our cottage patio at Gibbs Hill Farm we are not standing in that Roman legionaire's sandals. We're looking south towards the Wall! Can we be the barbarians? Well at this point the whole vicarious fantasy begins to fall apart. With accommodations like these it is impossible to imagine the barbarians flinging themselves at twenty one feet of stone cold inhospitality. While those Latin chapies are getting chilblains up on their towers, we are toasting our tootsies in front of a most cleverly conceived contraption called a woodburner, in this case hand-somely engulfed in a massive stone fireplace. There are modern fireplaces like this in all three cottages, each built in massive proportions as variations on a traditional theme. When Little Caesar decides to hit the hay...a sack of heather on a plank if he's lucky...he can't even dream of the comfort we barbarians are experiencing in our lovely carved pine bedroom suites up here at Gibbs Hill Farm. I don't imagine there's too much of this deep pile fitted carpeting over in those mile forts either.

The Edwards family, who offer courses in traditional farm skills, are ecologically minded and invite you to share their environment in all its richness, from horseback, mountain bike or on foot. There's fishing, shooting and golf...Hadrian's lads never had it so good!

ETB 4 Keys; Highly Commended & Deluxe

E&H
FPS
LT
TELcs
TV
W/Ds
NS P-
MS
OPEN
TA
£150-379
S 2-4

Contact John Edwards, Gibbs Hill FArm, Bardon Mill, Northumberland NE47 7AP
TEL 01144-1434-344-030 or FAX 01144-1434-344-641

BEACON HILL FARM   Longhorsley

Beacon Hill Farm is a 350-acre estate on the site of an ancient beacon and, incidentally, a traditional lookout for Scottish border raiders, among them the infamous clan Armstrong! There are commanding views here of the Cheviot Hills, forming the border with Scotland, and the beautiful Northumbrian coastline. One will find more castles here than anywhere else in England. Hadrian's Wall runs to the west, Newcastle and Durham, with its splendid Cathedral, are just to the south. Alnwick Castle, the stronghold of the Percy family, is nearby. This is an area of traditionally farmed land, with hedgerows, woods, and fields forming an attractive patchwork which has changed very little in generations, except to say that Armstrong cattle raiding has been on the wane since many of my more scurrilous ancestors migrated to the Americas.

In the shadow of some forty acres of ancient beechwoods, Clare and Alun Moore have converted old barns to create some truly magnificent accommodations. Indeed, they won the prestigious Country Landowners Association Prize in 1987 for their renovation design, and then went on to capture the English Tourist Board's Self Catering Holiday of the Year Award in 1991. There is a general feeling of open spaces, interior and exterior, at Beacon Hill Farm. You will find a forty foot heated indoor swimming pool, sauna, solarium and gymnasium, as well as all weather tennis and even cricket facilities in case you want to warm up for Lords. Riding? You bet; horses and ponies of all sizes from Little Dot, the miniature Shetland, to old Flint, the Clydesdale. Supervised riding is offered from Whitsun to mid-September at no extra charge.

There are eight cottages at Beacon Hill Farm. Quarry House is one of the two 5-Key Deluxe cottages on the Farm; indeed, it was the first holiday property in all Northumberland to earn the English Tourist Board's supreme grading. Quarry House is a single story sandstone building with a slate roof; rather modest, I should say, from the outside, harboring a very

| E&H |
| FP* |
| LT |
| TELc |
| TV V* |
| W/D* DW* |
| MW |
| P-BA |
| S-S   MS |
| E/HC* |
| TA |
| £160-850 |
| S 2-6 |

pleasant
surprise! It sits on its own grounds
a short walk through the gardens from the other cottages. A
brace of twelve foot patio windows offer wonderful views to the south and west.
Parenthetically, I should note here that the drama of sunset as seen from Quarry
House is not to be missed. There are three spacious and beautifully decorated bedrooms, a double and two twins, as well as two bathrooms, one with bath and bidet,
and both with showers. As for the kitchen, this is no *elbow knocker;* it was designed
and equipped for folks who know the joy of cooking, even (especially) on holiday!

The full measure of Beacon Hill Farm and the extraordinary taste the
Moore's have put into creating it is evident in the spacious drawing room of Quarry
House. Begin with the open fire and the classically inspired mantel, with fine dentil
moulding. Feel the soft maroon oriental carpet under foot. Consider the Georgian
Lancashire chest, the George Second mahogany tea table and washstand, the
Victorian chest on chest, the divine watercolors and the J. F. Slater oil painting.
Library, pictures, flowers; the detail is so delicious you may never go outside again.

There are seven other cottages on the Beacon Hill estate which sleep from
two to six people. Beacon Hill Cottage is another 5-Key Deluxe accommodation in
a much more modern idiom, with bold windows and very gay furnishings; actually it
is rather *Caribbean.* Each of the cottages is an individual, having in common only
the extremely good taste that has made Beacon Hill Farm one of Britain's premier
holiday properties.

This area offers much for touring. History here was not all war and pillage;
apparently there was a lot of praying, as well, if we are to judge by Brinkburn Priory
(said to rival Tintern Abbey) and the wealth of holy shrines in the neighborhood. At
Holystone village, in fact, the holy water still flows on tap for visitors. Also, a visit
to the nearby Armstrong estate, Cragside, may help to redeem my family name, as
this was the first dwelling in the world to be electrified. Well, that's our story
anyway! ETB 4-5 Keys; Highly Commended & Deluxe

Contact Alun & Clare Moore, Beacon Hill House, Longhorsley, Morpeth, Northumberland NE65 8QW
TEL 01144-1670-788-372

THE BANQUETING HOUSE
Nr Newcastle-upon-Tyne

The Landmark Trust "discovered" this unique building on the Estate of the Earl of Strathmore and date it to 1746, when it was commissioned by a local coal mogul and ancestor to the present Queen. Perched like an oriental doll house at the edge of a grassy knoll overlooking the rolling countryside of the Derwent Valley, The Banqueting House is once again an amazing decorative on the landscape. The spiritual perspective of this exotic quasi-folly is southerly, turning its back on the sooty materialism of Newcastle, now as in the 18th century.

During the period of ruination much of the Banqueting House's ornamentation was apparently lost. The Trust's restoration has probably been more restrained in decorative embellishments than the original, perhaps rendering the interior a bit more classically correct/elegant and less exotic than the exterior flights of fancy might suggest. The original layout, with a Great Room and only two anterooms, may have presented a spatial challenge to the adaptive restoration, but the Trust's superb decorating department solved the problem of combining twin bed accommodations with the central living space by installing the most complementary period furnishings. One of the chambers became the en-suite double bedroom; the other kitchen. The result is utterly charming and eminently workable for a party of four.

I.B-d
B-t
F-1
F-3
E&H
FP
LT
S-S   MS
INS
£337-671
S 4

Contact The Landmark Trust, Shottesbrook, Maidenhead, Berkshire SL6 3SW
TEL 01144-1628-825-925 or FAX 01144-1628-825-417

GALLOWHILL FARM Whalton

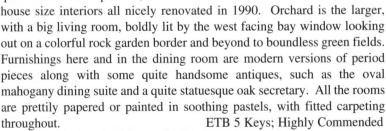

ORCHARD
I. F-1
II.B-q
B-t
B-s [2]
F-3
£260-385
S 6
PADDOCK
II.B-d
B-t
F-3
£190-250
S 4
BOTH
E&H
FP
LT
TELc TV
W/D
DW MW
P-
S-S

Gallowhill is very much a busy working family farm, with six hundred acres of livestock and grain. There are two attached cottages here on the farm; sturdy cut stone buildings with precise quoin work and spacious, house size interiors all nicely renovated in 1990. Orchard is the larger, with a big living room, boldly lit by the west facing bay window looking out on a colorful rock garden border and beyond to boundless green fields. Furnishings here and in the dining room are modern versions of period pieces along with some quite handsome antiques, such as the oval mahogany dining suite and a quite statuesque oak secretary. All the rooms are prettily papered or painted in soothing pastels, with fitted carpeting throughout.   ETB 5 Keys; Highly Commended

Contact Mrs. A.P. Coatsworth, Gallowhill Farm, Whalton, Morpeth, Northumberland NE61 3TX
TEL 01144-1661-881-241

COUPLAND CASTLE TOWER   Wooler

Every Anglophile's dream of stepping back in time to live in a castle may be realized here in the Coupland Tower. The ancient tower, adjoining the resident owners' Grade I Listed castle, has been made into an extraordinary holiday accommodation and is surrounded by ten acres of private grounds...battlegrounds of yore.

We are at the edge of the famous Cheviot Hills. This borderland south of the Tweed seems so wonderfully remote and peaceful now, but the landscape everywhere bears reminders of the centuries of fighting that went on here in these badlands. Some of the struggle was over big dynastic stakes; much of it was merely the secondary havoc and pillage of traversing armies; and then there was the daily vigilance against brigand lawlessness which gave us that chilling expression, *a man's home is his castle.*

The Tower, with its spiral staircase, occupies four floors. On the ground floor are rooms now designated for your use in the idle pleasures of billiards and table tennis, though one can easily imagine a mob of the estate serfs huddled here through a long and bloody siege. The second floor contains the present day kitchen and dining room. Here we also find a large Court Room with a massive stone fireplace bearing the inscription "1619". The Tower is, in fact, considerably older than that, and we may wonder at the thoughts those 1619 occupants may have had about their predecessors' lives in this room. History tells us that three centuries of relentless war between the local lords had come to an end about this time. Was the inscription perhaps in celebration of more civil times to come? Continuing our ascent, the quarters above the Court Room have been made over into two bedrooms, both with four-poster Jacobean beds...just to keep you in a period mood! Another bedroom on the top floor accommodates three.

This region has many opportunities for exploring the past and present: Holy Island is a paradise for bird watchers; nearby is Yeavering Bell, an Iron Age hill fort; and, if you have an appetite for more castles, don't forget Dunstanburgh and Bamburgh.

II. F-3
III. B-d
B-d+s
F-3
IV.B-t+s
E&H
LT
W/D
MW
P-
$1280-1745
S 7-8

Contact Mary McCanna, Westminster Lodgings, 160 Westminster Dr., W.E., Jamestown, NY 14701
TEL 800-699-0744 or 716-484-0744

THE PELE TOWER
Whitton Nr Rothbury

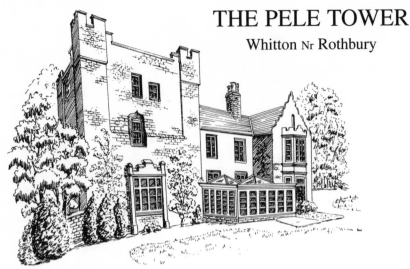

In Devon it's the *long-house;* in Kent it's the *oast*; and in Northumberland it's the *pele tower*. Vernacular abodes, quintessential steads...*when in Rome!* There is unquestionably something very special about holidaying in one of the genuine landmarks of a region. Just such a place is David and Agnes Malia's Pele Tower at Whitton on the Edge of Northumberland National Park. Although the holiday accommodation is an annex to the Tower from the last century, the main body of the Tower, with its ten foot thick walls, was built around 1380 as a fortification against the marauding Scots and Border Reivers. (It's those bloody Armstrongs again!) The crest of the ancient Umfraville family can be seen high up in the stonework.

One enters the "cottage" to an absolutely stunning kitchen with a flagstone floor and a low vaulted stone ceiling that would enable the most nervous cook to continue his/her culinary work in peace, no matter what the rapacious northern hordes were hurling overhead. One end of the kitchen features a massive round, kiln-like, stone wall, and the masonry arches over the bright kitchen windows are equally impressive. Readers already know that the kitchen is my favorite room of any house, and the Pele Tower kitchen lacks for nothing: cuisinart, blenders, juicers, an espresso maker and various kinds of toasters...there's even an automatic rice cooker! No wonder my marauding ancestors kept coming back!

The living room/dining area is handsomely furnished, and, like the kitchen, lacks nothing in electrical appointments: teletext TV, video, CD music setup, plus lots of games and books to pass the time in front of the cozy wood stove. Upstairs, the bathroom comes with whirlpool and the bedrooms have color TVs, a trouser press...even a facial sauna and foot spa (just what a marauding tourist of Scottish descent needs after a long day afoot!). So get a horse, Armstrong! No problem; there are stables just down the lane, and golf, tennis, mountain biking, as well as fishing are easily accessible from the Pele Tower.

ETB 5 Keys; DeLuxe

II.B-d	
B-t	
F-3	
E$m	
H	
FPS	
LT	
TELc	
TVV	
W/D	
DW	MW
NS	P-
S-S	MS
£248-467	
S 4	

Contact David & Agness Malia, The Pele Tower, Whitton, Rothbury, Northumberland NE65-7RL
TEL 01144- 1669-620-410 or FAX 01144-1669-621-006

AINTREE COTTAGE   Bruern Nr Milton-u-Wychwood

Lost in paradise is Aintree Cottage. Tucked away in the very heart of the Cotswolds, the tiny hamlet of Bruern is overlooked even by the Road Atlas, yet it is within five minutes or so of the meccas of Stow-on-the-Wold, Burford, Bourton-on-the-Water, the Slaughters and the Swells. The cottage has been fashioned out of the stable block of Bruern Abbey, a fine 18th century country house risen from the ruins of a medieval Cistercian monastery.

Though Aintree cottage is, strictly speaking, a stable conversion, one would think one was in the mansion itself. Exceptional imagination, taste, and careful attention to detail have gone into this project. And expense! No *unbox and assemble* here. To begin with, the color scheme is at once bold and soothing. I am told this is owed in part to paint finishes by Jocasta Innes, but as well we must credit a sophisticated manipulation of light...and, more important yet, shadow that creates atmosphere. Curled up in front of the elegantly framed Georgianesque open fire, with the gilt mirror over a mantel of pretty plates and Staffordshire figurines, it is rather hard to imagine that a horse once lived here. Rich fabrics in the soft furnishings and elegant drapery, pictures hung to be admired (not just to cover walls), truly fine antique pieces, and carefully chosen decoratives everywhere...nope, this is not a tack room!

The Aintree Cottage kitchen is *country* and *complete*. Good use has been made of the old beams, a terracotta tile floor has been laid, and some lovely antique pieces installed to disguise the functional modernity of the kitchen. The private terrace off the kitchen will undoubtedly inspire some alfresco dining. Another lovely terrace is accessed from the living room, and both have nice outdoor furnishings.

The cottage has three bedrooms upstairs. In the master suite you will find a wonderful mahogany four-poster bed with beautifully coordinated canopy, bolstered headboard, dust ruffle, linen and duvet in heritage blue stripes and prints. The twin bedrooms were not left wanting for the touch that makes Aintree such a joy. One features a pair of extraordinarily interesting marbled Victorian beds with antique patchwork quilts.

Bruern Abbey's exterior amenities include a heated outdoor pool, a games room with snooker and ping pong facilities, a delightful Victorian playhouse for the children, and a tennis court. As for hospitality, a complimentary basket of food and a bottle of wine awaits your arrival. ETB 5 Keys; Highly Commended

II.B-q
B-t [2]
F-2
F-3
E;   H$m
FP
LT
TELc
TVV
W
DW MW
P-
F-F   MS
TA
£328-530
S 6

Contact Cottage in the Country, Forest Gate, Frog Lane, Milton-U-Wychwood, Oxford OX7 6JZ
TEL 01144-1993-831-495 or FAX 01144-1993-831-095

THE MILL AT BURFORD

Burford

The Mill at Burford is an 18th century watermill which has been converted into five cheerful holiday cottage/apartments. It's all very picturesque: the mill-stream, the waterfall and water wheel...and for a backdrop you have this fascinating 900-year-old Cotswold town. Burford High Street, with shops, restaurants and pubs is a mere five minute walk away. In the other direction, foot paths take you into the idyllic countryside along the Windrush Valley where flocks of sheep graze peacefully.

Tail Race Cottage sleeps four adults and a child. It has a bright kitchen, opening onto a small patio beside the water where swans come to be fed. The dining/sitting room has a log burner, with comfy soft furnishings and walls handsomely decorated with blueware, country antiques and original pictures. The main bedroom has a lovely canopied pine four-poster bed. There is a second bedroom with twins and a single bed on the upstairs landing. *Windrush* is a two bedroom unit with an open airy living room and very modern furnishings. Ruth Jennings has an exceptional eye for detail and, again, one must comment on the delightful choice of pictures, books and bygones. The Windrush balcony overlooks the millstream and waterwheel. Upstairs is *Millstream,* a one bedroom accommodation with bright tongue 'n' groove pine ceilings and plenty of light flooding in from the glass door leading out to a small balcony over the rippling water of the Mill's tail race. Looking out over the secluded garden and the wooded wilderness beyond are *Cider Press* and *Lime Tree,* two studio apartments.

The sound and *feel* of the water never escapes you at the Mill. There is a small boat and a canoe for paddling around on the mill leat. Each spring a pair of swans return to raise a new family on the banks of the mill pond, happy to allow the Mill residents the privilege of entertaining their crop of cygnets. Ruth Jennings provides touring and walking maps for her guests, and will suggest interesting tours up and down the Cotswolds.

Burford is an ancient wool town and still one of the finest market towns in the Cotswolds. There is a good selection of antique shops and galleries, as well as a range of craft outlets. And, of course, there are all of the attractions of the Cotswolds within minutes, and Oxford only a half hour away.

ETB 3-4 Keys Highly Commended

E&H
LT
TELin*
TV
W/Ds
P-BA
E/HC*
S-S OPEN
MS
TA
£140-440
S 2-5

Contact Mrs Ruth Jennings, The Mill at Burford, Witney Street, Burford, Oxford OX18 4RX
TEL 01144-1993-822-379 or FAX 01144-1993-822-759

BADGER COTTAGE Nr Chipping Norton

Badger Cottage is set in the parklands of the Heythrop Estate, originally owned by the Duke of Shrewsbury. You will no doubt recall that it was Charles Talbot, the then Duke, who orchestrated the importation of William of Orange to be King. Badger Cottage served originally as stables for the Estate's giant Shire Horses and their grooms. Which is to say that you are in shadow of the great horses of king-makers in Badger Cottage. You're also in for a wonderful tranquil holiday set amidst 25 acres of secluded gardens and wood. However, you will have to share the grounds with the peacocks which roam freely as if by royal prerogative.

You enter Badger Cottage through a heavy plank door into a bright and airy sitting room with the lovely honey colored cut stone walls of the Cotswolds. There is a nice collection of period furnishings here: a cottage size Victorian breakfront, an old leather chesterfield with broad rolled arms and back, and a beautiful Adams pine mirror and mantle framing an open fire. The entertainment necessaries (TV & video) are happily concealed in a Victorian carved walnut cabinet. There are beige velvet curtains framing the 3 over 6 small pane window with views of the traditional country garden. The deluxe Axminster carpeting throughout gives the cottage a complete and cozy feel.

The bedrooms are on the same level; one double (with large brass bed) and a twin, with dark brown velvet curtains and interesting period pieces and decoration. The kitchen is fully fitted with all the modern conveniences and has a quarry tile floor. Of particular interest is a lovely collection of Victorian bottles.

Nearby is the classic Cotswold village of Great Tew and the famous old wool town of Chipping Norton, known as the *Gateway to the Cotswolds*. There are lovely Georgian houses in Chipping Norton, along with a marvelous Tudor Guildhall, and even remnants of Norman and Saxon times. A bit further down the road is Banbury of nursery rhyme fame, and, of course, the spires of Oxford are ever on the horizon of this area.

I. B-d
B-t
F-2
E$m
H$m
FP
TVV
W
MW
P-
S-S   MS
INS
BK$
£177-354
S 4

Contact Discover Britain, Shaw Mews, Shaw Street, Worcester WR1 3QQ
TEL 01144-1905-613-744 or FAX 01144-1905-613-747

THE LITTLE COTTAGE   at Churchill

Churchill is situated in the north-west corner of Oxfordshire in the rolling Cotswold hills. The village, itself, is most noted for its fine 19th century church, the tower of which is a two thirds scale replica of Magdalen College Tower at Oxford. Little Cottage is an attractive vine-covered traditional Cotswold stone dwelling, probably 18th century. Flanked by two larger homes, the little cottage resolutely follows the curve of the road, which contributes an extra dimension to its quaintness.

One enters directly into a cozy living room which is furnished primarily with antique style dark oak pieces; the chairs and sofa are covered in dark floral Liberty fabrics matching the curtains. There is a large, flush to wall, open limestone fireplace with a substantial stone lintel. Off the small ground floor lobby is the fully fitted kitchen with an antique pine table and a plate rack adorned with willow pattern crockery. There is a snug little dining room, as well; again with nice pine furnishings.

Upstairs we find a relatively spacious bathroom with a cast iron enamel tub (which no doubt stood its ground through the renovations) and very cheery pine paneling and flooring complemented by pale blue decorations...all very light and airy in feel. Across the landing is the bedroom through old plank doors (still with the original blackened iron latches). This room is open to the roof, with exposed oak beams and old dark floor boards graced by some rather pretty cotton rugs. The bedroom is done in a lovely Laura Ashley pale pink, with waxed pine furnishings.

In addition to touring the classic Cotswold villages, there is much fine walking in the vicinity, most notably the Cotswold Way, which runs along the escarpment, affording magnificent views towards the Welsh Mountains and Malvern Hills. The Oxfordshire Way is closer at hand, running from nearby Bourton-on-the-Water to Henley-on-Thames--which may be a tad further than you should venture and hope to get back to Little Cottage by night fall!   ETB 3 Keys; Highly Commended

I. CS
II.B-t
F-2
E&H
FP$
LT$
TV
P-
S-S
INS
£160-255
S 2-4

Contact Cottage in the Country, Forest Gate, Frog Lane, Milton-U-Wychwood, Oxford OX7 6JZ
TEL 01144-1993-831-495 or FAX 01144-1993-831-095

CAVALIERS COTTAGE
Culworth

This is another one of those *George Washington Slept Here* opportunities. No, of course, the great American revolutionary hero didn't sleep here, though, coincidentally, GW's ancestors did sleep just three miles down the road at their family estate, Sulgrave Manor. Rather, it was the great English anti-revolutionary hero, Charles I, who slept here in this fine early 17th century manor house to which Cavaliers Cottage is attached. To be perfectly candid, Charles slept in quite a lot of places (a matter of military exigencies rather than moral turpitude), though, as he prepared for an appearance on the battlefield of nearby Cropredy Bridge on June 27, 1644, I rather expect he did not rest as well as do contemporary guests at Cavaliers Cottage.

This was hotly contested territory during the English Civil War, and this Manor House was well prepared with a pair of siege cellars, three wells, and a stone lined secret tunnel out of the cellar and under adjoining fields. In fact, Royalist troops had occasion to use these exit facilities during the strife, but present day guests at Cavaliers Cottage are most reluctant to leave by any means.

Cavaliers Cottage is situated peacefully on the Green of the character village, Culworth. The Cotswold stone facade of the Manor House is covered in pretty virginia creeper and climbing roses, a promising beginning for the traditional charm that lay within. Afternoon arrivals will likely find a tray with tea and Scottish shortbreads awaiting them. The sitting room has an open fire suitable for coal and small logs, which can be bought in the village shop or gathered on the many delightful walks around the property. Typical of the tasteful furnishings are the two comfortable sofas covered in Sanderson linen...also plenty of games and books with which to amuse oneself in the event of a siege. The kitchen is well equipped and decorated prettily. There is a small breakfast room adjoining the kitchen with a farmhouse table and an old pine pew. Upstairs is the main bedroom with a pine canopy bed and a homey patchwork quilt, as well as a lovely old pine wardrobe and dresser. Up another set of quite steep stairs one finds another twin bedroom done up in pretty Liberty floral fabrics, with en-suite bathroom, complete with bidet.

The Manor has its own marvelous orchard, which, incidentally, has just been planted with 18,000 daffodils, and there are lovely walks in every direction. The touring opportunities from Cavaliers Cottage are endless and Stratford-upon-Avon is only a half hour's drive away. ETB 4 Keys; Highly Commended

I. F-1
II. B-d
III.B-t
F-4
E&H
FP
LT
TELin
TV
W/D
MW
F-F MS
INS
TA
£215-363
S 4

Contact Mrs Beth Soar, The Manor House, Culworth, Banbury, Oxfordshire OX17 2BB
TEL 01144-1295-760-099 or FAX 01144-1295-760-098

THE OAST HOUSE   East Hagbourne

This village dates from the 12th century when the church was built, and derives its name from the Saxon chief, Hacca. Cromwell is said to have marshalled his troops in the churchyard during one of the many civil war battles that raged across this land. Not far away is the remains of Donnington Castle, a Royalist stronghold that endured three sieges in the conflagration. The Oast House dates from the 18th century and, though sitting in the churchyard on one side, is in the farm yard on the other, with its own walled garden and pretty flowering tree out front. The farm, itself, has a defensive moat around it and foundations going back to pre- Norman times. All of which is to say that the situation of the Oast House is as historic as it is lovely.

The building, itself, is of considerable architectural fascination. The cruck framing is exposed on the exterior and there is a rich herringbone mosaic of brick inlay peeking through a wall of vines reaching up to the eaves under a most magnificent red tiled roof. The hue and undulation of this roof reminds me so much of Burgundy, though I should be thinking beer, not wine. A small cupola stands the place of the more common oast cone, but this very perpendicular structure did indeed, for a time, serve the function of drying hops for fine English "wine".

Pretty to look at, the Oast House is pretty to look out from. The view from dining room is of the garden and the ancient church. French doors from the living room bring in (or exit to) the lovely secluded garden. The downstairs study-cum-bedroom has windows that again frame the lovely church. Upstairs there are four bedrooms, one with a galleried bed area in the old kiln.

The Oast House is not only an ideal location for exploring the Berkshire Downs, it is only about a half hour's train ride to Paddington Station London, for the pleasure of a day in the city without the hassle of parking.   ETB 5 Keys; Highly Commended

| I. B-s |
| F-3 |
| II.B-k |
| F-1 |
| B-t |
| B-d [2] |
| B-s |
| F-2 |
| E$m H$m |
| LT |
| TELc TV |
| W/D |
| DW MW |
| S-S |
| INS TA |
| £360-700 |
| S 8 |

Contact Cottage in the Country, Forest Gate, Frog Lane, Milton-U-Wychwood, Oxford OX6 7JZ
TEL 01144-1993-831-495 or FAX 01144-1993-831-095

COXWELL HOUSE   Nr Faringdon

Coxwell House is the superb front part...the grand part!...of an elegant Georgian house built in 1760 as a hunting lodge. It is set at the edge of the village in an attractive secluded walled garden with beautiful trees behind palatial gates. Little Coxwell itself is an unspoiled farming village of thatched cottages and vine covered stone walls with views across the Vale of the White Horse to the 2000 year old Horse God cut into the chalk hillside.

One enters the house up stone steps through a Cambridge blue door into a spacious entrance hall with a flagstone floor. The drawing room has a window seat with a petit-point cushion to match the cream silk curtains, French watered silk wall paper and sofas. There are old Irish hunting and racing pictures in gilded frames mounted on colored velvet. The dining room features a mahogany table, an antique spinet, and cheerful yellow striped paper with toning brocade curtains. Both rooms have high ceilings and interesting plaster work. Library shelves flank the stone fire-places. These are wonderfully proportioned rooms with typically Georgian floor-to-ceiling windows to flood the living areas with light and bring nature inside.

The three well appointed bedrooms are upstairs and reached by a wide traditional staircase, with yet another library selection on the landing. There are twin beds in each of the spacious bedrooms, which can be zipped together to form six foot doubles. One of the bedrooms is en-suite, and both have tub and shower facilities. Pleasant views of the garden are to be had from each bedroom.

The kitchen has every modern convenience and there is a lobby leading out to the garden. The flowers include brilliant yellow massed aconites, daffodils, wisteria on the side of the house, acacia trees and numerous shrubs making for privacy.

Use of the tennis court and indoor heated pool may be arranged with the owners, who occupy the Victorian wing to the rear of Coxwell House. This is a lovely area for walks and picnics. A nine hole golf course and riding stables are just down the lane.

ETB 4 Keys; Highly Commended

II.B-t/q [3]
F-3 [2]
E&H
LT
TELm
TV
W/D
DW MW
P-BA
S-S
TA
£350-650
S 6

Contact E.A.G. Crossley Cooke at Little Coxwell House, Faringdon, Oxfordshire SN7 7LP
TEL 01144-1367-241-240   or FAX 01144-1367-240-911

BLUEBELL COTTAGE

Great Tew

Great Tew just sounds like a Merry Ole England village; and indeed it is! Here you will find a honey comb of vernacular architecture dating from the 1600s...all thatched and creamy hued with the local stonework. Photo opportunities at every turn! Though wrongdoing seems a bit improbable in such an idyllic spot, the old village stocks are even on display.

Bluebell Cottage, which sits just at the edge of the village on a quiet lane, just sounds like a Merry Ole England cottage; and (guess what) it is! With a cosy open fire in the living room, comfortable cottage style furnishings, and oodles of interesting knickknacks, Bluebell is a very *friendly* cottage. And, as with all the Rural Retreats cottage offerings, guests will be welcomed with a basket of victuals and a bottle of wine.

Country Club membership at Walton Hall is complimentary, and trout fishing can also be arranged. And don't forget to set aside a day for the cerebral attractions of Oxford, just a twenty-five minute drive away.

| II. B-q [2] |
| B-s |
| F-3 |
| E&H |
| FP |
| Lt |
| TV |
| W/D |
| DW MW |
| OPEN MS |
| INS |
| £360-615 |
| S 5 |

Contact Rural Retreats, Station Road, Blockley, Moreton-in-Marsh, Gloucestershire, GL56 9DZ
TEL 01144-1386-701-177 or FAX 01144-1386-701-178

THE COTTAGE at Islip

The Cottage is a homey little 16th century Cotswold stone building tucked into the center of the ancient village of Islip. Islip's most famous son was King Edward the Confessor, whose heirless demise in 1066 invited the Norman invasion. Although only five miles from the busy university town of Oxford (7 minutes by train), walking around Islip is like stepping into the past. This is definitely a character village, with narrow winding lanes and crooked little houses; the rivers Ray and Cherwell come together here, occasioning an annual rafting event.

| I. F-3 |
| II.B-d |
| B-s |
| E$c   H |
| FPS |
| LT$ |
| TEL-BA |
| TV |
| W/D |
| S-S |
| INS   TA |
| £180-250 |
| S 3 |

One enters the cottage through the be-flowered patio area to the rear. The kitchen/dining area is a happy merging of modern fitted cabinetry and old walls with a mind of their own. One steps down to the living room which has a cavern-size inglenook fireplace (with wood stove) and modest, but comfortable, furnishings. There is a spacious downstairs bathroom and two bedrooms upstairs; a single with a black cast iron firebox and a double with a pine bed and wardrobe, as well as a nice window seat overlooking the village green and the churchyard.

Contact Cottage in the Country, Forest Gate, Frog Lane, Milton-U-Wychwood, Oxford OX7 6JZ
Tel 01144-1993-831-495 or Fax 01144-1993-831-095

KEEN'S COTTAGE

Kingham
Nr Chipping Norton

Kingham is one of those places that even people who know the Cotswolds may not have ever heard of. It is an altogether underrated little hamlet with a charming village green, local shop, a good hotel (The Mill at Kingham), post office, and, necessary of all necessaries, a village pub. However, if this secluded tranquility begins to get a bit wearisome, or should you grow lonely for the sight of tourists in substantial numbers, Stow-on-the-Wold is only about five minutes away!

Originally this was a pair of tiny cottages without plumbing. The owner has recently combined and developed them into an extraordinarily handsome country property. We'll begin in the hallway: on the left you have the staircase and to the right a cozy and very comfortable sitting room. Your eye will be drawn immediately to the wonderful inglenook fireplace and bread oven. There is an open fire grate and iron chimney inserted now, with a most impressive wood lintel spanning this massive cavern. Exposed stone walls, open beams, fitted maroon carpeting, nice wall sconce lighting...all very cozy, indeed.

My favorite room in this cottage is actually outdoors...well, sort of. The huge conservatory dining room, glassed on three sides and overhead, makes every meal alfresco, and that is my idea of holiday dining. Three picnics a day, the weather be damned! The conservatory is nicely furnished with antiques: oak table and chairs, a handsome sideboard, pretty pictures and oriental vases, as well as a pair of lovely table lamps which will encourage the picnic to go into the night. Transoms open to regulate the heat in this south-facing suntrap and there are broad French doors opening onto the paved garden. The garden is enclosed and has many colorful flower baskets, as well as suitable patio furnishings.

Upstairs you may choose between the double and twin bedrooms, both with pretty rose patterned duvets and dust ruffles, and charming wall sconce lighting with little pink satin shades. These rooms have a nice feminine *ambiance,* and both are en-suite.

Keen's Cottage is nicely situated for touring the Cotswolds. Just up the road is Chastleton House, with links to the infamous Gunpowder Plot. Prehistoric sights like the Taston monolith and Hawk Stone are nearby, and a pleasant, car-less, day up to Oxford takes only 25 minutes by train from the Kingham station.

ETB 4 Keys; Highly Commended

II.B-t	
F-2	
B-d	
F-3	
E$m	H
LT	
TEL-BA	
TV	
W/D	
P-	
F-F	MS
INS	TA
£170-340	
S 4	

Contact Cottage in the Country, Forest Gate, Frog Lane, Milton-U-Wychwood, Oxford OX6 7JZ
TEL 01144-1993-831-495 or FAX 01144-1993-831-095

WHITE HALL

Minster Lovell

The old village of Minster Lovell is one of the most picturesque in the Cotswolds, with its street of honey stone and thatch houses, the 500-year-old Swan Inn, and the classic ruins of the manor house built by the 7th Lord Lovell in 1431. Herein starved the sad ill-fated Francis Lovell, hidden and forgotten for centuries in a secret room, awaiting the royal ascent of the pretender Lambert Simnel...just one of the many romantic tragedies of this enchanted land of color and light.

The Brodtmans of White Hall operate a plant nursery just outside the village and offer two well designed cottages, prettily covered by climbing roses, pyracantha and Virginia creepers. The decor is simple, with an open fireplace and good quality contemporary furnishings. Sky-lighting and broad French doors to the patios give good light to both Orchard End and The Stable. There is a tennis court on the property, as well. ETB 4 Keys; Highly Commended

ORCHARD
II.B-t [2]
F-3
STABLES
I. F-3
II.B-d
B-t [2]
F-2
E$m H$m
FP   FPE
LT
TELc TV
W/D*
S-S
INS   TA
£150-340
S 4 & 6

PIMLICO FARM COTTAGES

Tusmore Nr Bicester

Pimlico Farm is not far off the main road linking Buckingham, a county town dating from the reign of Alfred the Great, and Bicester, the hunt capital of the Oxford moors. The Harpers have developed four exception-al cottages out of the 18th century granary on their 370-acre farm. The cottages are open plan in design, with well chosen contemporary furnishings and up-to- date fixtures. There is a good choice of upstairs or downstairs (or both) sleeping arrangements, and April Cottage (sleeping 2-5) has been designed for handicap accessibility. This immediate area is off the beaten track of Cotswold tourism and is more noted for holiday activities than sight seeing. The Harpers will happily direct their guests to golf, tennis, fishing, riding...even gliding and clay pigeon shooting are readily avail-able. ETB 4 Keys; Highly Commended

E&H
LT
TELc
TV
W/Ds
DW MW
P-BA
E/HC*
S-S MS
INS TA
£140-395
S 2-6

Contact Cottage in the Country, Forest Gate, Frog Lane, Milton-U-Wychwood, Oxford OX6 7JZ
TEL 01144-1993-831-495 or FAX 01144-1993-831-095

THE OLD PARSONAGE   Oxford

These two Landmark Trust properties in Oxford closely approximate the split personality of this ancient academic city by the Thames.

In The Old Parsonage we find the cloistered dignity of dons and clerics; walled off and exclusive, not to say reclusive, a venue for quiet reflection and gentlemanly dialogues on the great ideas of all times; a sherry sipping sort of place. To be sure, The Old Parsonage is no monastery; one need not suffer the rigors of strict asceticism to feel a twinge of ecstasy in these rich interiors of paneled walls and ornate plaster.   Here is a place of privilege, beauty, and truth...consider the Latin motto which is inscribed around the cornice of the living room: *For we know that, if our earthly house were destroyed, we have a building of God, a house not made with hands, eternal in the heavens....*Easy for the old clerics and dons to say, but one suspects they would have been most grievously moved by the destruction of this particular house!   Well, no danger of that now that the Landmark Trust has moved in and widened access to these noble quarters for holidaymakers, which, existentially speaking, is probably what The Old Parsonage in Oxford always was.

The Old Parsonage dates, in part, from around 1500, though has undergone several modernizations, most particularly in mid-Victorian times. The public rooms are spacious and *thoughtfully* furnished (naturally, this is Oxford!). A separate stair tower takes us up to twin and double bedrooms on the second floor, and thence to a third floor tower bedroom with thrilling views over the spires of academe.   The Old Parsonage's walled garden extends to the River...take your sherry for a stroll!

II. B-d
B-t
F-2
III.B-t
E&H
FP
LT
M-M F-F
MS INS
£546-852
S 6

#7 St. Michaels Street

The *other* Oxford, the Oxford of youthful vigor and some considerable mischief, encompasses the Trust's second floor flat on St. Michaels Street.   Here we are adjacent to the famous Oxford Union, where it all *happens!*   To be sure, these wonderful rooms are no less historic and barely less refined than The Old Parsonage.   Here resided the Steward of the Union, who traditionally kept a measure of order in the affairs of the enthusiastic collegians.   You will find these Edwardian quarters handsomely scholarly in decoration and atmosphere.   Indeed, this too is a sherry-sipping environ with a private amphitheater view of the round-the-clock bustle of college life.

II.B-t
F-2
E&H
LT
M-M or F-F
MS
INS   TA
£280-430
S 2

Contact The Landmark Trust, Shottesbrook, Maidenhead, Berkshire SL6 3SW
TEL 01144-1628-825-925 or FAX 01144-1628-825-417

HEATH FARM   Swerford

Pretty geometry is the essence of Heath Farm. David and Nena Barbour obviously have a Moorish passion for angle and design and have fashioned Heath Farm as a most splendid architectural mosaic. I have a feeling that every inch of this extraordinary puzzle in honey stone and tile, wood grain and glass, was drawn over and over (reams and reams of drafting paper!) before a brick was ever laid or a board cut. This was definitely not a *call in the builder and have him do us a barn conversion* project.

Indeed, the Barbours began collecting the materials (and the ideas) for Heath Farm Cottages years before construction began. A joinery was set up on the farm to custom build furnishings and fittings from patiently cured English hardwoods taken from the Barbour's own woods. Traditional craftsmanship set to work on traditional materials in the fulfillment of an artisan's vision...the result is I think a most worthy extension of the Cotswold vernacular form, which, after all, begins with an intricate mosaic cut from golden stone. The Barbours have simply turned the kaleidoscope (around and around!) and discovered many new rich geometric patterns to lay upon the land in architectural and landscape forms that will have a place in the future. Perhaps five hundred years from now some astro-yuppie will discover the Heath Farm ruin and respectfully restore it to its *former glory*, a temple from a temple-less time. Well, you needn't wait to enjoy the *present glory* of Heath Farm.

There are four apartments around a central courtyard, which has been laid out with Archimedean precision....*Beechnut, Chestnut, Hazelnut, and Walnut*...like stations in a wood-worshipper's cross. The first apartment is entered beneath the dovecote through a heavy plank door with a wrought iron grill. The bedroom has stone mullion arched windows; more medieval arches and a stone passageway take

| B-q [all] |
| F-4* |
| E&H |
| FP |
| LT |
| TEL   TV |
| W/Ds |
| NS   C-BA |
| P- |
| S-S   MS |
| INS   TA |
| £180-350 |
| S 2-4 |

you to the living room. In Hazelnut you will find custom made ash furnishings and a wonderful bathroom reached through a hidden door in the wooden paneling. Chestnut offers an unusual fireplace, African slate floors and a bathroom with a bidet and an inviting window seat overlooking the valley below. Walnut is the Barbour's pride and joy (hard choice!). It occupies the top two stories with sunlit oak framed windows over the courtyard and stone arched windows over the fish pond and valley. Which-ever cottage you choose, get to know the neighbors so you can also have a gander at their hand crafted abode.

Contact Cottage in the Country, Forest Gate, Frog Lane, Milton-U-Wychwood, Oxford OX6 7JZ
TEL 01144-1993-831-495 or FAX 01144-1993-831-095

THE SUMMER HOUSE

Eyton-on-Severn

Here we are deep in the land of black and white half-timbered Elizabethan houses. The Summer House is Tudor also, though built in the red decorated stone of the region; inspired by considerable ostentation and even more romantic imagination. This was the Jacobean garden house of Sir Francis Newport; the only surviving component of his once great Tudor mansion. And, The Summer House survives only because of the care and craft of the benevolent Vivat Trust.

| I. F-3 |
| II.B-d |
| E&H |
| FP |
| LT |
| TV |
| W   MW |
| S-S |
| INS |
| $640-735 |
| S 2 |

The hexagonal pavilion is two stories high with a roof terrace to take in the lovely views of the Severn countryside. The ground elevation, with its three beautiful keystoned arches, has been glassed in to form an exceptionally bright dining/sitting area and kitchen. Original oak stairs lead up to the living room/bedroom which features a beautiful pine canopy bed with romantic pink drapings and an open fire. Interior design and furnishing can only be described as luxurious, which has become a Vivat Trust trademark.

Contact Haywood Cottage Holidays, P.O. Box 878, Eufaula, Alabama 36072
TEL 334-687-9800 or FAX 334-687-5324

THE BOTHY Clun

The Bothy is a Grade II Listed cottage attached to Cresswell House at the center of this ancient village. How ancient, you ask? Well, on this ground the Romano-Briton chieftain, Caractacus, made his stand against the Romans. The same sort of greeting was offered up by Edric the Wild for the Normans when they arrived. Alas however, the Normans prevailed and built their castle here overlooking the River Clun. Undaunted, the Welsh succeeded in breaching it four times in the 12-14th centuries, and finished things off by burning the town down on each occasion. Yes, Clun is just a spot on the map now, but what a history(!) and it's all on display now in the town's fascinating museum.

Well, things have toned down a bit since then, and your welcome at The Bothy will definitely not be in the tradition of Edric the Wild. You will find the customary bottle of wine and basket of grub (the Romans and Normans never had it so good!), and a compact little cottage that is steeped in rustic charm. Downstairs there is an inglenook fireplace nearly as big as the living room, and upstairs a cozy gallery bedroom awaits the weary warrior...or contemporary traveller.

| I. F-3 |
| II.B-q |
| E&H |
| FPG |
| LT |
| TVV |
| MW |
| P- |
| OPEN |
| MS |
| INS |
| £290-425 |
| S 2 |

Contact Rural Retreats, Station Road, Blockley, Moreton-in-Marsh, Gloucestershire, GL56 9DZ
TEL 01144-1386-701-177 or FAX 01144-1386-701-178

BROMFIELD PRIORY GATEHOUSE

Ludlow

Ludlow, an ancient *planned* town sandwiched in between the Rivers Teme and Corve, is noted for its black and white timbered houses and its tragedy filled Castle. Indeed, the Castle has been on guard here since around 1085, a sentinel over the so-called *Marcher Lands* which bound the English and Welsh in a bloody history of conflict that continues to have its sore spots (happily fought out on the linguistic front now). The original town grid plan, which supported the bastion with a productive populous, is still evident in the narrow medieval alleys and the broad Georgian streets that came later. But Ludlow's long history is not all gun and gore; there is a literary tradition here as well. Milton's famous masque of *Comus* was given birth here in a performance within the Castle, and one of my favorite poets, A.E. Housman, was laid to rest here by his own determination. A place to *be!*

Up the River Teme a couple miles is the estate village of Bromfield. The Priory here was originally a Benedictine property and the lower stone-built part of the gatehouse dates from the 14th century, while the timbered addition above came after Henry VIII had his way with the monasteries. In the centuries following Dissolution the Priory Gatehouse served as a manorial court, school, and even a parish recreation hall. Today the Gatehouse faces quietly onto the church green and is a wonderful base for visitors touring this fascinating region.

There are actually two levels in the stone elevation, containing an en-suite double bedroom off the entrance hall, and above that a twin room. The timber-built span over the arched gate is comprised of a long spacious great room under open beams and a peaked ceiling, with another twin bedroom at the end (upper right in drawing). The great room features an ornate Tudor fireplace with a wood stove at one end, and an open plan kitchen at the other. As with all the Landmark Trust houses, the furnishings are all in a comfortable older style with many period accent pieces.

I. B-d
F-3
II. B-t
III.B-t
F-2
E&H
FPS
S-S MS
INS
£371-602
S 6

Contact The Landmark Trust, Shottesbrook, Maidenhead, Berkshire SL6 3SW
TEL 01144-1628-825-925 or FAX 01144-1628-825-417

MUSIC MASTER'S HOUSE
Ironbridge

Certainly one of the major motivations of North Americans to visit Britain is to *soak up some history*. There is a vague sense that our modern lives have been indelibly shaped by the course of English (read "British") history, whether those Isles were the departure point for our particular ancestors or not. From Stonehenge to Hadrian's Wall, from the battle sites of Norman Conquest and Commonwealth to the castles of warriors and the stately homes of the nabobs of empire, we cling to *that* history much as we cling to *that* language.

The British tourist industry is most grateful for our loyalty to their history, and they have put out the welcome mat for us in every corner of the land. Even Shropshire! But let's face it, Shropshire is not upper most on the minds of prospective visitors to Britain from North America. And more's the pity, because here was born the industrial revolution, and no ancient battle nor heroic personality has more shaped our lives than what transpired in the Ironbridge Gorge through the 18th century. Today, the life and times of Ironbridge have been dramatically *museumified* to a standard on a par with Canada's Louisbourg or America's Williamsburg. What is more, the early scars of ruthless industrialism have been healed by the reassertion of nature; Shropshire is lush with the color of seasons and the charm of tranquil old villages. Ironbridge is a perfect base for exploring this important and wonderful "undiscovered" part of England and *our* history.

Music Masters House is, as the name suggests, the mid-19th-century brick home of the village music teacher, one W. Timmins. The house has been divided into two (connectible) holiday flats, rather compact in parts, and irregular in layout, but rich in the working class character of the period and the place. The spiral iron stairway, the original Victorian porcelain plumbing, wood furnishings reminiscent of my old school, (electrified) gas wall sconce lighting, brass beds, homey pictures, and patchwork quilts render an ambience that is really quite unique...part museum, part campy, but definitely not a designer idiom for yuppie tastes. Children, on the other hand, will love the place for its fixed and decorative curiosities and for features like the crawl up sleeping alcove in the smaller "Timmins Cottage". Music Master's House is sited on the steep hill overlooking the Severn Gorge, and there is a walled garden, beyond which is a jungle of forest park leading down to the ruins of the old Bedlam Blast Furnaces and the River Severn. More fun for the kids!

ETB 2 & 5 Keys; Commended

MUSIC M.
I. B-t
F-3
II. CS
F-1
III.B-d [2]
F-2
W/D DW
£165-315
S 6
TIMMINS
I. B-t
F-2
II.B-t/d
£95-175
S 2-4
BOTH
E&H
LT
TELc
TVV
MW TA

Contact David Phillips, Hundred House Hotel, Norton, Shropshire TF11 9EE
TEL 01144-1952-730-353 or FAX 01144-1952-730-355

WALCOT HALL   Lydbury North

Here is the Georgian home of Lord Clive of India, he who put the capital
"E" in British *Empire*. There have, in fact, only been four families to own Walcot
Hall, beginning with the Walcots themselves, who traced their presence in the area
back to the departure of the Romans. Clive arrived in Shropshire in 1764, fresh from
his bold military victories that had wrested the states of India from the grasps of the
French, not to mention the Indians themselves, to find the Walcot family fortunes at
a low ebb. As for fortunes, Lord Clive's had risen just a tad from his first assignment
in India as a modest 5 pounds per/year clerk. Suffice it to say that India had been *very
good* to Lord Clive, who, in the tradition of the time, lined his pockets on a scale that
made him arguably the richest man in the Kingdom, and, incidentally, brought him
under the scrutiny of a Parliament which was, itself, hardly a chamber of unblemished
public servants. Public inquiry or not, it suited Caesar to make over the already very
substantial Tudor mansion of the Walcots in the grander fashion of the Georgians.
Clive was by then on his way to Parliament and a long dynastic run at Walcot Hall.
Indeed, the Conqueror's descendants did carry on at Walcot Hall for 170 years,
adding on to the estate in a ambitious style that would have thoroughly pleased their
lineal founder. Not least was the contribution of Lord Clive's son, who put POWs of
the Napoleonic War to work digging the mile long lake in front of the house.

Today, there are three flats and a ground floor wing, with 2-4 bed-

E&H
FPS*
LT
TELc
TV
W*
DW
P-BA
S-S MS
TA
£168-250
S 2-8

rooms, available for holidaymakers. Accommodations are very *English,*
full of Laura Ashley and Colefax & Fowler colors, with eclectic homey
furnishings. The catholic tastes and interests of the owners of the past
forty years (Major M.W. Parish and family) are everywhere in evidence.
This is far from a typical tourist accommodation; indeed, there is a kind of
unstructured *make yourself at home* atmosphere. Quite likely you will find
the flower vases empty, with a note encouraging you to "pick your own
decor" from the arboretum and gardens.

Contact The Estate Manager, 41 Cheval Place, London SW7 1EW
TEL 01144-1715-812-782 or FAX 01144-1715-890-195

ASHWOOD
Nr Whitchurch

A stay at Ashwood could well be the most memorable holiday you have ever experienced. This is because the cottage, which is the self contained wing of a 16th century farmhouse, is uniquely rich in historic detail, and, more particularly, because the owner, Richard Hughes, is prepared to take you on a very special week-long journey into history itself. First the cottage:

For fear of going no further, one hesitates to begin by describing the fireplace, which is not so much a museum piece as a whole museum in itself, proudly wearing the altered tastes of every period from the Tudors on. It is an inglenook model large enough to accommodate a couple sturdy Jacobean chairs, a full complement of brass accouterments, and a good sized Georgian iron hearth with hood. Best of all are the intricately carved pilasters carrying the ceiling high mantel. Here are found the initials of ten generations of Mr. Hughes' family [he is the twelfth generation in this house!] and the Hughes family crest. Nearby is an oak blanket chest (c 1600) and many more museum quality pieces: a warming pan, skimming dishes, a sword, and various other weapons.

The kitchen of Ashwood was once the farm cheese-making room. Note the marks of the cheese press on the low ceiling beams (5'10"). The adjoining cheese storeroom has since been converted to a downstairs bathroom with separate WC. Upstairs there are three bedrooms, two doubles and a twin. Colors here are restful greens and whites, with coordinated drapes, carpets and bed linen...and, yes, more interesting antique pieces with old oil paintings by local artists. Exterior amenities include three acres of lovely garden and wood, with a spring show of more than 5000 bulbs!

Richard Hughes very tellingly describes himself as "the present *yeoman* owner" of Ashwood, and offers an optional *Teach-In Holiday*, which covers the local architecture (from Romans on), the manorial history (since the Conquest), and the Hughes family record (at Ashwood since 1515). Two hours a day in the company of such a yeoman spirit is not your everyday tourist fare....too too rare is the merry perspective on Merry Old England!

| I. F-1 |
| F-2 |
| II.B-d [2] |
| B-t |
| E$ H$ |
| FP!!! |
| LT |
| TEL TV |
| W/D MW |
| S-S MS |
| INS BK$ |
| £185-369 |
| S 6 |

Contact Discover Britain, Shaw Mews, Shaw Street, Worcester WR1 3QQ
TEL 01144-1905-613-744 or FAX 01144-1905-613-747

LYDFORD HALL
East Lydford

Once upon a time an impressionable seventeen year old Canadian school girl (a delegate to a vigil of remembrance for the patriotic dead of the World Wars) spent the night atop the Glastonbury Tor and fell forever in love. Perhaps it was the solemnity of the occasion, more likely it was the ethereal morning rising out of the Somerset Levels, but the view across the Poldern Hills towards Lydford was the makings of a lifelong passionate Anglophile. As I vaguely recall, we were billeted in a historic mansion, not unlike Lydford Hall...but then, that was quite a while ago.

Lydford Hall was built not long after Henry VIII hanged the Abbot of Glastonbury and ordered the Abbey broken up. Indeed, it is even possible that some of the stones from the magnificent Abbey, with its legendary associations with the Holy Grail, may have found their way into Lydford Hall. Today, the resident owners offer two truly splendid parts of the estate for holiday accommodations.

The East Wing of the Hall is beautifully furnished and decorated. The living room is done in a more or less Victorian idiom, with an oval mirror over the mantel, plenty of rich mahogany and a pair of deep blue sofas highlighted by creamy yellow walls and good natural light. The master bedroom features a very handsome four-poster canopy bed and an interesting spindle settle in front of an expansive window with a lovely view of the grounds. As with the public rooms, the bedrooms of the East Wing put rich dark woods against soft pastel decors (pink and lilac) for a wonderful romantic effect.

The Old Coach House offers single story accommodation under a vaulted ceiling. Again, the furnishings have been carefully chosen and arranged for an elegant uncluttered effect. The Coach House opens onto the courtyard with access to the a heated indoor pool...just the right shape for the early morning laps now preferred by aging tor climbers.

EAST WING	
II.B-q	
F-2	
B-d	
B-t+s	
F-3	
COACH H.	
I.B-d	
F-2	
B-t [2]	
F-3	
E	H$
LT	
TELc	TV
W/D	
DW	MW
C-BA	P-S-S
INS	
£288-642	
S 6-7	

Contact Classic Cottages, Leslie House, Lady Street, Helston, Cornwall TR13 8NA
TEL 01144-1326-565-656 or FAX 01144-1326-565-554

WEST LODGE   Cricket St. Thomas

Ah, it's an old and tragic story! The gentle-spirited Manor Born are resting comfortably on the laurels of their ancestors when suddenly they are displaced by some turnip and celery mogul. The moral of the story is clear enough: beware of upwardly mobile greengrocers! Before you know it, the *nicoise riche* have bought up the Old Manor and packed the blue bloods off to the Gate Lodge with nothing more than the timeless loyalty of an old retainer to call their own.

I. B-t
F-1
II.B-d
F-3
B-t
F-3
E   H$
FP
L
TEL TV
W
DW
P-
F-F MS
INS
$760-1265
S 6

Well, one could do a whole lot worse than be packed off to West Lodge, as Penelope Keith was in the BBC's long running series *To The Manor Born*. Anglophiles with intravenous tele-feeding via PBS will immediately recognize every room of West Lodge and enjoy their stay all the more now that the somewhat overbearing Penelope has moved back up to the big house as the Manor bride...*Mrs. Nicoise*, as it turns out! If you're thinking of strolling up to the Manor for tea, be prepared for roaming wallabies, llamas and all sorts of wild critters (excluding Ms Keith), as the real Georgian Manor at Cricket St. Thomas has become a wildlife park and home to the very interesting National Heavy Horse Centre.

Contact British Travel International, P.O. Box 299, Elkton VA 22827 USA
TEL 800-327-6097 or FAX 703-298-2347

UNDERWALL   Langport

This is a perfect base for a couple, honeymooning or otherwise, to explore the endless sights of central Somerset and to do a little fishing in the bargain. On the hill, with frontage (actually *backage*) on the River Parrett at the bottom of the steeply sloping garden, Underwall boasts views of a dozen church spires across the Somerset Levels. The *cottage* is, in fact, a Gothic annex to the owner's home, with entrance through the gazebo. The galleried sitting/dining room is a veritable den of exquisite little treasures, books, miniatures...all sorts of *objets d'art* and Spanish, as well as English, antiques, including fine Chippendale dining chairs. Up the oak spiral staircase is a double bedroom with a lovely 18th century four-poster bed.

I.B-d
F-3
E&H
FPG
LT
TELc
TV
W
C-BA
S-S
INS
$360-615
S 2-3

Contact Chapel House Cottages, P.O. Box 878, Eufaula, Alabama 36072
TEL 334-687-9800 or FAX 334-687-5324

GINGERBREAD HOUSE   Nr Ilminster

Character with a capital "C" is this Grade II Listed gem which sits amid the five hundred acre estate of the Speke family...descendants of him of Burton/Speke, searchers after the source of the Nile. Constructed from the golden stone of Somerset's Ham Hill (the so-called *hamstone*), with a cruck skeleton, Gingerbread House was built for the game keeper. In fact, there is still plenty of game about in these rolling dairy farmlands, and pheasant shooting is offered to the guests in the appropriate season and away from the Friesian dairy herd.

As one might expect, a hexagonal building makes for rather interesting interior design.   The architectural choices in the restoration were especially thoughtful: leaded diamond shaped windows in the best Gothic tradition, stone mullions, pine interior shutters.   Even the curious overhanging thatch terrace supported by un-hewn posts affects the interior atmosphere...*Gothicizing* the lighting and perspectives.   The same care and planning is evident in the choice of country style furnishings, Laura Ashley and Colefax & Fowler print upholstery and drapery.

The downstairs of Gingerbread House consists of a little hallway with a characterful studded front door. Off the hall is a WC and basin, as well as two sitting rooms (one with an open fire) and a contemporary kitchen with a Rayburn and laundry facilities. Three bedrooms upstairs are reached by a rather steep curved stairwell....more character! There is a large bathroom up here as well, and leaded pane dormer windows under thatch brows with delightfully Victorian views into the copper beech woods that surround the cottage.

Somerset offers a wealth of things to do and places to see. Some very nice wine and traditional cider is made in the neighborhood, and, for the antique shopper, it will take a full week to just poke your nose in all the shops of Honiton (twenty minutes away).

I. F-1
II. B-d
B-t [2]
F-3
E$c
H$c
FP
LT
TV
W/D
DW
C-BA
S-S   MS
INS BK$
£190-435
S 6

Contact Helpful Holidays, Coombe, Chagford, Devon TQ13 8DF
TEL 01144-1647-433-593 or FAX 01144-1647-433-694

OLD HALL
Croscombe

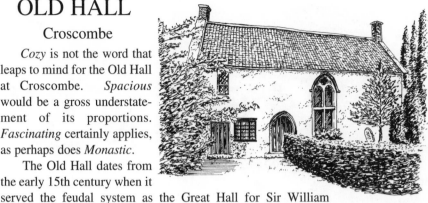

Cozy is not the word that leaps to mind for the Old Hall at Croscombe. *Spacious* would be a gross understatement of its proportions. *Fascinating* certainly applies, as perhaps does *Monastic*.

The Old Hall dates from the early 15th century when it served the feudal system as the Great Hall for Sir William Palton. The rest of the manor has long since disappeared, and for most of the last three centuries the Old Hall has been a baptist church. The Landmark Trust has taken the Hall back to its earlier design, albeit now in the service of the holiday trade. This is definitely not a *watch your head* cottage, though there are plenty of exposed beams, not least in the great arch braced open ceiling, with Gothic cathedral windows to fill all this vertical space with floods of light. On this scale the mile long refectory table and benches almost pass without notice. Massive double doors take us from the Great Hall into a very spacious kitchen, above which are the sleeping accommodations.

Now, if all this ecclesiastical elbowroom leaves you a bit claustrophobic, you can regain your perspective by visiting the nearby Abbey at Glastonbury or the Cathedral at Wells. There, you see, your Old Hall of Croscombe is really just a *cottage*.

I. F-2
II.B-t
B-t+s
E&H
FPS
LT
S-S MS
INS
£338-587
S 5

Contact The Landmark Trust, Shottesbrook, Maidenhead, Berkshire SL6 3SW
TEL 01144-1628-825-925 or FAX 01144-1628-825-417

COMER COTTAGE
Nr Ilminster

This lovely home-away-from-home is associated with the family estate that encompasses Gingerbread House. There is a great deal of house pride in the decoration of Comer Cottage, with double lined Colefax and Fowler curtains, Baker prints, deep feather sofas...smart furnishings and fittings from top to bottom. Rooms are spacious with high ceilings, an open fire in the living room, and gracious French windows from the formal dining room to the patio. Upstairs there are two en-suite bedrooms, one with a queen sized pine poster bed, and both with lovely views of the estate.

II. B-q
B-t
F-3 [2]
E$ H$
FP
LT
TV
W/D
DW MW
C-BA P-
F-F MS
INS BK$
£190-435
S 4

Contact Helpful Holidays, Coombe, Chagford, Devon TQ13 8DF
TEL 01144-1647-433-593 or FAX 01144-1647-433-694

CUTTHORNE   Luckwell Bridge

Cutthorne is smack in the middle of Exmoor. There is a quite extraordinary feeling about being in the middle of Exmoor, like being awash in prehistory or a self conscious dot in an ethereal painting. This is *Lorna Doone* country, the English "Bad Lands", rich in legends projected onto a landscape which is so markedly different from all the popular images of Merry Ole England.

Ann and Philip Durbin operate a Bed & Breakfast with two additional self catering cottages not far from Exford, the hunt capital of the moors. Indeed, the larger of the cottages is called the *Ballroom* from the time when it was used for hunt balls. What stories these quarters could tell; echoes of *Tom Jones*, rowdy and ribald fetes celebrated with plenty of after-ride exuberance and no sparing of liquid refreshment. Chances are that many a spent huntsman ended his hard day and night curled up in the hay next door in the Shippon. The Ballroom and the Shippon continue to be welcoming havens today, no less convivial steads, and a whole lot more comfortable than in the bumptious days of yore.

The Ballroom retains all of its original character, with solid oak floors and the large open fireplace. Nowadays there are French doors opening to the kitchen-dining hall and beyond that to a private patio. There is a double bedroom and another with adult size bunks.

BALLROOM	
II.B-d	
B-b	
F-3	
SHIPPON	
I. B-d+t	
F-3	
E	H$m
FP	
LT	
TV	
MW	
W/D-BA	
MW	
TA	
£200-425	
S 2-4	

The Shippon is nicely situated on the cobbled yard next to the pond. A rustic stone stairs brings you to what was originally the stable door. Inside is a large open plan lounge/diner with an oak fitted kitchen. The original beamed ceilings have been retained throughout and the old huntsman's hayloft has been redesigned for more dignified repose.

Cutthorne has plenty of animals, barnyard and others, but the Durbins invite you to bring your own horse and dog if you wish. They also invite you to their table, along with the B&B guests, for candlelight repasts that do full justice to all the legends of Exmoor hospitality. ETB 4 Keys; Deluxe

Contact: Ann Durbin at Luckwell Bridge, Wheddon Cross, Exmoor, Somerset TA24 7EW
TEL 01144-1643-83255

DRUMS HILL COTTAGE   Mells Nr Bath

Mells is a beautiful village in its own right, but I must confess that what always stands out in my memory is the glee on our seven year old's face when he discovered that the great Tudor mansion in the village belonged to the Horner family and was the source of the Little Jack Horner nursery rhyme. The aforementioned Jack with the sticky thumb would no doubt have visited Drums Hill Cottage in his time...in fact, you may want to get right into the rhyme of things and bake a Christmas pie yourself in the absolutely super country-style kitchen that comes with this property.

This 400-year-old sprawling thatch and stone house is situated at the end of a quiet lane amidst vines, gardens and wood. At one end is a large well-planted and nicely furnished conservatory with dining facilities opening onto an elevated patio (with barbeque). The movable feast opportunities at Drums Hill Cottage are endless and, personally, very appealing. Back inside, there are two sitting rooms in the house, with beam ceilings and fireplaces (one with wood stove). These are very homey, lived-in rooms, with soft furnishings in loose covers of William Morris fabric, scatter rugs on terracotta tile floors, good quality French provincial chairs, brass wall sconces, and a number of notable antique pieces, offering a nice *period* mood. The dining room features a handsome French cherry dining table, and there is yet another set of table and chairs in the kitchen.   Eat... eat...eat! Well somebody will have to get to work in the kitchen, and this is a kitchen made to cook in. There is plenty of counter space, excellent under cabinet lighting, good wash up facilities, and both gas and electric stoves.

Upstairs there are four bedrooms with zip/lock beds to make twin and king combinations according to need. The large bathroom is fitted in mahogany and has a power shower as well as bidet. There is another half bath upstairs and a WC & basin downstairs adjacent to the laundry room.

Should you ever want to leave this property, there is a wealth of touring opportunities within minutes: Bath, Longleat, Castle Combe, etc.

I. F-1	
II.B-d	
B-t	
B-t/q [2]	
F-4	
E	H$
FP	FPS
LT	
TEL	
TV	
W/D	
DW	MW
S-S	
INS	
BK$	
TA	
£420-660	
S 8	

Contact Mary Spivey, The Independent Traveller, Thorverton, Exeter EX5 5NT
TEL 01144-1392-860-807 or FAX 01144-1392-860-552

THE DOVE COTE
Somerton

Somerton is situated on the gentle flowing River Cary and has one of Somerset's most attractive townscapes. The church and almshouse date from the 17th century and the ancient octagonal market cross was *rebuilt* in 1673. On the outskirts is Dovecote Cottage, in the courtyard of the Lynch Country House, a noted B & B. Formerly part of the stables, Dovecote has been domestically refitted to a high standard, with beamed ceilings, stripped pine doors and truly elegant windows installed in the old arched stable door frames. The living room features a raised dais with comfortable furnishings. A twisting staircase takes one to the bedrooms, one of which is furnished with an impressive Victorian brass bedstead.

The Dovecote is an ideal base for touring the *must see* Cathedral and Close of Wells; Glastonbury, the legendary burial site of King Arthur; Longleat, Cheddar Gorge, Wookey Hole and much much more.

II.B-d
F-3 [2]
B-t
E
FPS$
LT
TV
DW MW
S-S
INS
£237-492
S 4

Contact Classic Cottages, Leslie House, Lady Street, Helston, Cornwall TR13 8NA
TEL 01144-1326-565-656 or FAX 01144-1326-565-554

MUTTLEBURYS MEAD
Thorncombe

This delightful little cottage is situated in a picturesque *Miss Marple village* which is off the tourist route, yet within a few minutes drive of all the tourist high spots of the Dorset coast. Muttleburys Mead Cottage is attached to the owners' home and surrounded by two acres of wonderful landscaping, which includes a rock-garden pond and even an aviary. The cottage itself is compact, tidy and bright, with beamed ceiling, polished pine doors and whitewashed walls. It is carpeted throughout (including the bathroom) and prettily furnished, albeit eclectically, with lots of interesting decorative bits, as well. The cottage comes with official greeter: a chubby, dear white lab, whose name ought to be Pickwick...just the sort of chum for a *Muttleburys Mead!*
ETB 3 Keys; Highly Commended

II.B-t/q
F-2
E&H
LT
TELc
TV
MW
C- P-
S-S
£140-245
S 2

Contact Mr. Ernest Smith, Muttleburys Mead, Chard Street, Thorncombe, Somerset TA20 4NB
TEL 01144-1460-30651

STOGURSEY CASTLE
Stogursey

In a book filled with unique holiday properties, Stogursey Castle Cottage is among the most unusual. The cottage is actually built into the ruins of the twin gate towers to Stogursey Castle, once a stronghold of William de Courcy, Steward to Henry I. The Castle has long since fallen to rubble, and, indeed, only after Landmark Trust was well into the dig was the moat dredged and the remains of the bridge discovered. The cottage, itself, probably dates to the 17th century and is entered now across a bridge that once brought knights to their liege lord's bidding.

The sitting room shape follows the rotunded stone wall of the old tower and features an impressive inglenook fireplace. Also on the ground floor is a spacious kitchen/dining room, off which circular stairs take us to a pair of small twin bedrooms overlooking the moat. There is something quite dreamy about the cottage and grounds of Stogursey Castle. This is a good place to just relax and pitch pebbles into the drink. Alternatively, you may make forays into the Quantock Hills, just to the south, or cast your eye out over Bridgewater Bay, just to the north.

II.B-t [2]
F-2
E&H
FP
LT
F-F MS
INS
£497-849
S 4

Contact The Landmark Trust, Shottesbrook, Maidenhead, Berkshire SL6 3SW
TEL 01144-1628-825-925 or FAX 01144-1628-825-417

WINTERSHEAD FARM   Simonsbath

This lovely 19th century farmhouse stands statuesque and glowing pink against the green expanse of Exmoor. Jane and Barry Styles offer three spacious cottages around the courtyard to the rear, plus a cozy bed sitter flat. The largest, Well Cottage, sleeps six in three sizable bedrooms, prettily furnished in pine with cheerful floral curtains and duvets. There are lovely exposed timbers in the living rooms and high quality contemporary furnishings. All cottages are carpeted throughout, and, though there is central heating, both Well and Spring Cottages have wood stoves encased in handsome fireplaces. There are truly wonderful walks along the River Barle nearby.
ETB 2-4 Keys; Highly Commended

E&H
FPS*
LT
TV
W
P-BA$
S-S MS
TA
£120-465
S 1-6

Contact Jane & Barry Styles, Wintershead Farm, Simonsbath, Exmoor, Somerset TA24 7LF
TEL 01144-1643-83222

SMITHY COTTAGE   Crowcombe

This is definitely a cottage for the literary pilgrim. These Quantock Hills have provided inspiration for so long and so many of Britain's finest penmen. Within ten minutes' drive of your base at Smithy Cottage, Samuel Taylor Coleridge wrote his best and Evelyn Waugh wrote his last. Lamb and Hazlitt visited often, and when Wordsworth took up residence the locals figured him for a French spy. Actually, Wordsworth was just an inveterate walker and nature observer, pastimes which remain the principal attractions of the Quantocks.

Smithy Cottage is at the center of Crowcombe, which is a handsome village at the bottom of the hills, with a Tudor church and some fine Georgian structures, as well. From atop the steep lane leading out of the village the view extends to the sea, where Coleridge launched his *Ancient Mariner*, and beyond to the Welsh Hills. The old 18th century smithy has been converted into a charming cottage, with spacious accommodation for adults and a *ladder-up* attic nook to delight the younger set. There is a large inglenook fireplace for cozy evenings, and a big garden for play or a quiet doze in the sun.   ETB 3 Keys; Commended

II.B-q	
B-t	
F-2	
E$m	H$
FP$	
LT$	
TV	
S-S	MS
INS	BK$
£144-342	
S 6	

Contact West Country Cottages, The Geminids, Priory Rd, Abbotskerswell, Devon TQ12 5PP
TEL 01144-1626-333-678   or   FAX 01144-1626-336-678

BOXBUSH COTTAGE
Wells

Wells is a town with a heart, and in Boxbush Cottage you are in the heart of the town. Just across from the Cathedral Green, this Grade II Listed cottage dates from the 1400s and has been renovated with a keen eye to architectural detail and creature comfort. The artisan owners have left their marks of good taste everywhere in the cottage. Notable antiques include a stained glass screen with links to Lord Nelson, a rocking horse, and a number of Victorian pieces. Bright casement windows, carefully restored wood and stone surfaces, nice decoratives...altogether a lovely romantic hideaway in the shadow of England's largest ecclesiastical precinct, filled with quiet and inspiring walks by day or night. However, don't expect to park at your front door; the rental comes with a prepaid ticket for the town carpark several blocks away.

II. B-d	
F-2	
III.B-s	
E$m	H$
LT	
TELc	TV
W	
DW	
P-	
S-S	MS
INS	
BK$	
$510-850	
S 3	

Contact Meta Voyage, 1945 Pauline Plaza, Suite 14, Ann Arbor, MI 48103-5047
TEL 800-771-4771 (East) 800-538-6881 (West)   or   FAX 313-995-3464

GEORGIAN TOWNHOUSE
Wells

No tour of the West Country can be called complete without a leisurely exploration of Wells. I admit that Wells can sometimes be a bit frustrating for mobility. Like all of the great medieval towns, Wells is seriously at odds with the internal combustion engine. In fact, its grand Cathedral notwithstanding, Wells is really just a country town, yet its traffic congestion can reach city proportions at their worst. Your notion of an idyllic holiday may not include a half hour squeezed in between a couple fuming lorries on a narrow ancient street, with thousands of pedestrian bodies also using the street as a sidewalk.

My most emphatic advice is *park it, don't miss it!* Become one of the multitude on the hoof; actually, I suspect that this cacophony has always been the Wells scene...substitute overladen carts for trucks, dung for diesel, and throngs of pilgrims and traders for the grockles of today. Indeed, Wells still draws both pilgrims and traders in great number. The former are on their way to stand in awe, religious or otherwise, of the truly magnificent 12th century Cathedral, which is surrounded by a fascinating array of other ecclesiastical buildings (the Chapter House, Lady Chapel, Vicar's Close, et al), all set back across a lush green commons with swans cruising the moat beyond. The latter, that is the traders, are on their way (generally in a hurry!) to the open air market. Go with them! (Save the historic sites for a couple other days; make one of them a Sunday, if possible). For me, market day in Wells ranks in the top ten most memorable scenes in over two decades of traveling Britain. Medieval cacophony with color, congestion, conviviality; gawkers and hawkers ...amble over to the butcher's auction and bid on a *lot* of pork chops...just be ready to catch them if the auctioneer closes on your nod! **"Next Lot...Leg of Lamb!"**

Well, where are you to cook those pork chops? You are about a five minute walk from *home*. You're staying in a three story Georgian terrace house on the Wells-Bath Road; actually it feels like the country out here away from the din of town, with your own private garden of roses and honeysuckle. There are even some herbs to enhance those chops. Your abode is exquisitely furnished with fine antiques, original art, and a bibliophile's library. One look at the kitchen and dining room and you will wish you had been a little more adventuresome and bid on the leg of lamb. Upstairs you will find an en-suite four-poster bed(room), among others, with views of the Somerset countryside all the way to the Glastonbury Tor. ETB 5 Keys; Highly Commended

I. F-1
II. B-d
F-3
B-s
III.B-t
B-s
F-3
E$ winter
H$ winter
LT
TELm
TV
W/D
DW MW
P-
F-F   MS
BK$
£300-600
S 6

Contact Celia Hutton, Bath Holiday Homes, 3 Frankley Buildings, Bath BA1 6EG, TEL 01144-1225-332-221

LITTLE QUARME   Nr Wheddon Cross

Got that *climb the wall* feeling?   Want to break out into wide open spaces, take long quiet walks and feel yourself disappear into nature?   Doctor Armstrong prescribes a healthy dose of Exmoor!   Moorland walks have been our preferred therapy year after year, and, though our heart belongs to Dartmoor, some of the Exmoor rambles are unsurpassable anywhere in the world (even Dartmoor!)...and there are over 600 miles of marked footpaths in Exmoor!   A personal favorite: the Tarr Steps trail along the River Barle in autumn when the bracken has gone all russet.

Little Quarme offers a wonderful base to "do" Exmoor on foot, horseback, bicycle, or (if you can't break all the bad habits!) even by car.   Indeed, one need only step out the doors of the six Cody-Boutcher cottages to feel you are a part of the grand space that is Exmoor.   We write so much about *views,* but this is a view you can get into! If you need an excuse for a walk, just say you're going to pop across the fields to the village of Wheddon Cross to post a letter and pay your respects at the friendly pub. It's only a half mile.

The Little Quarme cottages have risen out of the 1708 barns on the Cody-Boutcher's farm. They are spacious and conveniently modern; tastefully furnished and uncluttered. There is fitted carpeting throughout and electric fires to take the chill out of a spring morning. The kitchens, done in oak or knotty pine, are completely outfitted and have ceramic tile floors. There are 1, 2, & 3 bedroom cottages, with Country Diary and Jenny Wren design bedding. Little Quarme is very much family oriented, with donkeys and ponies for the children to ride, and ducks on the front step to give you a friendly quack in the morning. The nearby medieval village of Dunster is one of England's most picturesque and always seems to be abuzz with some festival....in June it is open-air Shakespeare theater in the Castle grounds.

| E$c H$c |
| LT |
| TVV |
| W/Ds |
| MW |
| F-F S-S |
| INS |
| £145-400 |
| S 2-6 |

ETB 4 Keys; Highly Commended to Deluxe

Contact Tammy Cody-Boutcher at Little Quarme Country Cottages, Wheddon Cross Nr Minehead, Somerset TA24 7EA   TEL 01144-1643-841-249

INGESTRE PAVILION   Nr Tixall

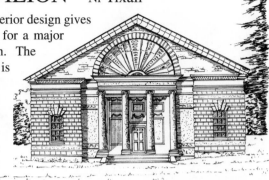

If classical architecture and interior design gives you goose bumps, then prepare for a major outbreak in the Ingestre Pavilion. The octagonal galleried room here is reminiscent of Monticello, and I am quite sure that, had Jefferson visited this perfect miniature during his architectural explorations, he would have copied it in his own work. However, for me there is a big difference between the Ingestre Pavilion and Monticello. Though I have often visited and sketched Jefferson's beloved domestic temple, I was never invited to sleep over!

As miniatures go, Ingestre Pavilion is quite large and spacious, with adequate sized bedrooms flanking the upper cavity of the octagonal saloon, and another twin bedroom on the ground floor. The kitchen is also quite large and work-

I. B-t
F-2
II.B-d
B-t
F-2
E&H
FP
LT
S-S   MS
INS
£422-604
S 6

able, and there are bathroom facilities upstairs and down. What is *sacrificed* is any pretense in the tiny tuck-away staircase--Jefferson would have approved! The Landmark Trust interior decorators have, however, sacrificed nothing in the decoration and furnishing which is wholly faithful to the intelligent elegance of the Age. The surrounding parklands are worthy of Capability Brown, which is not coincidental as both Brown and Wren were drawn into building schemes on the Chetwynd-Talbot estates.

MARTELLO TOWER   Aldeburgh

Now here's a place to sleep sound and secure; entombed, as it were, in a pile of a million bricks. Of course this is not just a random pile of masonry; its design was meant to be singularly inhospitable...well, at least uninviting as far as the Little Emperor across the water was concerned. The military life span of Martello Towers was as short lived as the Napoleonic era, but happily these were structures which could be more easily declared *obsolete* than actually demolished, and many have survived around the world. Landmark Trust has done a noble job bringing this Suffolk landmark back to life as a unique holiday venue by-the-sea. Indeed, *by-the-sea* is the sound, smell, taste, and feel of this echo chamber cottage, with an expansive roof terrace that offers you a private horizon on the all elements in their fullness, be it sun, mist, wind or fog. What is more, the cavernous tunnels make for fabulous games of hide 'n' seek... that is, if there are youngsters aboard for your holiday.

B-t [2]
F-3
CS
E&H
FP
LT
S-S   MS
INS
£431-683
S 5

Contact The Landmark Trust, Shottesbrook, Maidenhead, Berkshire SL6 3SW
TEL 01144-1628-825-925 or FAX 01144-1628-825-417

LODGE COTTAGE

Badwell Ash

Lodge Cottage is a Grade II Listed building and stands in the grounds of the owners' residence, Badwell Ash Hall, a handsome Tudor building in the ancient village of Badwell Ash. The board-sided, tile roofed *cottage* originally housed the coachman and the stable block, and has a half acre of private gardens of its own.

The interior decor of Lodge Cottage is clean and simple. There are two sitting rooms; one small and cozy and the other spacious enough for large family gatherings. Both have open log fires and lots of books and games to while away the tranquil hours. The dining room, which is a large convivial room featuring a big old pine table, is also paired with a smaller, more intimate dining area, which, incidentally, houses the piano. The kitchen contains all the modern conveniences and service accouterments, including pretty blue and white patterned china. Upstairs there are three twin and one double bedroom. All beds have duvets covered in pretty country flower prints. There are two bathrooms, both with full size tubs and one with a separate shower cubicle.

We return to the garden, as you will many times. Guests are invited to partake of the interesting array of fruits in the garden, including Old English Quince, and to use the good selection of herbs for cooking. The glassed over Fig House contains a prolific Brown Turkey Fig tree, and also houses the indoor barbeque. In fact, this is a delightful alternative dining venue on warm summer evenings, the white stone walls and trailing geraniums giving a positively Mediterranean atmosphere. There is a separate games house, with billiards, ping pong, and various pub games.

This part of Suffolk has many unspoiled medieval villages, where timbered houses lean tipsily together in a collage of soft colors. We are on the fringe of *Constable Country* here, an area to see at a leisurely pace as if we were a part of Constable's own landscape. On the way back to the Lodge we can stop for fresh produce at the farm gates. Market day at nearby Bury St. Edmunds will provide a good excuse to do a bit of formal tourism by taking in the ruins of the Great Abbey where the Barons of England drew up the Magna Carta.

ETB 5 Keys; Highly Commended

II.B-t [3]
B-d
F-2
F-3
E$m   H$
FP [2]
LT
TELc
TVV
W/D
DW MW
P-
S-S MS
£250-420
S 8

Contact: Mrs Madeline Castro, Badwell Ash Hall, Badwell Ash, Bury St. Edmunds, Suffolk IP31 3JG
TEL 01144-1359-259-643

PRIMROSE COTTAGE

Otley Bottom

It has always seemed to me that Suffolk is rather overlooked by tourists. Perhaps this old county doesn't have as many distinctly tourist attractions, which, of course, is to miss the point that Suffolk, in its gentle rolling rusticity, *is* the attraction!

II.B-q
B-t
F-3
II &III
B-t
B-s
F-3
E&H
FPG
LT
TV
W/D
DW MW
F-F MS
INS
£450-640
S 4-7

Primrose Cottage, near the quaintly named hamlet of Otley Bottom, is quintessentially Suffolk. Nestled in amongst the trees, with climbing roses and honeysuckle, the cottage is a picture of tranquility. Inside, you will find exceptional furnishings in a gallery atmosphere of fine paintings and sophisticated decoratives. The conveniences and utilities are completely modern, as is the decor, albeit studded with very handsome country antiques and pottery. Separate staircases lead to prettily decorated bedrooms offering soothing pastoral views. As with all Rural Retreat cottages, guests are greeted with a basket of victuals and a bottle of wine.

Contact Rural Retreats, Station Road, Blockley, Moreton-in-Marsh, Gloucestershire, GL56 9DZ
TEL 01144-1386-701-177 or FAX 01144-1386-701-178

GREEN COTTAGE

Market Weston

Green Cottage was built in the reign of the first Queen Elizabeth and is one of the oldest buildings in the this rural village. Tudor construction is much in evidence in the interior beams and framing, as well as some wattle & daub walls. The sitting room has a wood-burning stove in the inglenook fireplace and is furnished in a comfortable homey style with a rather interesting table made from an 18th century French cart wheel.

For the walkers and naturalists, Redgrave and Lopham Fens are close by; also there is Knettishall Heath, an attractive Breck landscape. Nearby is Thelritham Windmill, which has been restored to working order and is open to the public. The market town of Diss (8 miles away) is one of East Anglia's prettiest, with a six acre *mere* (lake) standing in for a village green.

I. B-s
F-2
II.B-d
B-t
E$m
H$m
FPS
TV
NS
S-S INS
£145-312
S 5

Contact Coast & Country Holidays, 15 Town Green, Wymondham, Norfolk NR18 0PN
TEL 01144-1953-604-480 or FAX 01144-1953-606-671

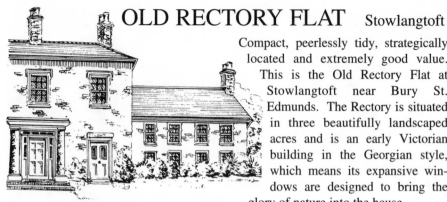

OLD RECTORY FLAT   Stowlangtoft

Compact, peerlessly tidy, strategically located and extremely good value. This is the Old Rectory Flat at Stowlangtoft near Bury St. Edmunds. The Rectory is situated in three beautifully landscaped acres and is an early Victorian building in the Georgian style, which means its expansive windows are designed to bring the glory of nature into the house.

The Flat is bright and airy, with furnishings in gay florals and warm pine. The sitting room is accented by a rich royal blue settee with pink piping. There is a step down fully fitted kitchen with a dining table for four. The bedroom offers twins with apricot duvets and views of the adjacent 13th century church. Guests are welcome to use both the tennis facilities and the owner's swimming pool, which, incidentally, is heated from Easter and late in the season until October.

ETB 4 Keys; Highly Commended

I.B-t
F-3
E
FPE
LT
TV
W/D
DW
NS
TA
£110-200
S 2

Contact: Mrs Jenny Godfrey at The Old Rectory, Stowlangtoft, Bury St Edmunds, Suffolk
IP31 3JY   TTEL 01144-1359-230-857 or 01144-1359-270-536

HAMPTON COURT PALACE   East Molesey

Your invitation to *Come to Court* is on behalf of the Historic Royal Palaces and reads thus: *The opportunity...to become part of this life, to go past the security barrier, to make yourself at home in a palace. Hampton Court is so much a part of our history that it needs no new introduction. The details are best learned (t)here, slowly and first hand: our visitors are free to explore the gardens and most of the courtyards at all times, early and late, and the public rooms of the palace during opening hours...*

FISH CT.
II.B-t
F-3 F-2
III.B-s [2]
B-d
GEO.H.
II. B-t
B-d
B-s
F-2
III.B-t
B-s
F-2
E&H
FP*
LT
S-S   MS
INS
£549-995
S 6-8

Your choice of accommodations (there are only two!) include a cozy apartment tucked in off Fish Court, where in days of yore the Pastry Officer held forth by the *Grace and Favour* of Henry VIII. The second floor living room looks down on the Master Carpenter's Court and the three additional bedrooms in the attic are reached by separate stairs. Or choose the Georgian House, built by the Prince of Wales in 1719. This elegant detached three story home comes with its own wall garden, and handsome furnishings from the Georgian and Victorian periods.

Contact The Landmark Trust, Shottesbrook, Maidenhead, Berkshire SL6 3SW
TEL 01144-1628-825-925 or FAX 01144-1628-825-417

SEAPOINT

Brighton

We owe the Coast Guard an historic debt. Not only has this valiant service saved so many lives, but they cleverly situated themselves in the most delightful marine viewplanes to do their important work. Now that rowing to the rescue has been replaced by the helicopter, the Coast Guard has left us a legacy of superb holiday accommodations. Actually, in this instance it was our friend Richard T.S. Harris' grandparents who received and passed along the *inheritance*.

Seapoint is one of eight terraced cottages built in the early Victorian Period, a mile or so east of Brighton. Brighton by-the-sea was as popular then as now for the holiday makers, and, no doubt, this fine terrace of professional vigilance recorded plenty of action, spotting and pulling amateur mariners out of the drink...saturated spirits, soggy petticoats, and all. Gosh knows, the keen eye of the coastal wardens could hardly miss much from up here; the view, then and now, would challenge the peripheral sight capacities of a fly. It can be said that the contemporary fly has more to see from Seapoint's commanding position, though happily not at the expense of the boundless blue of the English Channel which has always been the *raison d'etre* for this place. Today, there is a golf course out front, and a 2,000 berth yacht marina.

You approach the cottage from below with the sea to your back; indeed there is a pervasive sense of elevation here, both physical and emotional. *Up* through the pretty rock garden; *up* the broad front steps to the *upper* patio. (Feel it?). Well, you're up here now; might as well turn around and take it *all* in. See what I mean about the fly? Can't take it all in, can you, without screwing your head almost all the way around! I expect you'll end up spending most of your time out here under the parasol or on the patio on the chaise, just breathing deeply and seeing far; but first let's go in and get settled. From the patio we enter a south facing sun room...same view, double glazed for off season recreational vigilance. Through sliding doors into the living room...only marginally reduced view...with bright seaside furnishings in pine and rattan. There are a pair of settees and some pretty watercolors painted by Richard's grandmother. Further along there is a good workable kitchen with a dining table, Edwardian sideboard and Welsh dresser. *Up*stairs to a pair of bedrooms. *Up* front is the master bedroom...there's that view again!

ETB 4 Keys; Commended

I. CS	
F-1	
II.B-d	
B-t	
F-3	
E&H	
FPE	
LT	
TEL	
TV	
W/D	
MW	
NS	
S-S	MS
TA	
£255-485	
S 4	

Contact Richard T.S. Harris, Best of Brighton Cottages, Horseshoe Cottage, 2 Whipping Post Lane, Rottingdean, Sussex BN2 7HZ   TEL 01144-1273-308-779 or FAX 01144-1273-300-266

HANOVER CRESCENT

Brighton

There's no avoiding the use of the "L" word for this truly magnificent post-Regency home on Hanover Crescent. *Luxurious!*

Readers will, no doubt, be interested to know that Charles Dickens stayed in this house during his *Little Dorrit* period. I can say, without the slightest reservation, that this Hanover Crescent home did not assist Dickens one little bit in his brilliant portrayal of The Marshalsea, that dreary, squalid debtors' prison where poor Little Dorrit's papa (Alec Guinness, if you *waited for the movie*) languished, year after year, page after page. My god, what powers of imagination Dickens had! What a capacity for transcendence!

Hanover Crescent is centrally located within the city, but enjoys an expanse of green commons, undisturbed in modern times except for the parking arrangements for residents. Today, most of the houses in the long crescent have been made over into flats, albeit I should think rather up-market and stylish. Not so with this handsome property, which is a complete home on four floors and has been entrusted by its proud owners to the discretionary rental management of Richard T.S. Harris. *Best of Brighton*, indeed!

Overall the architectural detail, furnishings and decorating give the home very much a Renaissance air. Front and back, there are wide bright windows set in bays & bows, including some leaded small pane beauties like the masterpiece in the reception hall. Even the basement kitchen is wonderfully lit, with life-like landscape murals painted on the walls of the sunken patio. The latter, incidentally, is only one of three delightful places to sit out and enjoy the carefully managed tropical flora from the comfort of very stylish garden furnishings. There is a private little piazza garden with fountain and fishpond off the grade level entrance hall, and a spacious wrought iron railed balcony off the second story master bedroom.

Beginning with the below grade floor (one hardly wants to say *basement!*) we have a country style kitchen, an idiom which is somewhat out of step with the Regency elegance of the rest of the house, but which is, at any rate, very fashionable these days and tastefully done here with an antique pine table, big butcher block and plenty of country decoratives. Also on this level is a single bedroom with en-suite shower, and a sitting room with a double bed convertible sofa. This garden apartment, incidentally, may be rented separately, when the whole house is not taken.

The street level rooms are the height of Regency elegance, with some

Edwardian touches and even a bit of art nouveau in the statuary, and some strictly modern paintings, as well. The furnishings are individually noteworthy and work well together: a Hepplewhite style dining table and chairs, a handsome mahogany *secretaire*, many fine accent tables and cabinets with period flavor, crystal chandeliers, large ornate mirrors, heavy swagged drapery framing garden views through the bay windows, and blueware floor vases begging floral treatments which

I. B-s
F-3
CS
III..B-d [2]
F-3
IV. B-d+s
F-2
E&H
FPG
LT
TEL
TV
W/D
DW   MW
NS-prefered
OPEN
MS
£225-995
S 2-8

these rooms wear like jewelry. The living room walls are done in a bold red, and feature, among other fineries, a massive tapestry. Fireplaces in the living room and dining room are framed by classically white mantels.

Up the nicely turned side hall stairs to the second floor bedrooms. The bedrooms are distinctly masculine and feminine; the latter having a baroque queen sized bed accented by lacy pillows and a duvet, with a screened corner bath and bidet. The master's bedroom is situated in a paneled library stylized room, with a period four-poster bed canopied in striped fabric, and a Jacobean blanket chest. There is a separate bathroom as well. On the top floor you will find a family room with sleeping accommodations for three and another bathroom.

The letting arrangements on the Hanover Crescent home are notably flexible and accommodations can be structured for parties of two to eight, with pricing to match.

Contact Richard T.S. Harris, Best of Brighton Cottages, Horseshoe Cottage, 2 Whipping Post Lane, Rottingdean, Sussex BN2 7HZ   TEL 01144-1273-308-779 or FAX 01144-1273-300-266

BLACKSMITHS COTTAGE
Rottingdean Nr Brighton

This long time home of the village smithy is located on Vicarage Lane in historic Rottingdean by the sea, just three miles from the heart of Brighton. Blacksmiths Cottage (windows far left in drawing) is modest and homey, with comfy older style furnishings and a cozy traditional fireplace in the low ceiling living room. The dining area features an interesting Victorian painted dresser/hutch with a pretty display of china and pottery for daily use. Upstairs there are two tidy and unpretentious bedrooms under the exposed beam ceiling. The Grade II Listed cottage has a small secluded garden area with appropriate furnishings.

II.B-d
B-t
F-2
E&H
FP
LT
TV
W
NS   P-
S-S   MS
TA
£195-355
S 2-4

Contact Richard T.S. Harris, Best of Brighton Cottages, Horseshoe Cottage, 2 Whipping Post Lane, Rottingdean, Sussex BN2 7HZ   TEL 01144-1273-308-779 or FAX 01144-1273-300-266

EYEBRIGHT COTTAGE
Brighton

Eyebright is a traditional fisherman's style cottage in the residential Kemp Town section of Brighton. Visitors are close to Brighton's beaches and the historic Palace Pier, and within easy walking distance of downtown and the famous Royal Pavilion. Not least of the advantages of Eyebright Cottage is the parking which comes with the cottage, always a problem in Brighton during the busy tourist season or when the town is hosting a major convention.

The Cottage is small and compact but comfortable, with a spacious kitchen/dining room, a small living room, and three bedrooms upstairs with vanity basins. The second floor double bedroom has French windows leading to a wrought iron balcony overlooking the little front garden.

II. B-d
B-s
F-2
III.B-t
E$c   H$
LT
TV
W
MW
S-S
TA
£225-395
S 5

MARINE HOUSE   Brighton

This very handsome Regency Period townhouse was the long time *home away from the road* for the famous Shakespearean actress, Dame Flora Robson. Tucked away on a narrow little street near the beaches, Marine House is both a handsome retreat, and a centrally located base for forays into the sights and sounds of Brighton, by day and night.

The cottage is laid out on four floors, beginning with kitchen and dining facilities at the street level. Above this is the living room, which is exceptionally airy and bright with a pair of classic bow front windows as well as French doors leading to a romantic little balcony over the tiny street. The room is mirrored at one end, magnifying the elegantly compact proportions and reflecting the tasteful decor and furnishings. On the third floor there are two bedrooms, a double and twin, and a bathroom complete with bidet. One of Marine House's many pleasant surprises is the fourth floor garden/studio room, opening out on to a wonderfully private sun terrace where you can enjoy the sea atmosphere (and a bit of a view of it, as well) on your own terms. Top to bottom, Marine House is a treat and very good value for ever-popular Brighton.

II. B-d
III. B-t
F-4
IV.CS
E&H
LT
TV
MW
OPEN
£255-425
S 4 +

Contact Richard T.S. Harris, Best of Brighton Cottages, Horseshoe Cottage, 2 Whipping Post Lane, Rottingdean, Sussex BN2 7HZ   TEL 01144-1273-308-779 or FAX 01144-1273-300-266

PEKES MANOR

Chiddingly

Pekes is a stately brick and red tile Tudor manor house set back on 28 acres of secluded tranquility about ten miles from the South Coast. The estate has been in Eva Morris' family since 1908, and four very distinctive satellite buildings are offered as vacation rentals. These are not barn conversions, though, of course, the Oast House began life in the 19th century as a hops drying facility. However, hops didn't fare well in these parts and Eva's grandfather made over the old oast house as a dower house for Eva's great-grandmother. Eva's mother still resides in the oast, in life size portrait form, that is; one of many familial and homey aspects of these unique properties.

Of course, the thrill of oast houses are their round rooms, and the Pekes Oast has four beauties, each seventeen feet in diameter. On the ground floor there is a circular living room with parquet floors, fireplace, comfortable chairs and a semi-circular bar. The dining room is also circular and has furnishings customized to maximize the effect: curved side tables and a round dining table. The room is spacious enough to still accommodate a handsome settee that converts into a double bed. The kitchen is not, alas, in the round, but it is huge and has an oak table with seating for twelve! You will also find all your china here, openly displayed on a handsome pine dresser. Upstairs we are in the round again. Firstly in the master bedroom, which has a splendid four-poster bed and period style furnishings to match. The other circular bedroom is bound to be appropriated by the children in the party, and to minimize the conflict you will find three single beds here. Two other bedrooms are *regular* in dimensions, and comparably furnished in country style pine and decoratives.

Tudor View Cottage is a curious brick and tile building, all on one floor, with beveled ends, appearing a bit like a Victorian train station. It is set apart from the manor house and surrounded by its own flowery terrace garden and lawn. The double and twin bedrooms are interconnecting in-line, and the double bedroom opens on to the terrace. The cottage is carpeted throughout and comfortably furnished in a country style. Central heating and hot water is provided by a Trianco boiler which is hopper fed.

Other opportunities to holiday at Pekes Manor include a character wing of the Manor House, itself, and the sweet little gate house, set in its own garden behind a picket fence. Recreational amenities include an indoor pool, atmospherically planted in all sorts of greenery; sauna, badminton, hard tennis courts, and a sunbed/exercise solarium. ETB 4-5 Keys; Commended

Contact Eva Morris, 124 Elm Park Mansions, Park Walk, London SW10 0AR
TEL 01144-1713-528-088 or FAX 01144-1713-528-125

OAST
I. CS
F-3
II.B-d
F-t+s
B-t
B-s
F-2
FP$
£650-1065
S 8
TUDOR
I.B-d
B-t
CS
F-3
£290-590
S 4-5
BOTH
E$m   H
LT$
TELm
TV;   V$
W/D
DW   MW
S-S   F-F
MS   INS

BULL RIVER COTTAGE Nr Chiddingly

These are the South Downs, where the land drops off abruptly into the Channel in those improbable chalk cliffs known as the Seven Sisters. There is an improbable feature typical of South Downs architecture, as well...the tile hung wall (why don't they fall off?). Bull River Cottage has a tile hung gable, but that is not the end of improbability in this unique little cottage. What we have here is a one of a kind character cubby for two.

Set in secluded grounds, with a heated outdoor pool, the cottage begins with a conservatory filled with friendly plants and wicker. Then there is a spacious sitting room which becomes an improbable bedroom, with twin beds that fold out of the wall. Some easy chairs are gathered around a pleasant wood-burning stove in typical cottage fashion, but then there is a wholly improbable spiral step-cum-ladder (brilliantly fashioned out of pine) going to an equally improbable reading and wardrobe gallery above. Finally the kitchen; you probably wouldn't expect to find a beautiful new Aga, but there it is, all pleasantly surrounded by honey pine and bold blue tile! For all its improbability, I think you will probably remember Bull River Cottage as a perfect base to explore the South Downs, from the pleasure palaces of Brighton to battle scars of Hastings.

Contact Mary Spivey, The Independent Traveller, Thorverton, Exeter EX5 5NT
TEL 01144-1392-1860-807 or FAX 01144-1392-1860-552

```
I.B-t
 F-3
FPS
LT
TEL   TV
W
MW
E/HC
OPEN   MS
BK$    TA
£200-360
S 2
```

ABOVE PAR   Crawley

Above Par is a *convenience,* rather than *character,* cottage. Its proximity to Gatwick Airport should be noted by travellers who want to see a bit of the South Coast of England during a connecting flight layover on the a Continental European holiday. Stays can be for any number of nights. The owners offer a very economical alternative to bed and breakfasting it...or, if you're like us, a private and spacious place to repack the cargo (booty!) before the long flight home. As the name suggests, you can even have a round of golf on the par 72 course just across the street. Bridge enthusiasts should make themselves known to Tony Hodgkinson, who will happily arrange a social bridge game or introduce guests to duplicate bridge clubs. Suffering bridge spouses will be happy to know that the beaches of Brighton are only about twenty minutes away.

```
I. F-1
II.B-q
 CS
 B-t
 F-2
E$m  H$m
FPE
LT$
TELm  TV
W/D
DW  MW
NS  P-
OPEN
MS
£120-200
S 5
```

Above Par is a semi-detached home in the Forestfield subdivision ...quiet, secure, modern, and so very *convenient.*

ETB 4 Keys; Highly Commended

Contact Mrs Barbara Hodgkinson, "Hodge's Lodges", 52 Kelso Close, Worth, Crawley, West Sussex
RH10 7XH   TEL 01144-1293-882-008 or FAX 01144-1293-883-352

LAUGHTON PLACE Nr Lewes

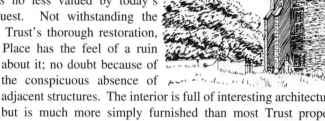

A solitary promontory on the Downs is Laughton Place. The ancient family Pelham may have had security in mind when they built this tower (actually *re*built) in 1534, but the perspective from up here is no less valued by today's holiday guest. Not withstanding the Landmark Trust's thorough restoration, Laughton Place has the feel of a ruin about it; no doubt because of the conspicuous absence of adjacent structures. The interior is full of interesting architectural features, but is much more simply furnished than most Trust properties. The circular castle stairs and tower bedrooms will delight the children, and the close proximity to all the sights and activities of the South Coast make this an ideal venue for a family holiday.

| I. F-3 |
| III.B-t |
| IV.B-t |
| E&H |
| LT |
| S-S MS |
| INS |
| £391-614 |
| S 4 |

FOX HALL   Charlton

It seems that in all cultures and times gentlemen (and surely some not-so-*gentle* men) have fashioned for themselves fraternal retreats, rustic venues away from polite society *(sans* ladies, if not female companionship entirely), there to enjoy the revelries of male bonding, ostensibly with the aim of reenacting the pageants & rituals of ancient (and once necessary) brutalities. In England, for the *gentle* classes, it was *The Hunt.*

It also seems that whatever man (gentle or otherwise) does, be it noble, ignoble, or just plain silly, he is inclined to leave an architectural monument. Thus it was that Fox Hall came into being as the hunting *camp* of the Duke of Richmond (circa 1730). Such an enthusiast was the Duke that he wanted a sleeping quarters right on site for what was then probably the most fashionable fox hunting ground in the realm. The Landmark Trust, who have restored the Duke's lodgings, has dubbed Fox Hall "Britain's premier bed-sitter." And so it is, with a magnificently domed baroque alcove off the upper hall wherein the sporting Duke could recline in slumber with happy images of little foxes bounding through his besotted cranium. Downstairs there is another bedroom, possibly once the footman's lodgings, as well as a spacious bath (presumably the Duke had his *toilette* upstairs in the splendor of the Great Hall, which, incidentally, is not so great in space, but lacks nothing for grandeur in classical decor. The Duke, after all, was a *gentleman!* Tally Ho!

| I. B-t |
| F-2 |
| II.B-d |
| E&H |
| LT |
| P- |
| S-S MS |
| INS |
| £377-610 |
| S 4 |

Contact The Landmark Trust, Shottesbrook, Maidenhead, Berkshire SL6 3SW
TEL 01144-1628-825-925 or FAX 01144-1628-825-417

BRUNSWICK SQUARE Hove

Brighton has a unique place in the British Isles, not unlike Los Angeles in the development of American culture. Like the *City of Angels,* the sunny perspective and broad sandy beach of this place probably destined it to be a pleasure venue and an aesthetic--some would say *moral*--frontier. A place to kick off the shoes, figuratively speaking, and make ones own peculiar tracks in the sands of time. And, if the footprints proved to be too *peculiar,* beyond even the respectable bounds of *avant-gardism,* or just plain silly, the surf could always be counted on to wash away the embarrassment (which, of course, is pretty much what has happened to Hollywood Gothic, though, gratefully, not so much to Brighton).

Back at the early adolescence of the 19th century, the then Prince Regent was very susceptible to the urge to kick off his shoes (among other bits of apparel) and in many ways he was a natural for the environmentally inspired decadence inherent in Brighton. Among the many Royal residences, the Regent favored the steads down in Brighton. The only rub was that, in the eye of the princely beholder, the local Palace just didn't have enough...enough...well, call it pizazz!

Actually, the prominent architects of the day, men like John Nash and C.A. Busby, were already taking some pretty fanciful diversions from strict Classicism and the Prince, no doubt, thought all that was jolly good. (Unlike our present Prince, also an aesthetically willed man.) But the future George IV wanted more than a cautious diversion; he wanted a bold stroke for the Picturesque and beyond, a bizarre Oriental fantasy palace, and he chose Nash to bring his whim to life by remodeling the old Brighton Palace. No doubt every architect longed for juicy Royal commissions, but I can't help thinking that Mr. Busby, et al, may have breathed a sigh of relief when they were passed over for this particular job. Besides, the Prince's enthusiasm for Brighton had set off a general building boom along the adjacent seaside, and there was work for everybody. Well, Nash really did go the whole hog and delivered up a Royal Pavilion for his Prince that set tongues wagging and has been called everything from wonderfully *exotic* ("symbol of far-flung Empire!") to shamefully *erotic* ("Potentate's harem house!"), and there is certainly no sign of it being washed away in the surf of time (though the same can not be said for Brighton's exotic pleasure piers). But, alas, the party Prince tired of his toy almost immediately, and architectural fashion returned to more elegant, less eclectic norms. Which is exactly where Mssr. Busby was, aesthetically speaking, as he was building Brunswick Square in the adjacent village of Hove just at the time the new King was recanting and decamping from Brighton for good. It would seem that Mr. Busby's clientele wanted abodes by the sand & surf which were imaginative and elegant, *sans* the exotic and erotic. Well, Busby's creation was, indeed, imaginatively picturesque and remains tastefully elegant by today's standards, while potentate harems are even today a bit edgy for domestic occupancy, even on holiday.

Brunswick Square occupies a lovely south facing position fronting on the Channel. The lasting integrity of the massive square of statuesque and richly pilastered terrace houses has been maintained, in part, because the founders covenant, that all the homes be painted a uniform sandstone color, has been rigorously upheld. The sweeping elegance of the bow fronts serves a special utility here, in that all the houses around the square, even those sited at right angles to the Channel, have a view

III.B-t
F-1
IV.B-d
B-t
F-3
F-4
E&H
LT
TEL
TV
W
DW MW
OPEN
MS
£295-575
S 6

of the sea. This is true of the penthouse (third & fourth floor) of #7 Brunswick Square, which also has a wonderful roof terrace with commanding views by daylight or starlight. Just below this superb cocktail bridge are three bedrooms, with the master bedroom enjoying one of the bow front bays. The third floor bow front belongs to the living room, which is furnished in a cool seaside idiom with a contemporary floral soft suite and decorated by pretty impressionist prints. The dining room features a Regency style table and chairs, and the kitchen is fitted with nice extras, like the Miele dishwasher. Inside and out, top to bottom, this is a very handsome flat, just short of luxurious, but right at the top of the *most for the least* list. I don't know of any property by the sea where a hundred dollars will buy such delightful accommodations for six in June.

Contact Richard T.S. Harris, Best of Brighton Cottages, Horseshoe Cottage, 2 Whipping Post Lane, Rottingdean,
Sussex BN2 7HZ   TEL 01144-1273-308-779 or FAX 01144-1273-300-266

GLEBE COTTAGE Patcham Old Village

Glebe Cottage is a Grade II listed building situated near the 13th century church in the quiet conservation area of the old village of Patcham. The ground floor has a modest sized living/dining room, with exposed blackened beams and an original brick fireplace. The white walls (with some interesting prints and engravings) and a large window/glass door leading to the terrace make for an airy well lit feeling. There is a double aspect kitchen, also overlooking the sunny walled garden. Up a small spiral stairs one finds a double bedroom and a second bedroom fitted with 3 ft. bunks. The bathroom and shower are also upstairs. This is not a large cottage, but if additional sleeping space is required, the living room sofa converts to a comfortable double bed.

I. CS
II.B-d
B-b
F-3
E$c   H$c
LT
W
MW
S-S MS
TA
£160-300
S 6

Patcham is a quite delightful village, only three miles from the tourist mecca of Brighton. Patcham is noted for its apparitions; the tall thin lady who lingers at All Saints Church on frosty evenings, and one Anthony Stapley, Esq, who distinguished himself by signing the warrant that relieved King Charles I of his head. ETB 3 Keys; Commended

Contact Mrs. Joan Deacon, 38 Ridgeside Ave. Patcham nr Brighton, East Sussex BN1 8WB
TEL 01144-1273-554-440

SOUTHERHAM OLD BARNS

Lewes

Designer at Work! Going through the four "cottages" of Southerham Old Barns is like a stroll through *Architectural Digest*. Each room is a canvas of imaginative furnishing and decor. Don't expect white paint that is less than *whiter than white*; the peach hues are so rich they almost have the fragrance of peaches; the aqua so *aqua* you want to dive in. All this in a barn conversion! To be perfectly frank, the original flint and brick barns, historic and handsome though they may be, are far from being the architecturally most interesting starting point for a development which has ended up being darn near perfect. In the courtyards of these barns, situated in the rolling countryside of the South Downs, are leisure facilities including an outdoor heated pool, a sauna, jacuzzi, small gymnasium and solarium. In addition, the Southerham offices provide a number of business services, including typing, telex, fax, photocopying, catered entertaining, and chauffeured transportation, as well as a self-drive car hire.

The cottages are spacious and have the atmosphere of country houses. Each cottage has its own garden or patio area. Of the four properties, Oxsetton is the smallest, sleeping four in two double bedrooms, with one bath. Furnishings here are ultra modern, with a colorful soft suite in the living room and a glass dining table. The open beam ceiling is painted a brilliant turquoise, rendering an airy Mediterranean feeling. Granary Cottage is designed for six, with three bedrooms and a living room/dining room partition which folds back to make a 32 foot reception room for entertaining. The contemporary designed living room features antique Victorian lady's and gentleman's chairs for accent, and you will find an attractive black lacquer dining suite in the adjoining room. Kemp's Barn, sleeping eight, shifts gracefully to a more traditional idiom, with an antique cast iron fireplace, exposed beams and a number of antique accent pieces. There is a double bedroom and shower facility downstairs, and three double rooms upstairs, plus two bathrooms.

Finally we come to Maudlyn *Cottage* (drawing above), which is anything but either a cottage or maudlin! Featuring a two story high wall of window (formerly the barn doors), the rooms here are huge, with brilliant contemporary and period style furnishings in lovely fabrics (flame stitch admirers will be especially pleased). With two bedrooms down and three up off the gallery landing, Maudlyn accommodates ten in absolute luxury.

ETB 5 Keys; Deluxe

E&H	
PF	
LT	
TEL	TV
W/D	
DW	MW
P$	
OPEN	MS
TA	
£365-1535	
S 2-10	

*Contact Richard T.S. Harris, Best of Brighton Cottages, Horseshoe Cottage, 2 Whipping Post Lane,
Rottingdean, Sussex BN2 7HZ   TEL 01144-1273-308-779 or FAX 01144-1273-300-266*

STABLE COTTAGE
Litlington

I. B-s
II.B-d+s
B-s
F-3
E$m
H$m
FPS
LT
TELin
TV
W/D
S-S
INS
$370-790
S 5

Stable Cottage is a lovely proportioned Victorian building with characterful flint walls and brick quoin-work. The cottage sits amidst the well tended grounds of a large 18th century manor house not far from the duck pond. There are three bedrooms; a single downstairs and another up, and a nice double/plus bedroom with balcony. The living room features a wood-burning stove.

There are many interesting sights in the area: the Saxon Long Man cut in the chalk is just across the Cuckmere River; the 14th century Clergy House in Alfriston, which was the first acquisition in the National Trust collection; and, of course, the great chalk cliffs of the Seven Sisters.

Contact Haywood Cottage Holidays, P.O. Box 878, Eufaula, Alabama 36072
TEL 334-687-9800 or FAX 334-687-5324

WEPHAM FARM STABLES
Wepham

Wepham is a small hamlet nestled on the South Downs with views of Arundel Castle, the traditional home of the Dukes of Norfolk. Wepham House is the center of the hamlet and the cottage was converted out of the 1841 stables last year. Stable Cottage overlooks a nice courtyard with a sunny terrace and barbeque. The kitchen theme is *country*, with farm animals adorning the tiles, pottery and curtains. There is a wood-burning stove in the sitting room with pleasant pine and soft furnishings in floral patterns. Upstairs you will find a double bedroom in blue pastels with adjoining bathroom featuring a large corner bath. Downstairs is a twin bedroom, adjoining a children's bunk room done in soldier and jungle themes. This is a splendid touring area with numerous historic sites & sandy beaches. If pubs are in your plan, be sure to try the old smugglers favorite, The George & Dragon.

I. B-t
B-b
F-3
II.B-d
F-2
E$ H$
FPS
LT
TV
W/D
DW
P-
S-S
INS BK$
£213-425
S 4-6

Contact Discover Britain, Shaw Mews, Worcester WR1 3QQ
TEL 01144-1905-613-744 or FAX 01144-1905-613-747

DUCK BARN
Telscombe Village

Duck Barn Cottages nestle in the very heart of the tranquil little hamlet of Telscombe, only 15 minutes drive from Brighton with its crowded piers and promenades, the exotic Royal Pavilion and famous Theatre Royal. In high season there is probably no more frenetic tourist area in all England; if Brighton is to be a focal point of your agenda, the respite of Telscombe Village might be a life-saver.

Anne Kennedy and her husband are both designers, and they have obviously had a delightful time doing up their three holiday buildings. The Duck Barn, itself, is a listed building with flint walls, a slate roof and the combination weather boarding typical of the south coast. The Barn, which accommodates up to twelve, seems to peek out of the hillside amidst a wild and romantic garden, with Italianate terraces that were once the fancy of the squire of the manor. There is a garden swing on which to idle the day away, and rope swings for the children in the mini-wilderness.

The interior of the Duck Barn revolves around the Great Hall, a splendid 30 foot square room with a high vaulted and beamed ceiling and French doors leading on to the terrace. The flagstone floors are decorated with colorful Oriental rugs and there are three large country style settees grouped around a cozy open fire. Books, pictures, pottery and duckish decoratives are in good supply and artfully displayed. A staircase takes one up to two small bedrooms (double and twin) with pretty Laura Ashley paper and antique pine furnishings. Bedroom three normally comes with a pair of twins, but for larger families four bunks can be installed for the children. The bathroom on this level features a white sunken bath. Another short stairs leads to the master bedroom which has a large internal window overlooking the Great Hall as well as a large dormer window framed by chintz curtains with views of the Manor House Tower and surrounding hills.

The Kennedy's also offer the Coach House Cottage, sleeping four, and the economical Gardener's Cottage, which is tucked away in a sea of roses and sleeps two in a gallery arrangement.

ETB 3-5 Keys Commended

```
DUCK-
BARN
I. F-1
   CS
II. B-d
    B-t
    B-b
    F-3
III.B-d
    F-2
E$c  H
FPS [2]
L;  T$
TELc
TV
W/D
DW  MW
F-F  MS
£120-575
S 2-10
```

Contact Anne Kennedy at Appletrees, 51 Firle Village, Lewes, East Sussex BN8 6LF
TEL 01144-1273-858-221 or FAX 01144-1273-858-200

COBBLE COTTAGE Rye

This cottage gives me the feel of a Robert Louis Stevenson novel, with its ancient low ceilings, half timber and plaster walls, and darkened beams. I can imagine him sitting here by a flickering tallow light penning a novel called *BEACHED*, a tale about some rogue left behind by the passing tide, as indeed Rye itself has been left up the creek by a receding sea since the 16th century. Actually, Rye's literary luminary was not Stevenson, but rather Henry James, the American of distinctly Georgian tastes, who I suspect would have found Cobble Cottage a bit claustrophobic; too Jacobean! Perhaps I'm wrong, for James certainly loved medieval Rye, with all it's smokey smuggler's environs and history stained cobble streets.

This 15th century Grade II Listed building oozes with character from the floors up...especially the floors which are all ancient polished plank wood, with colorful scatter rugs here and there. These are not floors that get lost under foot; you are ever conscious of the floors in this cottage, as if they were historic ground, just as the original paneling of the walls can be felt to contain you in historic space. This cottage has its own atmosphere. To get into a Stevensonian mood you might want to strike up a wood fire; there is an open log fire in the inglenook and a woodburner (plus gas stove) in the kitchen, which, incidentally is a quite pleasant farmhouse style room with pine units and table. There is a downstairs WC with bath off the kitchen.

Bedrooms begin up a steep stairs. Mind the head! The first is a bunkie room for two (probably favored by Stevenson's beached rogue because he could hear the creak of steps on the stairs!). The second bedroom is a double with a pretty floral duvet and a white dust ruffle against the darkened floor. Some nice Jacobean chairs and end tables restore the period feel. Along the hall is a WC. Up more steep stairs to a third bedroom, a double, with electric heater. Always the eye goes to the ancient beams, crooked by nature and age and inscribed by pilgrims from the past, possibly even Edward, Prince of Wales, whose crest appears rudely carved in the oak and suggests that the future king might have dallied here for some uncourtly assignation.

Rye, itself, is full of interesting sites: a photograph of the Quarterboys beating out the quarter-hour on the clock of the 12th century Church of St Marys is a *must;* a visit to Henry James' Lamb House for literary insights; and, of course, you'll want to lift a pint at the old Mermaid Inn amidst the shadows of smugglers and wayward princes.

I. F-2
II. B-d
B-b
F-1
III.B-d
E&H
FP   FPS
L$
TV
S-S
INS
$395-720
S 6

Contact Haywood Cottage Holidays, P.O. Box 878, Eufaula, Alabama 36072
TEL 334-687-9800 or FAX 334-687-5324

HATHAWAY HAMLETS

Nr Stratford-upon-Avon

Here we are in the village of Shottery where The Bard came to court young Anne at the Hathaway farm just down the road from our holiday cottage. The two miles from Stratford probably seemed further in Will's day, though in the anxious mood of his enterprise perhaps not. I'm sure that Shakespearean pilgrims of the present day will find the distance from the center of the Shakespeare industry just about right.

We enter this pretty little Listed cottage via a low doorway and find ourselves in a surprisingly large room (not referring to head room). The sitting room features a huge inglenook fireplace and is beautifully furnished to reflect the character of the cottage. A kitchen with stripped pine cabinetry has recently been added. Up the steep stairs and we are in a large bedroom under the open beams, with a double bed and a convertible divan.

I. F-2
II.B-d+s
E$m H$m
LT
TV
MW
P-
S-S MS
INS
$475-695
S 2-3

PRIEST'S HOUSE

Nr Stratford-upon-Avon

This cottage was already well over a century old when Will Shakespeare was penning his little ditties just four miles down the road in Stratford. The onetime monastic lodging sits in the privately owned character village of Preston-on-Stour.

It doesn't get much more *Ye Ole England* than this! Not a straight wall or floor in the whole cottage. Low beamed ceilings, low doorways, twisting uneven oak stairs, huge inglenook fireplace with bread oven, and original stone floors. As you enter the front door, the bathroom is on the right and is relatively modern in design. Through a door into the combination sitting/dining room which is surprisingly spacious, and beyond that to the tiny, albeit up-to-date, kitchen. The steep oaken stairs are off the hallway and lead to a pair of very pretty bedrooms with *watch-your-head* doorways and *seagoing* floors. Holiday Inn it is not! (Thank God). "May The Bard be with you"... and at the Priest's House he just might be!

I. F-2
II.B-d
B-t
E$m
H$m
FPS
LT
TV
MW
S-S MS
INS
$570-855
S 4

Contact British Travel International, P.O. Box 299, Elkton VA 22827 USA
TEL 800-327-6097 or FAX 703-298-2347

THE BATH HOUSE Nr Stratford-upon-Avon

The Bath House was built in a time when gentlemen regularly assembled for a bracing dip followed by a warming nip...well, perhaps several nips. The chilling dip was regarded as theoretically healthy, while the restorative powers of the nip could be confirmed without resort to promising abstractions. This bath house, with its grotto pool beneath and elegant chamber above, was built for Sir Charles Mordaunt in 1748.

The octagonal drawing room above is as handsome as handsome gets; and humorous! The Landmark Trust restoration team have outdone themselves recapturing both the elegance and the humor of the age with fine Georgian plasterwork fashioned into a dome of dripping icicles and garlands of seashells planted like ornamented quips on a backdrop of strict classical propriety. A second bed trundles out from under the day sofa for sleeping amongst some nice period style living room furnishings and a cozy fire in the Georgian fireplace. There is a cubby kitchen in an alcove and modern bathroom facilities upstairs above the foyer. With its secluded woodland setting, the Bath House is a perfect little hideaway.

I. CS	
II.F-2	
E&H	
FP	
LT	
P-	
S-S	MS
INS	
£313-481	
S 2	

Contact The Landmark Trust, Shottesbrook, Maidenhead, Berkshire SL6 3SW
TEL 01144-1628-825-925 or FAX 01144-1628-825-417

COACH HOUSE COTTAGES Lichfield

These in-town cottages are only a short walk from the Lichfield Cathedral and the historic city center, yet offer country quiet. There are three exceptionally well designed cottages in this renovated 1740's Coach House. Courtyard Cottage, with its own garden, has two double bedrooms (one up, one down) with views of the Cathedral, plus a single bedroom and a small child's room. Chestnut Cottage also has three bedrooms, two en-suite, as well as a spacious living room with beamed ceiling and good quality modern soft furnishings. The dining area features a very handsome mahogany breakfront and dining set. The largest, Honey Cottage, opens up through double doors from a hall conservatory into a spacious living room with fireplace. The dining room, with a Victorian style fireplace, overlooks the courtyard. The decors, throughout, mix nice floral patterns with soft solid colors (greens, pinks, wedgwood blues) and tasteful modern furnishings, many in interesting period styles.   ETB 3-5 Keys; Highly Commended

E$m	H$m
FPG	FPE
LT	
TVV	
W	D*
DW*	MW
OPEN	
£195-350	
S 2-6	

Contact Mrs Marlene Elson, 50 Sherifoot Lane, Four Oaks, Sutton Coldfield, West Midlands B75 5DT
TEL 01144-1213-088-352

THE OLD CHURCH
Manningford Bohune Common

The Vale of Pewsey sweeps across the barrenness of the Salisbury Plain like a grand geological sash. On the grassy hillside of Pewsey Down is the famous White Horse, which can be seen from the lovely church at Manningford Bohune in the valley below.

The tiny hamlet of Manningford Bohune Common has but four houses to go with its old chapel, hence the deconsecration of the statuesque Old Saints Church in 1973 after a hundred and sixteen years of ecclesiastical service. What followed was a period of makeshift domestic occupation until the present owner took over with a bold plan for architectural renovation. I must confess to having long had a passion for church conversions, where the opportunity for the creative manipulation of space seems boundless. This church redesign, recently completed, ranks very near the top of the many such projects we have drawn and photographed...brilliantly conceived and very skillfully executed!

This unique Grade II Listed house is situated in an acre of garden, with a small wood to the east, providing shelter from the winter winds sweeping across the Salisbury Plain.   Internally, space has been re-arranged to provide rooms on two levels at the east and west ends, with a towering openness over the living room in the middle. At the west end, on the ground floor, is the dining room, complete with a valuable oak dining table, reputed to have come from the home of Ann of Cleaves. A purpose built staircase rises to the main bedroom, a huge room lit by large skylights framed in between black Tudor style rafters against pristine white plaster.   The en-suite bedroom, with a clutter free walk-in closet, has its own wood-burning stove and a queen size bed, as well as a lovely mahogany dresser, wardrobe and various other antiques. The polished bare softwood floors are graced by some of the owners collection of oriental carpets.

At the east end ground level there is a guest suite. This has twin beds and it's own bathroom with a glass walled shower. The guests have their own fireplace

II. B-t
F-3
II.B-q
F-3
CS
F-3
E&H
FP FPS
LT
TV
W
OPEN MS
£450
S 6

in what was the old vestry. Above, is the studio/third bedroom, with a pretty sofa-bed, more bold skylighting and a separate bathroom. From the galleries one looks down on the living room with its pair of comfortable sofas, shelves of books, and even more lovely oriental carpets.

Nearby are the all-services market towns of Devizes and Marlborough, with historic Salisbury only a half hour's drive to the south. The BritRail station at Pewsey, three miles away, will deliver one into London's Paddington Station in an hour. Trout fishing, tennis, golf and riding are all available in the neighborhood, as is a very *serviceable* pub in a quaint thatched building.

Contact Rosamond Rose Properties, 22A Upper Addison Gardens, Holland Park, London W14 8AP
TEL 01144-1716-032-704 or FAX 01144-1716-031-710

THE DOWER HOUSE   Nr Bradford-on-Avon

The Dower House is actually a modern home built in the traditional style on the grounds of medieval Burghope Manor, which sits at the edge of Winsley village. Owners Elizabeth & John Denning have spared nothing in fitting out their Dower House to the same high standard as is evident in the manor house, itself. Everything is in the English country house style, with exquisite mahogany pieces, lovely chintz and velvet soft furnishings, and a wealth of interesting decoratives. The rooms are bright and cheery with peaceful views over the grounds of the manor in front, and a walled private patio and lawn to the rear. There is a proper dining room, with a refectory table seating eight and lovely china on display, as well as a full size kitchen. Up the central hall stairs one finds three bedrooms, two of which are en-suite.

I. F-1
II.B-d
B-t [2]
F-3 [3]
E&H
FPG
LT
TELm
TV
W/D
MW
NS
C-BA P-
S-S MS
TA
£350-550
S 6

The Dower House is only a ten minute drive from Bath and is well situated for exploring the many notable sites of this region. One should not overlook Bradford-on-Avon, itself, with its curious chapel on the bridge (later used as a gaol), impressive tithe barn, and wealth of both Tudor and Georgian architecture.

Contact Elizabeth & John Denning, Burghope Manor, Winsley, Bradford-on-Avon, Wiltshire BA15 2LA
TEL 01144-1225-723-557 or FAX 01144-1225-723-113

JASMINE COTTAGE   Marlborough

Designer at work! And good works they are. This is a very cheerful little cottage in a fashionable modern idiom, within a Grade II Listed 18th century exterior; and all this tucked away in a quiet corner of strategically situated Marlborough. Clean lined, pristine white walls, with brilliant yellow floral drapery on wooden rods and the same fabrics appearing in some of the soft furnishings. The living room also has a small (flush to the wall) gaslit fire and delightfully cushy matching sofas with simple striped covers. Dining is under a fitted glass canopy, which is a fine bit of architectural neo-Georgian*ism*. The kitchen is, again, pristinely white, showing off the French fruit wood table and chairs, with yellow themes returning in counter tile backs, terracotta floor, and even picture mattings. There is a twin bedroom on the ground floor, and a double upstairs under the eaves, with a pretty chintz covered headboard and a hand embroidered bed cover.

I. B-t
F-3
II.B-d
E&H
FPG
LT
TELc
TV
W/D
DW
P-
S-S
INS
$490-855
S 4

*Contact Chapel House Cottages, P.O. Box 878, Eufaula, Alabama 36072
TEL 334-687-9800 or FAX 334-687-5324*

COACH HOUSE   Melksham

Melksham sits on the River Avon a few miles upstream from Bath and is noted for its 18th century bridge. Nearby are the old weaving centers of Bradford-on-Avon and Castle Combe, the latter being widely acclaimed as *the prettiest village in England.* However, be warned, some people have been known to argue that Castle Combe is only the second or even third prettiest village in England. There is simply no accounting for the irregularities of personal bias.

COACH .
I. F-1
II.B-k
B-t
B-s
F-2
FP
DW MW
£360-615
S 2-5
CH APT.
II.B-d
F-3
£320-485
S 2
BOTH
E & H
LT
TV
W/Ds
OPEN MS
INS

The Coach House sits on the preservation listed Sandridge Park Estate and enjoys its own impressive driveway and a courtyard on three sides. The interior design is open-plan, with living, dining and kitchen areas flowing together and rendering an overall bright, spacious quality. The Coach House is furnished in a cheerful cottage style, with interesting pictures and decoratives, pretty rugs and up-to-date kitchen fittings.

Also available is the Coach House Apartment, a self contained wing with second floor panoramic views of the estate. Decor and furnishings here are more on the elegant side, with the accent on nice antiques and the same good decorating taste evidenced in the larger Coach House. Both properties offer large and prettily fitted bedrooms.

*Contact Rural Retreats, Station Road, Blockley, Moreton-in-Marsh, Gloucestershire, GL56 9DZ
TEL 01144-1386-701-177 or FAX 01144-1386-701-178*

THE WARDROBE

Salisbury

Most memorable church service? No question for us...Palm Sunday in Salisbury Cathedral. Heaven sent! But then the whole ecclesiastical precinct at Salisbury is heaven sent; truly a remarkable and serene environ, despite the ebb and flow of a multitude of the seriously faithful and the simply curious. The feeling that comes with strolling these grounds in the shadow of that Great Spire is nothing short of *blessed* (and this from a person with limited religious sensitivity) and the intensity of that aura grows exponentially after evensong. The opportunity to live here within The Close, even for a week or so, is truly unique. The Landmark Trust flat on the third story of The Wardrobe (above the museum) will install you front row center for the *scene, sound,* and, yes, even the *sense* of this blessed place. The living room dormer windows (see drawing) perfectly frame the Cathedral Spire, which verily glows through the night!

III.B-d	
B-t	
F-2	
E&H	
LT	
P-	
S-S	MS
INS	
£345-548	
S 4	

Contact The Landmark Trust, Shottesbrook, Maidenhead, Berkshire SL6 3SW
TEL 01144-1628-825925 or FAX 01144-1628-825417

THE STABLES

Netheravon

The village of Netheravon lies in a valley amidst the Salisbury Plain, only twelve miles from the great Cathedral City and five miles from that *must see* of all English prehistoric landmarks, Stonehenge. The Stables is a recent conversion of a two hundred year old building; all new and tidy, compact and convenient. There are lovely gardens with 45 varieties of roses!

Downstairs is a gleaming white tiled kitchen with all the culinary necessaries. Living and dining areas are at opposite ends of a 25-foot long room which opens through French windows onto the latticed patio. The furnishings include a very pretty red striped sofa and side chair and an 18th century oak corner cupboard. The walls are pristinely white, showing off several paintings by local Wessex artists. An exposed pine staircase leads to three upstairs bedrooms (one with wash basin). All are small, with sloping roofs and original beams exposed. The bedrooms are furnished simply and tastefully in pine, and the main bed has a strikingly beautiful Welsh patchwork quilt. There is an upstairs WC and a bathroom/shower downstairs, adjacent to the kitchen. Mrs Thatcher will also provide home cooked meals on request. ETB 4 Keys; Highly Commended

I. F-3	
II.B-d	
B-t	
B-s	
F-1	
E&H	
FPS	
LT	
TELc	TV
W/Ds	
DW	MW
S-S	MS
TA	
£220-350	
S 5	

Contact: Mrs AA Thatcher, Ivy Cottage, Netheravon, Salisbury, Wiltshire SP4 9QW
TEL 01144-1980-670-557

ACADEMY COTTAGE
Tisbury

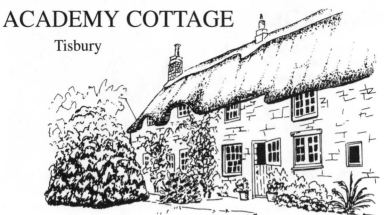

I. CS
II.B-d
B-t
B-b
F-3
E&H
FPS
LT
TELc TV
W
MW
P-
S-S
INS
$620-1090
S 6-8

Characterful thatch over neatly cut grey Chilmark stone; pretty ivy on the walls and a quiet garden retreat...just minutes away from the peerless Georgian splendor of Bath, Salisbury's *spireful* Cathedral, and Shaftsbury's picturesque Gold Hill...Bingo! Academy Cottage, which is conveniently attached to the owners' home, is a spacious yet homey abode, with an absolutely huge inglenook (now occupied in part by a cozy wood stove), higher than normal beamed ceilings for a 400 year old veteran, flagstone floors in the hall and kitchen and fitted carpets for the rest, and furnishings (such as mahogany dining table) that show age but respect.

MORTIMER COTTAGE   Wootton Rivers

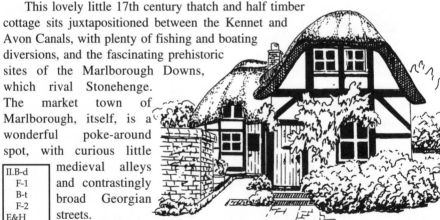

This lovely little 17th century thatch and half timber cottage sits juxtapositioned between the Kennet and Avon Canals, with plenty of fishing and boating diversions, and the fascinating prehistoric sites of the Marlborough Downs, which rival Stonehenge. The market town of Marlborough, itself, is a wonderful poke-around spot, with curious little medieval alleys and contrastingly broad Georgian streets.

II.B-d
F-1
B-t
F-2
E&H
FP
LT
TELc TV
W
P-
S-S
INS
$450-785
S 4-5

Mortimer Cottage is prettily decorated in honey pine and has a small open fireplace. Separate stairs lead to the two bedrooms, a double and a twin; both en-suite. Wootton Rivers is a quaint little canal village with a friendly pub near the cottage.

Contact Chapel House Cottages, P.O.Box 878, Eufaula, Alabama 36072
TEL 334-687-9800 or FAX 334-687-5324

DALEGARTH COTTAGES

Buckden

```
I.I. B-t
   F-3
   Sauna*
II.B-d
   CS
   F-3*
E$m H$m
FPE
LT
TELc  TV
W/Ds
NS*  P-
BA
S-S  MS
INS  TA
£274-426
S 4-6
```

The village of Buckden is situated in the heart of the Yorkshire Dales National Park and much of the surrounding countryside is owned and administered by the National Trust. These Dales are a tapestry of moorland and gentle, green hills; of ruined abbeys, crumbling castles and haunting patterns of dry stone walls; of grey sheep and black and white cattle...a landscape that both moves and soothes...the landscape which PBS watchers in North America have come to know as *Herriot Country*.

Dalegarth varies from most of the cottages in this book in that it was purpose built, and I should say without hesitation that Susan and David Lusted have a keen sense of *purpose;* to provide a comprehensive base for the holidaymaker to relax and explore these beautiful Dales. Dalegarth is nestled in the charming village of Buckden, which in turn is nestled in a deep valley, as if it had been here a thousand years. Built of local limestone in an old Victorian walled kitchen garden alongside a tumbling stream, these village homes are truly part of the landscape. The eleven cottages are designed with the living rooms upstairs to take advantage of the views...and what views they are (!) regardless of season: of lush green pastures dotted with spring lambs, or sweeping dales painted with autumn color, or whitened with snow. Each cottage has an individually designed stone fireplace; most have glass patio doors out onto balconies; several even have their own saunas. All the cottages are handsomely furnished and have many nice touches, such as original oils by local painters. There is an indoor pool, combined with a solarium, gymnasium and games room, as well as barbeque facilities.

THE GHYLL is comprised of three cottages designed especially for holidaying families with a member having mobility problems. All ground floor doorways are extra wide to accommodate wheelchairs, and downstairs bedrooms are en-suite, with level-deck showers and seats, as well as spa baths to relax in. None of these compensations are done at the expense of otherwise fine accommodations. You will find fresh Laura Ashley decors, with plush velvet drapes, deluxe furnishings, and very generous kitchens. Pool and other recreational amenities are shared with Dalegarth, which is only a couple hundred yards away.

```
I. B-t/q
   F-3
II.B-t/q
   F-3
E$m H$m
LT
TELc
TVV
DW MW
NS*  P-
E/HC
S-S  MS
INS  TA
£286-409
S 2-6
```

Contact Susan & David Lusted, Dalegarth, Buckden, Nr. Skipton, N. Yorkshire BD23 5JU
TEL 01144-1756-760-877

CLIFF HOUSE COTTAGES   Ebberston

Nicely situated for touring the Yorkshire coast or exploring the Yorkshire moors, Cliff House is a Grade II Listed building with seven holiday cottages fashioned out of the old farm buildings. With its red tiled roofs and stone walls set against the gentle slope I am reminded of some small hamlet in the Cote D'Or. Alas, no vines, though there are many other amenities, pleasant to the eye and to serve the holiday interest: indoor pool, jacuzzi spa, games room, tennis court, and an assortment of critters to delight the children. The cottages vary in size and accommodate from two to six. They are comfortably furnished in a more or less contemporary idiom, and have either oil fired or gas central heating. In addition, there is a recently converted self contained flat in Cliff House, itself, which accommodates two.   ETB 4 Keys; Highly Commended

E&H	
FP*	FPS*
LT	TV
W/D$s	
DW*	MS
P-	
S-S;	F-F
MS	TA
£160-630	
S 2-6	

Contact David & Angela Wilcock, Cliff House, Ebberston, nr Scarborough, N.Yorks YO13 9PA
TEL 01144-1723-859-440

VINE COTTAGE   Bellerby

Jan & David Ward are potters and create *Victorian Fragranced Pottery Gifts* from their characterful 17th century compound in this quaint little village. They share the compound and a couple acres with various equine friends and with guests from afar who want to be a part of James Herriot's glorious Yorkshire Dales for a time. Such good hosts are the Wards that they will even share their equine friends with guests who are truly experienced riders.

Vine Cottage is definitely a charmer. All the good old character elements are here: massive stone fireplace on a raised hearth set in a wall of exposed stone (the rest of the walls are freshly whitewashed), deep casement windows, and oak beams. The furnishings are equally characterful: Jacobean Welsh dresser, mahogany desk and corner cabinet, a Victorian chaise and an Edwardian highchair. And, as one might expect, lovely paintings and frameables, some old and some new. The kitchen features mahogany cabinetry, and upstairs there are two bedrooms with antique pine furnishings and floral fabrics.
ETB 3 Keys; Highly Commended

II. CS	
F-1	
II.B-d	
B-b	
F-3	
E&H	
FP	
L;	T$
TVV	
W/D	
MW	
P-	
S-S	MS
£180-295	
S 4-6	

Contact Jan & David Ward, Vine Cottage, Bellerby, Leyburn, North Yorkshire DL8 5QP
TEL/FAX 01144-1969-22184

BEE-BOLE COTTAGE

Countersett

Quaint name; quaint little cottage. Bee-Bole's name dates back to Elizabethan times when bees were kept in straw baskets (*Bee-Boles*) which were place in the recesses of the walls of this building to shelter them from the wind and cold. Today, the recesses are still there, preserved along with the character beams, inglenook fireplace and undulating plaster walls of this utterly charming hideaway. The cottage is prettily stenciled, and furnished in a homey style with lots of lace and embroidery. Equally pleasing is Bee-Bole's situation in the garden grounds of Countersett Hall, overlooking the original Quaker Hall, where meetings are still held monthly. The village, itself, is nestled on the edge of Countersett Lake, a beautiful venue for walking and riding.

I.B-t/q
B-s
F-3
E&H
FPG
LT
TV
MW
S-S MS
INS
£175-265
S 3

Contact Mrs. Linda Nash, All Cottages Great & Small, High Thirn Farm, Thirn, Ripon
Yorkshire HG4 4AU   TEL 01144-1677-460-287 or FAX 01144-1677-460-210

VIRGINIA COTTAGE

Grinton

James Herriot recalls the townscape of Grinton as an *unforgettable image of age and mellowness and grace.* Everybody's favorite Vet could well be speaking of Virginia Cottage, which sits in this quaint Swaledale village not far from the 12th Century church and the ancient stone bridge over the River Swale. This semi-detached village house, which is Grade II Listed, was built in 1648 and has enjoyed complete refurbishment by its present owner, an American interior designer. You will find a stone flagged dining hall furnished with a number of antiques, including a heavy oak trestle dining table, a chapel pew, and an old Persian rug laid out before the Victorian fireplace. The kitchen is farmhouse style, under a low beamed ceiling, and has an adjacent breakfast area. Another brass canopied fireplace is featured in the sitting room, which is handsomely furnished and decorated and leads through an ancient stone arch to an elevated study overlooking the back garden. Upstairs bedrooms enjoy pretty views over the countryside and of the stream flowing through the village. There are small private gardens to the front and rear of the cottage, and a nearby footpath leads up to the glorious heather clad moors.

I. F-2
II.B-d [2]
B-t [2]
E$m
H$m
FP$
L
TV
W/D
S-S MS
INS
$690-1140
S 8

Contact British Travel International, P.O. Box 299, Elkton VA 22827 USA
TEL 800-327-6097 or FAX 703-298-2347

GREAT BURLEES Nr Hebden Bridge

Wool is king in this part of Yorkshire; indeed this is the wool capital of Britain as much today as in previous centuries. Think sheep, yes; but also think mills, mill towns, and mill wealth. Great Burlees was built in a grand scale on the sunny side of the valley by a wealthy wool merchant in the 17th century. Today the house has been carefully restored and divided into five spacious cottages. Retaining the old oak beams and stone mullioned windows, the cottages are tastefully furnished and well equipped. Most of them have old stone fireplaces and sleep from two to six people. They are fitted with modern kitchens and bathrooms, and have cozy, tastefully decorated living rooms. From it's site high on a hill overlooking Hebden Bridge, the house gives spectacular views over the gardens, stream and duck pond and the beautiful Calder Valley beyond. Picnic tables and chairs have been provided in secluded spots in the garden.

This is a walker's paradise, with the Pennine Way passing just the other side of Hebden Bridge. The next village, Heptonstall, has an octagonal chapel where Wesley often preached, and five miles away is Haworth, home of the Brontes.   ETB 3 & 4 Keys; Commended

E$m
H$m
FP*
TV
W*
$250-665
S 2-6

Contact Mary McCanna, Westminster Lodgings, 160 Westminster Dr.,W.E., Jamestown, NY 14701
TEL 800-699-0744 or 716-484-0744

WESTFIELD FARM Haworth

The farming enterprise at Westfield has probably been going on since Norse times. Today, under the stewardship of Gordon & Wendy Carr, Westfield is still very much a working farm, with something in the order of 350 new lambs dotting its stone partitioned lush hillside pastures each spring. Farm modernization made for redundant buildings, and of these the Carrs have made five very comfortable holiday accommodations. They vary in size from Stable Cottage which sleeps two (and is wheel-chair accessible) to the Farmhouse, which sleeps six. The cottages are furnished in a contemporary style and offer truly splendid views over the valley to Haworth, home of the Bronte family. This is wonderful walking territory, and you can start out with a very detailed guide prepared by Wendy and Gordon which pretty nearly names every bit of flora and fauna along the way. The Pennine Moors, Top Withens (*Wuthering Heights*?) and Bronte Falls are all within walking range from the cottages. ETB 3-4 Keys; Highly Commended

E$m
H$m
L; T$
TV
W; Ds
MW
P-BA
E/HC*
F-F OPEN
MS
£130-300
S 2-6

Contact Wendy Carr, Westfield Farm, Tim Lane, Haworth, West Yorkshire BD22 7SA
TEL 01144-1535-644-568

LOW GREENFIELD FARM COTTAGES

Langstrothdale Chase

Low Greenfield Cottages nestle in the folds of limestone uplands at the source of the River Wharfe. This is a wonderful venue, away in the hills, so to speak, for ambling along the Dales Way, or trout fishing, or caving in these limestone cliffs.

The five cottages, which are approached through the National Trust's Upper Wharfedale Estate, have been designed to suit varying requirements, ranging from a cozy cottage for two, to one accommodating six, having three double bedrooms and bathrooms in equal measure. Formerly stone barns, with two feet thick walls to keep the rooms cool in summer or cozy in winter, they have been crafted into superb holiday accommodations by the same hand that created Dalegarth (see earlier entry) from scratch. The interiors are bright and welcoming and nicely furnished. The kitchens are lavishly spacious, light, airy and well equipped. However, when the urge comes to dine out, you will be pleased to know that, even in these remote parts, there is a large country estate house (turned guest house) right next door, which offers good local cuisine and the *sine qua non* of hospitality, the unmanned bar...based entirely on trust! Likewise, I trust you will enjoy your stay at Low Greenfield Farm.

E$m
H$m
LT
TV
NS* P-
S-S MS
INS
TA
£244-349
S 2-6

Contact Susan & David Lusted, Dalegarth, Buckden, Nr. Skipton, N. Yorkshire BD23 5JU
TEL 01144-1756-760-877

HILLTOP COTTAGE Langthwaite

I say; is that Tristan Farnon we see slipping out of the surgery and stealthfully making his way down to the Drovers Arms...? Devoted viewers of *All Creatures Great and Small* will recognize many scenes from this village where the James Herriot series was filmed. The opening scene of James' jalopy zipping over the picturesque little stone bridge is also patented Langthwaite.

Hilltop cottage, dating from the mid 18th century, was once a miner's cottage and is presently owned by two sisters living several doors down, who are fourth generation born and raised in the village. *Cozy* is the word for Hilltop Cottage, with an open fire in the living room and a Rayburn stove in the kitchen. There are open pine beams throughout and a decor that runs to browns and greens, accenting apple white walls. The walk-in larder next to the kitchen is filled with books and games for the enjoyment of visitors. Upstairs, the king size bed is in a yellow toned room with views over the patio and hills to the back.

I. F-1
II.B-d
B-t
F-2
E$m   H$
LT
TV
S-S MS
INS
£215-280
S 4

Contact Mrs. Linda Nash, All Cottages Great & Small, High Thirn Farm, Thirn, Ripon,
Yorkshire HG4 4AU   TEL 01144-1677-460-287 or FAX 01144-1677-460-210

RIVULET COURT   Pateley Bridge

When I first heard about Rivulet Court I naturally assumed the property was one of the premier British self-catering resort complexes...a sort of Abbots Court North. Rivulet Court's reputation is almost larger than the cottage itself. Yes, there is only one cottage, but it has turned out a legion of happy guests who continue to spread the good word about this very charming little holiday den.

The setting for Rivulet Court definitely hasn't hurt its reputation, particularly with those holiday makers who want to experience village life at the same time as being *lost* in a grand and remote landscape. (It's OK to want it ALL; you're on holiday!) The cottage is tucked away in its own garden courtyard just off the High Street of Pateley Bridge. This is a picturesque village (a frequent winner of the *Britain in Bloom* awards) with old stone buildings, nestled in the valley of the River Nidd with a veritable sea of heather-covered moorland around. *Lost* in the Yorkshire Dales! It's all here for exploration, by car, on foot, by mountain bike (available for local hire), or, for those who want to get on top of it all, there are even hot-air balloon excursions. For the more *civilized* pursuits, you will need to set aside several days for the wealth of stately homes to visit in the neighborhood: Skipton Castle, one of the most complete medieval castles; Castle Bolton, where Mary Queen of Scots was imprisoned by Queen Bess; and my favorite, Harewood House (home of the Earl and Countess of the same designation and former home of the Prince Royal), which is a sort of Longleat North, *sans* the zoo (human and otherwise). The cities of Harrogate and York, museums, galleries, public gardens, a host of children's attractions...all easily accessible from your hideaway in the *lost* village of Pateley Bridge.

After all this touring around it is time to get home to Rivulet Court. The cottage, which was once part of the estate of the Archbishop of York and administered by the Manorial Court, is approached through a stone arch and up a wooden spiral staircase from the courtyard. The living area is thus on the second and third floors, with a utility room at ground level. The wood paneled dining room on the second floor opens onto a most wonderful private terrace, literally in the tree tops, with long views over the roof tops and the sound of the rivulet below. The living room features a cozy fireplace in big cut limestone blocks, exposed stone walls and beamed ceiling. The furnishings are eclectic, with some truly outstanding pieces: a grandfather clock that has been in the Rack family for generations, a mahogany dining table, good paintings, old lace and embroidery, etc.

ETB 5 Keys; Highly Commended

II. F-3	
CS	
III.B-k	
F-3	
B-t [2]	
E&H	
FP [2]	
L; T$	
TELc TV	
W/D	
DW MW	
S-S OPEN	
MS	
INS TA	
£180-400	
S 6-8	

Contact Mrs Anne Rack, Blazefield, Bewerley, Harrogate, HG3 5BS   TEL 01144-1423-711-001

UPPER MYTHOLM BARN Luddenden Dean

Upper Mytholm is a traditional grey stone farmhouse with attached barn and a weaver's cottage built in 1775. It is nicely sited on a slope with a moorland stream running through the garden, and its mullion weaver windows give pleasant views of the wild but beautiful rolling Yorkshire countryside. However, the exterior views aren't a shade on what lies within the Upper Mytholm Barn, attached to the owners' home. Here, quite simply, is one of the prettiest cottages in all of England; the ETB rating of *Deluxe* is the best they give, but it is an understatement.

The Denton's have taken every advantage of the stone and beamwork of the old barn. Where the keystone-arched stable door was, they've installed a dramatic window framing the dining table in a panoramic vista. The accommodation is on three levels, making for interesting interior perspectives, peek-around corners and surprises to the eye. The super cozy sitting room features a wall size stone hearth with an impressive timber lintel and a hooded open fire. The soft furnishings are covered in a rich black rose fabric that invites a curl-up and snooze....but no time to nap; there is much much more to see!

The kitchen, with its own arched window over the sink, is spacious and done in custom pine with green ceramic tile counters and backs, and a stone floor. All the extras are here, both utilitarian and aesthetic: good country patterns in the crockery and decoratives, plants, lamps on the hutch, etc.

The bedroom decor goes to pretty small-print papers and fabrics shown off against the grey stone. There are neutral fitted carpets and wash basins in each room. The upstairs bathroom has a power shower as well as a whirlpool. Upper Mytholm Barn is very special, indeed! And, if you are able to tear yourself away, there is much to see in the area. On foot, by old fashioned train or horse drawn canal boat, the Yorkshire Pennines are full of wonderful sights.

ETB 4 Keys; Deluxe

I. B-t
F-1
II.B-d
F-3
III.B-t
E&H
FP
LT
TELm
TVV
W/Ds
DW MW
NS P-BA
OPEN MS
£260-450
S 6

Contact Mrs. Dorothy Denton, Upper Mytholm, Booth, Halifax, West Yorkshire HX2 6XB
TEL 01144-1422-882-240

BELL END FARM
Rosedale Abbey

Bell End Farm is one of England's most respected mini-resort complexes. It is hard to think of a tourism, design, or renovation award that the thoughtful management of this North Yorkshire property hasn't won.

This, however, is not Disneyland; the character and charm is real and in-scale....there are, in fact, only five cottages, though the communal amenities could accommodate many more.

Set amid two acres of grounds, the Farm is all built from colorful Yorkshire stone, with the characteristic pantile roofs. The grounds offer many pleasures: easy nature walks, barbeque and picnic facilities, paddocks. The pool is indoor and heated year round. There are even mountain bikes available for those who want to venture further afield in the lovely rolling moorland of the Yorkshire Dales. In fact, Bell End Farm is situated at the geographical center of the North York Moors National Park in the pretty village of Rosedale Abbey, which grew up on the foundations of an ancient Cistercian Abbey.

The row cottages are all designed on the "upside down" model; bedrooms below, with day-time living above to take advantage of the marvelous views. There are plenty of open beams, exposed stone walls and characterful little architectural curiosities. Redshank's Retreat sleeps six in three bedrooms. Typical of all the cottages, it has an open plan living room with low exposed beams and an open fire. Robin's Roost, Falcon's Folly, and Owls' 'Ouse sleep four and five. Park's Delight, which is detached, is the most luxurious and the delight of many honeymooners.

Bell End Farm could not be more strategic for touring. You are minutes from numerous English Heritage and National Trust sites, including Rievaulx and Byland Abbeys, not to mention Castle Howard for those who long to *Brideshead Revisit*. For the whole family there is the North Yorkshire Steam Railway and a wildlife park. Sports will revel at the nearness of nine golf courses and a half dozen race courses.

ETB 4 Keys; Highly Commended & Deluxe

E&H
FP$*
FP$*
LT
TELc
TV
W/Ds
MW
S-S; OPEN
INS
£208-813
S 2-6

Contact: Bell End Farm, Rosedale Abbey, Pickering, North Yorkshire YO18 8RE
TEL 01144-1751-417-431 or FAX 01144-1751-417-124

CULLODEN TOWER   Richmond

Monuments to and by the Hanover Dynasty are a-plenty. This one is particularly impressive for its tastefully scaled design and for the fact that it is one man's tribute to his monarchs. The man was John Yorke, a Parliamentarian, and he commissioned the tower on his estate overlooking the rushing waters of the River Swale in 1746.

The craftsmanship in Culloden Tower is sumptuous, which probably deserves to be said twice because the Tower, as we see it now, is a faithful restoration by the Landmark Trust plasterers, carpenters, and masons. The ground floor is occupied by a twin bedroom and separated bath and WC. A spiral staircase, breaking the octagonal form of the Tower on the exterior only, takes one up past a mezzanine kitchen to the drawing room. Here, under the exceptionally high ceilings, are eight walls richly ornamented by wood and plaster in the Gothic style, deep casement cathedral windows, and the usual Landmark Trust assemblage of comfortable period style furniture. On the level above (the fourth, counting the mezzanine) is the high ceilinged master bedroom, again richly ornamented, though this time in the Classical idiom. The many faceted views reach out over Richmond (a short walk away) and Yorke's pretty parkland leading down to the river. Though built in the Age of Reason, Culloden Tower is all *romance!*

```
I.  B-t
    F-2
III.B-d
    E&H
    LT
S-S  MS
INS
£403-741
S4
```

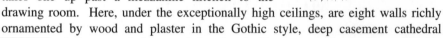

THE PIGSTY   Robin Hood's Bay

The man who wrote the book on classicism in architecture, Andrea Palladio, would have relished this tasty bit of column mongering...and quite likely he would have relished this building's tasty inhabitants, as well. While Squire Barry of Fyling Hall, who built The Pigsty a little over a century ago, may have set his neighbors to snickering, Palladio would have wholeheartedly endorsed the extension of strict (well, sort of *strict*) classical form to the porcine realm. *"What's good for the goose is good for the gander,"* he might have said, delicately sidestepping a more obvious metaphor.

Landmark Trust's interior decoration team, who are masters of setting a period ambiance for each of the Trust's properties were obviously challenged by this one. In the end they apparently decided they couldn't make a silk purse out of a sow's ear, though they have had a bit of fun in the swine idiom. You will find this pigsty very comfortable, with a large kitchen/diner, a compact twin bedroom, and a small living room with magnificent views over Robin Hood's Bay, partially blocked by a half dozen of Palladio's finest Doric columns.

```
I.B-t
 F-2
E&H
 LT
 P-
F-F  MS
INS
£289-512
S 2
```

Contact The Landmark Trust, Shottesbrook, Maidenhead, Berkshire SL6 3SW
TEL 01144-1628-825-925 or FAX 01144-1628-825-417

JASMINE COTTAGE   Sedbusk

Jasmine Cottage is in the heart of the Yorkshire Dales. Sedbusk is a small attractive hamlet situated on the sunny side of Upper Wensleydale. It looks across the valley of the River Ure (which, incidentally, has some excellent fishing) toward Hawes, the highest market town in all of Yorkshire. Epicures will recognize this as the home of Wensleydale cheese. This countryside is distinctive for its dry stone walls and paved footpaths cutting across the open fields. The region is steeped in history, from nearby Iron Age and Roman forts to Hadrian's Wall somewhat further afield. Medieval castles and abbeys are also in "good supply".

Jasmine Cottage is a mid-Victorian detached stone house, standing in its own grounds at the head of a quiet country lane. Enclosed by dry stone walls, the garden is a mixture of lawns, herbaceous borders, shrubs and mature trees. The hillside behind rises steeply onto a heather clad grouse moorland, above which is a craggy limestone escarpment providing superb views. Inside, the cottage has two attractive stone fireplaces forming focal points of the sitting and dining rooms. The former contains a Victorian corner cupboard and a brass log box with a window seat bookcase and a comfortable three piece suite. The dining room features an ornate, mahogany Victorian sideboard, together with an early 20th century dining table and chairs. Pictures of local scenes and cathedral plates adorn the walls. Off the living room is a double bedroom with mahogany furnishings and an en-suite bathroom. This bedroom is optional for an extra charge. The kitchen of Jasmine Cottage is to the rear, adjacent to a large utility room.

Upstairs, the master bedroom features a walnut Queen Anne style suite. Across the landing is a room with three single beds, fitted cupboards and other mahogany pieces. To the rear of the house lies another double bedroom with pine furnishings and a spacious bathroom with bidet. The cottage is centrally heated and has fitted carpets throughout.

ETB 4 Keys; Highly Commended

I. B-d
F-3
II.B-d [2]
B-t+s
F-4
E$c   H$
FP$
LT$
TEL$c
TV
W/D
MW
P-BA
S-S MS
£150-345
S 7 [+2]

Contact Mrs. A.D. Moore, 79 Cookridge Lane, Leeds LS16 7NE
TEL 01144-1532-679-332

BEAMSLEY HOSPITAL

Nr Skipton

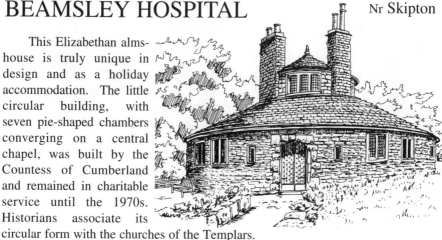

This Elizabethan alms-house is truly unique in design and as a holiday accommodation. The little circular building, with seven pie-shaped chambers converging on a central chapel, was built by the Countess of Cumberland and remained in charitable service until the 1970s. Historians associate its circular form with the churches of the Templars.

An entry hallway leads directly to the the tiny chapel with access then to each room. Simple white plaster walls, modestly trimmed in accord with the historic mission of the structure, set the decorative tone. However, as with all the Landmark Trust properties, the furnishings are chosen to lend a period ambience, and in this instance holiday guests may rest assured that the hospice is rather more comfortably fitted out than it was in its earlier function. There is a good sized kitchen and a separate dining room interconnected to the living room, with a large open stone fireplace.

The exterior setting is pleasant and countrified, and Skipton is both rich in historic sites of its own and a good base for exploring the Dales.

I.B-t [2]
B-s
F-1
F-2
E&H
FP
LT
S-S   MS
INS
£470-784
S 5

Contact The Landmark Trust, Shottesbrook, Maidenhead, Berkshire SL6 3SW
TEL 01144-1628-825-925 or FAX 01144-1628-825-417

LIME TREE COTTAGE   Sowerby

Sowerby and Thirsk are the villages so delight-fully fictionalized by James Herriot in *All Creatures Great and Small*. Lime Tree Cottage has a very welcoming feel, with its crooked 18th century walls and irregular hand made bricks. The lounge/dining area, under exposed oak beams, is done in autumn colors with attractive pictures of the area.

There is a coal effect gas fire to take the chill off the Yorkshire morning, and a galley style pine fitted kitchen to practice the fine art of preparing a hearty English breakfast before setting off across the Dales on Herriot's undulating country roads. (Can't you just hear the violins in the *All Creatures* theme music!). Up the curvy little stairs and you are in the double bedroom with simple pine furnishings and views across the Village Green. Incidentally, the cottage name is taken from the avenue of lime trees planted around the Village Green to commemorate Queen Victoria's Jubilee in 1877.

II.B-d
F-3
E&H
FPG
LT
TV
W
DW MW
S-S
INS
BK$
£190-260
S 2

Contact Discover Britain, Shaw Mews, Worcester WR1 3QQ   TEL 01144-1905-613-744 or FAX 01144-1905-613-747

BEECH FARM COTTAGES   Wrelton

The buildings at Beech Farm date back to the late 17th century, and are arranged around a gravel courtyard which features a contemporary dove cote. The complex has been developed from redundant farm buildings with many of the original features being kept, particularly the old oak beams which appear through the cottages, upstairs and down. Beech Farm is especially well situated, right opposite the tranquil village green of Wrelton. It is just two miles to the busy market town of Pickering, which offers a good choice of shops and an open air market on Mondays.

Each cottage is individual. Chris and Julie O'Hare, who sold their antique business and left other careers to take on the transformation of Beech Farm, endeavor to make a friendly *home away from home* atmosphere in each of their cottages. Fresh fruit and flowers will await your arrival, along with a welcome tea tray.   A quick look at their guest comments tells us that they have made quite a success of it, and, indeed, they took the *England For Excellence* Silver Medal, as well as Yorkshire top honors, in 1993 for their model operation.

You will find Beech Farm cottages very prettily furnished: comfy armchairs and settees upholstered in bright country chintz, lots of good country pine, and little added touches to bring individuality and brightness to each cottage. There are lots of dried flowers and fresh greenery, as well as pictures. The bedrooms are light and airy, with bed linens being in delicate pink floral designs with matching curtains.

In total there are seven cottages, from the cozy (not so little) Fat Hen Cottage, which sleeps two, to Shepherds Lodge, which will accommodate up to ten. There is a heated indoor pool and jacuzzi, as well as a sauna. Mountain bikes are available on the Farm for hire, and, indeed, this is a wonderful landscape to pedal, as well as hike, across.

In addition to the National Parks to explore, there is no shortage of tourist destinations reached easily from Beech Farm. Visitors or *Revisitors,* will want to take in *Brideshead's* Castle Howard, just ten minutes away. Also, the steam train from Pickering across the moors to Grosmont will delight children and adults.

ETB 4 Keys; Deluxe

F-3
E&H
FPS*
LT
TV
W/Ds$
DW* MW
P-
S-S   MS
TA
£225-1250
S 2-10

Contact Chris & Julie O'Hare, Beech Farm Cottages, Main St., Wrelton, Pickering YO18 8PG
TEL 01144-1751-476-612 or FAX 01144-1751-475-032

THE TEMPLE Swinnithwaite

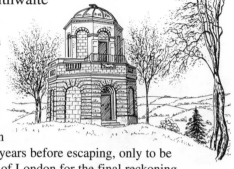

It doesn't get much more atmospheric than this! This historic folly was built in 1792 by the architect John Foss to ornament the gardens of nearby Swinnithwaite Hall. It stands in the privacy of its own walled garden over-looking the historic, 1100 year old castle of the Earls of Bolton. Here, Mary Queen of Scots was imprisoned for some eight years before escaping, only to be recaptured and transported to the Tower of London for the final reckoning.

I. F-3
II.B-d
E
FP
LT
TV
P-
S-S MS
INS
BK$
£220-315
S 2

The layout of the accommodations in The Temple are somewhat unusual due to the octagonal shape of the building and the balustraded set-back of the upper story. Downstairs is a large kitchen/dining area, as well as a characterful living room with natural wood and floral design furniture, and an open fire. The shower and WC are also on the first level.   The upper chamber is reached by an internal spiral stone staircase mounting to the balustraded walkway, with shuttered doors entering back into The Temple. The upstairs bedroom has a dome ceiling and peerless views over the beautiful Dales, with Bolton Castle below.

Contact Mrs. Linda Nash, All Cottages Great and Small, High Thirn Farm, Thirn, Ripon, Yorkshire HG4 4AU   TEL 01144-1677-460-287 or FAX 01144-1677-460-210

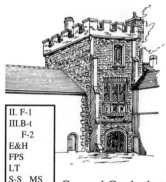

CAWOOD CASTLE Nr Selby

II. F-1
III.B-t
F-2
E&H
FPS
LT
S-S MS
INS
£252-417
S 2

A great deal of history has been made in this castle, which is most closely associated with the powerful Archbishops of York. The roll call of Royals parading in through these portals to enjoy the hospitality of Cawood Castle include Henry III, Edward I, Queen Isabella, Henry VIII and Queen Catherine Howard. Cardinal Wolsey was not so welcome and exited under the tower arch in irons. A history rich in intrigue and indigestion...it was here at Cawood Castle that the greatest (non-royal) feast on record occurred back in September 1465, when one George Neville celebrated his enthronement as Archbishop of York with a little feast for 2500 well wishers. The Castle survived the party, but it didn't fare well after the Civil War, and all that remains is the 15th century gatehouse above.

Today, Landmark Trust offers the handsomely restored medieval rooms on the second and third floors, as well as the tower roof terrace, for holiday let. A later Georgian stairwell (in building to right in drawing) takes one up to the Tower drawing room, where there is also small kitchen. Here we find beautiful latticed stone mullion windows, a fireplace, tile floors with oriental rugs and some interesting Jacobean furnishings. Ascent to the third floor en-suite bedroom and the roof terrace is via a medieval spiral stair.

Contact The Landmark Trust, Shottesbrook, Maidenhead, Berkshire SL6 3SW TEL 01144-1628-825-925 or FAX 01144-1628-825-417

TURKS HEAD COURT

York

Here, within the medieval city walls and in the shadow of the York Minster, stood the ancient Turks Head Inn, witness to centuries of York history. Today's accommodations are all new construction with sufficient traditional imagery to garner architectural awards for contributing to the on-going historic development of this landmark city. There are four townhouses offered for holiday fare, three with 2 bedrooms and one with 3 bedrooms. Each is bright and modern, with fitted carpets, central heating and pretty pine furnishings. Each unit has its own garage. The larger townhouse offers a nicely framed view of the Minster Tower. ETB 3 Keys; Highly Commended

E&H	
LT	
TELin	
TV	
W*	D
S-S	
INS	
$400-900	
S 4-6	

45 MONKGATE

York

Number 45 is the end townhouse in a handsome Victorian row standing just outside the eastern gate to the City, only a three minute walk from York Minster. The whole block has been nicely restored, and the three flats in #45 are no exception. You will find plenty of elegant period detail, with deep cove molded ceilings, wide casement

shuttered windows, and marble fireplaces (now fitted with gas fires). The interior decoration has been tastefully undertaken in nice heritage colors, coordinated carpeting and drapery, some carved antique pieces, and modern soft furnishings which

E&H	
FPG	
LT	
TV	
W*	D
S-S	
INS	
$400-875	
S 4-6	

are very complementary to the period. The bath/shower rooms are very contemporary, with gold fittings; the kitchens are conveniently laid out with all the necessary up-to-date conveniences and pretty blue & white crockery. The ground floor and second floor flats have two bedrooms, and four bedroom accommodation is offered in the third floor flat, which includes space in the dormered fourth floor. ETB 2-3 Keys; Commended

Contact Meta Voyage, 1945 Pauline Plaza, Suite 14, Ann Arbor, MI 48103-5047
TEL 800-771-4771 (East) 800-538-6881 (West) or FAX 313-995-3464

BAILE GATE HOUSE
York

York is one of the great historic cities of Europe, not simply by *comparison* to other European cities, but in the sense of being a part of historic Europe, just as it is also so much a part of historic England. York was a Roman town and a Viking town before it was an English town, and bits and pieces of half a dozen cultural/political ascendencies show clearly through the complex fabric of contemporary York. There is just so much to see here that one wants to get settled-in quickly and *hit the bricks*...after all, if you've only allocated a week to York, you're already behind schedule!

The Hodgkinsons' Baile Gate House couldn't be easier to settle in to, nor could it be more central to the whole enterprise of conquering the sights of York. Part of the 1988 development known as Bishop's Wharf, this townhouse is a thoroughly modern *period* style structure on the banks of the River Ouse. Just across the street is the medieval city wall; just across the bridge are the elevated Tower remains of York Castle, built by Henry III on the footings of battlements erected by William the Conqueror. (Yes, all Europe has beat its path to York at one time or another!)

The townhouse is laid out on three floors, with a quite clever modern glass conservatory suspended over the interior close. The second floor living room and dining area are south facing with wood framed sliding glass doors out to the conservatory. There is a very refreshing indoor/outdoor feel about these merging living spaces, which I'm sure is all the more welcome in the off seasons of this northerly city. Furnishings are in the Danish modern idiom, all teak and stream-lined, and there is a very commodious floral sofa that converts into a queen-sized bed. The kitchen is top drawer for anyone with culinary priorities...even the washing up can be inspired by the over-the-sink panoramic view of the historic city wall. I must especially commend Barbara Hodgkinson on her choice of the Portmeirion Botanic Garden Dinnerware, having ordered the same for ourselves the first time we saw it in a National Trust property down in Cornwall. The sleeping arrangements are divided, making the Baile Gate House particularly convenient for multiple family sojourners. There is a double bedroom on the ground floor, and queen and twin bedrooms on the third floor.

Alright, now you're moved-in; get your camera and let's go. Of course you want to begin with the York Minster, the largest Gothic cathedral in Northern Europe...then on to the Jorvik Viking Center and the National Railway Museum...after that there's the *ARC* for a little hands-on archeology...York wasn't built in a day!

ETB 5 Keys; Deluxe

I. B-d
F-1
II.CS
III.B-q
F-3
B-t
E$m H$m
LT$
TELm
TVV
W/D
DW MW
NS P-
S-S
£180-620
S 6-8

Contact Mrs Barbara Hodgkinson, "Hodge's Lodges", 52 Kelso Close, Worth, Crawley, West Sussex RH10 7XH
TEL 01144-1293-882-008 or FAX 01144-1293-883-352

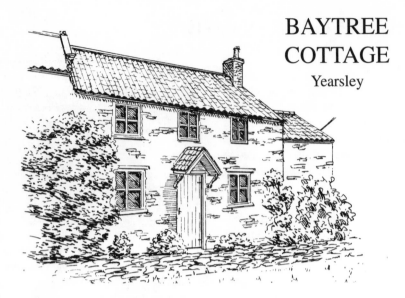

BAYTREE COTTAGE
Yearsley

Yearsley is a lovely village to choose as a base for either riding or walking. There is a riding school just opposite Baytree Cottage, and ramblers will be interested in partaking of both the Cleveland Way and Ebor Way in the nearby hills.

Baytree Cottage was the one time bakehouse of the village and dates back to the early 18th century. The gardens are surrounded by an old stone wall and one may pursue pleasant walks right from the garden gate. Inside, the cottage features stone floors throughout with rugs over, and a buttermilk decor which makes for a light and airy atmosphere. There are interesting furnishings and decoratives, including a large antique pine dining table for six, as well as original drawings and oils by local artists. The master bedroom features a king-size pine bed, fitted wardrobes and white walls, with a blue carpet and blue striped curtains. The twin bedded room is pale pink with carpeting to match.

I. F-1
II.B-d
  B-t
  F-2
E$m
H$
LT
TV
S-S MS
INS
£215-280
S 4

Contact Mrs. Linda Nash, All Cottages Great and Small, High Thirn Farm, Thirn, Ripon, Yorkshire HG4 4AU   TEL 01144-1677-460-287 or FAX 01144-1677-460-210

Welsh Counties

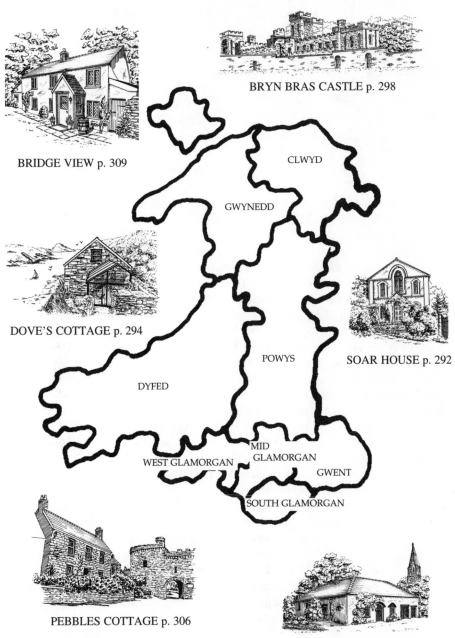

BRYN BRAS CASTLE p. 298

BRIDGE VIEW p. 309

CLWYD

GWYNEDD

DOVE'S COTTAGE p. 294

SOAR HOUSE p. 292

POWYS

DYFED

MID
GLAMORGAN

WEST GLAMORGAN

GWENT

SOUTH GLAMORGAN

PEBBLES COTTAGE p. 306

THE OLD SMITHY p. 294

SOAR HOUSE Aber

There is a bit of *deja-vu* here; flashes of Italy; coming around a corner in the back streets of a big city (Rome, maybe, or Naples) and suddenly finding oneself in a tiny closely tended paved garden with a pretty little neo-Palladian building, and all of it submerged in a sea of taller, ugly structures and unpleasant urban cacophony. Well, the last bit of the vision is definitely off base; there is nothing urban, ugly, or unpleasant about the neighborhood of Soar House. This is Aber in Wales, up a gorgeous valley near the 150 feet of cascading water known as Aber Falls.

The rest of the image, however, remains true. The garden is small, formal and Italianate, with a bit of comely statuary and a fountain...even the flora and fauna is vaguely Mediterranean. The neo-Palladian building in our little garden is a chapel, or rather a converted chapel, vintage 1830. Soar House is, I think, atypical of most of the little neighborhood ecclesiastical buildings in Britain, which tend to be either strictly unadorned (all *Method-ness*, no madness), or Gothicized miniatures, a bit comic without meaning to be. No, this little chapel is full of upright dignity, without a hint of pomposity. The quoinwork is to proper measure, as is the pitch of the gable and the keyed arches. The building has generosity as well as geometry...it invites.

Much of the chapel flavor has been left in the interior renovations. The rather perpendicular and richly paneled lectern remains *in situ*. The kitchen is on two levels, with a pew-seated dining nook backing onto the living room. Wood from the other pews is said to have been used for the wainscotting around the whole of the spacious living room. Furnishings are homey with some interesting bric-a-brac, bridge lamps, throw rugs, etc....church bazaar finds, in the best sense. One curiosity is an electric fireplace in a raised corner of the living room, with a superfluous polished copper hood, looking a bit altar-ish in a Neapolitan way.

Soar House has two bedrooms on the ground floor, both doubles, and a bathroom with corner tub. Upstairs there is a balconied mezzanine sitting room with a sofa bed and an additional single bedroom.

With the sea only a half mile away and the mountains of Snowdonia to the back, Aber is well situated for wonderful walks or day tripping. Good beaches are just up the road at Llanfairfechan, and just down the road is the National Trust's Penrhyn Castle, with its seven miles of wall and fabulous collections of everything from locomotives to dolls.

I. B-d [2]
F-2
II.B-s
CS
E$ H
FPE
LT
TV
W-BA
MW
P-
S-S
INS
$320-555
S 5-7

Contact Haywood Cottage Holidays, P.O. Box 878, Eufaula, Alabama 36072
TEL 334-687-9800 or FAX 334-687-5324

CLYTHA CASTLE

Nr Abergavenny

Strange as it may seem, many of the most delightful follies were built in the spirit of an Irish wake; as anti-dotes to grief, memorializing the departure of a loved one. So it was with Clytha Castle, an "L" shaped fantasy facade raised in 1790 by William Jones of Clytha House in com-memoration of his recently departed wife.

I. B-d
Fl
II.B-t [2]
F-2
E&H
FP
LT
S-S   MS
INS
£612-949
S 6

The square tower is comprised of a spacious sitting room, with a handsome fireplace and ornate gilt mirror on the ground floor, and a twin bedroom above, which is reached via the circular stairs in the adjacent tower. Separate kitchen and dining rooms occupy the inner knee of the "L", and a master bedroom is located in the ground floor round room of the turret to the right in the drawing. Elegant drapery, stylized furnishings from Jacobean to Victorian, and colorful rugging keep Clytha Castle in good taste, as its architecture keeps it in good humor.

Contact The Landmark Trust, Shottesbrook, Maidenhead, Berkshire SL6 3SW
TEL 01144-1628-825-925 or FAX 01144-1628-825-417

FRON FAWR Boncath

Fron Fawr means *big hill,* which is a good indication of the panoramic perspectives from this 65-acre working farm (soft fruit and sheep) on the fringe of the Pembrokeshire National Park. This is an area for outdoor activities (walking, pony trekking, fishing, birding, golfing) or outdoor *inactivity,* such as snoozing on the sunny patios of one of the three attractive accommodations fashioned out of this large old stone barn. I don't want to emphasize the *old* as regards Fron Fawr, because the quality factor here is strictly modern, designer modern from the architectural transformation of the original structure to the distinctly contemporary furnishings and decor. The emphasis is on good natural light, open space, and clean lines. As an integral whole, the Fron Fawr cottages are the opposite of *busy,* which is a pretty good idea for a holiday. Fay Cori will help you get *not busy* by having a home cooked meal in your microwave when you arrive; it's complimentary, as is the bottle of wine that also says, *welcome* and *relax!* WTB 5 Dragons

E$m
H$m
LT
TV
MW
P-
S-S   INS
£142-489
S 2-6

Contact Fay Cori, Fron Fawr, Boncath, Pembrokeshire, Dyfed SA37 0HS
TEL 01144-1239-841-285 or FAX 01144-1239-841-545

THE OLD SMITHY

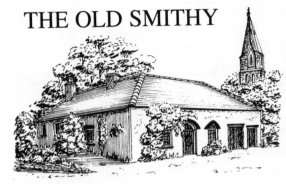

Nr Beaumaris

The Isle of Anglesey is more accessible than the Scottish Isles, but no less rich in mythic lore and ambiance. Know as *Mona* (Mother of Wales) since prehistoric times, Anglesey can be a destination venue or a base for touring Snowdonia and the North Coast. Anglesey is also the ferry gateway to Ireland.

About a mile from the famous castle at Beaumaris is The Old Smithy in the hamlet of Llanfaes. This unassuming old stone and hip roofed building contains a wealth of surprises; wonderfully spacious rooms, with massive fireplaces (in both kitchen and living room), galleried bedrooms (reached via circular stairwell), soaring rafters & exposed beams, and furnishings that include some fine antique pine pieces. There is a small conservatory and a delightful enclosed garden with a barbeque and appropriate furnishings.   WTB 4 Dragons

I. B-t
B-s
F-3
II.B-d [2]
E   H$
FPS
L
TV
W/D
DW MW
F-F   MS
BK$
£230-640
S 8

Contact Leonard & Margaret Rees, Quality Cottages, Cerbid, Solva, Haverfordwest, Pembrokeshire SA62 6YE TEL 01144-1348-837-874

DOVE'S COTTAGE   Nr Abercastle

Looking for an inexpensive romantic little hideaway by the sea? Look no further!

Dove's Cottage is down a steep flight of stairs from the Coastal Footpath and about a mile's walk (or drive) from the hamlet of Trefin, with its village shop and restaurant/pub. In days of yore, this cottage was no less inviting in its service as a grog shop for passing sailors. The waves still gently lap on the incoming tide and the private steps from the cottage terrace take you right into the sea. In fact, there are two secluded little terraces, making it possible to follow the sun through the day. During the winter the whole scene can be enjoyed from the warmth of the little conservatory. The cottage, which is completely open plan, has a galley kitchen with a Rayburn oil-fired stove, shower room & WC, and a gallery double bedroom. If your romantic holiday includes a chaperon, there is even a comfortable sofa bed. However, because of its hillside positioning, the cottage is not really suitable for *chaperons* under the age of six.   WTB 3 Dragons

I. CS
F-3
II.B-d
E&H
L
TV
MW
C-BA
S-S   MS
INS
BK$
£136-375
S 3

Contact Coastal Cottages of Pembrokeshire, Abercastle, Pembrokeshire SA62 5HJ TEL 01144-1348-837-771

ESTUARY VIEW COTTAGE

Nr Cardigan

The Pembrokeshire Coast Path ranks as one of Britain's finer walking challenges for serious hikers, as well as offering many viewful strolls for the casual walkers. It begins with a rather arduous ascent up 600 foot high Cemaes Head, which is the lower lip, so to speak, of the estuary formed by

I. B-t [2]
F-2
II.B-d
B-t
F-3
E&H
FPS
L
TV
W/D
DW MW
S-S MS
BK$
£245-690
S 8

the River Teifi. Across the way is barren Cardigan Island against the misty sea, with Cardigan town and its dilapidated Norman castle and busy market at the head of the estuary. This is an area of panoramas without end, not least from Estuary View Cottage, itself. The view and the remarkable ambience of this cottage have been greatly enhanced by the professionally designed renovation and extension. Every opportunity has been seized to bring the panorama right into the rooms. The view is the focal point of the living and dining rooms, even the upstairs bedrooms. The fashionable contemporary furnishings show well against polished wood floors and bright white walls. It is hard to imagine a more sunny and cheerful holiday stead. WTB 4 Dragons

Contact Leonard & Margaret Rees, Quality Cottages, Cerbid, Solva, Haverfordwest, Pembrokeshire SA62 6YE TEL 01144-1348-837-874

BWTHYN Y BONT

Fishguard

Fishguard (Nordic for *Fish Town*) is the market town for North Pembrokeshire and has the historic distinction of being the last place Britain was invaded (by the French in 1797). These days Fishguard is distinguished by its beautiful location, its artists' colony, and by the array of music and marine festivals it hosts for the many visitors to this shore. And, if it is *seashore* one seeks, Bwthyn Y Bont has a patent on some of the prettiest. The old cottage has been carefully renovated to preserve its stone and beam character, and has been furnished in a complementary fashion with antiques in the vernacular pine tradition. The owner, who is a watercolorist, has captured the magic of the area with her brush, and that work is on display throughout the cottage. The views from the house are matched by those from the garden, which, incidentally, will have surprises for the ornithologically inclined seeking new and rare species for their sightings list.

WTB 4 Dragons

II.B-d
B-t
B-s
F-2
E$m H$m
FP
L
TV
W
S-S MS
INS BK$
£152-484
S 5

Contact Coastal Cottages of Pembrokeshire, Abercastle, Pembrokeshire SA62 5HJ TEL 01144-348-837-771

THE SMITHY & TY HWNT

Llanthony Valley

Our first visit to the Llanthony Valley was by accident...actually, *navigational incompetence* was the initial indictment for the high crime of bearing left, rather than right, coming out of Hereford. We were on our way to Hay-on-Wye, where helpless bibliophiliacs from around the world congregate to fix their book buying addictions. Well, we *were* on our way to Hay-on-Wye, but, as it *left-turned-out*, we found ourselves on the way to Abergavenny (where to the best of my knowledge there is not even a particularly good bookstore). In fact, we were almost to Abergavenny before the mistake was noticed and, in the heat of the moment, a detour up through the the the wild Black Mountains was proposed by the penitent navigator. Visions of the Donner Party crossed my mind; did we bring the Swiss army knife? "Look, the road follows some kind of a stream; maybe we can chill the wine and cool off." (An exercise in feeble plea bargaining!) Suffice it to say, the road up through the Black Mountains is not a major thoroughfare, but the sheer and wondrous beauty of that drive was more than enough to inspire a general amnesty...even before we got to the wine! And, to this day, I haven't a clue what the A438 (right turn) out of Hereford looks like; we always go to Hay-on-Wye via the scenic route.

About half way up the Valley are the romantic ruins of a thousand-year-old Abbey, described by Giraldus in the twelfth century as "more truly suited to the monastic discipline than any other monastery in the British Isles." In this instance I don't think we should be fooled into thinking remoteness, which the Llanthony Valley certainly was and remains, is synonymous with "hard duty". Those monks knew a good thing! The Valley is bordered on the east by a memorable stretch of Offa's Dyke Footpath and is topped on both sides by heather clad moorland. It is not surprising that poets and painters (not to mention clever monks and wayward bibliophiliacs) have been captivated by this area.

| II.B-d |
| B-t [2] |
| F-2 |
| E$m   H$ |
| FP |
| LT |
| MW |
| P- |
| F-F OPEN |
| TA |
| £220-390 |
| S 6 |

The perfection of the Llanthony Valley is equalled by the Elliotts' two properties. The Smithy, which is just a short walk from the Abbey ruin, is situated in a tiny village setting comprised of four houses, an old church and a cloistered pub. You will find the "village" cluttered with pheasant pens in the making, hay, tractors, a car being repaired, hens and ducks clucking and quacking about, and the game keeper's dogs snoozing in the sun. The Elliotts live in an entirely separate part of the medieval smithy, but that in no way encroaches on the privacy of the cottage or its private garden. One enters the cottage by way of a country kitchen where the modern amenities are purposefully made unobtrusive; for example, the modern stainless steel sink is set in a teak worktop of an old laboratory unit. This room, under a sloping beamed ceiling, is open plan. The dining area has a handsome refectory table and chairs, a lovely long window seat, and a large antique hutch with a fine collection of pink and white china.

You will find the living room both elegant and cozy. From the outside, The Smithy has a *lost-in-garden* feel; yet this room is very well lit and has an unusual bottle kiln chimney and a large open log burning hearth. Pretty floral soft furnishing, lots of flowers in season, white Indian carpets on polished wood floors, a games table with chess, draughts, etc, and a bow window featuring a fascinating collection of antique printing blocks...pretty particulars everywhere the eye turns. Did I mention the baby grand piano? Outside there are wonderful places to sit in the garden, and everywhere there is the sound of the water gurgling by in the aforementioned wine chilling stream. Incidentally, there are trout in there too, if you're clever enough to catch them.   WTB 4 Dragons

Ty Hwnt is an old

stone-built farmhouse situated high on a sunny hillside. This is a simply idyllic spot with wonderful perspectives over fields of frolicking lambs in the spring, and in the distance is the heather covered moor. I would love to hole up here for a year, pretending to write, but actually just counting birds.   One guest recorded thirty-three species sighted in a single week from the upstairs loo window. Of course, I couldn't bird watch all the time, I'd have to take advantage of some of the fishing that comes with the property.

Compared to The Smithy, Ty Hwnt is architecturally rustic, and the Elliots have appropriately filled the house with antiques, more or less in the primitive idiom, including some very interesting Scandinavian farmhouse pieces and a buffalo hide studio couch. Did I mention there is a piano here too? Up the steep staircase there are three large bedrooms, plus an under-eaves room suitable for a child. You will find pretty antique pine beds with patchwork quilts; there is even a dear old pine cradle. This is a house with wonderful stone fireplaces. There is also a Rayburn, but Gaynor Elliot warns that winter visitors should bring some woolies as there is no central heating in Ty Hwnt.

I hope I haven't left the impression that The Smithy and Ty Hwnt are only suitable for chronic bibliophiliacs and procrastinating writers. There is plenty to do here, from pony trekking and hiking to fishing and golf (nearby). And, if for some strange reason you should stray beyond the Llanthony Valley, you have all the fabulous Brecon Beacons to explore. WTB 4 Dragons

I. F-2
II.B-d
B-t
CS
F-1
E$m
H$m
FP$
LT
W/D
S-S
TA
£220-390
S 6

Contact J. Elliott, The Smithy, Llanthony, Abergavenny, Gwenmt NP7 7NN TEL 01144-1873-890-781

BRYN BRAS CASTLE   Llanrug Nr Caernarfon

Bryn Bras Castle, in the foothills of Snowdonia National Park, was designed by the noted architect, Thomas Hopper, who subsequently gave us Britain's most perfect Neo-Romanesque structure, Penrhyn Castle in Bangor. If the 1829 Bryn Bras Castle was a practice run, then it is pretty near perfect itself! Architecture buffs holidaying here may never leave the grounds.

There are eight self contained apartments in the Castle, which is also the owners' home. This is definitely not a case of putting the pilgrims up in the stables. These spacious apartments have been fashioned out of the most interesting rooms. The circular living room in Flag Tower Apartment, for example, was a drawing room in Victorian times which became a grand billiard room during the Regency. Today, Flag Tower is approached up a ten foot wide spiral staircase, entering the extraordinary Neo-Romanesque lounge which is 23 feet in diameter. The walls are garlanded with twenty-three decorative arches and pillars. This room can only be described as *delicious;* all ivory, gilt and green, with cream fitted carpets. These dimensions are echoed in the bedroom above (a favorite of Prime Minister David Lloyd George), with colors giving way to rich Burgundies, including the four quadrants of the circular ceiling set above broad and complex cove moldings. A brass half-tester double bed and an elegant slate fireplace dominate the room.   The route continues up to the castellated tower itself, where you may survey the thirty two acres of historic gardens and parkland, and perhaps fantasize just a little. Not surprisingly, Flag Tower is a favorite of honeymooners.

E$c
H
L; T$
TELc
TV
DW MW
C-BA
OPEN
MS
INS
TA
£125-500
S 2-4

Bryn Bras was, of course, built to celebrate and enjoy country and domestic life, not withstand a siege. It is a lived-in castle, filled with an eclectic mixture of furnishings and mementoes (Victorian, Art Deco, even 1950s), arrived at rather more by accumulation than commercial design. This is neither a hotel nor a clever tourist resort; it is the Gray-Parry's home, and their warm invitation to "come for a visit at our castle" has a uniquely homey ring. Come for the night, the weekend, a week...stay on for a fortnight.

WTB 5 Dragons

Contact : Neville and Marita Gray-Parry, Bryn Bras Castle, Llanrug, nr. Caernarfon, Gwynedd,
N. Wales LL55 4RE   TEL/FAX 01144-1286-870-210

NEUADD FARM COTTAGES

Llwyndafydd

Cardigan Bay is a grand sweep of ethereal greenness mirroring the equally grand sweep of ethereal high moorland. These beautiful moors are drained by regular arteries, trickles into brooks into rushing streams, all bound for the Bay. At that juncture are to be found some of Britain's finest beaches. Unfortunately, in Wales these natural treasure coves have in many cases also become trailer havens. I hope that this observation doesn't come across as too snobbish, but it is a fact. The point is, one is not usually forewarned and first impressions are often off-putting. Invariably the novitiates are left wondering why it is that so many of their friends swear by Wales and make it their holiday destination year after year, eschewing all the other wonderful options in Britain and elsewhere. The answer is quite simply that, in its vastness, Wales swallows the less attractive human exploitations, and, in its extraordinary natural grandeur, it also invites the most tasteful sorts of holiday enterprises. Neuadd Farm Cottages is a case in point.

Malcolm and Karina Headley chose Wales, they didn't inherit it. What is more, they started from scratch, and *scratch* in this case was pretty rudimentary; to wit, an old farmhouse with a bunch of derelict barns and cow sheds. The good part was that, starting with an empty canvas, they could paint the picture the way they wanted...and, hopefully get it right, in the eyes of the beholders and in their own judgement. The verdict is in: The Headleys got it right! Very right!

There are ten cottages at Neuadd Farm, sleeping from two to six. I would not say that, architecturally, these were compelling buildings originally...pretty ordinary, actually, as old stone barns go. But what the Headleys have done, architecturally, is truly remarkable. Every nook and cranny, opening and level...every bit of texture in wood and stone or opportunity for light and shadow...has been exploited to the maximum, and then furnished and decorated with equal imagination. What is more, they have used the whole canvas. This is not a case of *nice cottages & nice garden;* its a case of a unified whole...interiors flow into exteriors, decoration and landscaping don't just meet like strangers at the door or window, they melt into each other. The whole scene is so integral that it is almost deceiving to take it apart and point to special amenities (like the expansive pool or cozy wood-burning stoves or large beds or private barbeque nooks or the tame rabbit warren for the delight of children). Nor should we attempt to list the many pretty particulars (like handmade lamp shades or original watercolors by noted artists or sumptuous fabrics and drapery or the wealth of games and books). So we just won't do that.
WTB 5 Dragons

E&H
FPS*
L; T$
TELc
TV
W/D$s
DW* MW
P-BA
F-F; S-S
MS
VAT$
TA
£160-600
S 2-6

Contact Malcolm & Karina Headley, Neuadd Farm, Llwyndafydd, Llandysul, Dyfed SA44 6BT
TEL 01144-1545-560-324

CRAIG Y MOR   Newport

The Royal Borough of Newport was settled by the Flemings and was once the center of the wool industry down here. All that is long gone, leaving Newport with its wide sandy beaches and dunes, and its protected little harbor, favored equally by local fishermen and holidaying boatsmen. Craig Y Mor couldn't get any closer to the water or the boats. It could, on the other hand, get closer to the road (though that wouldn't be nearly so much fun), which is to say that access to the cottage is by way of a hundred yard long pedestrian causeway. For loading and unloading purposes, one waits on the low tide and drives to the foot of the cottage's private slipway.

The cottage is really a good sized house, very handsomely fitted out for large family holidays, with endless marine attractions to occupy the kids and a secluded garden for the adults to relax in. Craig Y Mor is an all season venue, and has a conservatory for inclement days, along with a bright sea-facing living room. There are four bedrooms on the second floor, sharing a five-piece bathroom, and another en-suite bedroom up in the rafters, also with bidet.

In between long reads (or snoozes) in the garden and endless pokey walks along the shore, one might want to try their hand on the near-by fairways, or taste the fare at Newport's lovely tea shop. WTB 5 Dragons

```
I.  F-3
II. B-d
    B-t [3]
    F-4
III.B-t
    F-4
E$m  H$m
FPG
L
TV
W/D  DW
P-
S-S  MS
INS  BK$
£187-729
S 10
```

BWTHYN MAWR   Newport

Above Newport on the Hill of Angels is Bwthyn Mawr. The cottage is romantically situated on an old shepherd's path; indeed, Bwthyn Mawr, along with its neighbor, provided shelter for shepherds over many many generations. The view over the sea has not altered, but ye ole shepherds wouldn't quite know what to make of the renovated interior of the cottage. The stone walls and the huge inglenook are still in place, but today these rustic forms are decorated prettily and furnished with nice antiques. There is a lovely bedroom, all decked out in lace and pretty decoratives, and even the garden is full of flowers. Now, just where is Ole Shep supposed to bed down in a place like this?   WTB 4 Dragons

```
I.B-t/q
F-3
E$m
H$m
/fps
L
TV
S-S   MS
INS
BK$
£121-286
S 2
```

Contact Coastal Cottages of Pembrokeshire, Abercastle, Pembrokeshire SA62 5HJ
TEL 01144-1348-837-771

LLANERCH VINEYARD COTTAGES

Nr Pendoylan in the Vale of Glamorgan

It is not likely that many of our readers living in Phoenix or Atlanta or New England or the Midwest have had an opportunity to try the fine wines of England and Wales. Yes, I said *fine!* In fact, I've been saying it often and vociferously since my first magazine assignment to tell the story of English vineyards nearly twenty years ago. The wine keeps getting better and better, but you still won't find it in Phoenix or Atlanta or, for that matter, many places (even in Britain) except near the vine. Trust me, it's worth the trip, and a good place to begin this pleasant journey of discovery is with Peter and Diana Andrews in the lovely Vale of Glamorgan.

Llanerch Vineyard Cottages (and B&B) provide a convenient location for visiting South Wales and the western counties of England, being only fifteen minutes drive from Cardiff and another forty-five minutes from the city of Bath. Llanerch Vineyard sits astride the ancient parishes of Pendoylan and Miskin in the County of South Glamorgan. If you don't think there is some frontier romance in these parts consider the fact that in 1922 the land under this vineyard changed hands as a result of a horse race wager between the Lords of the Manors of Miskin and Hensol. Today, the winner, who happened to be the squire of Miskin, would be pulling a cork on a bottle of Llanerch Seyval Blanc to toast the nag and celebrate his good fortune.

The two cottages were converted from 19th century stables, retaining the handsome stonework and placing windows and doors to correspond with the old stable openings. Internally the cottages have been renovated to a very high standard creating two bedrooms upstairs under sloping ceilings with dormer views over the garden. Downstairs facilities are designed for handicapped access. The furnishings run to country pine and pretty florals, and the fully equipped kitchens will inspire the cook in the troupe to do great things with local produce. And here is the best part; you won't have to go far to find a truly *fine* bottle of wine for supper...or for an alfresco lunch...or both! WTB 5 Dragons

I. F-3
CS
II.B-t
B-t/q
F-2
E &H
LT
TELc TV
W/D
DW MW
NS
E/HC
S-S MS
TA
£280-500
S 6

Contact Peter & Diana Andrews, Llanerch Vineyard, Hensol, Pendoylan, South Glamorgan CF7 8JU
TEL 01144-1443-225-877 or FAX 01144-1443-225-546

FELIN PARC Nr Penrhyndeudraeth

There is a little voice in most of us that cries out for a journey into idyllic seclusion, there to unleash that great novel or painting which has been bound-up within our soul, heretofore imprisoned by the all too mundane priorities of just getting by in this miserable world. Felin Parc could be the place for me (as it has for some notable others), though the fact is that this place is so profoundly beautiful that I'd probably just sit in awe with my toes dangling in the cool rushing stream clutching a glass of wine, rather than a pen or brush. It's hard to chase immortality when life suddenly gets so darn good!

Felin Parc certainly meets the idyllic seclusion test, being situated three hundred yards up a private track, in a fairy tale wooded valley alongside the gurgling River Croesor, overlooking a small waterfall and pool. Further up the sheltered valley there are other fine waterfalls (all part of the drainage system of the majestic Snowdon Range) and views out over Cardigan Bay. Most of this land is today part of the Charitable Foundation Estate of the famous Welsh architect & conservationist, Sir Clough Williams-Ellis; he who fathered *New Towns* planning and whose great achievement at nearby Portmeirion is a *must see* for any traveler to Wales. Sir Clough's nephew, Owen, is our host and the present leaseholder to Felin Parc.

Felin Parc, which translates as *Parc Millhouse*, dates from the early 17th century and was a mill for knitting and weaving Welsh blankets until the turn of the century. In the river, right where I would dangle my toes, the millers undoubtedly washed their wool for a couple centuries. (No glass of Chardonnay in their hands!) The mill, itself, seems always to have been house sized and proportioned, with sturdy thick stone walls (whitewashed inside today) and characterful hand hewn beams of pine and oak throughout. At one end of the living room there is a large traditional stone fireplace with antique brass club fenders and the back boilers which feed the radiators throughout the house. (There are also electric fed night storage heaters.) The huge timber lintel wears many mementoes of retreat and visitation by Owen's family through the generations, as do walls and beams filled with plates, pottery, brasses, pictures and books. There is nothing less than an aesthetic aura here, with lived-in furnishings like the big old leather chesterfield where a body can curl up and let the mind cogitate in comfort. It is a measure of the integral effect of Felin Parc that one hardly notices what fine pieces some of these are, the antique Welsh dresser, the gate-leg dining table, etc. However, we have parked our materialism down the hill and wish not to think about *things*. Conveniently, the Williams-Ellises have made sure all the *things* are here

| I. F-1 |
| B-t |
| II.B-d |
| B-t [2] |
| F-3 |
| E$m H$c |
| L-BA |
| FP |
| TV |
| W/D |
| MW |
| P-BA |
| S-S MS |
| £175-500 |
| S 8 [+2] |

for us (actually, for themselves, as their personality is everywhere and this does not at all seem like a commercial venue). There is a good working kitchen, which is important because being so close to God and Nature always inspires the appetite (even when the typewriter is slow to kick-start). The subtly lit stone terraces right alongside the river are the perfect place for alfresco dining and romantic evenings. There are sleeping accommodations for eight or more, in three bedrooms with the sight and sound of the river ever present. Indeed, one lives intimately with the flowing waters here, be it the mill leat or the river. If, however, in a reckless moment of fraternalism one invites friends to share Nirvana there is an old granary, called *Penfelin,* behind the Mill that will sleep a couple in the 14 x 30 foot open room, which also has kitchen facilities and even a table tennis set-up (but, alas, no WC).

Now, if you've really let the cat out of the bag about your whereabouts, your chums just may have to make arrangements to rent Owen's other stone cottage, **Tan-Y-Clogwen**, which is about a hundred yards along the trail, lost in its own little

I. F-3	
II.B-d	
B-t	
E$c H$c	
FP	
L-BA	
TV	
D	
MW	
P-BA	
S-S MS	
£125-375	
S 4 [+2}	

wild garden. The literal translation (*dwelling under the rock*) is quite accurate, as the ancient little cottage, which sleeps four, is sited just above the river looking down on the old stone fording bridge, with the cliffs rising behind. More space for contemplation and aesthetic inspiration! Indeed, this cottage has its own little history in the world of letters, quite independent of Felin Parc. There is a quite tiny sitting room with an open fire and furnishings comparable to Felin Parc. Also a cubby kitchen with Italian decorative tiles.   **WTB 3 Dragons**

Contact Mr. & Mrs. Owen Williams-Ellis, San Giovanni, 4 Sylvan Rd, London SE19 2RX
TEL 01144-1816-533-188

PENYBONT BARN   Llangorse

If you have a hard time choosing between the pleasures of fishing and walking, a holiday in the Llangorse area will spare you the decision. A ramble along the thousand foot ridge rising between the River Usk and Llangorse Lake affords truly magnificent views over the Brecon Beacons. Below is Wales' second largest lake, which according to legend has a drowned city at its bottom. Also legendary are the enormous pike of Llangorse Lake, and that is no myth! Llangorse, the village, dates from the 1600's

I.B-t [2]	
F-3	
E&H	
L	
TV	
MW	
P-BA	
S-S MS	
INS	
£130-240	
S 4	

and its Church, which is adjacent to Penybont Barn Cottage, houses Christian relics dating from the 7th century.

Penybont Barn is separated from the ancient churchyard by a small stream. Stone window seats in the downstairs bedrooms overlook the tumbling water and churchyard through lancet windows. A quarry tile hallway leads us up to the spacious living room and kitchen. Another recessed nook with a pretty sofa offers yet more charming views over the enclosed garden and churchyard. The kitchen has been recently done in oak and offers all the modern conveniences.   **WTB 5 Dragons**

Contact Elizabeth Daniel, Brecon Beacons Holiday Cottages, Brynoyre, Talybont-on-Usk, Brecon, Powys LD3 7YS
TEL 01144-1874-87446 or FAX 01144-1874-87416

THE OLD BAKERY
Rhostryfan

The Old Bakery was once the exclusive domain of one Hugh Christmas Evans, master baker. The Yule-*ishness* of his name notwithstanding, local recollection is that Christmas Evans' specialty was hot-cross buns. Whatever, Hugh Christmas Evans must have been a happy old bunman, indeed, for living in this charming cottage.

Past the holly green Victorian front door you will find the sitting room dominated by a massive hearth under an equally massive slate lintel. There is an open hooded fire to make the cottage extra cozy (central heating is provided as well). Furnishings are mostly dark oak, against the earth tone walls of the living room. Owner Barbara Beaumont has decorated the rooms appropriately with Victorian horse and pony prints, an interesting collection of plates and an antique baker's shovel. A framed old deed copy reveals that the first owners paid the handsome sum of 6 pounds sterling for the cottage in 1860. The stairs and landing have been decorated in the Victorian style with a dado effect, glass lamp shades and rich red carpeting. Upstairs bedrooms each have a character of their own. The double bedrooms have original pine paneling and bumpy textured walls, as well as sloping floors...there isn't a characterless right angle in the house! The blue bedroom has a metal bedhead with brass knobs; the pale apricot and green room boasts a caned headboard. Bed linens are coordinated to the colors of the decorative cove friezes. The children's room is done in strong primary colors. Balloons, rainbows and a smiling sun are patterned along the border and repeated in the lampshade. Pine bunks have a removable ladder; assorted Teddies and a Victorian rag doll fill out the picture. The modern 3 piece bathroom is done in Laura Ashley paper. The kitchen returns to bold primary colors, red and white this time.

In the garden a felled tree has been made into a miniature table and stools for the small people, while the grown-ups have a more conventional picnic set. For alfresco lunches the little stream running through the garden is especially handy for chilling the wine. (If you've forgotten to bring wine, not to worry, Mrs. Beaumont has left you a bottle with her welcome note). Likewise, if you've forgotten to bring your pet, the Beaumont cat, Dragon, will happily move in with you, or at least come for lunch.

The Old Bakery is strategically located for day touring between Snowdonia National Park and Anglesey Island. The town of Caernarfon on the Menai Straits is a designated European Heritage resource, with its town wall, medieval castle and Roman ruins. The whole area is steeped in Celtic tradition and promises to be a most interesting and exciting holiday venue.

WTB 5 Dragons

II.B-d [2]
B-b
F-3
E&H
FP
LT
TELc
TVV
W/D
MW
S-S   MS
TA
£200-390
S 6

Contact Mrs. Barbara Beaumont, Fron, Llandwrog Uchaf, Caernarfon LL54 7RF
TEL 01144-1286-881-022

CALVES COT COTTAGE   Nr St. Davids

Calves Cot and No Name Cottages stand out for their architectural merit and meticulous interior appointments. Exquisite taste, combined with considerable expense, has yielded two of the most attractive cottages to be found anywhere, certainly in this price range.

We begin with a lovely setting, down a long lane to enclosed grounds with an array of interesting flora. The old stone built cottages are low and nestled into the landscaping. In the case of No Name Cottage most of the accommodations are on the ground floor peeking out pretty small pane windows. The living room could easily have fallen out of a decorator magazine, with its character fireplace, crowned by a crooked timber lintel, and undulating exposed stone walls. Furnishings here run to the truly elegant...French provincial wingbacks done in a delicious apricot, and polished wood floors bearing *Louis de Pootere* rugs. The eye is drawn to numerous interesting decoratives and pictures, and thence to the circular staircase leading to the gallery. The same *decorator-at-work* ambiance is to be had in the kitchen/dining room, with lovely antique pine pieces imaginatively placed under an open beamed ceiling. The best of the functional utilities are here, as well, for laying on a festive meal or zapping a quick bite in the microwave.

The sleeping arrangements in No Name are generously laid out to accommodate large families or perhaps separate families holidaying together. There are three first floor bedrooms and, off the mezzanine, a twin bedded room leading into a family style room with three single beds.

In Calves Cot Cottage (drawing above) we find an utterly charming living room situated in a separate single story wing, with a peaked ceiling, a massive stone fireplace and character windows. Again, wonderful expansive soft furnishings and no shortage of accent pieces (note the spinning wheel) and fascinating decoratives. As with No Name, sleeping is arranged both up and downstairs, with the master double bedroom featuring an antique brass bed, and another bedroom offering three singles. All in all, two superb large cottages.   WTB 4 Dragons

NO NAME
I. B-d
B-t
B-s
F-3 [2]
II.B-t
B-3s
£265-750
S 10

CALVES
I. B-d
B-t
F-1
II.B-t
B-3s
F-3
£245-690
S 9

BOTH
E&H
FP
L
TELc TV
W/D
DW   MW
F-F
BK$

Contact Leonard & Margaret Rees, Quality Cottages, Cerbid, Solva, Haverfordwest,
Pembrokeshire SA62 6YE TEL 01144-1348-837-874

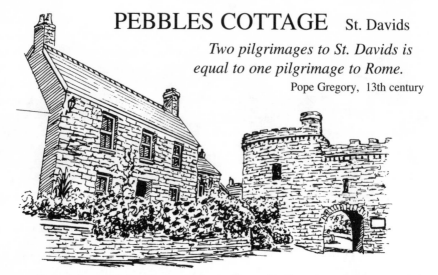

PEBBLES COTTAGE St. Davids

Two pilgrimages to St. Davids is
equal to one pilgrimage to Rome.

Pope Gregory, 13th century

Boy oh boy, did that Pope ever know his stuff! Once is probably enough for Rome, but St. David's is definitely a place you will want to go back to...again and again.

Someone else who really knows her stuff is Ann Eynon Cowie, who is an authority on Celtic history and a study leader for the Smithsonian Institute Travel Associates, based in Baltimore. "What a fascinating job," you're saying, perhaps with envy. Well, yes it is, but the down side for Ann is that she can not always live within the enlightenment of Pope Gregory's decree; to wit, she can't always be home at Pebbles (as I write, Ann is in Sicily)...and, when you really think about it, we're sorry for Ann, but glad for us, because she is willing to share her window on this blessed place when she's away.

And what a *window* it is! Right below the Norman gatehouse tower and within the walls of the 11th century Cathedral of St. David. Keep in mind that this *St. David's* is not your every day, down the street, name-borrowing house of worship. The Man, himself, built his settlement here in the sixth century! I can tell you, you don't have to be a regular church going type person to feel the extraordinary aura of these grounds. Have a dawn walk around the ethereal ruins of the Bishop's Palace (adjacent to the Cathedral) as we have...you'll feel it. Or take in the Bach Festival within the superb acoustics of the Cathedral during May...or the open air Shakespeare performances amongst the ruins of the Bishops' Palace throughout the summer ...you'll feel it!

I should hasten to add that St. David's, the City, is a *city* only by virtue of some arcane rule that Cathedrals can only be in a *city*. Officially, St. David's is the smallest *city* in Britain; probably the whole world. I suppose the alternative was to call this magnificent Cathedral a *chapel.* Well, there's no winning this one, but the fact is that St. David's is, demographically speaking, scarcely more than a village, and that scale of things probably has a lot to do with the enduring sagacity of the old Pope's decree. But, inasmuch as the Pope never actually took tea at Pebbles, which came along a bit later than his illustrious tenure in that other holy spot, we'd better tell you something about the accommodations.

The Cottage begins with a kitchen right out of *Country Living;* lots of fascinating clutter and worldly memorabilia along with every bit of cookin' paraphernalia to keep even Julia Child delirious. From here, French doors open out onto a pretty sun filled walled garden, where Julia (or you or I) might like to take a glass of wine and sit while the sauce reduced. Soup's on! Off to the dining room, with its antique pine table and chairs, old Welsh dresser lined with blueware and a pitcher collection, pretty tile-faced fireplace...all enveloped in forest green walls with super white trim and moldings, and, as everywhere, wonderful pictures and frameables of all sorts. Appetizing! But now it's time to retire to the living room, here to find comfy couches, an oriental carpet, fireplace of local slate...all overlooking the medieval wall and the valley. Pick out a book from the hallway library on the way up to the bedrooms; two in number, both en-suite (not "shared en-suite"), tucked away under the eaves with distant views of the sea and islands.

Don't forget to set your clock for that dawn amble around the Cathedral Close, and after that I suggest packing a picnic (include a nice bottle of Welsh grown wine) and spend the day on the peerless coastal walk that begins just down the lane. If this doesn't sound like paradise, then might I suggest the sweaty mobs on St. Peter's Square and a sleazy *pension* on the banks of the Tiber...only one visit required.

WTB 5 Dragons

I. F-1	
II.B-d	
F-2	
B-t	
F-2	
E H$	
FPG	
LT	
TELc	
TVV	
W/D MW	
NS P-BA	
S-S MS	
TA	
$600	
S 4	

Contact Ann Eynon Cowie, 7 The Pebbles, St. David's, Pembrokeshire, Dyfed SA62
TEL/FAX 01144-1437-721-819

KINGFISHER COTTAGE   St. Florence

Pride is the self evident measure of the village of St. Florence, which has parlayed community spirit into a steady stream of victories in the *Britain in Bloom* and *Best Kept Village* competitions. No less can be said for Kingfisher Cottage, which is done-up to a tee in a style that might well be called *storybook cute.* We begin with a pretty little fieldstone house set behind a wrought iron fence on a carefully landscaped terrace. We enter through a little *Miss Mouse* chapel door, peaked and Gothic, to a *neat-as-a-pin* cottage room with bright floral stencil work applied to pristine white walls and cheerful curtains to match. Overhead (which is not very far up!) there is a sweet little Edwardian chandelier with pink fabric shades, and more glow is projected by the cosy little wood stove engulfed in a wall of exposed stonework. Each bit of furnishing is a character piece...the Victorian ladies' chair, the tea table and shiny silver service, etc. Upstairs, two little bedrooms, a double bed for Mama & Papa Mouse, and a bunk room for the mouselings. And, just four miles away is the historic town of Tenby, with fascinations for all ages woven in and around its medieval walls.   WTB 4 Dragons

I. F-3	
II.B-d	
B-b	
E H$	
FP	
LT	
TV	
W/D	
MW	
P-	
S-S MS	
BK$	
£190-480	
S 4	

Contact Leonard & Margaret Rees, Quality Cottages, Cerbid, Solva, Haverfordwest,
Pembrokeshire SA62 6YE TEL 01144-1348-837-874

THE TOWER
Scethrog

But for an extra 26,000 feet or so, Pen-y-Fan could be Everest. OK, so the Brecon Beacons are not exactly the Himalayas, but there is a timeless, primordial aura to these magnificent Welsh mountains, nonetheless. The Romans must have felt it as they pushed their *civilization* up the Valley of the Usk to build a large fort near the present day town of Brecon. Centuries later the Normans gazed with equal awe at these seemingly impenetrable heights into which the savage natives evaporated with such ease, giving the invaders ground but not victory. The line of tension was held by a great feudal family, the Picards, who built their castle at Pencelli and placed a fortified watch tower at the fording place a mile or so downstream. In those days, The Tower was undoubtedly four stories or more high, and what excitement there must have been for the knights who garrisoned it when the unifying Welsh chieftain, Llywelyn, brought his bloody challenge down from the Brecon Beacons in 1277. Alas, however, the forces of King Edward I prevailed and the valiant Welsh irredentist fell in battle. With the passing of centuries, rather more blood was mixed than spilled, and gradually The Tower *fell* into an increasing state of domesticity. The Tower of Scethrog on the bend of the River Usk is Listed as the oldest inhabited building in Wales, though its *habitability* had definitely reached a low point when novelist Diana Melly discovered it in 1973.

With husband George, noted jazzman and arts critic, Diana Melly stripped The Tower back to basically three open high ceilinged rooms; one per floor. On the ground level are the convivial public areas for sitting, dining and cooking. *Professor Melly's Victorian Puppet Theatre* is also quartered on this level. A winding stone stairwell, recessed into the walls, was discovered during the renovations and leads to a first floor landing where there is now a well tuned piano. The second floor master suite features a brass double bed, fireplace, large convertible divan, sofa, and Gothic bookcases with packed shelves. As with every room, there is an eclectic array of antique farmhouse pieces, Moroccan rugs, cosmopolitan decoratives and original paintings. The upper floor accommodates guests in single and kingsize bedrooms and offers a wonderfully private working space under the open beams and skylights for the many artistically inspired guests who frequent The Tower, with or without the Mellys in residence. Such novelists as James Fox (*White Mischief*) and Bruce Chatwin (*On the Black Hill*) have worked here. Lady Arabella Boxer's *The Wind in the Willows Country Cookbook* recipes were tested in The Tower's rustic kitchen.

And, of course, The Tower has been a creative environment for the landlords, as well; Diana's *The Girl in the Picture* and *The Goosefeather Bed* were put to paper here; George regularly retreats from London to The Tower to scribe essays on art and music.

All of which brings us to the essence of the personality of The Tower. This is not a designer perfected country house, nor is it a rigorously restored historic site, despite all its architectural and historic interest. The personality of The Tower is very much the personality of its artistic owners; laissez faire, not luxury, is the essence of life at The Tower. One need not come for the highs of self realization; to think great thoughts or to write a book or to paint a picture. Plenty of rewards will come from just poking about in Diana Melly's wonderfully liberated garden, with its ancient roses, old breeds of fruit trees and berries of all sorts (all of which find their way into her much discussed country wines). Naturalists will be fulfilled by walks along the river, particularly as there are seventy-two acres adjacent to The Tower which have been set aside by the government as a *Site of Special Scientific Interest*. And, last but not least, four rods of fishing come with The Tower and one of the best trout & salmon beats on the River Usk...over a mile of fishing rights in waters that harbor trout in the five-six pound range.

I. F-3
II. B-d+CS
F-2
III.B-s
B-k
F-1
E&H
FP
LT
TEL
TVV
W
DW MW
S-S MS
INS
£350-600
S 4-6

Contact Elizabeth Daniel, Brecon Beacons Holiday Cottages, Brynoyre, Talybont-on-Usk, Brecon, Powys LD3 7YS   TEL 01144-1874-87446 or FAX 01144-1874-87416

BRIDGE VIEW COTTAGE

Nr Solva

Middle Mill lies about a mile up a rocky valley from the picturesque coastal village of Solva. The scene here is one of quieter times; even the little Victorian woolen mill still operating along the waters of the River Solva is a step into the past. Bridge View cottage is nestled in amongst terraced gardens with pretty views and complete privacy. The cottage, itself, has been very recently renovated and attractively furnished. Pristine white walls, blackened beams, bare soft wood floors with pretty rugs, a warming little fire...all the makings of a memorable holiday base. The cottage is deceptively spacious and offers a dining area in the kitchen, as well as a separate dining room. Or, dine on the patio, where there is a barbeque and garden furnishings.

You will find much to do and see along the Pembroke shore. Nearby there is a fascinating butterfly farm, the so-called *Nectarium*, occupying a deconsecrated chapel.

I. F-3	
II.B-d [2]	
B-s	
E	H$
FP	
L	
TV	
W/D	
MW	
S-S	MS
BK$	
£190-499	
S 5	

Contact Leonard & Margaret Rees, Quality Cottages, Cerbid, Solva, Haverfordwest, Pembrokeshire SA62 6YE TEL 01144-1348-837-874

CERBID FARMHOUSES

Nr Solva

The tiny private hamlet of Cerbid sits at the strategic center of the St. Davids Peninsula, just three or four miles from the north and south shores with their fine beaches, and about the same distance from the absolutely delightful village of St. Davids, Britain's smallest Cathedral "city". Solva, just five minutes to the south, once the quintessential Welsh fishing village, has become the equally quintessential up-market holiday center, much favored by the yachting and arty sets.

Leonard Rees' family ties to Cerbid go back centuries, and it was his restoration and conversion of the family farmstead here thirty years ago that began him on the road to developing one of Britain's most respected self catered holiday agencies. Today, in addition to representing perhaps a hundred other property owners in the area, Leonard still manages his own enclave of ever popular accommodations at Cerbid.

Cerbid Old Farmhouse sleeps six in character surrounds dating back to the 16th century. This is a traditional Welsh stone farmhouse, with grouted roof, exposed stone interior walls and beamed ceilings. This cozy cottage features a handsome fireplace with an ancient timber lintel and an open faced wood-burning stove. The Farmhouse is furnished for comfort in a mix of contemporary and period pieces, including an antique Welsh settle and, of course, the inevitable Welsh dresser with an array of colorful crockery. The kitchen is compact, but fully equipped. There are sleeping and bathroom/shower facilities on both floors.

The four bedroom Cerbid House (drawing above), is attached to the Old Farmhouse; a "modern" addition, as it were, dating from Georgian times. The two properties are independently oriented and each enjoys complete privacy. Here you will find the same homey furnishings, with a cozy open fire and pretty Edwardian style lighting. There are some nice decoratives, including a collection of local watercolors. One bedroom has a queen size bed and one of the twin rooms is designated as the *children's room* in acknowledgement of its exceptionally low ceiling.

E&H	
FP*	
FPS*	
LT	
TV	
W/D	
DW	MW
F-F	
MS	
BK$	
£215-799	
S 8-10	

Last, but by no means least, is Cwm Eithin, the former stone barn sitting on its own near the brook with expansive lawns and a secret garden. All accommodation is ground floor under a high peaked ceiling with a wall-sized stone chimney and fireplace. Furnishings here are most attractive, including a fetching Victorian button-back suite and many interesting accent pieces. Window seats under the bays offer charming pastoral views. Bedrooms include a queen, as well as a brace of twins. As with all the Cerbid properties, there is a very well outfitted kitchen. WTB 3 & 4 Dragons

Contact Leonard & Margaret Rees, Quality Cottages, Cerbid, Solva, Haverfordwest, Pembrokeshire SA62 6YE TEL 01144-1348-837-874

BRONLLYS CASTLE HOUSE
Talgarth

The Round Tower of Bronllys and remains of the old bailey castle date from the late 11th century. Castle House and its attached Coach House sit in seventeen acres of castle grounds bordered by the River Llynfi, which can be fished with a locally obtained permit. Accommodations here include a ground floor apartment in the Regency Period house, sleeping four in two en-suite bedrooms. The comfortably furnished living room has an open fire and the kitchen offers a complete range of conveniences for the self caterer, including a washer/dryer. Castle Cottage is attached and accommodates four in comparable quarters, while the detached Coach House (in drawing) provides accommodation for another six in an interesting layout of split level floors. The master bedroom in the Coach House features a handsome four-poster bed, and the sofa in the large open plan living room (upstairs) opens into a double bed. Gas central heating is provided throughout, and there is a games room with a full size billiard table, as well as a piano. WTB 5 Dragons

E&H
FP*
L
TV
W/D*
DW*
P-
E/HC*
S-S MS
INS
£180-325
S 4-6

HOPE COTTAGE   Upper Llangynidr

The village of Upper Llangynidr sits on the old Monmouth Canal, which has been reopened for holiday boating traffic from Pontypool to Brecon. The canal, itself, is a fascination for its intricate locks and tunnels, swinging bridges and towpaths. Good walking alongside good boating is to be had up and down the Usk Valley these days.

Hope Cottage is set right in the village, with a pretty detached garden and a walled-in little patio out front amongst the flowering shrubbery. The interior has been very handsomely done up, with good quality furnishings and interesting architecturals, such as the inglenook fireplace, oaken beams, and bright bay windows. There is electric central heating and both coal and logs are supplied for a cozy fire.
WTB 5 Dragons

II.B-d
B-t
F-3
E&H
FP
L
TELc TV
W/D MW
P-
S-S MS
INS
£180-295
S 4

Contact Elizabeth Daniel, Brecon Beacons Holiday Cottages, Brynoyre, Talybont-on-Usk, Brecon, Powys LD3 7YS   TEL 01144-1874-87446 or FAX 01144-1874-87416

BETWS-BACH   Ynys Nr Ciccieth

Betws-Bach is situated on that far side of Wales, beyond the rugged grandeur of Snowdonia National Park, with a southerly exposure to greet the warming Gulf Stream. Located in the tiny hamlet of Ynys, the large stone built farm cottage is nestled on a sheltered hillside overlooking green meadows that lead down to the wooded banks of the River Dwyfach.

Betws-Bach dates back to the early 17th century and is a Grade II Listed building with a preservation order on its authentic keep. The cottage begins with an entrance hall where you will be greeted by an old grandfather's clock and an understair cupboard containing various domestic necessaries. The sitting room is picturesque with an exposed beam ceiling and the original inglenook fireplace framed under an enormous timber lintel. There is a log burning stove in the fireplace now and a polished blue slate hearth with various brass and basketry accouterments. The cottage furnishings are an assemblage of mixed oldies and contemporary; homey rather than designer in inspiration.

The kitchen-dining area features an exposed stone wall and its own open fireplace. There are newly fitted oak cabinets and all the modern essentials. Upstairs you will find an "L" shaped main bedroom with an antique oak double bed and a three foot single. There is another pine paneled double bedroom with pleasant pastoral views, and a very small third single bedroom. The bathroom is done in floral tile and features a large deep tub and hand shower, as well as a bidet.

This land begs to be walked. The Dwyfach River meanders across the owner's adjacent farm, with waterfalls and rapids through a ravine which is a designated habitat for otters. There are deep and shallow pools which harbor salmon and sea trout, and fields of game: pigeons, woodcock, pheasant, hares and foxes. Venturing further afield you have the beaches of Tremadog Bay to enjoy.

Betws-Bach also has a *granny wing,* occupied appropriately enough by Mrs Jones' mother. The Jones have two other highly rated cottages to rent in the area: Rhos-Ddu House which sleeps five; and the adjacent Rhos-Wen Cottage, all on one level, sleeping six. WTB 5 Dragons

II.B-d+s
B-d
B-s
F-4
E$m
H$m
FP$ FPS$
L$
TV
W/D
DW MW
P-BA
S-S
£150-500
S 6

Contact Mrs. Anwen Jones , Rhandir, Boduan, Pwllheli, Gwynedd LL53 8UA
TEL/FAX 01144-1758-720-047

Scottish Counties

ORKNEY

SHETLAND

WESTERN ISLES

SKAILL HOUSE p. 335

HIGHLANDS

GRAMPIAN

TAYSIDE

FIFE

CENTRAL
SCOTLAND

LOTHIAN

STRATHCLYDE

SCOTTISH BORDERS

DUMFRIES & GALLOWAY

THE PINEAPPLE p. 318

ARROWDALE p. 328

KINMOUNT COURT
Nr Annan

Kinmount Court was another of the Clan Douglas seats, specifically that branch vested with the title *Marquis of Queensberry*. John Douglas, the Sixth Marquis, built the mansion in 1812 in a style that can aptly be described as a perfect meld of disciplined architectural formalism and strict Scottish propriety. Alfred, the Eighth Marquis, inherited the title and did his bit for formalizing the rules of fisticuffs; but propriety, Scottish or otherwise, was not generally his measure. It was at Kinmount Court that Lord Alfred Douglas entertained his friend Oscar Wilde... well, as they say, that's *another story!* Today, Kinmount Court is owned by Olympic Gold Medalist Steve Ovett, and I can not imagine a more splendid environment for keeping in shape. Not surprisingly, Kinmount Court offers its guests a generous array of recreational amenities, including a multi-gym, heated indoor pool, sauna, games room, and truly splendid grounds for those of us who prefer to work up a sweat by strolling through the azaleas and rhododendrons with a glass of sherry.

E$m	H$m
FPG	
L	
TV	
W/D	
DW	MW
P-	
E/HC*	
S-S	MS
INS	
$425-1870	
S 2-6	

Mr. Ovett offers his guests the choice of eight deliciously decorated accommodations in the Victorian servants' wing. Each apartment features a four-poster bed, sumptuous bedding fabrics and drapery, rich papering and carefully chosen ornamentation. Another gold medal for Mr. Ovett and team! And, for the literary pilgrim, the Wilde story is only the beginning of the offerings in this neighborhood. Museums   honoring Carlyle (at Ecclefechan) and Burns (at Dumfries) are nearby.

Contact British Travel International, P.O. Box 299, Elkton VA 22827 USA
TEL 800-327-6097 or FAX 703-298-2347

VILLAGE COTTAGE Banchory

Situated about an equidistant half hour between the handsome Georgian city of Aberdeen and the Royal's Scottish getaway at Balmoral is Banchory on the Dee...*Royal Deeside*, as it were. Castle Country!

Mrs. Rosalind Holmes began offering accommodation in her fine early Victorian

I. B-t
II.B-t
F-3
E&H
LT
TV
W   MW
£275-375
S 4

home (above), and continues to do so on a B&B basis. In addition, she has Village Cottage for self catering. Mrs. Holmes is a native Aberdonian, who knows how to lay on the tartan for a warm welcome! You will find the cottage nicely furnished, with deep rose carpeting and Sanderson curtains tied back in bows. The upstairs bedroom under the sloping ceiling is done in pine and pastels, very pretty, very feminine.   STB 4 Crowns; Highly Commended

Contact Rosalind Holmes, Village Guest House, 83 High St., Banchory AB31 3TJ TEL 01144-1330-823-307

BARJARG BACK LODGE Auldgirth

Of course, we all know that Scotland gave birth to golf, and each year thousands of North Americans make the pilgrimage to hack away at the sacred greens of the *Motherland. Well,* attention cyclists! We are very close here in Auldgirth to the source of the bicycle (No; the bike doesn't hail from China; that's the rocket!), and this Galloway countryside continues to be inspirational for the cycling enthusiasts. In addition, there is all manner of *fish'n* and *shoot'n* to be had on the large Barjarg farming estate, where this pretty cottage is situated. This 19th century cottage is built of sandstone, with lattice pane windows overlooking a small lawn, and offers a comfortably furnished sitting room with an open fire, as well as a small dining room. Upstairs, there are two bedrooms furnished in a country style.

I. F-2
II.B-d
B-t
E&H
FP
LT-BA
TELc TV
MW
S-S
INS
£135-205
S 4

BLACK CLAUCHRIE HOUSE Nr Barrhill

The approach to this century old, Arts & Crafts design shooting lodge is a dream, a four mile entry road through moorlands and forests to an oasis of lush vegetation where nestles this statuesque retreat. This house was expressly built to provide pleasure. An eyeful itself, Black Clauchrie House was meant to be a commodious base for exuberant outdoor*sey* types...that promise is as much alive today as in Victorian times. Wildlife abounds for the naturalist, trout and salmon await the fisherman, and there is deer and pheasant shooting, as well as clay pigeon facilities nearby for the gunner. The Estate has a curling pond and row boat. Indoor recreations take place in the billiard/ballroom, where there is also table tennis and badminton.

The house is completely paneled downstairs, with heavy timbered ceilings, a minstrel gallery, and a huge Victorian conservatory, and a barbeque area outside. There is no shortage of character rooms, not least being the original *conversation* bath/shower for intimate cohabitation, which is en-suite to the four-poster bedded room. Obviously the Victorians weren't all just *shootin'* and *fishin'*! As Black Clauchrie is the Watts' own home, it is well furnished with many homey and personal touches, and is centrally heated. Mrs. Watts is on hand, in adjoining accommodations, to act as provisioneer and/or part time chef according to the guest requirements.   STB 5 Crowns

I. F-1
II. B-q
B-d
B-t
B-s
F-3 [2]
III.B-d+s [3]
E&H
FP
LT-BA
TELc
TVV
DW MW
P-BA
£710-1100
S 16

Contact G. M. Thomson & Co., 27 King St., Castle Douglas, Scotland DG7 1AB
TEL 01144-1556-502-701 or FAX 01144-1556-503-277

HARBOUR ROW   Drummore

Here we are on the Mull of Galloway, Scotland's most southerly point, warmed by the Gulf Stream. When the noted conservation architect Tom Gray completed this project for developer Leonard Sculthorp, he received a number of written commendations for his imaginative restoration of the characterful old fishermen's cottages adjacent to the historic Coast Guard Station in Drummore. Alas, the little row of cottages, pristine white against the blue wash of Luce Bay, are not *re-*made, but *new-*made! Gray was able to find just the right balance of modern convenience and historic humility in the design of these accommodations. The seven cottages, named for the Western Islands (*Eigg, Rhum, Skye, Arran, Jura, Islay & Gigha*), have tartan carpeting, log fires and utility kitchens. Furnishing is comfortable, though not elaborate, and there are sunny south facing patios practically at the edge of the sandy beach. Drummore, itself, is a pleasant village with boats, wind surfing and guided fishing for hire. Just down the road is the Mull of Galloway lighthouse (1828), *Lands End* of Scotland. STB 4 Crowns; Highly Commended.

```
E$m  H$m
FP$
LT$
TELc  TV
W
S-S
£160-395
S 4-6
```

KIRKMAIDEN HOUSE   Drummore

Kirkmaiden House is a fine early Victorian home situated proudly on the hill overlooking the village and bay, with four acres of grounds and a lovely walled garden. Leonard Sculthorp purchased it in 1987 when he "retired" (when I spoke to Leonard recently he was in Florida doing a development!). Suffice it to say that the Sculthorps don't get much time to come down to Kirkmaiden House. The home has three stories with six bedrooms and is handsomely furnished in a mix of antiques and period styles. There are cozy open fires and deep casement windows with fold back shutters in the four public rooms. The kitchen is all newly done with bright pine cabinetry, tile floors, and all the necessaries for any kind of meal from hamburger to haggis. On the Kirkmaiden grounds there is also a stable complex, which has been converted to a three bedroom bungalow and can be rented separately or with the main house.
STB 5 Crowns; Highly Commended

```
I. F-1
II. B-t
   B-d [2]
   F-2
III.B-d
   B-s
   F-3
E$m  H$m
FP$
LT$
TEL  TV
W/D
DW  MW
OPEN
£ 850
S 10
```

Contact Mrs. S. Colman, 4 Coastguard Cottages, Drummore, Wigtownshire DG9 9QX TEL 01144-1776-840-631

ROSSLYN CASTLE Nr Edinburgh

One of the great ecclesiastical buildings in all Christendom is Rosslyn Chapel, just seven miles outside of Edinburgh. Rosslyn owes its existence to the passion of one man, William St. Clair, the last Prince of Orkney, who died in the decade before Columbus made his voyage to the East. St. Clair lived a most ostentatious life in nearby Rosslyn Castle, which is perched on a spine of rock rising out of the River Esk. The Castle proper is now 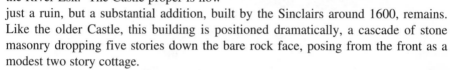 just a ruin, but a substantial addition, built by the Sinclairs around 1600, remains. Like the older Castle, this building is positioned dramatically, a cascade of stone masonry dropping five stories down the bare rock face, posing from the front as a modest two story cottage.

I. F-1
II.B-D
B-t
B-s
F-2
E&H
FPS
LT
F-F   MS
INS
£526-985
S 7

The "new" castle is still owned by the Earls of Rosslyn, though the property is managed by Landmark Trust. Here you will find a very personalized and graceful holiday home, with remarkable decorative touches, homey furnishings representing a span of periods from Jacobean onwards, and handsomely paneled walls under high and richly moulded ceilings. All this and easy access to Edinburgh too!

Contact The Landmark Trust, Shottesbrook, Maidenhead, Berkshire SL6 3SW
TEL 01144-1628-825-925 or FAX 01144-1628-825-417

BARNCROSH FARM Nr Castle Douglas

Barncrosh, which sits on the banks of the Dee and means *Place of the Cross,* has a long and curious history. In the 10th century there was a chapel on the site, made famous by one Father Damien, who, out of ecclesiastical ecstasy or a premature   scientific urge (I'm not sure which), adorned himself with feathers and took a dive off the castle wall. The result was less than full confirmation of the friar's faith, though it might be noted that his experiment preceded Galileo's less courageous effort by half a millennium. In the 14th century Archibald the Grim built Threave Castle nearby in the middle of the Dee, making it the Douglas stronghold for terrorizing the meek and confounding more distant dynastic authorities. It was a Douglas who beheaded the sheriff of Galloway and sent along the lower portions to the king with the percipient observation that the gent was "somewhat wanting in the heid."

Today, Barncrosh Farm is comprised of several hundred acres and incorporates a number of traditional stone-built tenant houses which have been renovated as holiday lets by Ronald and Liz Ball. The accommodations vary in size from a three bedroomed farmhouse to compact flats for couples. These are not luxury cottages, but they are comfortably furnished and represent good value as a base for exploring the legendary lochs and castles of Galloway. And, those of us with the blood of Black Douglases running in our veins will be glad to know that the warm hospitality of Ron and Liz Ball is not modeled on that of our ancestors.   STB 1-4 Crowns

E$m	H
FP*	
LT	
TV	
W/Ds	
P$	
S-S; F-F	
MS	TA
£85-350	
S 2-8	

Ronald Ball, Barncrosh Farm, Castle Douglas, Kirkcudbrightshire, Scotland DG7 1TX
TEL 01144-1556-680-216 or FAX 01144-1556-680-442

THE PINEAPPLE

Dunmore

The Pineapple is very special for me. While doing research for my children's novel, *The Mystery of Conch Cay*, I discovered that the very controversial last British Governor of Virginia, Lord Dunmore, personally assembled a valiant force of emancipated slaves to fight the planter aristocrats of the American Revolution. For the first few months of the War Dunmore's black army gave the rebel planters along the Virginia and Maryland shores quite a bashing. However, before long the force was reorganized, and Dunmore was packed off to Britain. With the final defeat in 1783, Lord Dunmore was appointed Governor of the Bahamas, where he promptly endorsed the re-enslavement of many of these very same black heroes of the Royal cause, who were by then, of course, part of the exodus of Tory refugees to Canada and the Bahamas. Lord Dunmore thus earned his anti-hero's black hat in my novel.

It was only later that I discovered exactly how the 4th Earl of Dunmore occupied his time in the interim between those colonial governorship appointments. He built The Pineapple, which must rank as one of the most humorous follies of all time! Even in his choice of vegetable metaphors, the Governor seemed to be making light of his troubles in America. The pineapple, now the accepted sign of hospitality, began its symbolic life in America, where sailors would mount a pineapple on their gate post to announce their return from a long voyage across the seven seas. Under the circumstances, one would have thought that Lord Dunmore might have played down his abrupt return to Britain. But clearly that wasn't His Lordship's style. In retrospect I must ask myself whether such a grand eccentric could have been all bad?

The Pineapple is a colossal garden pavilion, with a single holiday accommodation now occupying the two wings (see windows in drawing), which are at grade level from the rear. The living, dining, and kitchen areas are in the west wing, while sleeping and bathroom facilities occupy the east wing. Yes, one must go outside and cross the beautifully landscaped gardens to get from one part of the "cottage" to the other. This is a private garden for guests, separate from the public gardens in the foreground, which are open to the public under the auspices of the National Trust for Scotland. As always, the Landmark Trust interior decoration department has done a marvelous job of furnishing The Pineapple in a period idiom. You'll have no problem sensing the presence of Governor Dunmore. He's the ghost with the black hat.

| From Rear |
| I.B-t [2] |
| F-2 |
| E&H |
| FP |
| LT |
| F-F   MS |
| INS |
| £271-641 |
| S 4 |

Contact The Landmark Trust, Shottesbrook, Maidenhead, Berkshire SL6 3SW
TEL 01144-1628-825-925 or FAX 01144-1628-825-417

TRAPRAIN COTTAGE

Nr East Linton

There are some who come here to these East Lothian shores regularly in the manner of a great spiritual pilgrimage, to gaze with deep reverence out across the waters of the Firth of Forth, kneeling occasionally, laying hands upon the very ground itself, rising then and looking heavenward for divine intervention. They bear crooked sticks and they watch for bright little objects in the sky. They are known among their brothers as *duffers,* and they have come here to the Holy Land of Golf.

Traprain Cottage sits high looking out over the village of East Linton, out to spectacular Bass Rock and the Isle of May, out over a multitude of link shrines, sixteen in number, all within a short drive of the cottage. Among these holy pastures is Muirfield, where the British Open was played in 1992. Mecca! But wait. That name *Muir* recalls something to us (North Americans) besides crazed pilgrims, by twos and fours, scurrying about putting transcendental divots in the lawn. I speak of John Muir, of course, that child of Dunbar (just down the road from the cottage) for whom the local County Park is named, and who brought forth the transcendent concept of *park* onto our own land. Yosemite!

Traprain Cottage is a small stone built building from the last century. It is amazingly bright and airy, given its size, and has plenty of windows to bring in views of the rolling fields surrounding the cottage. There is a feel of seclusion here, which is actually conditioned by the quaint quality of the cottage rather than any real measure of remoteness. Mary Durkacz has done a nice job of renovating and decorating, retaining the cottage's essential modesty while making it a cheerful and cozy environ. Dainty prints, polished pine tables and chests, and floral covered wicker furnishings all make for an unpretentious *feel at home* cottage. Traprain is very much an all season abode, having both central heating and a multi-fuel stove which is particularly useful for taking the chill out of the evening...or drying out your Argyle golf puttees.

But what if golf isn't your cup of *tee?* Disciples of Muir will find plenty to do and see here, as well. The ornithologically inclined won't want to miss the hike out to St Abb's Head or a boat trip round Bass Rock. Castle hounds will have their hands full, beginning with the ruins of Hailes Castle right in East Linton and then on to Dunbar, Dirleton, Fast, and Tantallon Castles. Last but not least, there is Traprain Law, itself, site of an Iron Age fort and an ancient Celtic town.

STB 5 Crowns; Highly Commended

LCS
B-d
B-b
F-3
E&H
LT
TELc
TV
W/D
DW MW
NS
P-BA
S-S MS
INS
TA
£199-415
S 4-5

Contact Mary Durkacz, 10 Coltbridge Terrace, Edinburgh EH12 6AE
TEL 01144-1313-460-620 or FAX 01144-1313-133-198

ROYAL MILE MANSIONS
Edinburgh

I think it is generally the case that one pays more and gets less in the city, and in my experience over the past two decades Edinburgh is no exception. Though visitors to a metropolis generally resent this and typically think they are being exploited (paying a premium for proximity, as it were), the fact is that one pays more for less downtown simply because urban pressure makes downtown real estate out of sight, and if the landlord doesn't charge more for less he is subsidizing the holiday maker. It seems to me that, in the case of #22 The Royal Mile Mansions, the Fergusons are subsidizing their guests.

One thing is for sure, this flat puts us in the heart of historic Edinburgh, along the Royal Mile between Edinburgh Castle and the Palace of Holyroodhouse. St. Giles Cathedral is just around the corner, the John Knox House just up the street.... museums, galleries, theatre, or just poking about the narrow cobble streets and historic closes of the medieval city. In fact, it is said that the treaty which entrusted England to the Scottish king, James VI, was signed on the site of the Royal Mile Mansions. The present building has had a number of lives; prior to being completely renovated for prestige apartments in 1988, the building was the home of the famous department store *Grants of Edinburgh*.

One enters the building via an entry-phone security system and the apartment, which is on the third floor, may be reached by elevator or stairs. The flat, itself, runs through the building, with the living room and one bedroom perspective over cobbled Cockburn Street and the Corstorphine Hills in the distance, while the back bedroom faces on the inner well of the building and offers more quiet. The spacious and high ceilinged living room is strikingly decorated in lavenders and white, with a wooden dado rail and color coordinated wall to wall carpeting. The huge front bow windows are prettily draped from ceiling to floor. The furniture throughout the apartment is made of rose pinewood and includes a Duncan Phyfe style dining table for six with period style chairs, a writing bureau, and various occasional tables, in addition to the bedroom suites. The master bedroom is similar in proportions to the living room, and is decorated in sunny yellows and blue. The back bedroom is decorated in a really warming pink. In sum, Number Twenty-Two is near luxury accommodation at near hovel rates; ideal for a holidaying family, as well as the business traveller. STB 4 Crowns; Deluxe

III.B-q	
B-t	
CS	
F-3	
E&H	
LT	
TELc	
TV	
W/D	
S-S	MS
INS	
£225-450	
S 4-6	

Contact Mrs. Diane Ferguson, 139 Chalkwell Avenue, Westcliff on Sea, Essex SSO 8HN
TEL/FAX 01144-1702-77913

DRUIMARBIN FARMHOUSE

Fort William

Druimarbin Farmhouse is set in the heart of the Western Highlands in the foothills of Ben Nevis, Britain's highest mountain. Three miles away is Fort William, a focal point in the Jacobite Risings of the 18th century, where the name *Bonnie Prince Charlie* is still invoked with about the same reverence as *Robert E. Lee* in Virginia. If the history is big up here, so is the landscape; indeed these Highlands offer a wealth of outdoor attractions, be it fishing or sailing, climbing or walking.

Indoors, that is at Druimarbin Farmhouse, is no less a thrill. The German-Ribons

I. F-3
II.B-t [3]
F-3 [3]
B-s
E&H
FP
LT
TEL TV
W/D
DW
OPEN
£500
S 7

have done a masterful job of presenting this sturdy and spacious old farmhouse for the holiday trade. You will find all the quintessential Scottish themes in Mrs. German-Ribon's decorating, from the bold tartan fabrics, to the handsome array of sporting trophies and mountings, to the lovely landscape paintings and statuary. The furnishings are pure comfort, and plentiful; which is to say, it takes plenty of furniture to fill a home with a thirty foot drawing room and a dining room not much smaller. There are endless window views over the Loch and grounds, and French doors bring in the light and color of the garden. Splendid setting, splendid home...all the makings of a very memorable holiday in the Highlands.

Contact Mrs. Anthony German-Ribon, 57 Napier Avenue, London SW6 3PS TEL 01144-1717-364-864

THE MILLHOUSE

Girthon

The hamlet of Girthon was a thriving community in the mid-18th century, with the mill as a center of employment and a proud little *kirk* on the hill behind. These days the *kirk* is just a picturesque ecclesiastical ruin, but the

Mill House stands proud in a courtyard of cottages recently converted from the old mill complex. On the other side there is a wild garden with paths cut through to a large pond fed by two streams. The same *country* feel is carried right into the house, with its low window seats cut in the thick stone walls and bucolic views of the lambs in distant pasture and cattle trundling past on their way to be milked. Off the sitting room there is a cozy study, and throughout the cottage one finds lovely country pictures and family photographs to remind us of the pride of the owners in their Mill House. Upstairs there are four bedrooms furnished in pine, with still more pretty views over the rolling countryside.

I. F-4
II.B-d
B-t
B-b
B-s
F-3
E&H
FPE
TELin
TV
W
DW
P-
£200-380
S 7

Contact G. M. Thomson & Co., 27 King St., Castle Douglas, Scotland DG7 1AB
TEL 01144-1556-503-277 or FAX 01144-1556-503-277

52 CHARLOTTE
Glasgow

The industrial revolution was not kind to Glasgow, nor has the City's 20th century reputation always been very flattering. Well, a lot is happening in Glasgow as it becomes a *New European* cultural city for the coming century, and 52 Charlotte Street is exemplary of the best of it. This is a genuine 1790 Robert Adam house, completely restored by the National Trust for Scotland at a cost that is definitely not reflected in the tariff for any of the six modern holiday flats within. Tragically, this is the last of a two sided row of mansions, joined by pavilions, which were built for the returning mercantilist money of Empire; quite appropriately available these days for sojourning *colonists*. Now under the ownership and management of Simon Leslie-Carter, the one & two bedroom flats are handsomely furnished in period styles, with all of the timeless beauty of neo-classical architecture, hand stamped by the master himself, and respectfully restored by his most ardent contemporary disciples. Nearby amenities include theaters, cafes, galleries and the concert halls of the regenerated Merchant City.   STB 4 Crowns; Highly Commended

E&H
LT
TELc TVV
W/D
OPEN MS
£325-390
Daily £54-64
S 2-3

Contact Simon Leslie-Carter, 52 Charlotte St., Glasgow G1 5DW TEL/FAX 01144-1415-531-941

COLDSTRIFFEN COTTAGE   Glenbuchat

This is a *get away from it all* venue near the headwaters of the Don, about an hours drive up river from Aberdeen.   One thing you can't escape up here, however, is the castles.   Nearby are the remains of Kildrummy Castle, where Robert the Bruce's family narrowly escaped getting hung with the rest of the garrison

in 1306. Even closer is Glenbuchat Castle, a Gordon edifice that spoiled the ambitions of King George III.   Then there is Scotland's quintessential romance castle, Craigievar; and let's not forget Corgarff, Huntley, and the Royal favorite, Balmoral.

II.B-d
B-t [2]
F-3
E   H$
FP
LT
TV
DW MW
S-S INS
$575-950
S 6

Coldstriffen Cottage is rather more modest in scale than the aforementioned historic abodes, but a whole lot more comfortable, excepting Balmoral, of course; but then sleep-over invitations at Balmoral are somewhat restricted.   At Coldstriffen you will find all the modern conveniences, attractive furnishings, and complete peace...what crusty old Laird wouldn't trade his drafty castle for the likes of this? Plus that, there is a three mile private stretch of trout and salmon fishing that comes with this cottage! STB 4 Crowns; Deluxe

Contact Meta Voyage, 1945 Pauline Plaza, Suite 14, Ann Arbor, MI 48103-5047
TEL 800-771-4771 (East) 800-538-6881 (West) or FAX 313-995-3464

TIRORAN HOUSE
Isle of Mull

This beautiful estate definitely ranks high in the *get away from it all* category! We are forty minutes by ferry from Oban and another twenty-three miles from the landing at Craignure. Tiroran is nestled amidst sixty acres of impressive landscaping and inviting woods on the north shore of Loch Scridain, with a sunny southern perspective. A delightful brook wends its way across the lawn, hurriedly enroute to the loch below. One senses that it is perfectly respectable to be lazy here, unless, that is, one is the gardener!

The property is the pride and joy (both much in evidence) of Wing Commander and Mrs. Robin Blockey. Tiroran, once a sporting lodge, is now their home and the various out buildings have been converted to charming holiday accommodations. The largest, called *The Steadings*, is approached via a courtyard off which there is a private garden. The three bedroom apartment occupies the second floor of the original stone barn and is furnished in a very homey idiom with older style pieces as well as some handsome antiques. From this height there are spectacular views of the loch and the southern hills of Mull. Below is Stable Cottage, an open plan bed-sitter for two, with hand hewn pine posts and French doors leading out onto a private walled terrace overlooking the gardens and loch.

Stone Cottage has come a long way from its former life as a laundry, and is now, I think, the preferred venue for a holiday at Tiroran. There are some interesting architectural features, most notably a Bermuda style hipped ceiling in the living room, all done in polished pine. The furnishings in Stone Cottage are of impeccable taste: lovely arm chairs in blue florals, a large convertible sofa fabricked with pink florals, and several handsome mahogany occasional pieces. Once again, the views reach into the room like landscape murals, lit and projected from behind, as if Mother Nature begged your attention at all times. The dining table is fit-ended to one of these *picture* windows. The downstairs twin bedroom is prettily furnished in a very feminine fashion, and there is an additional single bedroom.

Pine Cottage, which is all ground floor, is in a different style entirely; more rustic, with pine paneling throughout and open shelving in the kitchen. There is an Annex between Stone and Pine, which may be opened to either to increase the accommodations by two people, with en-suite facilities.

E$m	H$m
FPS*	
LT$	
TV	
W/D*	
MW	
S-S	
TA	
£150-364	
S 2-7	

Contact Wing Commander & Mrs. R.S. Blockey, Tiroran House, Isle of Mull, Argyll
Scotland PAA 69 6ES   TEL 01144-1232-06815

LARACH BHAN
Kilchrenan

In the vernacular of the present day, Loch Awe is *awesome!* Vernacular aside, this Loch just east of Oban is, in fact, nothing less than awesome! And, much the same can be said for this marvelous house overlooking the Loch. Part of Larach Bhan dates from the 1300s, though Victorian is the architectural layout of today, and elegantly contemporary is the measure of its fittings and decor. With its baby grand piano, lovely antique accent pieces, and good library, Larach Bhan promises a most refined holiday. Adjacent to the house is a beautiful sunken garden, and the estate offers many fine walks among the rhododendrons and woods. At the water's edge is a private pier and, for the piscatorially inclined, arrangements may be made to hire the 15 foot boat.

Also on this secluded estate, reached by its own single track lane, is Cruachan House. This modern home is a page from *Architectural Digest,* with beautifully composed vertical space, floods of light, and elegant furnishings in a stunningly white decor. A pretty spiral stair takes us to a galleried sitting room with more of those *awesome* views.

LARACH B.
I .B-s
F-2
F-1
II.B-d
F-3
B-t [2]
F-3
E$m   H$m
FP
L
TELc   TV
W/D
DW   MW
S-S   MS
INS
$1180-2620
S 7-9

ARRAN VIEW   Isle of Bute

The 13th century Rothesay Castle on the Isle of Bute was razed by Cromwell's victorious Republicans, but the little island still claims a Royal "Dukedom", currently vested safely in the personage

of Prince Charles. The island has also claimed the hearts of many generations of holiday-makers, particularly the yachting set who favor the harbor at Rothesay.

I. B-t	
F-3	
II.B-d	
E$m	H
L	
TV	
W/D	
DW MW	
E/HC	
S-S MS	
INS	
$575-1200	
S 4	

Arran View is a born-again Georgian coach house on the west coast of the island, facing the Isle of Arran. Nearby is the two mile sand beach at Ettrick Bay and there are plenty of opportunities for golfing and fishing enthusiasts. The cottage is comfortably furnished and features a most handsome Victorian style conservatory accessed from the living room through pretty arched doors. The whole atmosphere is bright and airy, with the lovely gardens and grounds seeming to reach right in to the living area.

Contact British Travel International, P.O. Box 299, Elkton VA 22827 USA
TEL 800-327-6097 or FAX 703-298-2347

DRUMMUIR CASTLE ESTATE

Nr Keith

It has been said that Scotland's three principle *tourist* attractions are its salmon, its whiskey, and its ancestral roots. Come to think of it, the *natives* are pretty wrapped up in these attractions too! Biggest, best, and proudest, respectively. Yu'll nay expect me to take issue with these entirely legitimate claims!

All three of these attractions come together to make "Alex" Gordon-Duff's Drummuir Castle Estate a destination, par excellence, for a sojourn in Scotland. As regards fishing, we need only point out that the Drummuir Estate is sandwiched between the Spey and the Deveron. I should warn the readers that reports of the Spey standing third to the Tay and Tweed in the matter of Salmon are not held in much repute in these parts. With respect to the national libation, Drummuir is just off that pilgrimage byway known as the *Whiskey Trail*, with Glenfiddich Distillery a mere three miles away. Just a *hop and a skip* down the road, you might say (at least coming back). Finally, we come to the genealogical attraction. Drummuir Castle is the center for the Clan MacDuff. Indeed, the Duffs have held the estate since 1621. Robert the Gallant Duff spent his blood in the Cavalier cause in 1645, and *Admiral of the Red,* Archibald Duff, built the present castle in 1848, after a long naval career that began in a lieutenancy under Nelson. The Gordon cousins entered the picture when the Admiral died without issue in 1858, which, you might say, renders Drummuir Castle doubly proud, with two clans for the price of one.

Today, under the current Laird's imaginative management, Drummuir Estate is a little empire of hospitality enterprises. One may dine at the Mill Restaurant on the estate, and all sorts of hunting and sporting programs are offered as well. For the self caterer there are four traditional cottages scattered about the 10,000 acre estate, including Loch End Cottage, pictured above. Situated in splendid isolation alongside the estate's private trout lake, guests and supplies are initially delivered over a rough track by Land Rover. Be prepared for a twenty minute walk for mid term visits to *civilization,* that is if you should ever want to stray from this delightful cottage (furnished and decorated by spares from the Castle) and lake (*furnished* with trout and a boat to pursue them). Electricity is by generator and the spring water is crystal clear, should you wish to mix a little bit of it with the you-know-what...or even wash your face.

LOCHEND
II.B-d
F-3
E$
FPS$
L
W
OPEN
MS
£172-314
S 2

Contact Drummuir Castle, Keith, Banffshire AB55 3JE   TEL 01144-1542-81255 or FAX 01144-1542-81280

SADDELL CASTLE Kintyre

Displaced descendants of the Clan Campbell will surely be able to commune with the ghosts of their ancestors here at Saddell Castle. This very early sixteenth century tower house is a masterpiece of castle restoration, in a setting of battlements and shoreline that could not be more moving or memorable. There is, in fact, quite a large estate here under the umbrella of the Landmark Trust, with three other proper cottages lost in the woods surrounding the Castle. Even if the gathering of your clan runs to a regiment of 23, all can be accommodated, and in such a generous pattern of disbursement that ancient internecine schisms need not be tested unnecessarily. The Castle, itself, sleeps eight in very spacious quarters on the top two floors, with the battlement walk-around just above. Separate living and kitchen/dining rooms are located on the second floor, under beautifully paneled ceilings. Here you will find a massive arch lintel hearth and deep (deep, deep) stone casement windows. Should jealousies percolate amongst the tribe billeted in the estate cottages, rest assured the thickness of these Castle walls will secure you from everything short of a nuclear attack. You may, however, wish to lift the special Campbell welcome mat located just inside the front door. This will divert unruly visitors to the cellars below in a most rude fashion. To be sure, one does not find such security amenities in many holiday properties! Security, aside, castle life doesn't get much better than Saddell Castle. It is certainly on our family's short list for an extended stay.

| I. F-2 |
| III.B-d |
| B-s [2] |
| IV.B-t [2] |
| F-2 |
| E&H |
| FP |
| LT |
| F-F   MS |
| INS |
| £718-1452 |
| S 8 |

Contact The Landmark Trust, Shottesbrook, Maidenhead, Berkshire SL6 3SW
TEL 01144-1628-825-925 or FAX 01144-1628-825-417

DONLELLAN Loch Tummel

This is one of those cottages which will suit the activity oriented holiday maker as well as the couch potato. For the latter, Donlellan is a *windowful* cocoon, with glorious open views of the lake and moors...the metamorphosis can move lazily into the sunny conservatory and thence onto the terrace. For the busy bee, however, there are plenty of things to do, from sailing and fishing on the loch, to pony trekking and hiking on trails which will take you along the loch or into the mountain forests. Close by there are theatre festivals and highland games to take in, not to mention the quintessential Scottish pastimes: golf and distillery hopping. Donlellan, itself, sits in a sweep of pasture land about 200 yards from the shores of Loch Tummel. The cottage is actually quite old, but has been expanded into a thoroughly modern bungalow.

| I. B-t |
| B-s |
| F-3 |
| II.B-d |
| B-t |
| F-2 |
| E$m H$m |
| FPS$ |
| L; T$ |
| TELc TV |
| W/D |
| DW MW |
| P- |
| S-S MS |
| TA |
| £300-700 |
| S 7 |

Contact Mr Greg Poole, Bridge End Farm, Boot, Eskdale, Cumbria CA19 1TG TEL/FAX 01144-1946-723-100

MELFORT PIER HARBOUR LODGES
Kilmelford

Melfort Pier and Harbour is an all purpose marine holiday center. How *all purpose,* you may ask? Well, if you want to do it on or near water, this is the place: sailing, motor boating, canoeing, water skiing, knee boarding, windsurfing, yacht charters (up to 60 ft, bareboat or skippered), party boat trips through the Isles on a catamaran, deep sea fishing, loch fishing (all tackle available), wetsuit diving, etc. etc. If the Melfort Pier people can't directly provide the service, they will make the arrangements locally for their guests, usually at substantial discounts.

There are ten ultra modern holiday accommodations discretely situated on and around the old foundations of the Melfort Pier, with the water lapping at the front door and the spectacular hills to the rear. Accommodations are for parties of two to six, all with 2 bathrooms or more, all with their own saunas and jacuzzis. Furnishings are also modern in design, leather living room suites, with bright pine dining suites and clean line kitchens. Each cottage offers a different layout; some units are arranged with bedrooms on the ground floor and living-dining areas above for unobstructed views across the water, while others, like the Boat Houses, are literally built out over the water. The Piermaster units, pictured above, have handsome cathedral ceilings and either open fires or cozy wood-burning stoves. All the Melfort Pier units are centrally heated, as well. The Boat Houses and Quayside also suited for the elderly and have wheelchair access.

So, perhaps you are not much for water sports. Well, how about mountain biking, pony trekking, hiking, golfing, snow skiing, excellent castle touring, bird watching or just relax and enjoy a session of aromatherapy in your own lodge. Melfort Pier accommodations may be let for two days, a week, or more, year round.

STB 4-5 Crowns; Deluxe

E$m
H$m
LT
FP or
FPS
LT
TELm
TV
DW
MW*
E/HC*
OPEN MS
£395-895
S 2-6

Contact Mrs. L. Stewart, Melfort Pier Harbour Lodges, The Pier, Kilmelford, Nr Oban, Argyll PA34 4XD   TEL 01144-81852-200-333 or FAX 01144-1852-200-329

ARROWDALE Loch Shieldaig

It is customary to counsel the prospective visitor to western Scotland about the remoteness and rusticity of the Highlands. As the mountains get higher and higher, the villages further and further apart, and the roads narrower and narrower, one's hopes of finding "civilized" accommodations tend to diminish...indeed, panic may set in! "It's a trade off," you tell yourself; "a little hardship to accent the grandeur of Britain's wild outback." Groans are likely to be forthcoming from the city slickers in your touring party. Well, take heart! The MacDonalds of Gairloch don't think the world's greatest scenery has to come with the world's greatest back ache. In Arrowdale and Innis Bheatha, Dr. John has provided us with real homes away from home. Indeed, I wish *home* was like this!

These two wonderful houses are situated on the south shore of Loch Shieldaig, a couple miles from the picturesque village of Badachro, which has one of the finest natural harbors on the west coast. With the waters of the loch lapping at the shore below Arrowdale, and some dear wooly Highland cows grazing in the pasture, the properties are surrounded by twenty two acres of woodland filled with other little *deers* of the red and roe varieties. Each house is further enveloped by a couple acres of wonderfully landscaped gardens of camellias, azaleas and rhododendron. *Innis Bheatha* literally means *meadow of the birches,* and the name *Arrowdale* commemorates the legendary pair of archers who in the 16th century took up an impregnable position and repelled a dastardly seaborne attack. In fact, the steps in the rock on which they stood can be seen, as can their burial mounds on a heather covered isle just 150 yards off shore from the MacDonald property.

I. F-3
B-D
B-S
F-2
II.. B-D
B-T
F-2
III.B-T
E&H
FP
LT
TEL
TVV
W/D
DW MW
£240-500
S 9

Both Arrowdale and Innis Bheatha date from around 1840, being modest thatched cottages originally, then converted to traditional one and a half story Highland houses around the turn of the century. More recent extensions have made them even more commodious.

Arrowdale has a very large L-shaped living room with picture window, *reach out and touch it* views of the loch, and traditional small pane window perspectives over the garden. This is one of the most congenial rooms I've ever seen, filled with all sorts of homey soft furnishing, covered in bold colorful fabrics, no two alike...small prints and giant florals, as well as tartans in sufficient variety as to firmly establish the MacDonalds' aesthetic ecumenicalism as far as ancient clan rivalries may be concerned. Framed embroidery family crests confess to the MacDonald blood having been liberally mixed with that of the MacLeods and Munros, and I should think many genealogical pilgrims among our readers might want to explore the matter of ancestral ties with their delightful landlords.

The same flair for colorful decoration is carried through the rest of Arrowdale. Everywhere there are eye catching original paintings, brightly framed prints, and decorative plates. Wall papers and curtains, throw rugs and throw pillows, duvets and bed drapery...all off on a chromatic adventure, exploding with a gaiety that will surely be contagious for your whole holiday in Arrowdale.
STB 5 Crowns; Highly Commended

INNIS BHEATHA

Innis Bheatha, says the particular minded inspectorate of the Scottish Tourist Board, is even better! I'm not sure how that is possible, but, alas, the parsimonious inspector *only* gave Arrowdale five crowns, while Innis Bheatha was awarded "Deluxe" status. Perhaps it is the three fireplaces: the one in the living room blazing forth from a solid wall of colorful (what else!) field stone; or the cozy glow in the library from a Victorian coaler, surrounded by hand painted tiles with a pine mantle added for yet more color; or the wood-burning stove with the bright red tile back in the dining room. And, while we are on the subject of warming devices, we might as well address the question of the AGA. By this point in the book, readers already know that my admiration for Agas verges on idolatry. Well, imagine the thrill of coming home to worship before a highly polished, fire-engine red Aga...a veritable altar of culinary ecstasy! But then there is a good deal of ecstasy in the rest of Innis Bheatha, from the very feminine Laura Ashley bedrooms with beautifully draped corona beds, to the cozy green room, the perfect place to relax with a dram of the local restorative after a bracing walk along the loch shore.

This is truly an enchanted land, full of sandy bays and peaceful beaches...the word crowded has never been mentioned here! There are hundreds of nooks of rare beauty with Kodak ordered sunsets and a wild Highland grandeur to fill the soul. I can think of no better place to let it all sink in than Arrowdale or Innis Bheatha.
STB 5 Crowns; Deluxe

| I. F-3 |
| F-2 |
| II.B-d [2] |
| F-2 |
| B-t |
| B-s |
| E&H |
| FP [2] |
| FPS |
| LT |
| TEL TVV |
| W/D |
| DW MW |
| OPEN |
| TA |
| £240-500 |
| S 7 |

Contact Dr John MacDonald, Tigh Eibhinn, Easterton, Dalcross, Inverness IV1 2JE
TEL 01144-1667-462-792

EILDON HOLIDAY COTTAGES   Nr Melrose

Eildon Holiday Cottages are located about an hour south of Edinburgh on the slopes of the beautiful Eildon Hills. This is the Scottish borderlands, immortalized by Sir Walter Scott and other masters of romance, and dramatized by the real life *shoot'em-up* comings and goings of the Border Reivers. Virtually within sight of the cottages is Melrose Abbey, where tradition has it that King Robert the Bruce's heart is buried. The Eildon Hills also claim to be the burial site of none other than King Arthur...here interred with his knights and their horses, waiting for the sign to rise again, which should keep them on their toes down south!

Sue and Richard Oldfield have had a special mission in the development of what were until recently the Duke of Buccleuch's 18th century cattle courts and granary. Their aim was to provide first class holiday accommodations for the handicapped, all the while making those special facilities wholly unobtrusive for accompanying family and other guests. The five cottages are designed on the premise that everything must be accessible from two heights, standing and wheelchair...not so much either/or as both. Plug switches, all the kitchen facilities, even the picture windows, which offer magnificent views over the Tweed River Valley, are set low. Doors and passages are intentionally wide and bathroom facilities offer easy side loading and plenty of grab rails. There are genuine shower rooms, rather than tub cabinets, etc.

If all this sounds a bit institutional, let me hasten to correct that impression. All conveniences are subtly imbedded in what are by any standards very tasteful holiday accommodations. Take *Single Tree Cottage,* for example. The living room is very spacious and has two exposed stone walls, with bookshelves built into stone alcoves. There is an interesting antique oak carved chest and chintz covered soft furnishings. The three bedrooms are furnished in Yorkshire pine; they are jade green, apricot and blue, respectively, with color coordinated linens and towels. In the kitchen one finds all the special conveniences (eg. low wall oven) along with pretty touches, such as the Denby Regency Green crockery. Exterior flower beds contain fragrant herbs, alpine strawberries, and many other little delights.

STB 3-4 Crowns; Highly Commended

E$m H$m
LT
TELc
TV
W/D
NS* P-
BA
E/HC
S-S MS
INS
TA
£180-380
S 2-5

Contact Sue & Richard Oldfield, Eildon Holiday Cottages, Dingleton Mains, Melrose, Roxburghshire
Scotland TD6 9HS   TEL 01144-1896-823-258

BARROCK HOUSE
Lyth

I.F-3
II.Suite 1
B-d
B-s
Suite 2
B-t [2]
B-s
F-2
Suite 3
B-d
B-s
F-2
E$m H$m
FP
L
TELc TV
W/D
S-S MS
INS
$845-1870
S 10

Sinclairs in strength of numbers...Behold! Your ancestral steads await you, with *bairn* and cousins in *gatherings* of ten...even non-kinspersons are welcome at Barrock House, here in the Northern Highlands. This mid-17th century mansion is furnished with many original family pieces, in rich Jacobean and Victorian styles, with sleeping quarters regally divided up into three multi-bedroom suites. The ancestral presence of Clan Sinclair is registered in many noble portraits throughout. Real and vicarious Sinclair guests will be impressed by the grandeur of the ground floor public rooms and the baronial style staircase; and the vagaries of Sinclair history and fate may be comfortably debated in front of the cozy fires of the library and the card room. Have a Ceilidh!

Why do I get the impression that this branch of Clan Sinclair was not there with the Armstrongs amongst the huddled mass of immigrants who populated the hills of Cape Breton and Appalachia?

Contact British Travel International, P.O. Box 299, Elkton VA 22827 USA
TEL 800-327-6097 or FAX 703-298-2347

EARNKNOWE COTTAGES Lochearnhead

In many ways Loch Earn reminds us of the *Up North* lakes of the Midwest that slumber through winter and then burst to life with all sorts of summer holiday fare. Indeed, this loch is noted for providing the full range of summer recreation on water: fishing, canoeing, sailing, water ski-ing...there is even parascending. Earnknowe Cottages are also reminiscent of the camps of Wisconsin and Michigan, with a laid back, nothing too fancy, attitude; plenty of hill and dale for the children to explore, and, of course, the ever inviting water lapping at the shore in front of the cottages. There is a small jetty and a boat for guest use; a motor may be for a nominal charge. The cottages, themselves, are four in number, converted from the old stone barn and furnished comfortably in contemporary pine cottage furnishings, with wonderful views out over the lake. All very clean and tidy and a good economical place to put your feet up and relax or use as a base for exploring the Southern Highlands.   STB 3-4 Crowns; Commended

I. CS
II.B-d
B-t
F-3
E$c H$c
FP$
LT
TV
W/Ds
P-BA
S-S
TA
£100-335
S 2-6

Contact Lawrence & Pamela Hopkins, Earnknowe, Lochearnhead, Scotland FK19 8PY
TEL 01144-1567-830-238

SHENNANTON HOUSE   Newton Stewart

No danger of claustrophobic attacks at Shennanton House! Set in the Galloway Hills of southwest Scotland, Shennanton was designed and built in 1908 for a family of latter day nabobs and financed by the commercial success of plantation rubber. From a distance one might think Shennanton was one of those gigantic Elizabethan country estates, the self-glorifying repatriation monument of some swash-buckling mogul of the Mercantilist Age, aping royal ostentation, indeed, brashly upping the ante to the blue bloods. But the Age here is Edwardian, not Tudor, and the corporate revenue of rubber was nothing like the windfall riches of privateering or the bonanza of the opium trade. One may safely assume that the financial foundations of this ersatz mogul mansion rested firmly on the undramatic acumen of bookkeeping, rather than the dash and dare of commercial buccaneering. Yet the romantic megalomania of that earlier age of empire was certainly a part of the vision and aspiration of Shennanton's 20th century builders. In fact, Shennanton is not a sprawling spendthrift-built Tudor palace, but rather a good sized country house, albeit designed as a thoroughly domestic imitation of the former.

The official citation for this Grade A Listed building reads "Tudor/vernacular style", and, to be sure, Shennanton has about as much *style* as one could possibly load onto a house of its not unsubstantial, if not quite palatial, dimensions. The first principle of Shennanton's designer, the noted Glasgow architect H.E. Clifford, was *asymmetry,* which, of course, enabled him to multiply the variety of architectural features. I don't think Clifford missed much, inside or out; this is a *one of everything house:* castellated roof, Gothic archways, buttresses, a forest of rich wood paneling, pillars capitalized by all the orders, inglenooks, oriel windows, vaulted ceilings, pilasters, stone mullioned windows...all this and much much more in mix and match patterns, a veritable style book of Gothic imagination, cleverly divided up into four absolutely gigantic holiday suites. Incidentally, the four holiday accommodations comprise the whole of the mansion.

Each self catering suite will comfortably accommodate eight to eleven guests in grandly proportioned double bedrooms, with luxury en-suite bathrooms, most with jacuzzi tubs in various sizes and shapes. There are handsome furnishings throughout, new living room and bedroom suites in appropriate period styles, colorful carpets over polished wood floors, and some nice pictures. If furnishings seem scarce, in part it is because these are such huge rooms. In fact, the living room of Bladnoch Suite is situated at one end of what was the former billiard room, with the absolutely massive slate billiard table still in place, yet there is enough room remaining for most of the cast of *Brideshead Revisited* to mill about with cocktails in hand! All four of the suites have up and downstairs, with beautiful internal stairwells. Bladnoch Suite, however, has been designed for wheelchair access, with a downstairs bedroom adjacent to a wheel-in shower room. Each apartment offers nice perspectives over some thirty acres of lawn and gardens. The estate, in total, is comprised of a thousand acres, and outdoor amenities include a four hole putting green, croquet, tennis, fishing & boating, as well as many fine walks.

Shennanton House is outfitted, as well, for business clients, with computer facilities provided in each suite, and several suites have large multipurpose rooms for seminars or social gatherings. Bed and breakfast at daily rates is also offered, as is full catering and maid service.

E&H
FP*
LT
TVV
W/D
MW DW
E/HC*
OPEN MS
£690-950
S 8-11

Contact Shennanton House, Kirkcowan, Nr Newton Steward, Wigtownshire, Scotland DG8 0EG
TEL 01144-1671-830-494 or FAX 01144-1671-830-445

ACHNANDARACH LODGE   Plockton

Plockton, which is most often noted for its improbable palm trees, is one of Scotland's most delightful villages, sandwiched in a peerless setting between mountain and shore, and now largely under the guardianship of the National Trust of Scotland. Once a gathering place of pathetic crofters, victims of the cruelties of the Clearance, today Plockton is a much favored gathering place for holidaymakers and sailing enthusiasts.

Achnandarach Lodge peeks out from the forest with long views over the Inner Sound of Raasay and the Isle of Skye in the background. Indeed, the ferry across to Skye is only a short drive away. This is a modern chalet style home, which is every bit as spectacular inside as is its setting. Three levels, long beam spans, plenty of glass bringing in the natural environment, a wrap around balcony...*expansive* is the word! As one would hope in a *lodge,* there is a wealth of stone and natural wood in the construction, with polished pine floors, and a roaring open fire. The furnishing is all modern, again with the emphasis on bright pine. Pretty blue soft furnishings are featured in the living room and sun room. The kitchen is *loaded,* and the layout of sleeping and showering facilities is particularly geared for large parties.

B-q [2]
B-t [2]
B-s
F-1
F-3 [2]
E&H
FP
LT
TV
W/D
DW
MW
OPEN MS
INS
£850-1200
S 9

Contact Rural Retreats, Station Road, Blockley, Moreton-in-Marsh, Gloucestershire, GL56 9DZ
TEL 01144-1386-701-177 or FAX 01144-1386-701-178

ARDSHELLACH North Connel

The village of North Connel lies on the north shore of Loch Etive, in a peaceful crofting and farming area in the heartland of glorious Lorne. Within fifty miles there are over a dozen romantic and ancient castles, three seats of Clan Chiefs, scores of archaeological and early Christian sites and historic Glencoe, Appin and Iona. And Oban, the jumping off point for trips to the Hebrides, is only seven miles away.

Chris Paine and his wife are Scottish exiles in England, and commissioned an architect in 1970 to design them a comfortable, easy to run house for family holidays and eventual retirement on their spectacular site above the loch. So far, their exile continues, and when not escaping to the homeland for their own holidays, they offer it to other vacationers. The house and its secluded south-facing garden have wonderful views over the loch and mountains. There is a sun terrace, equipped with teak garden table and chairs--a wonderful place just to sit and relax. The loch, itself, is reached by a private road from the house.

Ardshellach is centrally heated, with thermostats in each room. There are beautiful beech wood floors in the hall and sitting room, and fitted carpets in every bedroom. The sitting room is comfortably furnished, with a turquoise and soft gold color scheme and William Morris *Wey* patterned curtains. The bay window view of the loch and hills is nothing short of spectacular. The scientifically designed Baxi fireplace can be used for log or coal fires if required.

I. B-t
F-1
II.B-d
B-b+s
F-2
E$m H$m
FP
LT$
TEL
TV
W/D
DW MW
P-
S-S
£150-370
S 7

The kitchen at Ardshellach is spacious and a pleasure to work in, with a bar counter dividing the kitchen from the dining area, which has nice pine paneling, as well as French doors leading to the terrace. The downstairs bedroom is a twin with pretty Sanderson fabrics in peach and almond. Adjacent is a cloakroom with WC and washbasin. Upstairs there is a landing with a couple interesting antique pieces. The master bedroom is done in cream and florals and has soft green carpeting. The other bedroom is a triple, with bunks and a single. Both bedrooms offer wonderful views over the loch.

STB 4 Crowns; Highly Commended

Contact Mrs. Aileen Binner, Ailand, North Connel, Argyll PA37 1QX TEL 01144-1631-71264

SKAILL HOUSE FLATS   Orkney Isles

The dramatic islands of Orkney lie twenty miles off the North Coast of Scotland. There are seventy islands in all, but only twenty are inhabited. The largest of the islands is, curiously enough, called *Mainland,* and here you will find Skaill House, the most complete 17th century mansion in the Orkneys. You are on the west coast of the island overlooking the spectacular sandy Bay of Skaill, with the Loch of Skaill immediately to your back. Only 350 yards away is Skara Brae by the seashore, Europe's best preserved prehistoric village, dating back 3000 years. The then Laird of Skaill House discovered Skara Brae in 1850.

There are two flats forming right-angle sides of the courtyard adjoining Skaill House. *Langskaill* is on the second floor with splendid views over Skaill Bay, while *Peerieskaill* is on the ground floor. The flats are entered through a large flag-stone hall with a conservatory and general utility room.

Langskaill sleeps up to seven people. There is a fully fitted kitchen adjoining the dining room with an open fireplace and also access into the the inner courtyard, down a stone stairway. The sitting room is also expansive, with pristine white plaster walls, breaking at shoulder height with the pitch of the roof. You will find a contemporary brick fireplace at one end, with a cozy grate fire. The furnishings are a nice mix of antiques (overflow from the mansion): mahogany *secretaire* and circular table, comfortable sofas and several nice occasional pieces. Bedroom arrangements include a double and twin (with electric blankets!), plus a small single and bunk room.

Peerieskaill sleeps five, also with a very cozy sitting room and open fire. The kitchen of *Peerieskaill* has direct access to the conservatory, which opens into the courtyard. The estate also has two privately owned lochs, with three boats available for guests with an inclination to go fishing.

STB 4 Crowns

PEER.
I.B-t
B-s
B-b
F-2
£230-300
S 5
LANG.
II.B-d
B-t
B-b
B-s
F-2
£340-430
S 7
BOTH
E$m
H$m
FP
TELc
TV
W/Ds
S-S
INS
BK$

Contact Discover Britain, Shaw Mews, Shaw Street, Worcester WR1 3QQ
TEL 01144-1905-613-744 or FAX 01144-1905-613-747

DRON COURT Nr St. Andrews

With St. Andrews one always thinks of golf. Presumably, that is what Leonard Sculthorp had on his mind as he was beating the ball around the Royal & Ancient Course while on holiday back in 1980. However, the peripatetic Mr. Sculthorp has a difficult time keeping his mind off interesting properties, particularly those worthy of restoration or creative rebuilding (see Drummore & Dunmore Court). It seems that Mr. Sculthorp can't resist a development challenge, and his holiday took a tangent the minute he saw the *For Sale* sign on the old South Dron farm near the golf course.

Out went the call to friend and architect Tom Gray in Edinburgh. Reconstruction began within the year, but it took until 1984 to complete the whole project. Gray made a thorough study of this centuries-old farmstead. It was discovered that the site began as a watering hole for pilgrimaging monks enroute to the holy city of St. Andrews, and, indeed, one of the original wells was discovered during the excavation, and now supplies the courtyard fountain. Various other architectural features were identified and marked as "keepers" before the rip and tear began. Stonework, slate floors, pantiles, which came as ballast from Holland, and a host of curiosities, like the old sandstone grinding wheel, the stone trough & pump, and the hen steps protruding from an interior stone wall to a loft...all elements to be worked into the final design.

The results were well worth waiting for. Today there are ten handsome cottages sleeping up to nine, with comfortable contemporary furnishings, efficient kitchens, open fireplaces and private patio furnishings. *Auchterlonie,* the largest with three bedrooms, was the original sandstone farmhouse and features a richly paneled traditional living room. The cottage names remind us that we are in the holy land of golf: *Hogan, Vardon, Jones, Thomson,* etc. All of the accommodations face onto the nicely landscaped courtyard; there to relax over a dram of the local libation and perhaps improve one's score in the retelling.

STB 4 Crowns; Highly Commended

E$m
H$m
FP*$
LT$
TELc
TV
W
S-S
£140-495
S 2-9

Contact Tom Scott, Dron Court, South Dron, St. Andrews KY16 9YA TEL 01144-1334-870-835

PAVILION COTTAGE

Rumbling Bridge

We're on the River Devon here with a sweep of moorlands above and rising hills beyond. But these are the Ochil Hills, not the bumpy tors of the West Country, and the sea of purple moorland here comes with a definite Scottish accent. The displaced River Devon has cut a deep gorge in this landscape, cascading dramatically over precipices, an audio-visual torrent surging under Rumbling Bridge on its way to the double waterfall at Cauldron Linn.

A half mile from Rumbling Bridge is the Briglands Estate, once the home of Lord Clyde. Here we find his Lordship's private little teahouse tucked away in its own gardens and now fitted out for holiday repose. The fully carpeted ground floor offers a living/dining room with access to the garden. The kitchen and two bedrooms share the same elevation, and above, reached by spiral stairs, is the featured chamber which once served for the ritual leisures of the leaf and is today a cozy second sitting room, where holidaymakers may partake of the libation of their choice. If the quietude becomes overwhelming, busy Edinburgh is only a short drive, and golf addicts have many options, not least the famous Gleneagles Course; only twenty minutes away.

I.B-d
B-t
F-3
E$m H$
TELc
TV
W
MW
NS
S-S
INS
$575-1200
S 4

Contact British Travel International, P.O. Box 299, Elkton VA 22827 USA   TEL 800-327-6097

KINTAIL Ratagan

If you've had the pleasure of seeing the touching film, *Ring of Bright Water*, then you will have a keen sense of the sheer grandeur of this landscape. Indeed, Gavin Maxwell was occasionally seen hiking past Kintail Cottage with his lovable chum, Midge the Otter, whose tragic demise still floods our house with tears every time we put on the video. But, never mind our grief, there are still plenty of wild Midges in this neighborhood for you to enjoy, and they too can be seen frolicking in front of the cottage, along with the deer and the seals and the porpoises and you name it in the wildlife idiom. Did I mention that this Loch Duich, flowing out to meet the shores of the Isle of Skye, is a boundless wilderness? Roads are far and few between up here, but you will come in by way of the A87 past the magnificent Five Sisters of Kintail, and these landmark peaks will accompany you right into the view-full windows of your cottage.

I. F-3
II.B-d+s
B-t+s
E$m H$m
FP
L
TELc
TV
W/D
DW MW
£316-373
S 4-6

Kintail Cottage is situated right on the shore of the Loch, and is pleasantly, albeit lightly, furnished. This is the Vyner-Brooks family's second home, and they've done all they can to make it a warm and comfortable get-away, with views...views...views!
STB 5 Crowns; Highly Commended

Contact V. R. Vyner-Brooks, Esq., Middle Barrows Green, Kendal, Cumbria LA8 0JG TEL 01144-1539-560-242

DUNMORE VILLA & COURT Nr Tarbert

Here in the heart of Kintyre is the remainder of the Dunmore Estate occupying 1200 acres along three miles of the north shore of West Loch Tarbert. Dunmore Villa is not to be confused with the large old mansion (once the seat of the MacMillan clan), which was partially burned a number of years ago. The Villa was built in 1969 in a bold contemporary style. It sits right at the edge of the loch, with a sweep of shingle beach on which to pull up the boat or sit in the sun. Big picture windows enjoin the exterior panorama with the spacious living room. In fact, even with two sets of furnishings, one focused on the massive stone fireplace and the other directed to the sea, there is room here to swing the cat or engage in some equally rowdy Gaelic reel. There is a similarly commodious dining room which will seat ten. The ground floor master bedroom also features a seaward picture window, and an en-suite bathroom with bidet. The upstairs is divided into two wings, making Dunmore Villa particularly convenient for traveling companion groups wishing their own zones of privacy. Each wing is comprised of two bedrooms and separate bathrooms.

I. B-t
F-4
II.B-t [2]
F-2 [2]
B-d
B-b
E$m H$m
FP$
LT$
TEL TV
W/D
DW MW
S-S
£340-695
S 10

Dunmore Court, originally the farm buildings associated with the Estate, sits entirely on its own and was the first of the collaborations between Leonard Sculthorp and architect Tom Gray. The four cottages are grouped around a nicely landscaped courtyard with a stable close entryway. The front two cottages, *Fraser* and *MacMillan,* are two stories, with skylight and dormered upstairs quarters, and sliding doors to the patios facing north toward the Castle. *Campbell* and *Ross* Cottages offer all-on-one-level accommodations with three bedrooms each.

E$c H$c
FP$
LT$
TELc
TV
W/D
S-S
£150-395
S 5-7

The long Kintyre Peninsula has a number of interesting sights and the western shore road is a continuous window on the Western Isles. Ferries leave from Kennacraig, near Tarbert, and from Tayinloan. At the northern end of the peninsula is the fascinating Crinan Canal, begun by the Duke of Argyll in the late 18th century and a tribute to Scottish audacity, if not exactly Scottish financial acumen. Today the canal is much favored by the sailing fraternity, connecting to the great cruising waters of the Firth of Clyde and the Firth of Lorne, without taking on the long run around the Mull of Kintyre. STB 4-5 Crowns; Commended

Contact Mrs Meg MacKinnon, Dunmore Home Farm, Nr Tarbert, Argyll PA29 6XS TEL 01144-1880-820-654

WESTER BALLACHRAGGAN Trochry

Wester Ballachraggan is situated by the Sma Glen in the Highlands, an area of outstanding natural beauty. The cottage is located a few miles from the historic town of Dunkeld which stands on the mighty River Tay, much renowned for its salmon fishing. Edinburgh, Perth and Pitlochry are all within easy driving distance. The setting for the cottage could scarcely be more panoramic, with an endless horizon of moorland and rivers. The wonderful sight of herds of red deer, pheasant, grouse and partridge can be observed on walks around the cottage. This is a land of domestic critters as well: cows, sheep and goats graze the hillside, with poultry ranging freely in the fields. There is a large fenced garden surrounding the cottage, with an abundance of trees and shrubs, as well as suitable garden furniture and a barbeque. Every window of the cottage is filled with the panoramic views of the mountains and the River Braan.

Wester Ballachraggan was built in the 18th century of local stone with a slate roof and has been meticulously maintained. The cottage is approached via a meandering drive up the hillside through the grounds, where there is a pond for ducks and geese. The welcoming entrance porch leads through to the sitting room where a blazing log fire might await you after a bracing ramble over the moorland. The furnishings are an eclectic mix of older styles, with comfy sofa and chairs, and handsome antique mirrors over the living room and dining room fireplaces. There is, as well, a video player for the TV and a CD. The dining room, adjacent to the sitting room, has its own log burning stove, and fuel for both fires is included in the rent. There is also central heating. The kitchen is completely modern, with all the mechanical amenities (including AGA) and nicely fitted oak cabinetry.

The master bedroom offers a king size four-poster bed, draped with fabric coordinated to the curtains and soft furnishings. There is, as well, a twin room and a bunk room for children. Indeed, Wester Ballachraggan is an extraordinary venue for children, a wide open and run-free environ which is all too rare in this age of theme parks.

STB 5 Crowns; Deluxe

I. F-3
II.B-d
B-t
B-b
F-1
E H$c
FP$ FPS$
LT
TELc
TVV
W/D
DW MW
S-S OPEN
MS TA
£300-500
S 6

Contact Dr. John Hooper, Wester Ballachraggan, Trochry, Dunkeld, Perthshire, Scotland PH8 0EA
TEL 01144-1350-723-207

RHIDORROCH ESTATE COTTAGES

Nr Ullapool

Want to get away from the maddening crowd? Just had it with people? Rather fish than talk? Want to walk all day and not see a soul? Well the Rhidorroch Estate is just the place for you. True, there are all of six cottages here, counting the Lodge (drawing above), a communal self-catering hermitage for ten. But not to worry about congestion; the three old shepherd's cottages (and one wooden chalet) are deposited at respectable intervals up the estate's private glen which stretches for fourteen miles along the beautiful Rhidorroch River. Four miles down river is the town of Ullapool, hard at work with lobstering and scalloping, but tourist conscious enough to offer summertime day cruises out to the Summer Isles, as well as deep sea fishing opportunities.

Ewen and Jenny Scobie manage the Estate and are always available to lend a hand, give directions, and arrange fishing. The Lodge is the largest of the Estate cottages and lies up river, four miles by paved road, followed by another four of gravel which delivers one to the foot bridge. Across the river, one follows the path into the Caledonian Pine forest for 180 yards to arrive at the handsome stone built Lodge and one adjacent cottage. The Lodge has gas heating, and electricity is supplied by generator. Not so with some of the other cottages, which are remote enough to require (Calor) gas lighting as well. The whitewashed stone cottage, Glastullich, which sleeps six, sits quietly in a deer filled glen and overlooks the loch and the River Ullapool. Cadubh Cottage (sleeping six) is further up the glen, idyllically sited under the towering cliffs within earshot of the soothing music of the Rhidorroch River tumbling over the rocks. Corry Cottage (sleeps six) is magnificently poised overlooking Loch Broom. Naturalists, and birders in particular, will be in seventh heaven up here. There are river beats and boats on the lochs for the piscatorially inclined guests, and more wildlife than you'll see in a zoo. And, most important, there is QUIET!

STB 1-4 Crowns; Commended

LODGE
B-d
F-3
B-t [3]
B-s [2]
E&H
FPS
LT$
TELc
W
S-S
£360-480
S10

Contact Rhidorroch Estate Office, Ullapool, Wester Ross, Scotland IV26 2UB TEL 01144-1854-612-548

CROSSWOODHILL FARM West Calder

Crosswoodhill Farm is well placed; a half hour's drive transports one from the peace of the hills into the heart of bustling, sometimes claustrophobic, Edinburgh. In my experience, this is just about the right distance if one chooses the height of the Festival Season for doing Edinburgh. Crosswoodhill is a large stone-built farmhouse dating from the 18th century, and is set in acres of sheltered grounds and woodlands on a 1700 acre beef and sheep farm in the bucolic Pentland Hills. The house is situated well back and across the road from the farm buildings, peacefully screened by dense rhododendron bushes and trees.

CROSSW.	
II.B-d	
B-b	
CS	
F-2	
E$m	H$m
FP$	FPS
LT	
TELc	TV
W/D	
S-S	
TA	
£140-300	
S5	

The self-catering unit comprises a self-contained wing with its own entrance at the rear of the property. Guests enter from their own garden into a quarry tiled, slightly old-fashioned but colorful, compact and well equipped kitchen. Adjacent is the downstairs living room which doubles as the dining room. You will find a multi-fuel stove here which burns home-produced peat, as well as coal and logs. When in Scotland...!

A short flight of stairs leads up to the more traditional part of the house, with old pine window panels, shutters and doors. Leading off the passageway, with views out over the lawn and trees, you will find a double bedroom, with a much-admired large gentleman's wardrobe, and a smaller room with bunk beds, as well as a bathroom with power shower over the tub. At the far end of the upstairs corridor is a spacious second living room, with an open fire and both single and double beds, heaped with floral cushions for sofa use during the daytime.

MID-CROSS	
I.B-d	
B-t	
B-s	
F-2	
F-3	
E$m	H$m
FP$	
LT	
TELc	TV
W/D	
DW	MW
P-	
S-S	
TA	
£150-285	
S 5	

Also on the farm is another self-catering property with a character all its own. The Hamiltons have just done a top to bottom renovation of this attractive single story traditional shepherd's cottage, dating from the 18th century. Actually Midcrosswood Cottage (drawing above) is quite secluded, with its nearest neighbor a half mile away, not counting sheep. The ovine idiom also finds its way into the cottage, with sheepskins on the handsome new maple floors that have been laid throughout. The living room stretches from one gable end to the other, with small pane window views and skylights, as well.

STB 5 Crowns: Highly Commended

Contact Mrs. Geraldine Hamilton, Crosswoodhill, West Calder, West Lothian EH55 8LP
TEL 01144-1501-785-205

WESTBEACH
West Ferry-Dundee

At the mouth of the Tay, between Dundee town center and Broughty Castle, Westbeach house was built by Lord Dalhousie about 1838. The fine old mansion has a splendid little garden terrace in front along the public walkway and stony beach. The accommodation comprises the half of the house on the left in the drawing, with marvelous views across the busy Tay from the living room, which has an impressive black marble fronted fireplace. Also note the upstairs balcony, off one of the bedrooms...a wonderful place to sit in the morning; like having your morning tea in the bow of a boat! Furnishing and decoration are a bit sparing, but the house is quite comfortable and exceptionally bright.

Westbeach offers a good functional base for chasing the great salmon of the Tay or the little white balls around the Royal & Ancient Golf Course at St. Andrews, just across the River. In fact, there are twenty five other accessible golf courses within as many miles...when in Rome! STB 4 Crowns; Highly Commended

II.B-d
B-t [2]
F-2
F-3
E$m
H$m
FP$
L-BA
NS
S-S MS
£280-420
S 6

Contact Jean Silvers, 23 Douglas Terrace, West Ferry, Dundee DD5 1JD   TEL 01144-1382-77982

CHANNEL ISLANDS

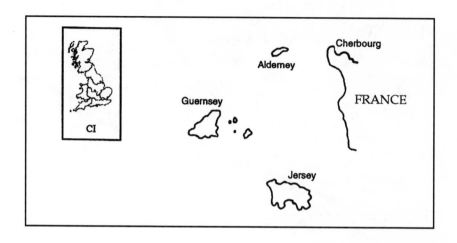

Alderney

F Forts
1. St. Anne
2. Hanging Rock
3. Golf Course
4. Airport
5. The Harbour
6. Nunnery

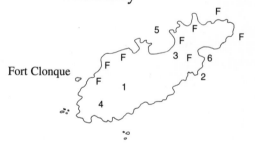

Fort Clonque

Jersey

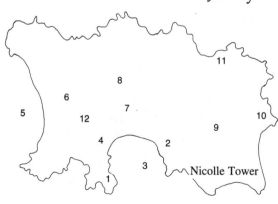

Nicolle Tower

1. La Tour de Vinde
2. St. Helier
3. Elizabeth Castle
4. St. Aubin
5. St. Ouens Bay
6. St. Peter's Bunker
7. German Underground Hospital
8. Fantastic Gardens
9. La Houge Bie
10. Mont Orgueil
11. Jersey Zoological Park
12. Airport

FORT CLONQUE
Alderney

Over here one raises the salutatory glass with a toast to "Our Queen & *Our Duke*". The latter reference is to the ancient Dukedom of Normandy, whence came the ever popular William the Conqueror, and an even earlier *William* (The First), who, in fact, conquered the Channel Islands over a century before his descendent got busy with the Normanization of the English Mainland. Therein lies the unique political identity and statutory relationship between the Channel Islands and Great Britain. It's a question of who is the conqueror and who the conqueree!

Fort Clonque was built in the middle of the 19th century, a bastion of "English Normans" against the French. Alas, history is rich with many such ironies, just as Alderney is rich with forts of all sizes, ages and political persuasions, from Roman to Nazi. Indeed, when Hitler arrived, the guns of Alderney were redirected back at the British, and old Fort Clonque was fortified as it had never been during its brief period of military utility in Victorian times. In fact, your spacious bedroom in this Landmark Trust restoration may well be one of the chambers formerly occupied by the formidable *Big Berthas* in the German arsenal. There are six bedrooms in all, scattered around in the various chambers of the sprawling fortification. This fort is particularly picturesque because of its glorious siting on the rock promontory across the (Victorian built) causeway, and because, structurally, the fort follows the ups and downs and ins and outs of its geologic foundation. The thrill of it all increases as the high tide submerges the causeway; *my home, my castle; my island, my home!*

Alderney can be reached directly by air from England. There are less than 2000 residents on the 2x5 km island, mostly living in the cheerful little village of St. Anne. The *national* mode of transport is bicycle, and I can think of nothing more delightful than spending a week pedalling around this bit of paradise. Well, on second thought, I guess living here forever would be better yet!

E&H
FP
LT
F-F MS
INS
£377-1350
S 12

Contact The Landmark Trust, Shottesbrook, Maidenhead, Berkshire SL6 3SW
TEL 01144-1628-825-925 or FAX 01144-1628-825-417

THE NICOLLE TOWER   Jersey

Folks have been visiting Jersey for many years; actually about 70,000 years, give or take a generation. Archeologists call that the *Old* Stone Age, not to be confused with the New Stone Age, which some of the locals argue returned to the island in the 1940s when a fresh swarm of goose-stepping barbarians arrived from the East.

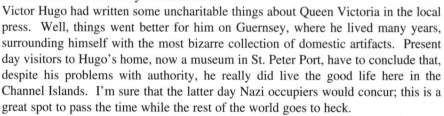

The occupations of Jersey have been many over the years since those paleolithic chaps. One notable occupant of St. Clements parish, wherein we find the Nicolle Tower, was none other than Victor Hugo. Strictly speaking, Hugo was not your regular tourist. France's great literary genius came to stay awhile in the Channel Islands because he and the French authorities agreed that he shouldn't live in France. The Hugo exile legend is everywhere in these islands. To put it mildly, Victor left an impression; in the instance of Jersey the impression was none too good, and the local constable was obliged to escort the *la miserable* penman to a waiting boat which carried Hugo further into exile on Guernsey. It seems that Victor Hugo had written some uncharitable things about Queen Victoria in the local press. Well, things went better for him on Guernsey, where he lived many years, surrounding himself with the most bizarre collection of domestic artifacts. Present day visitors to Hugo's home, now a museum in St. Peter Port, have to conclude that, despite his problems with authority, he really did live the good life here in the Channel Islands. I'm sure that the latter day Nazi occupiers would concur; this is a great spot to pass the time while the rest of the world goes to heck.

I. F-1
III.B-t
F-2
E&H
LT
P-
F-F MS
INS
£305-508
S 2

In fact, some of those very same German sojourners spent their war in the Nicolle Tower, back over on Jersey. When Philippe Nicolle built the somewhat comic little octagonal Gothic tower in his field in 1821 it wasn't quite as high as it is presently. The Hitler holiday gang added the top floor (complete with gun slits) for unobstructed 360 degree views over the surrounding sea. The view is every bit as good today, and the layer cake stack of character rooms (kitchen/dining, living room, bedroom) have been most comfortably outfitted by the Landmark Trust.

Exile, anyone? *Oui, s'il vous plait!*

Contact The Landmark Trust, Shottesbrook, Maidenhead, Berkshire SL6 3SW
TEL 01144-1628-825-925 or FAX 01144-1628-825-417

INDEX
by Cottage Name

TELL US !

about

Your Cottage Holiday Experience

We very much appreciate hearing from you about your holiday experience in Britain. Your comments may be incorporated into future editions of this book (with permission, of course), and, more importantly, your reflections will greatly assist us in making our cottage selections for future editions.

Did our recommendations measure up? Have you found other cottages which you think we should have a look at and consider for future editions? Whether your comments are laudatory or critical, please be specific in identifying the merits or demerits of particular properties. Your observations are important to us and will be handled with discretion. All letters will be gratefully acknowledged.

The Editors
Classic Media Publications
P.O. Box 710
Searsport, ME 04974

AN INCENTIVE OFFER

To underscore the importance we place in recruiting you onto our team of eyes & ears for selecting cottage properties in Britain, we make the following offer:

Those who write to us about their cottage experience will become honored members of the CHB team and will receive substantial discounts on the full range of Gale Armstrong artwork. With our letter of acknowledgement you will receive a brochure listing Gale Armstrong's currently available paintings and drawings (and a special *members only* discount price list). Gale paints a variety of subjects in water-colors and acrylics, as well as her pen & ink drawings of architectural subjects. Classic Media Fine Art Productions is the exclusive representative for Gale Armstrong's work in the United States and handles her limited edition prints and collector posters, as well as her remarkable original paintings. Gale Armstrong also does her *House Proud Originals* on a commission basis. Perhaps you would like such a portrait of your own home, or commission an architectural portrait as a gift for a friend. Or perhaps you would simply like a matted and framed print of that special cottage you called home while in Britain.

Help us with future refinements in *COTTAGE HOLIDAYING IN BRITAIN*, and Classic Media will help bring a fine Gale Armstrong picture into your own home. Welcome to our Cottage Holidaying Team!

HOW TO ORDER
COTTAGE HOLIDAYING IN BRITAIN

<u>Individual Copies</u> of this book may be purchased by personal check, money order, or VISA/MC (include number and expiry date).

      (US) $16.95, plus $3.00 shipping
      (CAN) $22.95, plus $3.00 shipping

Send to: Sales
                  Classic Media Publications
                  P.O. Box 710
                  Searsport, ME
                  04974 USA

Telephone orders are also accepted and may be charged to VISA/MC. This method is the most preferred and simple for orders originating outside the United States. Overseas orders add $4 shipping. Allow six-weeks for delivery.

CALL 1-800-499-3910

<u>Multiple copy</u> discounts are available on orders from Individuals, Organizations, Retail Shops and Distributors. Please call or write for Terms & Conditions.